MINOR
TRANSNATIONALISM

MINOR
TRANSNATIONALISM

Françoise Lionnet & Shu-mei Shih, *editors*

Duke University Press   *Durham and London*   2005

© 2005 Duke University Press
All rights reserved
Printed in the United States
of America on acid-free paper ∞
Designed by Amy Ruth Buchanan
Typeset in Janson by Keystone
Typesetting Inc.
Library of Congress Cataloging-
in-Publication Data and additional
permissions information appear on
the last printed page of this book.

CONTENTS

III. Reading, Writing, Performing

IV. Spatializing

Introduction

Thinking through the Minor, Transnationally

The conception of this collaborative project emerged from a serendipitous meeting on a cold and gray November day in 1998. We were both attending a conference that was being held in the Luxembourg Palace in Paris. The dark corridors and heavy security of this major site of political power in a European capital led us to a conversation on the state of "ethnic studies" in the United States and Europe. In a café, over cups of hot mulled wine, we continued the conversation on our personal and institutional backgrounds, allegiances, and dissatisfactions until late into the evening. One main dissatisfaction, we found out, was over the disciplinary boundaries that would ordinarily keep us on very different professional tracks, and thus not lead us to meet with each other. Our paths would not have crossed were we back in our home institutions, too busy fighting our own battles within our narrowly focused disciplines to understand the possibilities of working across these disciplines. One a Mauritian of French descent working in francophone, African, and African American studies, and the other a Korean-born ethnic Han working in Chinese, Sinophone, and Asian American studies, we were both in some sense "minoritized" in the major disciplines of French and Chinese. We were both too "ethnic studies" for the mainstream of our fields, but we would not normally have shared our common concerns and our common predicament. Had we not met through an arbitrary gathering in a major metropolis, the seat of power, our minor orientations would have remained invisible to each other. We realized, in retrospect, that our battles are always framed vertically, and we forget to look sideways to lateral networks that are not readily apparent.

Our encounter is symptomatic of the compulsory mediation by the mainstream for all forms of cultural production and interrelations among different minority communities. More often than not, minority subjects identify themselves in opposition to a dominant discourse rather than vis-à-vis each other and other minority groups. We study the center and the margin but rarely examine the relationships among different margins. The dominant is posited, even by those who resist it, as a powerful and universalizing force that either erases or eventually absorbs cultural particularities. Universalism demands a politics of assimilation, incorporation, or resistance, instituting a structure of vertical struggle for recognition and citizenship. Like many scholars we find universalist constructs wanting, but our reasons are specific to our locations as multiply diasporic subjects in the United States occupying a peculiar, transnational space.

One such universalism is the French version of Republicanism, which aims to assimilate immigrants and minorities into a particular version of "Frenchness." The official discourse flaunts an ideal of "Frenchness" as a promise to be achieved through the mastery of the French language and cultural codes. Thus to be "French" is to relate vertically to an ideal image of the French nation, not to find common ground with other immigrants who have embarked on this process of "becoming-French." There is a clear lack of proliferation of relational discourses among different minority groups, a legacy from the colonial ideology of divide and conquer that has historically pitted different ethnic groups against each other. The minor *appears* always mediated by the major in both its social and its psychic means of identification.

Globalization increasingly favors lateral and nonhierarchical network structures, or what Gilles Deleuze and Félix Guattari call a rhizome. The figure of the rhizome suggests an uncontainable, invisible symbolic geography of relations that become the creative terrain on which minority subjects act and interact in fruitful, lateral ways. Yet, even in these productive theoretical approaches, Deleuze and Guattari end up falling back into a recentered model of "minor literature." For them, the minor's literary and political significance rests on its critical function within and against the major in a binary and vertical relationship: "A minor literature doesn't come from a minor language; it is rather that which a minority constructs within a major language" (16).

French philosophers such as Deleuze and Guattari, Emmanuel Levinas, and Jacques Derrida have given us tools for thinking about otherness, tools that are all too often appropriated and depoliticized. It is important to remember that the historical and political context of poststructural-ist theory is the experience of decolonization with which many of these thinkers were familiar. Derrida's *Of Grammatology* mentions the word *ethnocentrism* in its first few pages before it even brings up the now much more central concept of logocentrism. However, we do not readily associate Derridean deconstruction with a critique of ethnocentrism, except as rarified philosophical musings on difference and otherness. Derrida's personal experience of growing up Jewish in Algeria at the time of decolonization has inevitably colored his intellectual choices in the same way that it did Hélène Cixous's. But it isn't until Franz Fanon traveled from the Caribbean to Algeria, which is to say from one minor space to another, that we can begin to see the emergence of the profile of a minor transnational intellectual linking spaces and struggles laterally.

Derridean deconstruction, even though marginal to the European center in the middle of the century, has become a dominant paradigm in French theoretical discourse in the United States and, by now, even in France. The deconstructive procedure has the paradoxical effect of exercising the muscles of the European philosophical and literary tradition, which becomes even more complex and indeterminate for an infinite play of meanings. Critiquing the center, when it stands as an end in itself, seems only to enhance it; the center remains the focus and the main object of study. The deconstructive dyad center/margin thus appears to privilege marginality only to end up containing it. The marginal or the other remains a philosophical concept and futuristic promise: the other never "arrives," he or she is always "à venir." The ethical implications of this approach are important in that they prevent the reification of the other, one of the major pitfalls of identity politics. However, when seen from this perspective, the other continues to exist more as a promise than as a reality. To say it bluntly, this promise of an "à venir" may be analogous to the illusive and elusive promise of equality in Republican universalism.

By contrast, Fanon's writings would instead help spur and partly undergird the civil rights movements of the 1960s, and by extension the discipline of ethnic studies in the United States. These writings inspired many other liberation movements and minority struggles in Asia, Latin America, and Africa, because Fanon was the first both to dissect the affective dimensions of oppression and to "translate" Hegelian or Sartrean definitions of alienation into a context where they could be used for nationalist struggles. These struggles were usually launched by those who were fighting for national and cultural autonomy and for racial equality. In the

United States, these struggles led to the recognition that minority populations are not just arriving, "à venir," but have already arrived and contributed to the definition of what the United States is. All minority groups are constitutive of the United States as a national entity; they are not just "playing in the dark" (Morrison) and should not be viewed as "perpetual foreigners" with second-class status because of their linguistic differences. They should be granted full citizenship with due recognition of rights and obligations. One of the salient results of these struggles was the establishment of ethnic studies programs in various universities, and the important research that these programs have facilitated. For tactical and strategic purposes, minority identities have been constructed in strong and bounded terms that have unfortunately rendered invisible subject positions that did not readily fall into such accepted categories as those of official minorities.

The paradigm of arrival in ethnic studies led, by necessity, to a more or less exclusive focus on domestic dynamics and hierarchies. On the one hand, new immigrants in general have been placed in a paradoxical position with regard to the claims of authenticity and cultural nationalism that have fueled the development of ethnic studies. On the other hand, vertical models of resistance have tended to impede interethnic solidarity and international minority alliances. For instance, scholars in ethnic studies very rarely communicate or collaborate with scholars in francophone studies, although there are many geographical and cultural points of convergence between the two. Likewise, ethnic studies and area studies continue to be caught in a fraught relationship: if pan-Africanism has provided a limited platform for African and African American scholars, pan-Asianism is politically too suspect and threatening to be viable as an institutional concept. Ethnic studies remain an American domestic paradigm, while area studies continue to subscribe to an outmoded view of continental territories. National-language departments rarely question the metonymical relationship between language and nation.

Increased pressures from transnational movements of peoples and cultures have, however, challenged the above nation-state–based definitions of ethnic and area studies. As scholars working both within and across area and ethnic studies, we not only want to bring intellectual questions raised in one field to bear upon the other, and vice versa, but we also want to raise new questions that address specific issues of transnationality in the twentieth century. This project is the result of such dialogues and multi-year collaborations among the contributors here under the organizational aegis of a Multicampus Research Group on Transnational and Trans-colonial Studies at the University of California, codirected by the editors of this book. Like our working group, this book aims to create a bridge between constituencies that have overlapping interests and porous borders but are under institutional constraints to defend established territories. Our intellectual work has convinced us, however, of the theoretical and practical benefits of looking at transnationalism from this "minor" perspective. It is indispensable to a better understanding of the general logic of transcultural and transdisciplinary approaches, and it troubles the prevalent notions of transnationalism as a homogenizing force.

Minor Transnationalism

In the last ten years or so, we have seen a new field of inquiry emerging in the name of transnational studies, aided by the increasing currency of theories of transnationalism in the social sciences, which are in turn legitimized by new theories of globalization. In general, it is understood that transnationalism as a consequence of the latest wave of globalization shares with globalization the historical moment of late capitalism, characterized by the logics of finance capital, flexible accumulation, and post-Fordist international division of labor (Hall 23; Harvey). Whereas the global is, in our understanding, defined vis-à-vis a homogeneous and dominant set of criteria, the transnational designates spaces and practices acted upon by border-crossing agents, be they dominant or marginal. The logic of globalization is centripetal and centrifugal at the same time and assumes a universal core or norm, which spreads out across the world while pulling into its vortex other forms of culture to be tested by its norm. It produces a hierarchy of subjects between the so-called universal and particular, with all the attendant problems of Eurocentric universalism. The transnational, on the contrary, can be conceived as a space of exchange and participation wherever processes of hybridization occur and where it is still possible for cultures to be produced and performed without necessary mediation by the center.

This definition of the transnational recognizes that transnationalism is part and parcel of the process of globalization, but also that the transnational can be less scripted and more scattered. In an effort to show the diverse ways that the transnational can work and is constituted, scholars have attempted to determine its parameters and track its movements. In one formulation, we have the so-called transnationalism from above, the

transnationalism of the multinational corporate sector, of finance capital, of global media, and other elite-controlled macrostructural processes
(Mahler). This transnationalism from above is associated with the utopic
views of globalization, which celebrate the overcoming of national and
other boundaries for the constitution of a liberal global market, the hybridization of cultures, and the expansion of democracies and universal
human rights. Dystopic visions of globalization, by contrast, point toward
such negative consequences as environmental and health hazards, "Mc-
Donaldization" of cultures, the exasperated disparity between the rich
and the poor, and the increased exploitation of Third World labor con-
tributing to the financial wealth of the North at the expanse of the South;
in other words, the hegemony of Western capitalism and, according to
Gayatri Spivak, the "untrammeled financialization of the globe" (262).
The dystopic views generate a resistant site that some have called "the
transnationalism from below," which is the sum of the counterhegemonic
operations of the nonelite who refuse assimilation to one given nation-
state, including "everyday practices of ordinary people" (Mahler). Michel
de Certeau's formulation of the quotidian and the everyday as the quintessential locus of resistance is an earlier formulation of this view from
below; so is James Scott's emphasis of "hidden transcripts" and everyday
forms of practice as always already resistant "weapons of the weak" (*Domination and the Arts of Resistance*; *Weapons of the Weak*). Neither de Certeau
nor Scott considers transnationality as integral to these resistant practices,
since theirs is a politics of the local. Similarly, local/global studies tend to
romanticize the local as not necessarily pure but stubbornly the site of
resistance. As has been pointed out, globalization is by no means a complete or thorough phenomenon, and neither does the global stand in
binary opposition to the local. What has changed, however, are the parameters of the national. The national is no longer the site of homogeneous time and territorialized space but is increasingly inflected by a
transnationality that suggests the intersection of "multiple spatiotemporal
(dis)orders" (Sassen, 221). The transnational, therefore, is not bound by
the binary of the local and the global and can occur in national, local, or
global spaces across different and multiple spatialities and temporalities.

We offer, in this volume, a conception of minor transnationalism that
intervenes in the above formulations in multiple ways. When we take a
minor or minoritized perspective, we inevitably need to shift the accents
and revise the above formulations. Major discussions of transnationalism
and globalization assume that ethnic particularity and minoritized per-

spectives are contained within and easily assimilated into the dominant forms of transnationalism. We concur that the minority and the diasporic necessarily participate, though differentially, in the moment of transnationalism, either from below or above, or that the minority and the diasporic live within the space of increasing global integration brought on by globalizing forces in communication, migration, and capital flow, within the circulation of global cultures, ideas, and capital. However, the minority and the diasporic peoples, even under duress, develop cultural practices and networks of communication that exceed the parameters of these theories. What is lacking in the binary model of above-and-below, the utopic and the dystopic, and the global and the local is an awareness and recognition of the creative interventions that networks of minoritized cultures produce within and across national boundaries. All too often the emphasis on the major/resistant mode of cultural practices denies the complex and multiple forms of cultural expressions of minorities and diasporic peoples and hides their micropractices of transnationality in their multiple, paradoxical, or even irreverent relations with the economic transnationalism of contemporary empires. Common conceptions of resistance to the major reify the boundaries of communities by placing the focus on action and reaction, excluding other forms of participation in the transnational that may be more proactive and more creative even while economically disadvantaged. By extracting the site of resistance and defining it as transnationalism from below, it appears that there are two different transnationalisms in opposition and conflict, when in reality the minor and the major participate in one shared transnational moment and space structured by uneven power relations.

We claim that theories of transnationalism continue to exercise a "politics of recognition" (see Taylor; Fraser) in valorizing the most dominant and the most resistant. The binary model presupposes that minorities necessarily and continuously engage with and against majority cultures in a vertical relationship of opposition or assimilation. The Foucauldian overemphasis on the capillary operation of power of the dominant contributed to this vertical model from which horizontal communication amongst minorities is made invisible. Thanks to the global reach of the media as well as the intensified migration of peoples, transnationality in minority cultures has become a given and their mutual communication is also enhanced. Minority cultures are part of our transnational moment, not a reified or segregated pocket of cultures and mores waiting to be selectively incorporated into what qualifies as global or transnational by the powers that be. What has prevented the admission of the integral role played by minority cultures is the politics of recognition exercised by theorists of transnationalism that in arguing for a borderless world have continued to adhere to a binary North/South, dominant/resistant model of culture.

Our emphasis is on transversal movements of culture that are distinguishable from the "arenas of postnational identification" (Joseph 17). This cultural transversalism includes minor cultural articulations in productive relationship with the major (in all its possible shapes, forms, and kinds), as well as minor-to-minor networks that circumvent the major altogether. This transversalism also produces new forms of identification that negotiate with national, ethnic, and cultural boundaries, thus allowing for the emergence of the minor's inherent complexity and multiplicity. New requirements of ethics become urgent, and expressions of allegiance are found in unexpected and sometimes surprising places; new literacies are created in nonstandard languages, tonalities, and rhythms; and the copresence of colonial, postcolonial, and neocolonial spaces fundamentally blurs the temporal sequence of these moments. This conception of minor transnationality differs from the postnational, nomadic, and "flexible" norms of citizenship (Appadurai; Joseph; Ong). Unlike the postnational or nomadic identities that are relatively unmoored from the control of the state and bounded territories, minor transnationality points toward and makes visible the multiple relations between the national and the transnational. It recognizes the difficulty that minority subjects without a statist parameter of citizenship face when the nation-state remains the chief mechanism for dispersing and regulating power, status, and material resources. Flexible or nomadic subjects function as if they are free-floating signifiers without psychic and material investment in one or more given particular geopolitical spaces. By contrast, minor transnational subjects are inevitably invested in their respective geopolitical spaces, often waiting to be recognized as "citizens" to receive the attendant privileges of full citizenship.

The postnational assumes that nations have discreet boundaries in order to go beyond them, but our conception of minor transnationalism takes as its point of departure Edouard Glissant's theories of relation. For Glissant, cultures are not monadic entities or bounded spaces tracing national borders. Such a conception was and is an illusion. According to his definition of creolization, within contact zones, the creolization of cultures occurs not because pure cultural entities have come into contact with each other, but because cultures are always already hybrid and relational as a result of sometimes unexpected and sometimes violent processes (*Poétique de la relation*). Therefore, the transnational is our language to designate this originary multiplicity or creolization, which foregrounds the formative experiences of minorities within and beyond nation-states. Nation-states are alive as mechanisms of control and domination even when transnational corporations are supposed to have dissolved their boundaries. Minority cultural workers are transnational not because they transcend the national, but because their cultural orientations are by definition creolized in Glissant's sense. Samir Amin, for instance, has also noted the hypocrisy of recent theories of globalization, as if prior to our contemporary moment all nations, cultures, and languages were separate and pure entities (*Capitalism in the Age of Globalization*; *Eurocentrism*). Jean-Loup Amselle's theory of "branchements," modeled on technological networks, and his study of the N'ko minority Islamic group, has also opened new avenues for the analysis of cultural change while demonstrating that transcontinental patterns predate contemporary definitions of globalization. If we posit, after Glissant, Amin, and Amselle, that creolization and mixture are the a priori conditions of culture, we can further evince minor expressivity as even more necessarily mixed and transnational. By virtue of their marginality within the nation-state and by their experience of migration and various forms of (neo)colonialism, they had to fall upon cultural resources outside the dominant ones (including those promoted by transnational corporations) that pretend to singularity and authenticity. Not that the dominant cultural resources are inherently monological, but the rhetoric, management, and deployment of these resources by the dominant aggressively assert their authenticity in order to rationalize the dominant's sense of entitlement. For the minor, however, authenticity is the "othering machine" (Suleri) that historically denied them access to full citizenship; it is also that mechanism that produces in the minor a reactive notion of authenticity in the form of cultural nationalism.

The question of authenticity is two-pronged, from our perspective. It includes a politics of retrieval and a politics of inclusion and exclusion. Insofar as the politics of retrieval allows subaltern groups to reclaim lost and suppressed cultural identifications, it is an empowering practice. But insofar as the politics of retrieval presupposes a desire to recapture a lost purity, it is a dangerous impulse that can lead to problematic forms of cultural essentialisms and mythical views of authenticity. Once authenticity is evoked or normalized, a politics of inclusion and exclusion sets in, where arbitrarily fixed categories of identity in the form of identity politics can police cultural expressions and practices. Differences within a given minority group are suppressed in the interest of forming a cultural unified front against domination. However, minor cultures as we know them are the products of transmigrations and multiple encounters, which imply that they are always already mixed, hybrid, and relational. It has been politically useful to disavow such multiplicities, but strategic uses of authenticity have a limited life span, as points of politicization change within a given minority group over time. Spivak's notion of strategic essentialism was never meant to be solidified or fixed into truth claims. Not that we do not need a strategic essentialism or a politics of authenticity, but that we need to be cognizant of its limited usage in changing contexts of application and its exclusivist tendencies even toward its internal members.

What makes it even more imperative now to rethink the politics of authenticity from a transnational or relational perspective is the increased speed, frequency, and expansion of cultural conjunctures and disjunctures in the formation of various spaces of contact, physical and virtual. The garb of authenticity today in the transnational context would fall prey to the "stranger fetishism" wherein the authentic stranger becomes a commodity whose difference is contained and consumed by those with purchasing power (Ahmed). A new global multiculturalism is thus engendered where strangers of various origins constitute the shopping list of cultures. As nationalisms decline on the transnational front, the hardening of minority identity becomes more visible and out of step with economic globalization and is soon ready material for global multicultural consumption.

Within the new formation of global multiculturalism, what constitutes the "minor" or "minority" needs to be reframed from the erstwhile nation-state–based model of understanding. When we juxtapose *minor* with *transnationalism*, a new field of meanings emerges with an array of combinations of issues that depart from existing notions of "minority discourse." The formulation of "minority discourse" emerged within American studies as a way of theorizing diversity. But this approach to diversity remains largely monolingual, even though multilinguality is a given within minority communities. When non-U.S. forms of transnationalism and transcolonialism are brought into play, the "minority discourse" model is helpful only to a limited extent. Not all minorities are minoritized by the same mechanisms in different places; there is no universal minority position as such. By looking at the way minority issues have been formulated in other national and regional contexts, it is possible to show that all expressive discourses (such as music, cinema, autobiography, and other literary genres) are inflected by transnational and transcolonial processes. Here transcolonialism denotes the shared, though differentiated, experience of colonialism and neocolonialism (by the same colonizer or by different colonizers), a site of trauma, constituting the shadowy side of the transnational.

Many European nations, such as Britain, France, Portugal, and Spain, and the Asian nations of China and Japan, along with the United States, all have a history of colonial and imperial dominance. As a result, their cultures, literatures, and languages have reached peoples and nations far beyond their borders. While postcolonial studies has proven to be an important tool for the exploration of colonized cultures, sociocultural developments since decolonization now call for better contextualization using transcolonial perspectives. For example, the very notion of postcoloniality seems insufficient in its focus on the historical period since independence was achieved. It remains concerned with the exploration of relationality between dominant (colonizing cultures) and dominated (colonized) spaces and therefore does not provide an adequate framework for the study of those cultures that remain effectively colonized or those cultures subjected to the colonizing effects of globalization and multinational capital and the accompanying cultural markers. Most importantly, postcolonial studies fails to foreground the productive cultural work of minorities resulting from their transcolonial and transnational experiences. Postcolonial cultural studies has been overly concerned with a vertical analysis confined to one nation-state, such as the effect of British colonialism in India, where the vertical power relationship between the colonizer and the colonized is the main object of analysis. Finally, it reinforces the hegemony of English as the language of discourse and communication.

In contradistinction, we recognize the persistence of colonial power relations and the power of global capital, attend to the inherent complexity of minor expressive cultures on multiple registers, take a horizontal approach that brings postcolonial minor cultural formations across national boundaries into productive comparisons, and engage with multiple linguistic formations. Methodologically, for this particular volume, this means dialogues on multiple fronts involving questions of theory, history, spatiality, culture, and disciplines across national boundaries and ethnic/ area studies divides. Nation-based research in American ethnic studies as well as area studies enters into productive encounters with traditional others, such as European studies and the field of "theory." For instance, how do we theorize an ethnic American subjectivity when it is situated elsewhere and is read as the representative of the global? How do we map the immigrant subject-in-process from being a national subject (at the place of origin) to an ethnic subject (at the place of settlement) when the two are porously interactive and, shall we say, intersubjective? Is the immigrant subject postmodern by definition? How do the two terms *minority* and *theory* inflect each other, when theory as such is Eurocentric? How do we then, "provincialize" theory (as Chakrabarty might say) so that universalizing theories will be returned to their contexts and exposed of their specificities?

Transformative Practices

Theory, *history*, *performance*, *spatiality*, *culture*, and *discipline* are posited here as terms of action that can be deployed outside of their conventional parameters and by inauthentic agents, those presumed to be "without history" and "without theory." "Theorizing" is a practice that challenges Eurocentric theories' universal claims while at the same time not giving in to naive empiricism and documentarity with assumptions of transparent representation of reality. Theories as such have always already implicated minoritized subjects, even if the modes of implication may merely be neglect, misrecognition, and disavowal. The other, as such, is constitutive of the self of theory; its absence at every moment calls for its emergence and arrival. Our modes of engagement with theory as such, therefore, are multiple, including critique, reinscription, and invention, not allowing theory to monopolize the power to make generalizations about our transnational world.

It is in this vein that Suzanne Gearhart delineates Etienne Balibar's notion of "interior exclusion" in her theorization of the intersection of the minority and the transnational. The minority and the immigrant are constitutive of the national in its status as the object of interior exclusion, integral to what the national means and how citizenship is defined. As the putative European self exercises exclusion of the minoritized other, it is involved in a "transindividual" or intersubjective and intrasubjective relation with the other, just as its subjectivization process requires the interior exclusion of the self from itself. This double process determines the ambivalence of identification in terms of national citizenship and belonging. Similarly, the immigrant and the minority are constitutive of the transnational — whether in its "good" or "bad" versions, corresponding to the distinctions between "transnationalism from below" and "transnationalism from above" — through its double engagement with their difference and sameness, exclusion and inclusion.

Literalizing the constitutive character of the minority in the formation of the transnational is the phenomenon of migration and traveling between the West and the non-West. While there have been adequate critiques of mainstream Western travelers to the faraway and not-so-faraway colonial and Third World sites tracing colonial, postcolonial, and neocolonial trajectories and routes (Clifford; Kaplan), very little has been said about the multidirectional travels by the other except in terms of immigration studies where the immigrants are granted subjecthood, albeit a problematic one, only when they enter the West. There are also the categories of the Third World cosmopolitan and the flexible citizen (Ong) who possess the wherewithal to float above national determinations of economy, politics, culture, and citizenship. But what about the others, whose travels and movements do not fall into these categories?

The nonwhite Western person who traverses the forces of globalization to the non-West presents one such subject position fraught with ambivalence, and so does the nonwhite, non-Western person en route to the West without intending to be an immigrant and without the wherewithal to be a Third World cosmopolitan or a flexible citizen. Globalization has brought many others home but also sent many abroad, producing alternate circuits of transnationality that have been largely undertheorized. David Palumbo-Liu's and Shu-mei Shih's essays ask questions about ethics in the transnational context when both virtual and face-to-face contacts between selves and others have increased to an unprecedented degree. What are the responsibilities of the self to the other? How may these responsibilities be expressed, concretized, assumed, or fulfilled? Does the other bear responsibilities also?

Framing his argument on transpacific circulation of intersubjective affect in the context of globalization, Palumbo-Liu begins his essay via a provocative critique of the two seemingly unrelated discourses — rational choice theory and American pragmatism — as holding up "the logic of self-interest and exclusivity." What is the role and function of literature in such a context? Can literature function today as the site of production of ethical affect against the dehumanizing forces of the global economy and media? How should it deal with sentimentality, which rational choice theory dismisses and pragmatism manipulates? The paradigmatic text in question turns out to be a minor text written by Japanese American writer Ruth Ozeki, *My Year of Meats*. Her postmodern novel, so to speak, retains the residual modern in its ability to lend information an ethical context and to imagine communities (albeit spatially and temporally discontiguous ones like the Internet or faxes) that are possible. The novel also does not shy away from deploying sentimentality but rather sees it as an expedient means of expressing and representing the regard for others. Here, the putative, racialized other within the United States — the Japanese American protagonist in Ozeki's novel — becomes emblematic of the Western self and its responsibility to the non-West as well as other ethnic minorities in the United States.

The circulation of ethical affect can also begin from the non-West, when the so-called Third World native other overcomes the reactive affects of nationalism and nativism and escapes from the binary logic of the politics of recognition. Shu-mei Shih analyzes the bind of binarism in the discourse of Orientalism and anti-Orientalism as well as the withholding of and the struggle for coevality as expressions of the paucity of Western liberal imagination about the other, and the ambivalent compliance of the other's response to that imagination. The other's compliance is most readily observable in the discourses of cultural nationalism and nativism, resisting and refuting the injustice of the totalizing discourses of Orientalism and the withholding of coevality, one important aspect of which for the Chinese in China is a deeply embedded sinocentrism. The frustration of this sinocentrism to effect a powerful rebuttal to the West is often displaced to its internal and external others: ethnic minorities in China, and those "inauthentic" people of Han Chinese descent residing elsewhere. Shih suggests that part of the ethical responsibilities of the continental Chinese is precisely to shed the burden of sinocentrism as a reaction against Western hegemony, just as the West also needs to shed its domineering ways and arbitrarily manipulated discourses of difference and sameness. Shih's example is feminism's negotiation across the China/West divide, a divide complicated by immigration, traveling, and diaspora, and that has thus become at least a tripartite construct. In a synthesis à la Emmanuel Levinas, Karatani Kōjin, and Li Xiaojiang, Shih then proposes a transversal and transpositional politics where to be ethical is to be able to shift positions to those of the other and many more others beyond the binary logic of First World hegemony and Third World nationalism.

Susan Koshy likewise questions the assumed universalism of Western globalization theory that continues to posit the Third World as the recipient of theory, emptying out what she deftly calls the "transformative agency" of Third World figures as well as their participation in the co-authorship of the global order. Conceptualizing minor transnationalism as the site of emergent, nonnormative regimes and "practical humanism," the framework for "aggregating numerous movements, groups, and discourses" engaged in a guerrilla war against a major transnationalism, and the network of "transnationalized communities," Koshy proposes a "sustainable universalism" that better marks the Third World's constitutive role in globalization. For example, the task of monitoring the transnational trafficking of sex slaves, having dropped through the cracks of national and transnational legal regimes into a legal void, has now fallen on minor transnational organizations that can exercise forms of practical and sustainable universalism to better represent the context-specific as well as transcontext situations of the postmodern subaltern: the sex slaves.

Equally important to the project of rethinking transnational ethnic and migratory relations is the urgent need to consider the disciplinary principles that guide the production of academic knowledge about minority subjects and their histories. By "historicizing" the field of minority discourse production, it is possible to show how transdisciplinary academic practices can construct transnational objects of knowledge, thereby transforming our established interpretive frameworks and disciplinary conventions, while also producing alternative genealogies and narratives of the past.

Tyler Stovall's essay adopts a historical and a critical practice that enacts a minor transnational critique. He brings insights from one field to illuminate questions raised in another, and thus demonstrates how traditional disciplinary paradigms would not allow for a complete understanding of the 1926 Crutcher murder case he examines. He uses perspectives from French, francophone, and African American studies, adopting a postcolonial and cultural studies approach to this Parisian murder case in which a white French woman murdered her black American husband. Stovall produces a historical analysis of the way dynamics of class, race, sex, gender, and violence were being destabilized by the arrival of non-white subjects in the metropole, and he reveals the new relations of power and the "fault lines" that were developing in the "années folles" of 1920s

French society. Stovall shows how it is necessary to consider this case "from three different geographical and theoretical perspectives" in order to fully understand it as an example of "postcolonial criminality" that involved metropolitan, colonial, and American contexts. His method of doing a cultural history that is simultaneously transnational and transcontextual allows him to show that "American-style patterns of race relations" were already developing in France in the interwar era. Such a reading proves that contemporary questions about race and multiculturalism in France have a longer genealogy than is generally understood.

In a similar vein, Kathleen McHugh brings together problems of theory, history, and geography to show how minoritarian filmmakers undo mainstream narrative and cinematic conventions that purport to capture the "truth" of coherent selves rooted in national space and historical time. She shows how "ethnic" American filmmakers set out to register "the representational absence and invisibility integral to transnational minority experience." The Japanese American Rea Tajiri's *History and Memory* does so by incorporating "historical modes of visual representation" that document this absence, whereas the Chicano artists Ramiro Puerta's and Guillermo Verdecchia's film *Crucero/Crossroads* uses space to "fracture the coherence of the subject." These experimental approaches to filmmaking and narration produce images that exemplify the fragmented consciousness common to the transnational minority experience of "border subjects" for whom the private and the public, the personal and the historical, the real and the fictional are closely intertwined. McHugh's careful analyses highlight the extent to which the minority experience lives out the theories that have developed about so-called postmodern narratives of absence and incoherence. But here, this absence, she points out, is given a presence, a past, and a possible future through visual representations of the racialized body. These filmic images expose the myriad ways in which "the fissures and inadequacies of the nation and the state locate themselves in the body of the transnational minority subject." But these representations do not reconfigure in an oppositional or essentialist mode the minority body as a cohesive or homogeneous entity; instead, the filmmakers keep to a logic of the fragment in their cinematic practice, thus illuminating the always already discontinuous and multiply coded forms of identifications that are those of "marginal" subjects.

Minority bodies matter: their visible (racial, sexual) difference has been instrumentalized by a variety of discourses. Bodies are put in the center of many disciplinary debates about the technologies of the self. Together with the body and physical appearance, language is a crucial marker of identity and nationality. But in Africa, where everyone is multilingual, the monologic approach to language and identity no longer obtains. Moradewun Adejunmobi surveys the debate about language and literacy under French and British colonial policies of assimilation or indirect rule, respectively. She argues that some anticolonial writers and critics framed the language issues "with the very same tropes" used by colonial advocates of vernacular literacy: "alienation," "respect for the past," and the need "to speak to each community" in its own language. She describes the territorial logic at work in colonial or "major" discourses of the vernacular that used it as a pretext for the containment and separation of different linguistic communities that were thus *constructed* as distinct. By questioning the oppositional status of the vernacular as a pure nativist space, she also demystifies the most common clichés about the "minor" politics of language choice. The vernacular does not automatically exist as an uncontaminated field; rather, it is either an instrument of colonial administrative control or part of a program to win political autonomy. It is rarely an end in itself for most African writers who usually see past the binary opposition between the European language and the mother tongue, being more interested in the concept of a lingua franca for transcultural communication. As a result, language use in Africa seems to be an interesting example of a de facto minor transnationalism that connects overlapping and multiply-identified communities who are more interested in a lateral cultural engagement with each other than in asserting themselves as purely ethnic and oppositional vis-à-vis the major transnational forms of economic global power.

In the section on "Reading, Writing, Performing," Françoise Lionnet adds another perspective on the uses of the vernacular in the Indian Ocean–African zone. Focusing on Dev Virahsawmy, the popular Mauritian dramatist who has produced radical adaptations and reinterpretations of Shakespeare's plays, she argues that his *Toufann* is best understood not just in relation to the Shakespearean original (*The Tempest*), its explicit intertext, but rather as a transcolonial critique of power that echoes the work of several sub-Saharan African authors, such as Chinua Achebe or Sony Labou Tansi. The play's success, when translated into English and produced in London in 1999, underscored the paradoxes of the reception of "marginal" cultural texts. A profound statement about the politics of knowledge, control, and power, *Toufann*'s critical and sexual edge was blunted by its travel back to the metropole, where it seemed to have become just another "cultural" manifestation of well-worn critical paradigms instead of the astute critique of such paradigms.

The questions of language, literature, and postcolonial modes of interpretive reading are underscored by what Ali Behdad calls "the predicament of reading 'minor' literature." What is at stake in the institutionalization of this literature? And to what extent do its themes of exile, mobility, and metaphoric vs. real displacements create a field of discourse that tends to idealize homelessness and the advantages of a free-floating subjectivity rooted only in language? The utopian impulse of postcolonial intellectual approaches to this literature has led to a romanticized view of the "seductive power of geographical displacement." In a self-reflexive move about his own critical practice, Behdad demonstrates the importance of social, economic, political, and historical contextualization for a thorough understanding of the real-life conditions and contexts of exile and immigration in the Algerian Driss Chraïbi's 1955 novel *Les boucs*, which depicts the fate of postwar Maghrebian immigrants in suburban France.

Postcolonial theory's aestheticization of displacement, as Behdad points out, marks a utopian dimension of transnationality. The transnationalism of elite and diasporic theorists can be read as a form of transnationalism from above. Michael Bourdaghs's essay deals with what is seemingly an aerial and ethereal form of transnational movement, that of jet-setting pop musicians over two metropolitan sites, but his reading of Sakamoto Kyū's "translations of rockabilly" points to the limits imposed upon the mobility and translatability of non-Western performers and artists in the American context. Although Sakamoto Kyū is not a "minority" subject in the United States, his music became culturalized and racialized to represent "Japaneseness." The universally understood culinary connotations of the imposed title of his song, "Sukiyaki," became part of an international lingua franca that trivialized an otherwise major voice in his home country. Translation produces differences and hierarchies that reinforce the difficulty of traveling from a major mode to a minor one. This ethereal Japanese pop traveler died in a plane crash and never got his star on the Hollywood walk of fame. What Michael Bourdaghs's critical practice also demonstrates is that there are fruitful and productive theoretical borrowings across "minor" transnational discourses. Indeed, it is the work of *Black Atlantic* theorist Paul Gilroy on black music that allows Bourdaghs to develop his own views on rockabilly music.

When questions of globalization, immigration, and transnational flows are discussed, there is a tendency to conflate the notion of the global with that of the urban, with the rural regions of the globe being perceived as existing outside of modernity and globalization. In our final section, "Spatializing," Jenny Sharpe's essay shifts the focus to rural Jamaica, providing a different take on Gilroy's work and alerting us to the persistence of old colonial patterns of exploitation that are now "driving a greater wedge between city and country." In the country, it is not cyberspace but radio that becomes the true site *and* metaphor for black female subjectivity and agency. If the major global forms of transnationalism tend to correspond to a virtual network of urban spaces, in Jamaica, dancehall culture, radio, and dub poetry are powerful forms of "minor" globalizations through which rural women express their material cultures and stay connected to national and international news about many daily struggles that echo their own. Thus, the dub poetry of Jean Binta Breeze "gives faces to the nameless women who are otherwise absent from our cartographies of transnational cultures and globalization." Sharpe's is a salutary reminder that there exist minor moods and modes of existing both musically and globally, and that women's performances make this plainly visible and audible.

If a major transnationalism flaunts the supercompression of space or the elimination of distance, minor transnationalism charts a much more complex configuration of space and heterogeneous "spatial practices" (à la Henri Lefèbvre). These practices occur in the nonspaces of boundaries and borders, spaces which are nonetheless infinitely expansive and full of possibilities. Seiji Lippit's essay delineates the conceptual limits of national culture by way of its paradoxical view of minority culture as the site of both abjection and incorporation. It reflects a particular form of organization of the inside and the outside, as Yuri Lotman's notion of "semiosphere" suggests, where the boundary between the two spaces both separates and unites the two spaces. One of these boundary spaces is the *roji*, the term used by novelist Nagakami Kenji to designate the outcaste village into which and out of which the Japanese subject wanders. Just as this space has an ambivalent relationship with other "authentic" national spaces as being both their outside (exclusion and abjection) and their inside (assimilation and incorporation), so does the minor culture have a paradoxical relationship with national culture. The abject has the "potential of becoming the sacred" at any moment within this national imaginary — thus the roji's "strange power" which has obsessed writers such as Nagakami.

Similarly, Elizabeth Marchant's piece uses a concrete historical site, the Pelourinho, the historic center of the city of Salvador, the "Black Rome," to examine the condition of the Afro-Bahian's simultaneous marginality and centrality to Brazilian national culture. Marchant's Pelourinho is Lippit's roji, in this sense; Lippit's "abjection" echoes Marchant's "subjection," as the Pelourinho is the site of black suffering and violence. The paradoxical prominence or centrality of the Pelourinho, Marchant goes on to expose, however, is the Brazilian nation's need to promote tourism to the area, which requires a romantic rhetoric of racial democracy and harmony and a cultural promotion of blackness. This romantic valorization of black culture does not change the conditions of blacks in terms of their class status; rather, it reifies ethnicity and culture. The valorization occurs at a level different from the socioeconomic; the cultural is decontextualized to carry the rhetoric of racial democracy and cultural mixing as part and parcel of the definition of Brazilian national culture. Marchant's essay provides an important perspective on the layers of meaning that subtend the appropriation of a "minor" space for a "major" purpose. It puts into question the very marginality of what this space is meant to represent historically and nationally.

The Chicano/a construction of the mythic homeland of Aztlán as an oppositional and alternative geography against U.S. territorialization likewise registers a challenge to normative citizenship. Rafael Pérez-Torres engages in a radical valuation of *mestizaje* and interstitiality within the transnational space of the border. Despite romanticization, on the part of some critics, of the tropes of borderland and mestizaje, Pérez-Torres shows that these ultimately resist fetishization. He argues that for Chicano/a artists, poets, and scholars, the trope of mestizaje is empowering and melancholic, ironic and ambiguous, all at once. Historical dislocations create ideological ruptures while embedding individual subjects within the material conditions of constraining social relations. That is why the mythic space of the homeland in Chicano expressive culture keeps on shaping individual projects in which anticolonial triumph and melancholy remain intertwined, articulating both a gain and a loss of embodied subjectivity. Pérez-Torres's essay brings in a crucial dimension within the field of U.S. ethnic studies. Unlike the Asian or African minorities, whose histories are those of displacement (whether through immigration or slavery), the Chicanos/as occupy an ambiguous space: their transnationalism is not one born of the movement from a national context to another but rather one produced by the historical realities of shifting borders in the southwestern United States. Pérez-Torres argues that Chicano/a art intervenes in the social production of space within the Southwest, and that it presents a challenge to "accepted notions of American identity . . . premised on the exclusion of the racial in the service of the national." This is an important point that, we feel, adds a unique dimension to this volume on "minor" transnational encounters. There are specificities here that do not echo those of the African (as discussed by Adejunmobi) or Mauritian (Lionnet) contexts, but rather describe a form of mestizaje that, had we more space to do so, would provide an interesting parallel to the kinds of geographical and political issues that the Basque people of France and Spain, say, are dealing with in their own cross-border multilingual cultural identities and dissident practices.

The constantly changing and troubling terrains of identities and cultures under contemporary transnational conditions echo both the specific material circumstances that we have described above and the shifting psychic identifications that border writers and artists are able to negotiate with acute sensitivity. This melancholic valence of the border is perhaps that which most resonates with the "minor" key in a musical sense. If the minor mood in music is an introspective and mournful tone different from the more triumphant "major" key, then "minor transnationalism" is perhaps the mode in which the traumas of colonial, imperial, and global hegemonies as well as the affective dimensions of transcolonial solidarities continue to work themselves out and produce new possibilities. Beyond the nostalgic and the melancholic, these solidarities point to ways of becoming more engaged with present and future promises of transformation through active participation in the production of local knowledges and global cultures. We offer this volume as testimony and as example of the dynamic possibilities of the work of border-crossing friendships, collaboration, and scholarship.

Works Cited

Ahmed, Sara. *Strange Encounters: Embodied Others in Post-Coloniality*. London: Routledge, 2000.

Amin, Samir. *Capitalism in the Age of Globalization: The Management of Contemporary Society*. London: Zed Books, 1997.

——. *Eurocentrism*. Trans. Russell Moore. New York: Monthly Review Press, 1989.

Amselle, Jean-Loup. *Branchements: Anthropologie de l'universalité des cultures*. Paris: Flammarion, 2001.

Appadurai, Arjun. *Modernity at Large: Cultural Dimensions of Globalization*. Minneapolis: University of Minnesota Press, 1996.

Chakrabarty, Dipesh. *Provincializing Europe: Postcolonial Thought and Historical Difference*. Princeton: Princeton University Press, 2000.

Clifford, James. *Routes: Travel and Translation in the Late Twentieth Century*. Cambridge: Harvard University Press, 1997.

De Certeau, Michel. *L'invention du quotidien*. 2 vols. Paris: Union générale d'éditions, 1980. Trans. by Steven Rendall as *The Practice of Everyday Life*. Berkeley: University of California Press, 1984.

Deleuze, Gilles, and Félix Guattari. *Kafka: Pour une littérature mineure*. Paris: Éditions de Minuit, 1975. Trans. by Dana Polan as *Kafka: Toward a Minor Literature*. Foreword by Réda Bensmaïa. Minneapolis: University of Minnesota Press, 1986.

Derrida, Jacques. *De la grammatologie*. Paris: Édtions de Minuit, 1967. Trans. by Gayatri Chakravorty Spivak as *Of Grammatology*. Baltimore: Johns Hopkins University Press, 1976.

Fanon, Frantz. *Les damnés de la terre*. Preface by Jean-Paul Sartre. Paris: Maspéro, 1961. Trans. by Constance Farrington as *The Wretched of the Earth*. New York: Grove, 1965. Trans. and foreword by Richard Philcox as *The Wretched of the Earth*. New York: Grove, forthcoming.

——. *Peau noire, masques blancs*. Paris: Éditions du Seuil, 1952. Trans. by Charles Lam Markham as *Black Skin, White Masks*. New York: Grove, 1967.

Fraser, Nancy. "From Redistribution to Recognition? Dilemmas of Justice in a 'Post-Socialist' Age." *Theorizing Multiculturalism: A Guide to the Current Debate*. Ed. Cynthia Willett. Oxford: Blackwell, 1998. 19–49.

Glissant, Edouard. *Le discours antillais*. Paris: Seuil, 1981. Trans. and intro. by J. Michael Dash as *Caribbean Discourse: Selected Essays*. Charlottesville: University Press of Virginia, 1989.

——. *Poétique de la relation*. Paris: Gallimard, 1990. Trans. by Betsy Wing as *Poetics of Relation*. Ann Arbor: University of Michigan Press, 1997.

Hall, Stuart, "The Local and the Global: Globalization and Ethnicity." *Culture, Globalization, and the World System*. Ed. Anthony King. Minneapolis: University of Minnesota Press, 1997. 19–39.

Harvey, David. *The Condition of Postmodernity: An Enquiry into the Origins of Cultural Change*. Oxford: Blackwell, 1989.

Levinas, Emmanuel. *Entre nous: Essais sur le penser-à-l'autre*. Paris: Bernard Grasset, 1991. Trans. by Michael B. Smith and Barbara Harshav as *Entre nous: On Thinking-of-the-Other*. New York: Columbia University Press, 1998.

Joseph, May. *Nomadic Identities: The Performance of Citizenship*. Minneapolis: University of Minnesota Press, 1999.

Kaplan, Caren. *Questions of Travel: Postmodern Discourses of Displacement*. Durham: Duke University Press, 1996.

Mahler, Sarah, J. " Theoretical and Empirical Contributions toward a Research Agenda for Transnationalism." *Transnationalism from Below*. Ed. Michael Peter Smith and Luis Eduardo Guarnizo. London: Transaction, 1998. 64–100.

Morrison, Toni. *Playing in the Dark: Whiteness and the Literary Imagination*. Cambridge: Harvard University Press, 1992.

Ong, Aihwa. *Flexible Citizenship: The Cultural Logics of Transnationality*. Durham: Duke University Press, 1999.

Suleri, Sara. "Woman Skin Deep: Feminism and the Postcolonial Condition." *Identi-*

ties. Ed. Henry Louis Gates Jr. and Anthony Appiah. Chicago: University of Chicago Press, 1995. 133–146.

Sassen, Saskia. "Spatialities and Temporalities of the Global: Elements for a Theorization." *Public Culture* 12.1 (2000): 215–232.

Scott, James. *Domination and the Arts of Resistance: Hidden Transcripts.* New Haven: Yale University Press, 1990.

——. *Weapons of the Weak: Everyday Forms of Peasant Resistance.* New Haven: Yale University Press, 1985.

Spivak, Gayatri, "Diasporas Old and New: Women in the Transnational World," *Textual Practice* 10.2 (1996): 245–269.

Taylor, Charles, and Amy Gutman. *Multiculturalism and "The Politics of Recognition":* *An Essay.* Princeton: Princeton University Press, 1992.

PART I
THEORIZING

SUZANNE GEARHART

Inclusions

Psychoanalysis, Transnationalism, and Minority Cultures

The questions before us today are simple and direct: do minority cultures exhibit transnational perspectives and, if so, how do these perspectives inflect our understanding of transnationalism? But despite their apparent directness, they are, of course, very difficult questions, whose terms are problematic and whose answers, therefore, are to say the very least complex. One of the things at stake in these questions is the meaning of the term "minority culture" itself. In this connection one of the first problems one encounters concerns the context within which any given minority culture is defined. We know that a group that might be called a minority within one particular national context can be a majority in another national context. But what does this mean with respect to its minority status? A related issue would be that of cultural groups that do not exist as a majority within any national context whatsoever. How would the different status of these two types of minorities within the general category of minority cultures inflect our understanding of the term "minority" itself? Does the term "minority" have the same significance with respect to each?

Still another question would concern the relationship between minority cultures and power. The question of minority cultures is inseparable from a question of power, or at least when we speak of a minority culture today it seems to me that what we have in mind are cultural groups whose members are not only fewer in number than those of the cultural majority but who are also relatively disempowered with respect to members of a more powerful majority culture or group. If one associates power with majority status and disempowerment with minority status, however, it is not logically inconceivable that there could be a "majority" culture that is also a "minority" culture, or a "minority" culture that is also a "majority" culture. In other words, there could be groups whose members are greater in number but are relatively deprived of power and groups whose members are fewer in number but are relatively more powerful.

The history of colonialism offers numerous examples of such majority/ minority inversions, in which a small minority made up of colonizers tyrannizes a large majority made up of the colonized. Postcolonial societies in which the former colonizers or their descendants still represent an overwhelmingly powerful minority — at least in economic terms — represent another example. But even cultures or nations that have existed for centuries as separate states and that have had no direct experience of colonization offer examples of such a "minority majority" or "majority minority" paradox. In saying this I am thinking of the way in which class and "racial" characteristics reinforce each other in the history of racism. Myths of race, it has been argued, refer not so much to the nation as a whole as to a class or an aristocracy within the nation — the criteria invested by racism with racial and cultural significance tend to be criteria of social class. Thus the dominant racial ideology of a given nation tends to coincide with the class ideology of an elite within the nation (Balibar and Wallerstein 60–61). In this sense, a "minority" culture becomes the "majority" culture, and elites become what might be called "minority majorities" or "majority minorities."

In order to pursue a bit further these and other questions about the possible meanings of the concept of minority culture, I now turn to the work of Etienne Balibar, not only because of his widely cited essays on contemporary nationalism, immigration, neoracism, and citizenship, but also because I would like to discuss the possible role of psychoanalysis in providing new approaches to such questions. For alongside the questions about minority culture I have already mentioned are still another group of questions about cultural identity or rather cultural identification and the formation of cultural groups. Questions that in turn lead to still other questions about the meaning of the terms "minority" and "majority" in relation to any particular experience of culture. Questions that have the merit — or the drawback, whichever you prefer — of making it even more difficult to determine what is meant or could be meant by the terms "minority" and "minority cultures."

These questions about the formation of cultural groups call, in my view, for a psychoanalytic perspective and language in order to be phrased, because they suggest that cultural identity is never given in itself, but rather produced by means of identification or identifications, and because psychoanalysis provides concepts and strategies that can be used to analyze this production of identity and to articulate its potential implications for our understanding of the first of the problematic terms and concepts that are our focus — "minority culture."

It might seem paradoxical to refer to the work of Balibar in connection with psychoanalysis, not only because he is known primarily as a political philosopher and cultural theorist, but also because in the one essay that he has devoted entirely to the discussion of psychoanalytic issues, his essay on Wilhelm Reich, entitled "Fascism, Psychoanalysis, Freudo-Marxism," Balibar explicitly discourages any attempt to revive what he calls "Freudo-Marxism," especially the Freudo-Marxism of Reich. However, Balibar also argues that it is important to "recall the necessity" of Freudo-Marxism (177), and many points in his political and cultural analyses take on even greater clarity and force when they are viewed in the light of this essay on psychoanalysis.

I will be focusing on two concepts that lie at the heart of Balibar's cultural and political analyses — "transindividuality" and "interior inclusion." As I read Balibar, both of these terms suggest that the point of departure for his political philosophy and cultural theory is a self that is not punctual and unified but rather complex and problematic, a self whose identity has been put into question from the very outset by the concept and process of repression. I recognize that it is virtually commonplace today to speak of a divided or split or complex subject, and that as a result many might ask whether a political philosophy that takes the idea of psychic repression as a starting point has anything new or different to teach us. I would respond by saying that it is not at all clear that the social and cultural implications of such a problematic form of subjectivity have been previously explored in the way Balibar explores them or with the same critical results.

In addressing questions about the links between psychoanalysis and cultural theory in Balibar's work, it is important to stress that his relationship to psychoanalysis is a critical one — critical, in particular, of the psychoanalytic model proposed by Reich and other Freudo-Marxists. What Balibar explicitly rejects is Reich's affirmation of what could be called the libidinal model of culture and politics: Reich's desire for a return to "the utopia of a psyche without an unconscious," a return in which "the objective of politics" becomes "the removal of repression itself" ("Freudo-Marxism," 187) and the total fulfillment of desire. What Balibar embraces, on the other hand, is the contrasting idea that repression and desire do not exist separately, which implies that the ego cannot be simply liberated from repression (or identified with repression) and that repression itself cannot be simply removed or overcome. In what I am tempted to call Balibar's version of psychoanalysis, the ego is "tied to the ambivalence of repression, to the double pressure of a desire and a censorship, or of an id and a superego with whom you have to 'negotiate' " (185). Repression, in other words, is necessarily negative and positive, neither purely negative nor purely positive, because what is positive from the standpoint of one "pressure" or psychic instance will be negative from the standpoint of the other and vice versa.

What in Balibar's terms are the social and cultural implications of this psychic configuration? The question is too simple, because it presupposes or risks presupposing that it is legitimate to analyze (or psychoanalyze) the conflict and interplay between the ego, the id, and the superego without asking the question of how they came to be what they are and to function as they do in the first place. It assumes, in other words, that the psyche is a *cause* of social relations and social structures when it may in fact be an *effect*. This is why Balibar argues that engaging in psychoanalysis without any supporting social analysis leads to results that are limited and reductive ("Freudo-Marxism," 185). But such concepts as the "collective unconscious" or the "popular unconscious" are equally limited and reductive, not only of the individual and the individual unconscious but also of the complexity of social and cultural relations. Rather than offering an alternative to the notion of the individual unconscious, Balibar argues, they mirror it to the extent that those who use such concepts construe the collective or popular subject (and its unconscious) as the mere sum of individual subjects, and the collectivity itself as a kind of superindividual. There is a Marxist individualism (or "whiggism") (180) as well as a Freudian individualism.

Thus while certain forms of social analysis seem profoundly dissimilar to traditional forms of psychoanalysis, from the political-psychoanalytic perspective that is Balibar's they appear profoundly similar, because each tends to neglect the ambiguity of repression. In psychic terms, this ambiguity means that the self is confronted by "the other" not only when it confronts society, but also when it confronts itself, a product of the "negotiation" between desire and censorship or, in other words, between the self and itself. In cultural terms, it means that society is confronted by "the other" in the form of individual selves, in the form of other collective selves, but also, and perhaps most significantly, in the form of its own collective "identity." In other words, the other of society is not merely the self, and the other of the self is not merely society. The other of both self and society is the "transindividual," a term used frequently by Balibar to denote a relation that is at once intersubjective and intrasubjective, that disrupts all forms of individual and collective identity.

Balibar's concept of repression and complementary concepts such as "transindividuality" and "interior exclusion" have a dual relation to culture in his work, providing the basis for his critical analyses of contemporary culture and politics and also for the model of civil society he proposes as an alternative to the nationalisms and "fictive ethnicities" (*Race, Nation, Class* 96) that dominate politics in many, if not all parts of the contemporary world. For example, a central preoccupation of Balibar is the question of the relation between violence and nationalism — that is, in our terms, the question of the violence against minorities and minority cultures perceived as not fitting into or belonging to a majority, national culture. There is, according to Balibar, a crucial issue to be explored in connection with this violence, one immediately linked to his perspective on repression. In Balibar's language it is the issue of "interior exclusion," which for him is implicitly the paradigmatic form of exclusion of minority cultures and therefore of violence against them as well. But what, exactly, does he mean by this term? Though Balibar never uses the term "exterior exclusion," the definition of "interior exclusion" obviously depends on an implied contrast between the two terms. According to the logic suggested by this contrast, exterior exclusion would be a form of exclusion in which the conflict created by cultural identification opposes those who identify with a given culture or nation to those who do not identify with it and who are therefore stigmatized and excluded by those who do. In other words, the concept of exterior exclusion would presuppose a purely positive (or a purely negative) form of repression (or identification), in which the self or the collectivity constitutes a unified totality, and in which "exclusion" would relate to what is "exterior" to that totality.

What if repression is neither simply positive or negative, however, but rather ambivalent? Clearly, if the "pressure" with which the subject "negotiates" is a contradictory one, then exclusion would involve not only what is "exterior" — those (minority) individuals or (minority) cultures that do not conform to the model of identity created by what might be called the dominance of one pressure over another in a given situation. It would also involve what is interior; that is, it would involve the subordination or the "minoritization" of one of the two pressures with which one has to negotiate in order to create a single self or identity that can relate positively (or negatively) to a culture or a nation. The exclusion of either one of these pressures would be an "interior" exclusion, in the sense that each of them corresponds to a part of the self.

The concept of interior exclusion obviously has a cultural and social meaning as well. In using it to analyze contemporary political and cultural conflicts, Balibar's suggestion is that cultural or political exclusion not only takes the form of conflict between members of one nation and another, or one ethnic group within a nation and another, but also takes the equally "inclusive" form of a conflict between those (but this would include everyone) who identify positively and those (but this would also include everyone) who identify negatively with the ideals of the nation or the ethnic group in question. In other words, the violence latent in cultural communities or nations may be directed not only at members of minority cultures but also against the community or the nation itself.

It is here that one can begin to answer the question of whether other forms of cultural analysis make it possible to confront the problem of the ambivalence of identification as squarely as Balibar's and whether the critiques of the subject that have been used to support various cultural critiques are really all the same. In many or almost all of the models of ambivalent identification that have been proposed, does not the "ambivalence" in question merely *mirror* a purely *cultural* hybridity and in this sense perpetuate the concept and logic of exterior exclusion that is the object of Balibar's critique? For as Balibar suggests, the source of cultural ambivalence is not only that one or more distinct cultures (that is, cultures that are "exterior" to each other) make conflicting demands on the subject. One's "own" culture is also the source of conflicting demands, or rather, one's relationship to one's "own" culture can be equally ambivalent, because subjectivity is not so much an identity as it is a process of negotiation and conflict.

But how exactly does the concept of interior exclusion apply to nationalism? It would seem that in this regard the logic of interior exclusion leads to an absurd paradox — that the nationalist is an antinationalist or, in the language we are using, that the "majority" culture is a "minority" culture. As implausible as it may at first seem, this is what Balibar in fact argues, for example, when he writes of the (antinational) nationalism and xenophobia of the National Front: "The 'carte d'identité' [or national identity card] is important, but we know that actually in the discourse of the National Front, as in all historical racisms and fascisms, the principal obsession is not with knowing who has the identity card and who does not have it and can therefore be turned back [*refoulé*] at the border. It is to know which Frenchmen are 'in reality' camouflaged foreigners inside French nationality." For the National Front, "potentially *anyone at all is a foreigner*" (*Droit de cité* 123–124; my translation).

The national identity card thus testifies to the existence of exterior exclusion and to a simple form of repression, but the fact that it is *not* the principal obsession of the National Front reveals that the form of exclusion at stake in the politics of the National Front is not an exterior but rather an interior one, which excludes not only "others" or "the other" but even the French citizen who possesses an identity card, and finally even the self (*"anyone at all"*) as other. Balibar makes a similar point in his discussion of the internationalist orientation taken by extreme forms of nationalism. For example, the attempt on the part of the Nazis to identify authentic Aryan Germans led them to a positive identification with an international (and therefore non-German or at least not exclusively German) Aryan group and a negative identification with other members of the German nation. Thus "by seeking to circumscribe the common essence of nationals, racism . . . inevitably becomes involved in the obsessional quest for a 'core' of authenticity that cannot be found, shrinks the category of nationality and de-stabilizes the historical nation" (Balabar and Wallerstein 60). Exclusion, in other words, cannot be analyzed in political or cultural terms alone. It can be analyzed only by a political or cultural theory supplemented by a psychoanalytic theory and informed and transformed by it, because the "differences" it concerns are as much psychic as they are cultural and political, as much "interior" as they are "exterior."

The questions of minority culture and transnationalism are intimately connected with the question of immigration, not just for Balibar, but for virtually every contemporary theorist interested in the subject of (trans)nationalism. At the same time, the contrast between Balibar's approach to the issue of immigration and the approach suggested by other theorists of nationalism is striking. According to the analyses of both Ernest Gellner and Benedict Anderson, for example, those excluded from the group created by the mechanisms of identification are in each case excluded because of some objective factor—Gellner's deliberately absurd but nonetheless revealing example is "blue skin" but he also cites "some deeply engrained religious-cultural habits" (65, 67, 71). Throughout *Imagined Communities*, Anderson stresses the role of language in creating the imagined community of the nation. In other words, Gellner and Anderson describe forms of exclusion and/or of identification whose mechanisms are "simple" and "exterior"—the exclusion of the "blues" by those of another color, the exclusion of Buddhists by Moslems, or the exclusion of speakers of Ukrainian by speakers of Russian. But from Balibar's standpoint such a perspective appears reductive and simplistic and could even be argued to support the spirit of exclusion. It does this, of course, not directly, by claiming that exclusion is legitimate, but indirectly, by suggesting that the differences that are claimed to legitimate exclusion are objective, when in fact it is just as plausible that nationalism itself creates differences, or creates a value system in which certain differences are held to be significant while others are not, and in doing so causes those particular differences to be seen as objective and determining.

In contrast, Balibar's notion of "interior exclusion" means that the primary significance of the immigrants' situation lies in their being not necessarily "others" in whatever terms one could invoke, but rather " 'others' who are not altogether foreigners" (*Droit de cité* 58)—that is, who are not altogether "exterior." In other words, immigrants are others who participate in the economic and cultural life of the European nations in many of the same ways that "native" Europeans do. This is why for Balibar the immigrant is not so much an outsider who needs to be welcomed or embraced by French or European society but rather the potential model for a new form of "citizenship" (*citoyenneté*) and a new form of collective belonging based neither on the total identification of citizenship with nationality nor on the abstraction of a culturally disembodied citizen-subject. In Balibar's words, immigrants in Europe today "appear tendentiously, . . . to typify a *new form of sociability and of citizenship* (*'citoyenneté'*), competing with national sociability and citizenship . . . The 'immigrants' who come from outside of the European community may well be *Europeans par excellence*" (*Droit de cité*, 51–52).

I have noted that Balibar himself never uses the term "exterior exclusion." The same is true for another term that his analyses suggest just as strongly—"exterior inclusion." And yet clearly, if exclusion can be interior, then inclusion can be exterior. This is precisely what Balibar suggests when he writes of immigrants: "What mobilized (and continues to mobilize) their support by intellectuals who want, above all, to act like citizens . . . is less than anything the irresponsible temptation to oppose to the *hatred* of foreigners cultivated and encouraged by the National Front the symmetrical proposition of a *love* of foreigners as such" (*Droit de cité*, 11). The "love" of the immigrant is not opposed to the "hatred" of the immigrant to the extent that love, like hate, can exclude, albeit in different ways. The opposite of "hate" is not "love," because both love and hate are "exterior" in that they imply a simple (positive or negative) form of identification and/or a simple form of repression. In other words, replacing negative stereotypes with positive ones represents no advance with respect to inclusiveness and may even represent a step backward, in the sense that it is the stereotype itself that is negative. The challenge of contemporary multiculturalism lies in the ever-present risk that it will only encourage the proliferation of stereotypes and thus prove to have been little or nothing more than an exterior form of inclusion.

Finally, if inclusion can be exterior, this implies that it can be interior as well — an idea that is born out by Balibar when he writes of violence: "Our society must *defeat violence*, and first of all *in itself*" (*Droit de cité*, 143). To defeat (rather than merely to "beat" [125]) violence means that the violence wrought by exclusion must be overcome not only in other individuals and in other groups "exterior" to oneself and one's own group but also in one's "own" group — and in oneself. But the idea of interior inclusion should not be regarded as utopian, for just as Balibar repeatedly distances himself from the utopianism of a libidinal community (in his critique of Reich, in his refusal to oppose a "love" for immigrants to the National Front's "hatred" of them, etc.), so he suggests that interior inclusion would not be the same as undifferentiated identification. Instead, it would have to be thought of as another form of "negotiation," in which a "double pressure" continued to differentiate not only the self from the other or the other from the self, but also the self from itself and therefore from all absolute forms of identification with the other.

I began by raising the related questions of whether minority cultures exhibit transnational perspectives and, if so, whether these perspectives can be shown to call for a new understanding of transnationalism. Up until this point, however, I have for the most part discussed the concept of minority culture and have had little to say about transnationalism or a transnational perspective. But much of what I have already suggested about the idea of a "minority" culture and both exterior and interior inclusion is directly relevant to the question of transnationalism. From the perspective I have adopted here, it is not of paramount importance to ask whether minority cultures exhibit transnational perspectives that call for a new understanding of transnationalism. Instead I would stress that the term "transnationalism" itself represents a new perspective on the issue of the nation as well as that of the international community, of nationalism as well as internationalism. When we invoke the concept of "transnationalism" today, we do so in order to be able to refer to phenomena taking place beyond the borders of the nation, phenomena that cannot be conceptualized in terms of the nation and its interests alone. But whereas in the past we might have tried to understand what was happening beyond the borders of the nation in terms of an international perspective, we now think in terms of "transnational" perspectives.

It seems to me that this development stems in part from a disenchantment with the internationalisms of the past, a recognition that they can reinforce nationalism because they are in many cases nothing other than a form of "super-nationalism" or a collective nationalism rather than an alternative to nationalism. But another aspect of the current situation that might lead us to choose the term "transnationalism" today when we want to talk about what is happening beyond the borders of the nation is that the "beyond" the borders of the nation is now also inseparable from a "within" the borders of the nation. In other words, just as the trans-individual is neither the individual nor the collective, so the transnational is neither the national nor the international. It is rather an "internationality" that lies within the nation and a "nationality" that is not — for better or for worse — overcome or dissolved in and by the international.

Do minority cultures, then, exhibit transnational perspectives that call for a new understanding of transnationalism? I would say rather that transnationalism is itself a new concept and offers a new perspective that has to some extent been thrust upon us in a world where seemingly every culture can be viewed as a "minority" culture, if only because, as Claude Lévi-Strauss once put it, culture should not be understood only or even primarily in terms of the production of homogeneity and the perpetuation of tradition, but rather as a continual mixing or *métissage* that works against the creation of what he called "monocultures" and what we might call "majority cultures" of all types. In other words, the cultural blocks that once seemed to provide the models for the nation and for culture itself now appear, for a variety of different reasons and in different ways, to carry the seeds of cultural diversity within them.

In short, I would say our situation today is not one in which a new transnationalism is beginning to emerge but rather one in which the newness of the concept and phenomenon of transnationalism is still making itself felt. Transnationalism, I would thus argue, is to the nation-state what transindividuality is to the subject (whether individual or collective). This means that the "exclusion" of one nation-state by another or others — that is, the creation or emergence of conflict and hostility between two nations or groups of nations — also inevitably goes hand in hand with the exclusion of a group within a given nation or nations, a group that is comprised of individuals who, however different they may represent themselves or be represented as being from other groups in the nation, are in fact also *similar*.

This also means that the inclusion of a given nation-state within the international community can take the "exterior" form that inclusion can take within the nation-state. An international "exterior inclusion" can reinforce the nation and nationalism all the more while pretending to respect shared, international standards. But just as inclusion can be exterior and exclusion can be interior in the case of the nation as well as the individual, so it is conceivable that the idea of interior inclusion could be meaningful with regard not only to the subject but also to the community or communities that lie both within and beyond national borders. That a "transnational" community — or perhaps I should say a "noncommunity" or, borrowing from Jean-Luc Nancy, an "unworked" community, in which the other would be included not only as different but also as same, not only as other but also as self — is not only possible but even, one could argue, has already begun to emerge. It is just such a (non)community that makes itself heard and felt when we use terms like "transnationalism," "transindividuality," "interior exclusion," "interior inclusion," or still another of Balibar's terms — "fictive ethnicity."

Indeed, one of the most valuable of the many suggestions contained in Balibar's work relates to his idea of what could be called "transnational culture." For Balibar's statement that the immigrant today is perhaps the "European par excellence" implies that the long-standing conceptual opposition between assimilation and separatism in terms of which the question of culture was frequently addressed in the past and is still often addressed in the present needs to be rethought. The choice that faces not only Europe but also other regions in the world today is not necessarily one between cultural assimilation and cultural separatism, even though there are many forces today that would seemingly be at work to preserve these options — which of course are not true options at all. The idea of a cultural competition evoked by Balibar when he writes that immigrants in Europe today "appear tendentiously, . . . to typify a *new form of sociability and of citizenship*, competing with national sociability and citizenship" seems to me to be important in this connection, not because Balibar is advocating the imposition of a market model on culture, but rather because he is arguing that cultures can and even must produce ideals of community, but that those ideals need not have a purely restrictive or repressive function. They can be, rather, the means of assessing and reassessing (national) culture. In this process of critical reassessment, different cultural strands within national life do not necessarily need to be kept separate *or* tied into one single knot. Instead, each can contribute to the creation of cultures or even of a national culture that are new both from the standpoint of the dominant culture or cultures and from that of minority cultures, that are not merely a cultural common denominator embodying what may be the least attractive element or elements in each culture but rather a cultural project that asks something more or better of us instead of merely returning to us what in cultural terms we already know or have.

Our contemporary sense that we live in a transnational world is inseparable, I would argue, from our collective experience of the changes in it that have been brought about by the patterns of immigration over the last two decades, changes that have made the idea of the nation, understood as a homogeneous cultural configuration, seem still more problematic than it did a century or even several decades ago. As a result, it seems to me impossible to treat the issue of transnationalism without also addressing the status of newly created minority groups and cultures as well as those created by immigration in the past. The question today is how to respond to the emergent transnationalism and its attendant creation of minority cultures, to its potential dangers as well as to the opportunities that it presents.

For if it is important to recognize the opportunities created by the increasingly transnational nature of collective existence, it is also important not merely to celebrate it, or to assume that a good outcome is assured if we merely welcome it, that there is no need for a critical assessment when it comes to the transnational. If there is an urgency to all of these questions about the national, the transnational, the transindividual, as well as the minority and the majority, it is with reference to the violence that has been and is still today wrought by what I have been calling "interior" exclusion within the context of the nation and the world community. But it is also important, it seems to me, to acknowledge that nationalism and internationalism are not necessarily "bad" or "violent" and that transnationalism is not necessarily "good" or "nonviolent." The category of the "transnational" is, as Balibar has said with respect to nationalism, constantly dividing (Balibar and Wallerstein 47). There is a "good" transnationalism and a "bad" transnationalism, a transnationalism that is open to and tolerant of other nations and other cultures and a transnationalism that merely exploits the fragility of the nation in order to better exploit workers and markets, or even to better carry out violence against individuals and groups. It is important, in other words, to recognize that transnationality is not a panacea but rather a dilemma and a challenge.

Balibar's concept of civility seems to me to offer a well-considered response to this dilemma and to the questions connected with it. As Balibar defines it, civility relates not only to the duties and rights of the citizen in the ancient polis or the modern nation-state, but also to the development of "forms of life and of communication that permit us to take a certain distance in relation to the hystericization of identities which we are witnessing, which in truth besiege us ourselves" (*Droit de cité*, 129). Balibar's idea of civility thus calls for, among other things, a "democratization of the borders" (*Droit de cité*, 6) that circumscribe cultural identities as well as nation-states — and therefore, I would say, an active rather than a merely passive "transnationalization." If there is something worth affirming in the idea of transnationalism, it seems to me to lie in its potential to "dehystericize identities" or, in other words, in its ambiguous relation to nationalism and, therefore, to internationalism. Indeed, transnationalism in the best sense should perhaps be defined as an *ambivalent* or *ambiguous* nationalism, or an *ambivalent* or *ambiguous* internationalism. It should be defined, in other words, as a nationalism that embraces the impossibility of ever defining the nation in ultimate terms as a condition of national life and individual and collective freedom. Or as an internationalism that embraces the impossibility of ever defining the world order in ultimate terms as a condition of international cooperation and respect.

Balibar's analyses suggest that while the culture of immigrants who become minorities once they settle in a new nation would seem in many cases to encourage or even to exemplify an openness and tolerance not found in national culture, there are no guarantees that this is or will be the case. In other words, no one is *by nature* a member of either a minority or a majority, just as no culture is by nature a minority or a majority one. This means that no one is by nature or even by culture predisposed to embrace an inclusive, tolerant transnationalism. But another important implication of Balibar's concept of interior exclusion is that in a sense everyone has a firsthand experience of what it is to be a minority. This is because the minority is produced through a process of *interior* exclusion, and thus, as we have seen, exclusion involves not only the other but one's own self or group as other. Thus if no one is predisposed by nature or by culture to embrace an open, tolerant transnationalism, neither is anyone predisposed by nature or by culture to be a nationalist, let alone a nationalist of the most xenophobic type.

Civility, then, is not an attribute of nationality, of ethnicity, or of a "native" ability to speak a language, whether it is the language of a "majority" or a "minority." Instead, civility lies in the ambivalence of identification and the ambiguity of repression to the extent that they are viewed or lived not as limitations to be overcome but rather as conditions of sociability and freedom. This means that civility cannot be identified with national culture — but, equally important, it cannot be simply identified with minority or immigrant culture either. It is rather a matter and a manner of addressing the minor or the transnational in culture and in the self; it is interior inclusion of, as opposed to purely positive or purely negative identification with, the minor other. Through his analyses of interior inclusion, transindividuality and other closely related concepts that I have touched on more briefly, Balibar testifies to his engagement with the liberal tradition as well as with the critical thrust of contemporary cultural theory. But he also testifies to his engagement with psychoanalytic thought, by suggesting that the problem of the inclusion of minorities needs to be thought in terms of a transnationality and a transindividuality that cannot be identified with any collective or individual subject but that lie rather "within" each nation, each culture, each ethnicity, each majority, and each minority.

Works Cited

Anderson, Benedict. *Imagined Communities: Reflections on the Origin and Spread of Nationalism*. London: Verso, 1983.

Balibar, Etienne. *Droit de cité: Culture et politique en démocratie*. Paris: L'Aube, 1998.

——. "Fascism, Psychoanalysis, Freudo-Marxism." *Masses, Classes, Ideas: Studies on Politics and Philosophy before and after Marx*. New York: Routledge, 1994. 177–189.

Balibar, Etienne, and Emmanuel Wallerstein. *Race, Nation, Class: Ambiguous Identities*. London: Verso, 1991.

Gellner, Ernest. *Nations and Nationalism*. Ithaca: Cornell University Press, 1983.

Lévi-Strauss, Claude. *Race et histoire*. Paris: Éditions Gonthier, 1961.

Nancy, Jean-Luc. *La communauté désoeuvrée*. Paris: Christian Bourgois, 1986.

Rational and Irrational Choices

Form, Affect, and Ethics

I often teach the work of Chinua Achebe, and each time I do, I have the class watch an interview Bill Moyers taped with the author in 1989. Two topics covered during the interview inform the core of this essay. First, Achebe mentions time and again the issue of the First World dumping its toxic waste in Third World countries, Nigeria being one of the primary dumping grounds. Second, he speaks of the need for Africa to tell its story. Achebe articulates again his well-known critique of *Heart of Darkness*, deploring its reduction of Africans to mere ghosts, phantoms, ciphers. Instead Achebe demands that the West "listen" to Africa's human voice. I ask the class to think about the connection between the two topics — how does a lack of voice, or its suppression under another narrative, allow for or even facilitate the poisoning of a continent?

To drive home this point, I distribute copies of Larry Summers's infamous World Bank memo of 1991 (see Vallette). During his tenure as chief economist for the World Bank, Summers issued a memo suggesting that there was indeed a problem with pollution — the First World had too much of it, and the Third World too little. He proffered a number of rational choice arguments, among them the rationale that since the life expectancy of those living in the Third World was so far below that of those living in the First World, the human cost of breathing toxic fumes and consuming toxic food and water would be much greater in the First World than in the Third. After all, those living in the Third World couldn't expect to live as long as "we" do, so what would be the matter with reducing their lifetimes by a minuscule amount, when, on the other hand, if we were to actually breathe in the by-products of our First World lifestyle, it would decrease our lifetimes by a much greater proportion? This is the way Summers puts it:

> "Dirty" Industries: Just between you and me, shouldn't the World Bank be encouraging MORE migration of the dirty industries to the LDCS [Less Developed Countries]? I can think of three reasons [here I cite only the third]: The demand for a clean environment for aesthetic and health reasons is likely to have very high income elasticity. The concern over an agent that causes a one in a million change in the odds of prostrate [*sic*] cancer is obviously going to be much higher in a country where people survive to get prostrate [*sic*] cancer than in a country where under 5 mortality is 200 per thousand. Also, much of the concern over industrial atmosphere discharge is about visibility impairing particulates. These discharges may have very little direct health impact. Clearly trade in goods that embody aesthetic pollution concerns could be welfare enhancing. While production is mobile the consumption of pretty air is a non-tradable.

The response of Jose Lutzenberger, the Brazilian Minister of the Environment, upon reading this leaked memo seems to sum it up:

> Your reasoning is perfectly logical but totally insane . . . Your thoughts [provide] a concrete example of the unbelievable alienation, reductionist thinking, social ruthlessness and the arrogant ignorance of many conventional "economists" concerning the nature of the world we live in. . . . If the World Bank keeps you as vice president it will lose all credibility. To me it would confirm what I often said . . . the best thing that could happen would be for the Bank to disappear. (Vallette)

While one might applaud such a sentiment, it would appear Lutzenberger is offering a contradiction — aren't logic and sanity deeply affiliated? What could be their possible point of separation? Glossing the terms helps the class tease out the "rational" from the sociopathic, the "impeccable" ethics of business based upon some utilitarian notion of "the greater good" (particularly construed, of course) from the notion of an ethical system based on some sense of global community and the goal of a more democratic, just, and equal modality of interdependence.

We then talk about the power of stories and disaggregate the different types of stories found here — Summers's modest proposal and the stories Achebe believes might act as countervailing forces. We consider the case in "real" terms — what were the respective fates of Summers and Lutzenberger? Lutzenberger was fired after sending that riposte; Summers became Clinton's secretary of the treasury and then president of Harvard University. We then begin to wonder about the stories people hear, believe, and act upon; we wonder about this thing called "truth," how it is construed, and what it matters. And we talk about the transnational and global aspects of this case.

All this has a great deal to do with the topic of "minor transnationalisms," for if we expand the case outlined above to the most general level, then we can take the issues I have been writing about and repose the topic as such: if we allow ourselves a moment of Manicheanism, and see the topoi of globalization as differentiated across a grid of rich/poor, north/south, First World/Third World binaries (not to mention the gendered and racialized facets of the real distributions of power and wealth), then we need to ask, In what forms, rhetorics, discursive formulations, poetics, can the "minor" effectively represent its case across those differentiated spaces and hope to produce some sort of affect that will move people to act in ethical manners? Or, to borrow from Lutzenberger, how can we tell stories that motivate people to act sanely and humanely, rather than only according to a chilling bureaucratic logic that deprives others of their humanity, rights, and dignity? In this essay, I use Ruth Ozeki's novel *My Year of Meats* to explore these questions and add one more topic for our consideration: if, in the past, the modern novel was seen to be the instrument with which literature might instill a sense of cosmopolitical community, can it still do so when the very medium through which the new "global village" is linked is not literature, but information, advertising, and entertainment technologies? Furthermore, what do we do when "information" is rationalized and packaged in particular ways that seem to preclude precisely that sense of global community and shared obligation? That is, how can we "touch" our newly constituted community members when the terms of engagement seem to be radically different from those of the past? What different strategies of "reasoning" vie for the attention and commitments of the new global citizen? And what do modernist literary aesthetics have to do with such issues anymore? This essay is a preliminary attempt to address these questions.

Rational Choice, Literature, and the Sentimental

In this first section I want to set forth three key questions. First, how does rational choice theory attempt to account for how individuals act, and how does individual rational choice relate to social or "other-regarding" issues that may be either rational or intuitive? Second, how has the modern literary aesthetic been seen to enable and foster precisely that sense of relation to the other that goes beyond the rational/intuitive divide? And third, how is the ethical related to storytelling?

Peter Abell presents a useful sketch of rational choice theory in relation to sociology. As he describes it, rational choice theory (RCT) strives "to understand individual actors (which in specified circumstances may be collectivities of one sort or another) as acting, or more likely interacting, in a manner such that they can be deemed to be doing the best they can for themselves, given their objectives, resources, and circumstances, as they see them" (252). Here I want to draw out three aspects of rational choice theory as its discourse and assumptions about human action might relate to the issue of storytelling, affect, and ethics. I want to note that, first, rational choice theory tends to ignore or downplay the ways in which "other-regarding" interests might complicate or give a different significance to an individual's rational choice. Likewise, it does not well tolerate intuition, irregularity, and affect, and this of course puts it into a particularly fraught relationship to literature. Second, rational choice hinges upon the idea of adequate information and well-formed beliefs. I will argue that the issue of the particular *mediation* of information is something that requires closer consideration, as it might well create preferences in certain ways. Finally, I note that on the other hand one of the most useful aspects of rational choice theory is its interest in working back from individual action to a description of systems and structures. If we apply the same critique to rational choice "behaviorism," then we can look at the isolated example of the Summers memo and see at work a larger system of values, beliefs, and assumptions.

In seeking to arrive at an elegant, simple, "parsimonious" theory of human action, rational choice theory must discount certain kinds of behaviors that, on the contrary, literature focuses upon. Abell admits that "at times we act impulsively, which in retrospect we find distasteful, and we may also be possessed by our desires which then cloud our reason" (263). This, along with the ways that intersubjective influences might affect choice, simply falls beyond the scope of RCT's interests (outside of game theory approaches). As Abell puts it, strict RCT is "disinclined to accept the exogeneity of norms and values, rather seeking an explanation for their genesis and persistence from its own precepts" (254). He continues: "To my knowledge, there is no good theory of the genesis of and shaping of affects, though rational choice theorists are inclined to invoke some social contagion or learning model" (265).[1] That is to say, such social and intersubjective behavior as we are most interested in here tends to be understood by RCT within very specific and exclusive sociological regimes. "Quasi-exogeneous" explanations are often regarded with suspicion: "There are now many attempts to incorporate altruism, malice, and, more generally, relative utilities into a rational choice theory framework. Rational choice theorists remain, nevertheless, ever cautious about invoking such sentiments and are inclined to search for hidden self-regard when faced with apparent other-regard" (265).[2] This proclivity would seem to cut short any robust investigation into the relationship between individual preferences and notions of community, diverse values, preferences, and affects.

One critique of rational choice theory that is of particular relevance to the current essay is Michael Taylor's "When Rationality Fails." Taylor argues, "Rational choice studies of collective action, in particular, standardly ignore a range of motivations that can give rise to cooperation, or else treat them in a limited form in which they can be accommodated artificially within the rational choice framework. . . . This is an aspect of a very general and very large failing of rational choice work, including economics: its programmatic blindness to the rich diversity of ways in which humans value things" (224–25). Counterposed to the available preferences of RCT, Taylor offers what he calls "commitments": "We can say that commitment-driven behavior is *expressive* of a *self* constituted by commitments" (230, emphasis added). Here I consider this "self" within a framework of a culture of commitment that exceeds the limits of "rationality" read as self-interest in its narrowest and reductive sense. I will focus on the question of how a sense of commitment can be expressed through literary texts and other media, so as to have the effect of inculcating in others a similar and shared sense of commitment.

In this regard, again, the particular modalities of literary and media forms require special attention. It is not enough to rely solely upon the notion proffered by RCT about the need for "optimal belief formation," that is, the optimalization of information available to social actors so that they might have the widest range of "choices." Abell explains:

> Precisely what optimal belief formation implies is a complex mat-
> ter but usually means something like this: given an actor's affects
> (wants), the information available/collected is sufficient to enable
> the actor to form beliefs about the possible courses of action available
> and their consequences so that a better alternative (given the actor's
> affects) will not be ignored. In fact a great deal of contemporary
> rational choice theory is devoted to the impact of incomplete infor-
> mation . . . upon social action. . . . All can agree that modeling both
> the nature and causes of the prevailing information conditions in
> which actors find themselves or create for themselves, and their at-
> tendant beliefs and reasoning, is often at the heart of the sociological
> enterprise. (264)

While not ignoring for a moment the validity of this point, our task here is
to better understand how "information" is packaged in particular ways
(the rhetoric of information) so that it can enhance or diminish the attractiveness (or "logic") of any particular choice.

To bring this back to our discussion of Summers and Achebe: whence
does Summers derive his confidence that the information he provides to
bolster his case for toxic dumping will be transparent and lead inevitably
to the correct choice? And where do we get the sense that Achebe and
Lutzenberger's arguments are more acceptable, more "sane"? And what
do the kinds of choices presented and argued by either side have to do
with larger, systemic beliefs and values? Following the goals of rational
choice theory, Coleman notes, "the focus must be on the social system
whose behavior is to be explained. This may be as small as dyad or as large
as a society or even a world system, but the essential requirement is that
the explanatory focus be on the system as a unit, not on the individuals or
other components that make it up" (2), and here we might agree.

This also requires that, just as we have tried to understand the logic
which informs "rational" choices, so we must devote attention also to
the realm of the sentimental. Abell himself notes this (but not without
caution):

> There is an important message here. On the one hand, we should not
> ignore any independent evidence at our disposal concerning other-
> regarding sentiments. . . . Many rational choice theorists do run foul
> of this dictum in their zeal to promote an exclusive reliance upon
> self-regard and as a consequence construct overelaborate theories
> when there is no need and where the explanatory focus should shift

to the sources of the sentiments themselves. On the other hand, we should beware the cavalier invocation of "exotic sentiments." (266)

The use of the term "exotic" is doubly apt in terms of the present essay. First, it is of course cognate to "exogeneous," and thus underscores the otherness of sentiment to rational choice. But it also points to the link outward, beyond the individual, to an intersubjective space that is located upon another sort of terrain. And it is on this terrain that literature finds itself.

To conclude this discussion of rational choice theory, I turn to a text that both directly addresses the relation of RCT and storytelling, and, in a fascinating way, ends up implicitly validating (albeit in a qualified manner) not only literature, but collectivities and shared values of justice. No one has written more about the relation of rational choice theory and the emotions than Jon Elster. For this discussion, I turn to one of his most elementary books, but one that describes emotions and literature as a basic issue. In *Nuts and Bolts for the Social Sciences*, Jon Elster's discussions of storytelling and literature provide an interesting set of observations regarding the goals of rational choice theory, as well as its limitations. He points to both the benefits and the dangers of literature (and the kind of thinking it engages) within the rational choice enterprise. In all cases, his remarks bear importantly upon the topic of this essay. Elster gives credit to storytelling for its ability to present the individual with a set of options and a particular imaginative space for weighing those choices (and the example he gives is itself enormously revealing): "Storytelling can suggest new, parsimonious explanations. Suppose that someone asserts that self-sacrificing or helping behavior is conclusive proof that not all action is rational. . . . Could it not be in one's self-interest to help others? Could it not be rational to be swayed by one's emotions? The first step toward finding a positive answer is telling a *plausible story* to show how these possibilities could be realized" (7–8). But in the same passage, Elster cautions: "Storytelling can be harmful if it is mistaken for the real thing." Furthermore, "with some ingenuity — and many scholars have a great deal — one can *always* tell a story in which things are turned upside down" (8). In sum, storytelling allows us to increase the body of information upon which we form our beliefs, but fiction also may be deployed to instantiate false or irrational beliefs. It contributes to a body of emotions Elster calls "counterfactual emotions," "arising out of what could have happened but didn't" (63). In other words, the benefit that storytelling might offer rational choice making in terms of its speculative and hypo-thetical power is offset by its illusory quality, its tendency to be confused for fact, for turning things "upside down."

This cost-benefit analysis is carried over to his discussion of emotion, a discussion in which we can see the connection between the issue of story-telling with the topic of literature's ability to allow us to imagine others, and to put ourselves in their place (we will address this issue in detail be-low). Elster describes a powerful set of emotions — "other-oriented emo-tions." Such emotions are predicated on the belief "It could have been me" (64). We can see in these last two instances a connection that points directly at fiction and affect — storytelling allows the individual to specu-late on a range of possible scenarios; "other-oriented emotions" predicate stories in which the individual might feel the effect of actions upon a hypothetical stand-in for him- or herself. If we now have fiction and affect on the table for discussion, in his next paragraph, Elster completes the circle of this essay's core concerns — he speaks of justice, and the correlate issue of ethics:

> The related feeling of being unfairly treated deserves special men-tion. Sufficient conditions for the occurrence of this powerful emo-tion are the following. First, the situation is perceived as morally wrong; second, it has been brought about intentionally, not as the byproduct of natural causality or the invisible hand of social causal-ity; third, it can be rectified by social intervention. Thus the feeling of injustice rests on the combination of "It ought to be otherwise," "It is someone's fault that it is not otherwise," and "It could have been made otherwise," in addition to the general counterfactual con-dition "It could have been otherwise." (64)

Note that all the conditional elements here ("ought," and "could") take us back to a condition of narrative — the speaker is imagining not a single fact, but a set of interconnected circumstances in which others live justly. Within this set of discussions of storytelling, affect, and ethics, we are thus caught in a situation wherein storytelling, emotions, and the thoughts they make possible are all part of choice making, and yet their cost-benefit ratio is uncertain — how many possibilities can or should we entertain, on what basis can or should we rely on emotional data? Thus Elster writes, "Emo-tions matter because they move and disturb us, and because, through their links to social norms, they stabilize social life. They also interfere with our thought processes, making them less rational than they would otherwise be" (70).

Up to this point we have been speaking about individual choices (as is the large insistence of rational choice theory). When moved from individual choice making to social planning and collectivities, things simply get worse: "We cannot predict how rational people behave under conditions of uncertainty of multiple equilibria, nor whether their behavior will be governed by rationality or social norms" (168). Under such conditions of unpredictability, social change is almost impossible to carry out successfully, and it is to this topic that I turn now to close off this discussion of Elster and rational choice theory. Instead of placing any faith in large, sweeping reforms (which mobilize too many different individual responses), Elster recommends small steps, measured discretely and judiciously as one goes along. Large structural change creates a heightened sense of expectation, and people grow impatient for the benefits of reform to become manifest.

Nevertheless, Elster ends his book by suggesting one sweeping reform. He asserts that among social models, "an all-cooperative economy could be superior, perhaps by a great deal, to an all-capitalist one, even if isolated cooperatives do worse than capitalist forms in a capitalist environment" (170). But what about the aforementioned issue of impatience? The final sentence of Elster's book names the one thing that might motivate people to accept social change: "The only thing that could motivate people to suffer the transition costs would be perceiving the reform to be a matter of basic justice, not economic efficiency. In that case, however, we are not talking any longer about social planning, but about a movement for social reform" (170–171). We end thus with a belief that is stronger than any other—a belief that might provide the rationale for a preference or choice where no other will, the preference for "basic justice." If rational choice can thus accommodate this social value, then the positive aspects of storytelling and "other-oriented emotion" are redeemable. In other words, it may be precisely literature that stands available as a vehicle for social change. Let me now couple this inferable conception of literature and its function to a more "classic" notion of literary narrative, affect, and ethics.

Recently there has been a flurry of articles and essays defending the idea of modernism and its role in progressive politics. The argument is made that, far from being outmoded, the modern novel form is the sole instrument with which one can fashion a narrative commensurate with our historical situation and the goals outlined above. For instance, updating Georg Lukács, Marshall Berman claims: "Modern men and women must become the subjects as well as the objects of modernization; they must learn to change the world that is changing them, and make it their own" (33). According to Berman, to do so requires adhering to modern aesthetic principles. This turns out not to be too hard, since Berman will argue that the form seems nearly inescapable. Citing works by artists diverse as Maya Lin, Laurie Anderson, Les Levine, Anselm Kiefer, and Salman Rushdie, Berman claims that the efficacy of their works hinges upon a particular vision of what art is, what it does, and how it does it. This vision is "modernism."

And in an essay on "Fiction and Justice," Winfried Fluck draws the connection between form and social affect. He first inventories the salient features of modernist fiction: aesthetic modernism "focuses on fiction's potential for defamiliarization, boundary crossing, and cultural transgression. Fiction is regarded as experimental epistemology which permits the reader to cross existing boundaries, explore other worlds, and try out new identities" (23). Then he links these structural features to the notion that fiction conveys a hunger for justice. This hunger is instantiated doubly — the narrative represents an unjust situation, and we readers want justice for that person or group not only because of the specific grievance or dilemma which needs to be addressed, but also because, thanks to the particular dynamics of modernist narrative, we sense them as somehow similar to us and see in their depicted situation a situation that is at least structurally similar to one in which we might find ourselves: fiction "allows for the attachment of imaginary longings on the basis of structural resemblance" (31). It is important to note here that "imagination" works in (at least) three ways — we imagine the characters' situation, we imagine how we might feel, and we are then instilled with "imaginary longings" for a just resolution.[3] But how would this translate from the realm of a private experience of reading to the domain of public action? Interestingly, Richard Rorty turns to the notion of affective storytelling in his speech on human rights for Amnesty International.[4] I will conclude this section with a brief discussion of this lecture, for in it we may see the juncture of several of the main issues of this essay, namely the relation between the discourse of rationality and the discourse of affect, and the connection between storytelling, affect, and ethics. Coupled with our previous discussion of modern aesthetics and literary form, these topics form the analytic constellation in which I will approach Ozeki's novel.

To begin with, Rorty dispenses with the common notion that human beings are to be defined by their shared capacity for rational thinking: "Traditionally, the name of the shared human attribute which supposedly 'grounds' morality is 'rationality.' . . . Philosophers like myself, who think of rationality as simply the attempt at such coherence, agree with Rabossi that foundationalist projects are outmoded. We see our task as a matter of making our own culture — the human rights culture — more self-conscious and more powerful, rather than of demonstrating its superiority to other cultures by appealing to something transcultural" (117). Instead of trying to argue that human rights might be founded on any principle of transcultural, transhistorical commonality, Rorty focuses upon the pragmatic, contingent, and historical processing of "sad stories," which might produce in the listener or reader a sense of shared humanity on this issue or topic. He argues for the necessity of telling and listening to stories. This listening is not to be done (so much as) to gain knowledge of things as it is to feel sympathy with others: "We pragmatists argue from the fact that the emergence of the human rights culture seems to owe nothing to increased moral knowledge, and everything to hearing sad and sentimental stories" (118–119).[5] Finally, this is to be done so as to facilitate a wider sense of human-being, sympathy, and obligation. Rorty urges us to "concentrate our energies on manipulating sentiments, on sentimental education. That sort of education sufficiently acquaints people of different kinds with one another so that they are less tempted to think of those different from themselves as only quasi-human. The goal of this manipulation of sentiment is to expand the reference of the terms 'our kind of people' and 'people like us' " (123).

There is something attractive about this formula, for it collapses the distinction between the "rational" economistic model we noted above in the Summers memo and the "imaginative" and cultural.[6] Crucially, it does so with an eye toward ethics:

> Contemporary moral philosophy is still lumbered with this opposition between self-interest and morality, an opposition that makes it hard to realize that my pride in being a part of the human rights culture is no more external to my self than my desire for financial success. . . . Plato got moral philosophy off on the wrong foot. He led moral philosophers to concentrate on the rather rare figure of the psychopath, the person who has no concern for any human being other than himself. Moral philosophy has systematically neglected

the much more common case: the person whose treatment of a rather narrow range of featherless bipeds is morally impeccable, but who remains indifferent to the suffering of those outside this range, the ones he or she thinks of as pseudohumans. (123–124)

Thus the emphasis is no longer on the supposed boundary between "rationality" and morality, self-interest and altruism, but rather in seeing how the "human" can be universalized in a nonfoundational and pragmatic way so as to allow us to act toward others in the broadest and most humane way possible. If we revisit the Summers/Achebe issue set out at the beginning of this essay, we see that Rorty's appeal to "sentiment" seeks to neutralize the "rational" choice Summers wishes the World Bank to make by disabling the dehumanizing, "insane" partitioning of the world into human and "pseudo-human."

However, if stories are the vehicles that will at once convey and enable that sentiment, we are still left with a question that haunts persistently each of the theses we have discussed thus far—what makes a "good" story? How can information be mediated so as to affect people outside the logic of self-interest and exclusivity? The question of aesthetics and rhetoric is important because it leads to the production of an ethically informed affect. Yet, crucially, the "ordinary" question posed to literature is now problematic not only because of the possible lapse of modern forms before the onslaught of the postmodern (to adopt Berman's perspective), but also because of the *material* changes in culture and information. And it is to this entire set of questions that Ruth Ozeki addresses her novel.

My Year of Meats

Ruth Ozeki's novel attempts to ascertain the function of literature in a world of corporate mediazation. She is especially interested in the different ways in which people might be affected by literary texts and by media images so as to act ethically and with a sense of being together. *My Year of Meats* tells the story of Jane Tagaki Little, a documentary filmmaker barely scraping by, who is willingly recruited by a multinational corporation, Beef-Ex, to create a "documentary series" that is actually an extended series of commercials designed to hook Japanese consumers on American beef. The show will send the crew out into the American heartland to find "typical" American housewives, interview them about their lives, and have them prepare their favorite beef recipes to share with their

Japanese counterparts. Theirs will be not only a pedagogical relationship, but also an economic one. The company is anxious to "find" the "authentic" America because its exoticism sells well. Jane confesses, "Although my heart was set on being a documentarian, it seems I was more useful as a go-between, a cultural pimp, selling off the cast illusion of America to a cramped population on that small string of Pacific islands" (9). Asian-American relations are thus intensely and insistently mediated by both national and transnational economics: "Locating our subjects felt like a confidence game, really. I'd inveigle a nice woman with her civic duty to promote American meat abroad and thereby help rectify the trade imbalance with Japan" (35).

It is just this pernicious attempt to revise the Japanese diet, to infiltrate "culture" via food consumption in order to right a trade imbalance, that introduces Ozeki's indictment not only of the beef industry, but also of an entire range of interlinked corporate interests that show no reluctance to contaminate our bodies as well as our spirits. Drug companies at once sell unsafe growth hormones to feed companies and DES to pregnant women. In an interview included in the book, Ozeki writes: "I see our lives as being part of an enormous web of interconnected spheres, where the workings of the larger social, political, and corporate machinery impact something as private and intimate as the descent of an egg through a woman's fallopian tube. This is the resonance I want to conjecture in my books" (appendix, 8).

Ozeki's novel has been met with enthusiasm, especially for its wit, intelligence, and progressive politics. More specifically, as Shameem Black writes, "in drawing upon the political strategies of global feminism, the novel claims for itself the power of progressive action and the right to identify one positive form of cosmofeminism." This positivity is predicated on the novel's insistence on praxis. Black goes on to note that after demonstrating the possibilities of latching onto global media, "the novel asserts that not only can global media itself instigate cosmofeminist alliances, but that these alliances can and perhaps must leave the mediation of the screen and take root in lived social experience."[7] On the other hand, Monica Chiu finds that whatever progressive politics might occur in the novel are quickly reabsorbed into the dominant ideology: "The invisible, national (read: multicultural) ideology that the novel creates . . . reconstitutes the very localized, national framework that it initially attempts to subvert."[8]

I find myself agreeing at once with both these perspectives. Surely,

Ozeki has constructed an ambitious, progressive novel that seeks to educate, persuade, anger, and motivate its readers toward all sorts of what I consider positive action — anticorruption, anticorporate, antimisogynistic, antichauvinist, antiracist, antisexist, the list goes on. Yet it is precisely the completeness of this inventory that might strike one as formulaic and contrived. Ultimately, the novel can indeed be read as a failure to deliver on its promises, as all sorts of national, gendered, and racial norms seem to be reinstated. Furthermore, the protagonist's own ethics may be called into question, not for her lack of sincerity, but on her failure to account for her inconsistencies.

Nevertheless, I believe that Ozeki's novel is more complex, self-conscious, and interestingly crafted than it might appear. As we move through the novel, we begin to witness telling slippages that indicate a calculated critique not only of "the media," but also of the ability to tell effective stories in any pristine, transparent manner. We are reminded, with force, of Rorty's interest in the idea of and intent behind manipulating feelings — as *My Year of Meats* unfolds we see the complexities of what might be called "ethical manipulation." Indeed, one of the key themes of the novel has to do precisely with the line between the real and the contrived, authenticity and art, the documentary and the commercial. As Jane declares, this line necessarily has to become blurred, and in the melding of the two we find the most potent forms of persuasion: "The strategy was to develop a powerful synergy between the commercials and the documentary vehicles, in order to stimulate consumer purchase motivation" (41).

Such motivation relies on producing a certain affect, one that relies on particular stereotypes of the other: "Japanese market studies show that Japanese wives often feel neglected by their husbands and are susceptible to the kindness, generosity, and sweetness that they see as typical of American men" (13). Ozeki registers the effect of Jane's "product" not only on the general forms of perceiving images of difference, but also on the microcosmic sensory perceptions of it as registered on the body itself. In a fascinating passage we move the distance between the phonic to the ideology of consumption, from Japan to America: "She [Akiko] liked the sounds of the parallel Japanese r's, with their delicate flick of the tongue across the palate, and the plosive *pu* like a kiss or a fart in the middle of a big American dinner. She liked the size of things American. Convenient. Economical. Big and simple" (19). In a similar fashion, the aesthetic of difference prompts an attempt at mimcry: "What a beautiful name, thought

Akiko. Suzie Flowers [a person represented in one of the commercials] laughed easily, but Akiko was practicing how to do this too" (21).

Here we should insist on noting that the imitation of American life is of course not simply aesthetic — it links up with ideologies of race, nation, and gender in critical ways (why does she want to be like "an American"?). Yet I want to forestall a too easy transference out of the aesthetic realm as such, for it is in the vague, indistinct, and incompletely interpreted spaces of cross-cultural aesthetic transference that we find a more nuanced understanding of affect. This incompleteness is not necessarily a source of weakness; it may come to be an enabling one of appropriation and internalization: "It felt like Bobby Joe [Creely] was telling her a story and if only she could understand the words she would be able to identify with it perfectly. Unfortunately, there was no Japanese translation on the lyric sheet" (77). I want to pause here to linger over the phrase, "telling her a story," but also the qualifier, "as if." As the novel progresses, we see a slow detachment from the obsession with literal translation, and a greater indulgence in and sympathy for the incomplete, and sometimes incommensurate. I would suggest that this has a great deal to do with what we discover about affect. But we should not become too enamored of this moment of relative freedom and empathy — Ozeki never lets us forget the commercial outcomes to which the production of such affect may be geared: "The next day she took the bullet train to town and found the CD at Tower Records in Shibuya" (78). Again, "his songs made her feel reckless and even a little dangerous. . . . She'd never seen heat rising before, or met a woman like the one in the song who carried a straight razor. Akiko didn't know what a straight razor was, but suddenly she wished she could have one too" (79).[9]

In this highly commercialized environment, where art, truth, and affect are put into the service of raw profit and consumerism, Jane tries to salve her conscience: how can she accept complacency in "inveigling"? She rationalizes: "I had so many years, in both Japan and America, floundering in miasma of misinformation about culture and race I was determined to this window into mainstream network television to educate. Perhaps it was naive, but I believed, honestly, that I could use wives to sell meat in the service of a Larger Truth" (27). Nevertheless, we come back to our key question — what makes a good story? How is truth to be packaged so that it is attractive and compelling? Or, how can truth coexist with falsity? Are the very narrative strategies that deliver affect incompatible with truth? I mentioned above how the novel slowly unfolds a complex and ambivalent stance toward the possibilities of truth telling. In the following sequence, we can clearly ascertain that trajectory.

One of the first shows Jane tapes is of a Mexican family. If we look to this segment in hopes that we will find some example of the "truth" Jane wishes to convey, we will seem to have just such material:

> The boy, whose name was Bobby, lived there with his parents, Alberto and Catalina Martinez. Alberto, or Bert, as he now preferred to be called, was a farm worker. He'd lost his left hand to a hay baler in Abilene seven years earlier, a few months after he and Catalina (Cathy) had emigrated from Mexico, just in time for Bobby to be born an American citizen. That had been Cathy's dream, to have an American son, and Bert had paid for her dream with his hand. (58)

While here we have a non-white, laboring immigrant family, and the story conspicuously details the cost of the American Dream within one of the chief targets of Ozeki's indictment — agribusiness — we are still placed squarely within the "immigrant story." Alberto's preference for an Anglo name and the absence of any remark on his or anyone else's part about his accident remove any explicit critique — this "truth" seems too pale, as it fades to invisibility within a cliché.

It is that suppression of those kinds of truth that ultimately raises the segment above the material world — "Bobby smiled at the camera, a little Mexican boy shyly offering his American Supper to the nation of Japan. Everything was in slow motion." It was "surreal and exquisite" (61). And, indeed, it has produced the intended effect thousands of miles away: "Toes tucked neatly beneath her, she [Akiko] watched the screen, where a young Mexican child stood in the middle of a waving field of wheat. . . . Akiko felt the tears well up in her eyes as, pen in hand, she smoothed out the sheet of paper, ready to take down the day's recipe" (63). Jane's reaction reveals the limits and standards within which she operates. She writes to her employers: "I was very happy to hear about the high ratings for the Martinez show. . . . I will do my best to increase the Authenticity and General Interest of the program" (64). Now at this point I think we are meant to take this with a dose of skepticism — is Jane merely mimicking the commercial discourse she knows will be effective in allowing her to go forward with her "subversive" multicultural agenda?

Two kinds of cynicism emerge. The first has to do with the fact that no matter how profound and even uplifting the affect is, the ultimate issue will become the bottom line for some. This is nowhere more apparent than in the segment Jane shoots at a southern church filled with African American worshippers. Being present in the church meeting seems to produce another transformative moment, not only on Jane and her crew, but even on John Ueno, Jane's misogynistic, wife-abusing Japanese boss who has recently attempted to rape Jane:

> The ladies on either side responded, grabbing Ueno and me and wrapping us in their arms, then passing us off to another neighbor, to be similarly embraced. Catharsis was close at hand. I dimly understood it, felt it gathering all around me. And the miracle was, so did Ueno. . . . All around him, people were dancing and writhing and singing and shaking and speaking in tongues, and others were caring for them, laying on their hands, supporting their frenzy. Sweat was pouring down Ueno's face, pure distilled alcohol by the smell of it, and he was sobbing. (112–113)

Yet this affective "transformation" is quickly shown to be only transitory — Ueno ends up disallowing the show to be broadcast: "How could a Japanese housewife relate to a poor black family with nine children?" (130).

If we see this moment of cynicism as both a critique of capitalism and Jane's naïveté, it still does not seem to amount to much. Yet a second kind of cynicism that comes into play in the course of the novel is sharper and more devastating than this first, for it shows how even the reputed victims of capital and the profit motive can be turned into its subjects.

We find this in the story of the Bukowsky family, whose daughter Christina is paralyzed, indeed comatose, after being hit by a Wal-Mart truck. As the company has refused to assume any responsibility, it falls to the family to care for their daughter alone. But soon the townspeople take an interest. They in fact begin a collective ritual of empathy and transference: "Each person brought something that he or she loved" (134). These visits and the talismans that are brought for the girl to touch create a communal ritual that gradually works a miracle: Christina emerges from her coma.

Yet it does not end there, for Jane then tells us, "the media got hold of the story and pumped it for all it was worth from every angle, including the exploitation of small-town America by the corporate retail giants" (135). It is here that we begin to ask if this exploitation is anything different from what Jane has been doing, complete with the reliance on stock narrative devices. But what is even more significant is what follows:

The town of Quarry had discovered a new natural resource—compassion—and they were mining it and marketing it to America. Quarry became Hope, and Mr. Bukowsky was elected mayor. . . . The townspeople found jobs with the Center or started their own businesses as affiliated service providers . . . The Mayor and Mrs. Bukowsky starred in a promotional videotape, "Welcome to Our Living Room: The Bukowsky Method of Compassion and Renewal," and published a best-selling book by the same name (136).

The "affect," and what is mimed, has nothing anymore to do with compassion or sympathy, and everything to do with commercialism. Are we to take this positively, is this some sort of poetic justice, has the family finally received its due? Not exactly—because of the media attention, Wal-Mart does take responsibility. All this is rather a matter of profiting beyond justice, and commodifying what was originally an authentic act of compassion. Yet Jane offers no comment on this turn of events; instead she focuses on the efficacy of her docudrama and her own perspicacity: "I felt the warm smugness that comes over me when I know that there is another heart-wrenching documentary moment at hand, being exquisitely recorded" (175).

Ultimately, Jane not only recognizes the necessity to "manipulate" sentiment, she also recognizes precisely the need to be fictive: "I wanted to make programs with documentary integrity and at first I believed in a truth that existed—singular empirical absolute. But slowly, as my skills improved and I learned about editing and camera angles and the effect that music can have on meaning, I realized that truth was like race and could be measured only in ever-diminishing approximations" (176). Until the very end of the novel, Jane persists in rationalizing the need to deploy the rhetorical strategies of storytelling within the frame of televisual media, and in the process, the "real" becomes simply one ingredient among others: "The program was a good one, really solid, moving, the best I'd made. It could even effect social change. And so I continued, taking out the stutters and catches from the women's voices, creating a seamless flow in a reality that was no longer theirs and not quite so real anymore" (179).

We have thus far spoken about Jane's gradual admission that creating an effective story is a particular blend of myth, reality, and aesthetics. But what is to be effected by this mix? How do stories do their work? Once affect has been installed, how is it supposed to be harnessed to an ethical action? First, Ozeki makes the argument that stories can shift perspective.

Again, this is exactly in keeping with the effects mentioned by Fluck above: "Fiction is regarded as experimental epistemology which permits the reader to cross existing boundaries, explore other worlds, and try out new identities. In a key episode, we find the mother of a girl poisoned by hormones in cattle feed describing her complacency, and then the transformative work the film has done. Upon seeing Jane's film of her daughter, Bunny Dunn is transformed from a silent victim to a witness: "You just get used to it. Until something happens, that wakes you up and makes you see different. That's what happened when you all showed up. I saw her with your eyes, and everything looked different. Wrong . . . it was like I finally made a choice, talkin' for the camera, it felt good. Like I was takin' a stand" (294–295). And when she shows her husband the tape, it is "like finally he understood" (357). This reconfiguration of subjectivity comes about because the mediated narrative has allowed the subject to achieve an exterior point of view. This in turn allows the individual to take part in an affective community, one that is constituted precisely by a common experience of viewing both events and mediated images.

Jane thus embarks on a project of finding historical facts, suppressed information, and miscellaneous data, and forging stories that transcend "mere" facticity: they become aestheticized. Critical to this enterprise is the intersubjective validation of the narrative and its effect, and this intersubjective validation is done within a particularly construed affective community. As Akiko weeps over a program, she correlates the experience of those depicted with hers: "She realized that . . . these were tears of admiration for the strong women so determined to have their family against all odds. And tears of pity for herself for the trepidation she felt in place of desire and for the pale, wan sentiment that she let pass for love . . . something that the black woman had said . . . resonated in her. Something about impossibility and desire, or lack of it" (181). This circle of affect works its way back to Jane herself. After Akiko writes her (upon being moved by an episode of the program), Jane realizes that she is broadcasting to human beings: "Maybe it was because my shows were broadcast in Japan, on the other side of the globe, but up until now I'd never really imagined my audience before. She was an abstract concept: at most, a stereotypical housewife. . . . Now it hit me: what an arrogant and chauvinistic attitude this was" (231).

While the instantiation of these new communities is laudable, clustered as they are around a set of moral and ethical issues and geared toward specific actions, we should not lose sight of the fact that they are constructed around *stories*. While the key characters each eventually meet each other, their relations and their desire to be in those relations are prepared in advance by a narrative that captures both their imagination and their sympathy:

> "I think Akiko's story is touching," she [Lara] said, pulling Dyan gently to her stomach. "You should write about her. I mean, this woman has guts. Escaping from a husband who beat her, coming all the way here to America, to Northampton, Massachusetts, to have her baby, all because of us. . . . What was it she wrote? 'I feel such sadness for my lying life. So I now wish to ask you where can I go to live my happy life like her?' " (343)

This instance of storytelling and affect lends weight to Rorty's program of telling "sad and sentimental stories" to affect a sense of commonality, but it still leaves open two related questions. First, the question we have posed throughout: *What* stories? What exactly constitutes "human interest"? Are we forever condemned to mine that repertory, that stock of emotional hits? Second, at what point does direct human contact *replace* the story? And at that point, are we enriched, more "authentic"? Or, conversely, with the disappearance of the story (or at least its being eclipsed by the "real thing"), do we lose precisely that particular, contingent point of commonality that is effective in spurring ethical action? My suspicion is that this is a false choice, but we need to retain this question as a heuristic device to mark out the valences of stories and actualities.

What seems of greatest concern to Ozeki is not the conversion of virtual to real relations. Rather, what seems to concern her most is the discrete moral action that is made possible by the affect produced in her programs. At the end of the novel, she not only has come to accept that a combination of fact and fiction is necessary to get an audience, she has also construed this as the nature of the business, for better or worse. She poses the question: "It was not a TV show, which was what I'd become accustomed to. It was a real documentary, the first I'd ever tried to make. . . . There were no sociological surveys, no bright attempts at entertainment. So how to tell the story?" (334). Part of the problem about "how to tell the story" is, of course, how to make it attractive: "I still couldn't imagine what I would do with the tape . . . I mean, who would want to see it?" (335).

We will come back to that disingenuous statement at the end of this essay. Before that, it is important to attend to Jane's ending disquisition, which attempts to answer the question of form and truth, that is, the formal properties needed to make truth attractive, persuasive, and affective. Jane works backward from the "success" of her enterprise to a diagnosis of the pathologies of the media and the public:

> I had succeeded: I got a small but critical piece of information about the corruption of meats in America out to the world, and possibly even saved a little girl's life in the process. And maybe that is the important part of the story, but the truth is so much more complex . . . Like all the parts of the Gulf War that were never reported. That war was certainly a Thing That Gained by Being Painted. And like Suzie's tale, a small but Outstandingly Splendid Thing. I mean, I take a Japanese television crew to Iowa to film a documentary about this American wife, and we make total fiction of the facts of her life, and now, a year later she tells me that those facts have turned right around and aligned themselves with our fiction. So go figure. . . . In the Year of Meats, truth wasn't stranger than fiction; it was fiction. Ma says I'm neither here nor there, and if that's the case, so be it. Half documentarian, half fabulist . . . Maybe sometimes you have to make things up, to tell truths that alter outcomes. (360)

Armed with such perceptions of and conclusions about both audience reception and the requisite rhetorical tools of the media, Jane's question about "who would want to see it" is transparently disingenuous. In fact, as we have seen before, Jane possesses a sharp awareness of what kinds of stories people not only want to see, but seem *compelled* to see. Furthermore, she not only knows which buttons to push, she also has a fairly good sense of what will happen when they are pushed. Jane's "documentaries" are primarily geared toward eliciting interest and sympathy from a broad moderate and liberal audience already primed for an authentic multicultural moment that itself taps into a more traditional American narrative of self-improvement.

Nevertheless, the episode in question, the one that actually might have saved at least one life, the one that is the most graphic and disturbing indictment of the meat industry, relies not on that multicultural ideology but on a weird mixture of horror and voyeurism. The young girl's body is proffered as evidence, and that evidence is compelling not (only) because of the deformity of the body, but of the particularly sexual and erotic nature of those deformities and the way they are framed by her half-brother's actions.

It is here that we need finally to address the multiple layers of narrative point of view and authorial voice. We should not rush to then assume that Jane and Ozeki take on exactly the same point of view, for the slippages noted above should be evidence enough that Ozeki has set up a sympathetic, but not perfect protagonist. There are telling contradictions between what Jane says and thinks about any one issue and her actions and assessments at other points. If we can accept that point of difference, then the book is at once more complicated and more interesting. For it now appears that Jane cannot stand outside her own critique of the media. Surely, she makes critical remarks about the media and even incriminates herself from time to time, but these instances of explicit confession again run the risk of sounding both sanctimonious and ironic. It is the unselfconscious contradictions that strike me as most meaningful, as in Jane's disingenuous question. And it is in those moments that we might perceive an intelligence outside Jane's. It is this doubling that gives the book its true critical edge, a critical edge that allows us to return to our basic questions with a different sense of how the novel works to problematize notions of literary form, modernism, the media, ethics, and affect.

Ozeki claims: "By having Jane discuss the shortcomings of happy endings right smack in the middle of one, I was hoping to invite the reader into a more complex relationship with the ending. In essence, I point an authorial figure at the very thing that I am writing, and poke a hole in the seamlessness of the happy ending by making it self-referential and reflexive. Ironic" (appendix 13). However, that is itself only half the story. For while she endows Jane with this self-reflexivity here, at other points she disallows Jane that capacity, and the "authorial finger" is pointed not at the "thing being written" but at the point of view that guides it, Jane's own interior point of view. The novel thus unabashedly raises the question of modern storytelling and the ethical application of stories from a number of angles.

This is staged in a juxtaposition between Jane's book and Sei Shonagon's tenth-century text *The Pillow Book*. Throughout the novel, all three main women's voices quote *The Pillow Book*; Ozeki includes quotations from Shonagon, and both Akiko and Jane respond to and play off these quotations. Yet at the end, after all the communal acts of reading and writing have taken place, Jane finally decides that her stance toward her narrative will be different from Shonagon's — while Sei Shonagon hid her book, Jane will bring hers forward into the public realm. As opposed to Shonagon, who writes, "Whatever people may think of my book, I still regret that it ever came to light" (354), Jane asserts, "Whatever people may think of my book, I will make it public, bring it to light unflinchingly. That is the modern thing to do" (361). Here we need to underscore the historical, ethical, and aesthetic difference that this remark draws in order to delineate Jane's project. As opposed to what she sees as Shonagon's private text, Jane insists on the obligations the modern age places upon her. It is modern to be public, revelatory of the private. In particular, a certain kind of private knowledge is to be brought under the light of public scrutiny. Crucially, this information and knowledge are to be conveyed in a particular affective form.

But Jane's "book" seems to belie her claim to modernity — it seems rather an eminently postmodern text. For example, her repeated meditations on the notion that fiction and truth are at one with each other, that facts are randomly extracted from a mass of possible data. And yet the novel ends up focusing on that alignment between the world of fiction created in the ersatz documentary and the reality it seeks to expose, that is, on a modern resolution. While one might dwell on the postmodern world of the novel — the crisis of connection in an age of simulacra and fragmentation, media imaging and just-in-time production of affect, in this last statement Ozeki opens a historical question: is it only in the modern, with all its baggage, that we can locate ethics? Is the postmodern world of late capital actually unable to anchor a sense of belonging and obligation? Can the fragmentation and loss of grounding associated with the postmodern actually be exploited by and recuperated by the "modern"?

In fact, Ozeki's novel can easily be read as a calculated and persistent rebuttal of the postmodern. We find the constant activities of piecing together, which deploys a multiplicity of communication devices: the novel is peppered with transpacific faxes, telephone calls, answering machine recordings, cell phone calls from jet airliners, videotapes, office memos. The printed page of the novel itself replicates that of faxes, memos, and so on, but gathers those heterogeneous forms back into its dominant narrative space. What we end up with seems therefore an eminently modern project. However, how is this "modern" project actually given form? It is not as simple as it may appear. Ozeki constantly balances between Jane's film and her novel, and her novel and the texts and information which encase it.

Thus, when Jane says, "Whatever people may think of my *book*," it is here that Ozeki's voice emerges most clearly as distinct from Jane's — after all, Jane has not written a book, she has made a film. As this is the case, we can better understand at once Ozeki's authorial distance (which varies from moment to moment) from Jane's point of view, and the project of the novel itself. The very material form of the narrative that delivers this important ethical message to us is decidedly not the medium represented in the narrative. And yet the novel itself is embedded within another set of documents—we are provided with information sources on the meat industry, documentation on DES, women's health resources, as well as sample study questions for the novel. If Ozeki mocks the Beef-Ex series for attempting to blunt its sheer commercialism by couching the pro-grams as "documentaries" which proport to present cross-cultural under-standing (the segments include interviews with the families about their lives and habits, and there is a "sociological survey" that asks the Japanese audience to respond to the programs), her own text parallels these strate-gies. That is, it is "packaged" in a similar fashion. There is a novel, but the "book" is *not only* a novel, not *only* "literature."

Ozeki's text is linked both by the logic and symbolic structure of its diegesis and also through its surrounding texts, to the material history of the contemporary. This complementarity can be appreciated as Ozeki appropriating what Walter Benjamin called "technique" or "tendency," that is, the particular mode of cultural production within a specific social formation. It may also be seen as suggesting that in this historical age, neither of the two elements—what used to be called the "literary" and the "nonliterary"—can efficiently stand alone to deliver an ethically effective text. And we should be explicit here—the tension we have been speaking of all this time is between the particular imaginative function of literature and the global codifications and disseminations of *information*. Ozeki's literary narrative discloses her attempt to exploit our current registering of globalization as information and literature's modernist ability to lend new forms of information an affective and ethical content.

It may all come down to the fact that we simply do not yet know whether the very information technologies and entertainment and other cultural networks that form one set of powerful conduits through which we are incorporated into "the globe" are not at once habituating us to a different set of representational phenomena—sound and visual bytes, dif-ferently formatted images and information packages—or whether the residual forms of modernist aesthetics are not still the dominant modes of producing and receiving narratives. We need to ask: Do these different forms and their accompanying phenomenologies disable or revise our capacity to imagine others? How is otherness available to us, and what does it look like once it gets here? And how might the very technologies that bring us into some sort of contact allow for any sort of consolidated moral action? Ozeki's text is hardly a revolutionary one in any formal sense. And yet its formal presentation raises critical questions about the persisting role of a literary genre, or, indeed, *all* cultural forms in an age of increasingly extensive and intensive media.[10]

No doubt, the novel leaves itself open to two interrelated criticisms. First, as we have noted above, is its resort to stereotypical, liberal multi-culturalist clichés and plot devices. I have attempted to demonstrate how, by delinking Jane's point of view from the author's, we might comprehend a more complex critical strategy. But we have yet to confront a second criticism, namely that the novel exploits sentimentality.[11] This brings us back to Rorty's argument for "manipulating feelings." Rorty is not unaware of the weaknesses of such an argument: "It is revolting to think that our only hope for a decent society consists of softening the self-satisfied hearts of a leisure class" (130). While I do not accept wholeheartedly Rorty's argument, I do think it is worth considering the fact that, whether we like it or not, there seems to be some validity to the claim that it is precisely the emotional element that needs to be recognized positively as over and against the "perfectly logical but totally insane" rationality of the market. As I write this essay, the latest news is about the Terrorism Futures Market that the Pentagon has proposed. As one news article puts it:

> It sounds jaw-droppingly callous, not to mention absurd: An Internet gambling parlor, sponsored by the U.S. government, on politics in the Middle East. Anyone, from Osama bin Laden to your grandmother, can bet over the Web on such questions as whether Yasser Arafat will be assassinated or Turkey's government will be overthrown.
>
> If the bettors are right, they'll win money; if they're wrong, they'll lose their wagers. The site itself will keep numerical tallies of the current "odds" for various events.
>
> Why not just ask the guys at the corner bar whether or not we should invade Jordan, or play SimCity to make foreign policy decisions?
>
> But experts say the DARPA-backed Policy Analysis Market (www.policyanalysismarket.org) is based on a legitimate theory, the Efficient Market Hypothesis, that has a proven track record in predicting outcomes. Basically, the idea is that the collective conscious-

ness is smarter than any single person. By forcing people to put their money where their mouth is, the wagers help weed out know-nothings and give more weight to the opinions of those in the know.

"Markets are a great way of aggregating information that a lot of different people have," said Eric Zitzewitz, an assistant professor of economics at the Stanford Graduate School of Business. "One of the big issues with intelligence that was gathered before 9/11 was that information wasn't aggregated within the intelligence community. This is directly aimed at addressing that."[12]

Although the idea sounds offensive to some, "to the extent this has even a small probability of using valuable information to help prevent tragedies, that's got to be the overriding ethical concern," he said. (*San Francisco Chronicle*, 30 August 2003)

At least for the moment, in this case, those of us who affectively "wince" at the "callousness" of this scheme have won out — after news of this was publicized, congresspeople on both sides urged the defunding of the program, despite the ardent defense of it put forward by the Pentagon in exactly the terms used by Zitzewitz. Now why is that?

While we might cringe at the clichés and the "nationalist" sentimentality found in Ozeki's novel, I believe we ignore the sentimental at our own risk — rather than simple knowledge or "rationality" it might be the most powerful tool in persuasive storytelling, and progressives should reclaim that as a tool. To be effective, we need to think more closely about our inherited forms for sadness. At what do we rise in outrage? How is such affect produced? I know full well that this again borders on an apology for propaganda, for the aestheticization of politics. And yet, given our hypermediated age that draws "us" together precisely in its terms, is it not incumbent upon us to think through these questions, for the sake of our own political, and human, futures?

A critical point of examination would involve turning our gaze upon ourselves, as academics and intellectuals, and asking why it is we downplay, ignore, degrade the idea that the narrative of a Mexican fieldworker who has lost his hand is "cheap sentimentality" unless it is accompanied by a full exposition of the mode of production? While I am completely sympathetic to that critique (and have made it often myself), I think that at this point we have to also think of the ways in which we link the two together in a form that is compelling, and that works on several levels and registers. We need to understand much better both what might be our new forms of representation, especially those that do the bulk of the work in mediating (and indeed, creating) our sense of the "global," and the persistence of "old" ways of feeling ourselves in the world with others.

A Short Aside on "Propaganda"

While Rorty's open plea for progressives to learn how to "manipulate" the sentiments of others so as to move them to specific sorts of affect and ethical actions might well strike some as naive, misguided, or unethical (or all the above), as the reader can gather from my own remarks, I believe we ignore such a notion at our own peril. Not only has "rational choice" discourse seemed to permeate the economic, corporate, and political realm, but it has penetrated the forms of sentiment as well. Indeed, all sorts of bad sentimental arguments are loaded upon the more obviously bad rational ones (for example, the notion from the Stanford economics professor who argues that betting on terrorism futures is not only not morally repugnant, but both good market sense and, above all, ethical).

From this we might learn something from history. About seventy years ago, the brilliant literary critic and novelist Kenneth Burke addressed the American Writers' Congress. His speech was taken by many as an act of treason against the socialist cause. What was Burke's sin? It might be reduced to his simple suggestion that the rhetoric of the proletarian revolution, mobilized in the name of "the masses," be rededicated to the keyword "the people." If now we regard this as an eerily prescient view to the New Left and beyond into the 1970s and 1980s, Burke's statement was then taken as a repudiation of the fundamental principles of Marxism. His argument is well summed up by Frank Lentricchia:

> In 1935 Burke was saying to America's radical left not only that a potentially revolutionary culture must be culturally as well as economically rooted, but as well, and this was perhaps the most difficult of Burke's implication for his radical critics to swallow, that a revolutionary culture must situate itself firmly on the terrain of its capitalist antagonist, must not attempt a dramatic leap beyond capitalism in one explosive, rupturing moment of release, must work its way through capital's language of domination by working cunningly within it, using, appropriating, even speaking through its key mechanisms of repression. (24)

That is to say, capital had already interpellated its subjects according to certain hegemonic forms of imagination. To argue against it from an "alien" lexicon rooted in economistic nomenclature would be futile. Burke argues instead for an attention not only to the "cultural symbolic," but also to the precise forms of collective belief that such symbolism both taps into and replenishes:

> Myths may be wrong, or they may be used to bad ends — but they cannot be dispensed with. In the last analysis, they are our basic psychological tools for working together. A hammer is a carpenter's tool; a wrench is a mechanic's tool; and a 'myth' is the social tool for welding the sense of interrelationship by which the carpenter and the mechanic, though differently occupied, can work together for common social ends. In this sense a myth that works well is as real as food, tools, and shelter are. (87)

Most importantly for our discussion, Burke declares,

> I shall consider this matter *purely from the standpoint of propaganda* . . . Insofar as a writer really is a propagandist, not merely writing work that will be applauded by his allies, convincing the already convinced, but actually moving forward like a pioneer into outlying areas of the public and bringing them the first favorable impressions of his doctrine, the nature of his trade may give rise to special symbolic requirements. Accordingly, it is the *propaganda* aspect of the symbol that I shall center upon — considering the symbol particularly as a device for spreading the areas of allegiance. (89, emphasis original)

Burke thus thinks of propaganda "not as an over-simplified, literal, explicit writing of lawyer's briefs, but as a process of broadly and generally associating his political alignment with cultural awareness in the large" (93). This movement outward, *exotopically*, is in our age precisely the movement globally. Therefore, the true difficulty lies not in finding a universal "rationality" but rather in discovering not only a shared set of rational/sentimental values and affects that can steer us toward behaving humanely toward one another, but also the means by which one might convey them.

What I take from Burke is first the notion that we cannot simply dismiss "propaganda" or, to use Rorty's term, "manipulation," if by that we mean the careful attention to the ways images, narratives, and other media forms can and do draw upon specific beliefs, assumptions, and stereotypes. The point would be not only to "expose" those that to our mind work against "truth," but also to craft our own rhetoric so as to convey our sense of the truth in a compelling, effective manner. I am not suggesting that we subscribe to a uniform rhetoric, but rather that we entertain a more capacious set of rhetorics and vocabularies—even the sentimental.[13]

Conclusion: Structures of Feeling in a Global Age

We find ourselves at a moment when we need seriously to reexamine our "structures of feeling." In his exposition of this concept, Raymond Williams first notes a "frequent tension between the received interpretation [of new experiences] and practical experience. . . . This tension is often an unease, a stress, a displacement, a latency: the moment of conscious comparison not yet come, often not even coming. . . . There are the experiences to which the fixed forms do not speak at all, which indeed they do not recognize." Crucially, Williams settles on the aesthetic as the "unfixed" form most likely to be able to represent these "embryonic feelings":

> The unmistakable presence of certain elements in art which are not covered by other formal systems is the true source of the specializing categories of "the aesthetic," "the arts," and "imaginative literature." We need, on the one hand, to acknowledge (and welcome) the specificity of these elements—specific feelings, specific rhythms—and yet to find ways of recognizing their specific kinds of sociality. . . . The idea of structure of feeling can be specifically related to the evidence of forms and conventions—semantic figures—which, in art and literature, are often among the first indications that such a new structure is forming. (133)

It is exactly this barely conscious intuition that we are entering a new era of human being that may form the heart of an aesthetics of the global. Such an aesthetics would be pursued not simply as an inventory of forms, but as an attempt to see how such structures of feeling may or may not have any ethical effect or ramification. For we need to always remind ourselves that Williams's "structures of feeling" are not simply metaphysical, but rather produced within eminently lived, socially and historically concrete experiences. The question that haunts the present is exactly the question of how "feeling" is modulated, conveyed, and how it might be effective in consolidating a response from the margins and reaching across the border of the minor/dominant divide.

Notes

1 One attempt is Raimo Tuomela's *The Importance of Us: A Philosophical Study of Basic Social Norms*. Tuomela ultimately comes to the conclusion that: "all social notions are in principle reconstructible on an individualistically acceptable way. . . . ontological interrelationship does not postulate any social wholes and serves to give a naturalistic account of the social realm" (376). That is to say, this huge study comes back to the primacy of the individual modeling system.

2 For such an attempt, see Margolis's *Selfishness, Altruism, and Rationality*, which takes on, among other topics, the case of voting — why do people do this?

3 One can recall Elster's comments about storytelling and other-oriented emotions. There of course is a running debate, centered on the work of Martha Nussbaum, over the actual possibility of imagining others through literature. I must leave that matter aside for the purposes of this essay. What I wish to track is something more specific and evidentiary — the production of affect. Whether or to what degree that production takes place because one has sufficiently imagined an other is beside the point.

4 For an illuminating discussion of this essay, see Bruce Robbins, *Feeling Global*.

5 Cf. "Most of the work of changing moral intuitions is being done by manipulating feelings rather than increasing our knowledge" (118).

6 Michael Suk-Young Chwe notes that in modern sociology, a partitioning was instated by Vilfredo Pareto between economics and sociology. Chwe goes on to note how this division is contested in the works of Erving Goffman, Lévi-Strauss, and others (95–96).

7 I hasten to add that where I have here used elements of Black's positive evaluation of the novel, she is not uncritical of the text.

8 Chiu's essay makes similar points as mine with regard to the episode with the Mexican family (107), Jane's cleansing of images (108), and Akiko's train ride (109).

9 One of the few realms in which affect and mimicry do not lead to consumerism is in the realm of sexuality and pleasure. Here is Akiko looking at a soft porn magazine: "The girl stared boldly at her. Akiko stared back, moving her finger around a little. She liked looking at the pictures. Even though they weren't so authentic, she found them sexy — but she was not sure whether she wanted to make love to the girl or simply to be her" (188).

10 As Alan Liu puts it: "The vital task for literary study in the age of advanced creative destruction, I believe, is to inquire into the aesthetic value — let us simply call it the literary — once managed by 'creative' literature but now busily seeking new management amid the ceaseless creation and recreation of the forms, styles, media, and institutions of postindustrial knowledge work" (63).

11 Again, Black's chapter on Ozeki includes an extensive discussion of the idea of sentiment, especially as linked to the notion of "cosmofeminism."

12   For a rebuttal to this rationale, see Stiglitz.

13   Chwe's aforementioned book on "rational ritual" is a stimulating exercise in this vein. He writes, "This book tries to show that this distinction cannot so easily be maintained. It starts with a narrow, unadorned conception of rationality in the context of coordination problems and shows that the common knowledge required is substantially related to issues of intersubjectivity, collective consciousness, and group identity" (95).

Works Cited

Abell, Peter. "Sociological Theory and Rational Choice Theory." *Social Theory*. Ed. Bryan Turner. Oxford: Blackwell, 1996. 252–277.

Benjamin, Walter. "The Author as Producer." *Reflections: Essays, Aphorisms, Autobiographical Writings*. Ed. Peter Demetz. New York: Schocken Books, 1987. 220–238.

Berman, Marshall. "Why Modernism Still Matters." *Modernity and Identity*. Ed. Scott Lash and Jonathan Friedman. Oxford: Blackwell. 33–58.

Black, Shameem. "Cosmopoetics: Global Imagination in Contemporary Writing." Ph.D. diss. Stanford University, May 2004.

Burke, Kenneth. "Revolutionary Symbolism in America." *American Writers' Congress*. Ed. Henry Hart. New York: International Publishers, 1935.

Chiu, Monica. "Postnational Globalization and (En)gendered Meat Production in Ruth L. Ozeki's *My Year of Meats*" *LIT* 12 (2001): 99–128.

Chwe, Michael Suk-Young. *Rational Ritual: Culture, Coordination, and Common Knowledge*. Princeton: Princeton University Press, 2001.

Coleman, J. S. *Foundations of Social Theory*. Cambridge: Belknap, 1990.

Elster, John. *Nuts and Bolts for the Social Sciences*. Cambridge: Cambridge University Press, 1989.

Fluck, Winfried. "Fiction and Justice." *New Literary History* 34 (2003): 19–42.

Friedman, Jeffrey, ed. *The Rational Choice Controversy: Economic Models of Politics Reconsidered*. New Haven: Yale University Press, 1996.

Lash, Scott, and Jonathan Friedman, eds. *Modernity and Identity*. Oxford: Blackwell, 1992.

Lentricchia, Frank. *Criticism and Social Change*. Chicago: University of Chicago Press, 1983.

Liu, Alan. "The Future Literary: Literature and the Culture of Information." *Time and the Literary*. Ed. Karen Newman, Jay Clayton, and Marianne Hirsch. New York: Routledge, 2002.

Margolis, Howard. *Selfishness, Altruism, and Rationality: A Theory of Social Choice* Cambridge: Cambridge University Press, 1982.

Moyers, Bill. "Chinua Achebe." Public Affairs TV. Alexandria: PBS Video, 1989.

Ozeki, Ruth L. *My Year of Meats*. New York: Penguin, 1998.

Robbins, Bruce. *Feeling Global: Internationalism in Distress*. New York: New York UP, 1999.

Rorty, Richard. "Human Rights, Rationality, and Sentimentality." *On Human Rights: The Oxford Amnesty Lectures.* Ed. Stephen Shute and Susan Hurley. New York: Basic, 1993. 111–134.

Stiglitz, Joseph E. "Terrorism: There's No Futures In It." *Los Angeles Times* 31 July 2003.

Taylor, Michael. "When Rationality Fails." *The Rational Choice Controversy: Economic Models of Politics Reconsidered.* Ed. Jeffrey Friedman. New Haven: Yale University Press, 1996. 223–234.

Tuomela, Raimo. *The Importance of Us: A Philosophical Study of Basic Social Norms.* Stanford: Stanford University Press, 1995.

Vallette, Jim. "Larry Summers's War against the Earth." *Counterpunch.* http://www.counterpunch.org/summers.html.

Williams, Raymond. *Marxism and Literature.* New York: Oxford University Press, 1977.

Toward an Ethics of Transnational Encounters,

or, "When" Does a "Chinese" Woman Become a "Feminist"?

To begin, two narratives: A Chinese woman who had rehearsed for the lead role in the model opera *Red Azalea* (*Dujuan shan*) during the waning years of the Cultural Revolution in the 1970s decided to immigrate to the United States. Upon arriving in 1984, she struggled to learn the English language and to make a living. In the span of a few short years, she successfully mastered English sufficiently to accomplish the unlikely task of writing a best-selling autobiographical novel, *Red Azalea*, named after the opera. The autobiography chronicles the traumas of the Cultural Revolution from a female perspective and clearly proclaims that America is the end of the author's search for freedom and self-expression as a woman. Another Chinese woman, who in the 1980s had single-handedly created the discipline of women's studies in the hinterland of China, the city of Zhengzhou in Henan Province, and had freely drawn from Western feminist classics in her writings, was invited to come to an academic conference on Chinese feminism in 1992 at Harvard University. There, she disagreed strongly with the assumptions of Western feminism as represented by some of the conference participants and has since publicly repudiated Western feminism.

These two narratives seem to fall within two unrelated categories as objects of academic inquiry: the former belongs with questions of assimilation and multiculturalism in ethnic and diaspora studies; the latter raises questions of cross-cultural encounter and conflict in studies of First/Third World feminisms. The former may be construed as a domestic issue belonging to immigration studies or minority studies, since the author of the autobiography, Anchee Min, had clear intentions to stay in the United States and has since become a U.S. citizen; the latter may appear as an international topic, since the scholar Li Xiaojiang never intended to stay in the United States.[1] The main factor weighing in such a conventional academic categorization, it seems, lies in the *intentions* and the different *durations* of their stays, where one is construed as immigration and the other as travel.

What complicates this neat distinction between immigration and traveling, as is evident in the uneasy way in which the "sojourner mentality" of early Chinese laborers in the United States is dealt with in Asian American historiography,[2] is that the intention to stay and the duration of the stay are neither absolute nor useful markers of national, cultural, and individual "identity," whether for Chinese gold diggers and laborers of the nineteenth century or for Chinese women in the late twentieth century of mobile capital, traveling, and migration.[3] In the latter case, regardless of their national and legal citizenship, both women purport to speak as authentic Chinese persons representing China and Chineseness, the former from Hacienda Heights, California, who makes frequent trips to China, and the latter first from Zhengzhou, then Beijing and Dalian, China. Postcolonial studies, dangling over and between issues of immigration and travel, may be considered the fitting paradigm here that can accommodate both women's experiences — except that from the perspective of these Chinese women, their condition can hardly be considered postcolonial. *(Post)socialist*, in its implied, albeit limited, externality to capitalist-centric Western discursive practices, of which postcoloniality as theorized in the United States is an example, is a more appropriate descriptive term here. In the messiness of categorizing these two women vis-à-vis the artificial designations of disciplinary and methodological boundaries, we are coming closer to identifying the fluidity and complexity of our transnational moment, where migration, travel, and diaspora can no longer be clearly distinguished by intention and duration, nor by national citizenship and belonging. We are also witnessing, I think, the inability of postcolonial theory, which arose from capitalist postcolonies and hypercapitalist metropoles, to deal adequately with the (post)socialist condition.[4]

What happens, then, when we disregard the customary boundaries of immigration studies and cross-cultural studies and focus instead on the logics and politics of the transnational encounter with the other and difference? How do the border crossings of these two women expose and confront the West-centric regime of power and representation where difference is variously value coded in terms of time, space, ethnicity, and subjectivity (the backward/past, the underdeveloped/remote, the racialized/ethnicized, the oppressed Third World woman, each stereotypically attributed to the other)? What economy of subjection and subjectivization is implied in such value codings of time, space, ethnicity, and subjectivity, and what are its problematics? How might we, finally, imagine and practice an ethics of transnational encounter that is neither simply assimilationist nor conflictual, alternatives that a cursory summary of the two stories above seems to suggest?

By bracketing "when," "Chinese," and "feminist" to examine Western (mis)uses of difference in encoding values of time/space, ethnicity, and gender subjectivity at the moments and places of encounter, this paper argues, among other things, the prominence of affect as a subjective expression of desire, feeling, and emotion in discursive and political encodings of difference. Affect in turn seeks and produces legitimations of difference through interlinked discourses of modernity, ethnicity, and gender subjectivity that then posit such identifications as "Chinese woman," "Chinese feminist," "immigrant Chinese woman," and so on to embody by now specifically delineated differences. From the other side looking West, the non-West's mimeticism of the West consolidates Western universalism and passively participates in the colonial and neocolonial circulation of knowledge, at one extreme; at the other extreme, the affective technologies of nativism and cultural nationalism produce another set of legitimizing counterdiscourses that often reproduce and replicate the "very dynamics that are being opposed."[5] For others who reside in the West as racialized immigrants and minorities, their choices are often rigidly limited to the poles of assimilation (mimeticism) and resistance (disidentification), with the questions of what they assimilate to and what they disidentify from left uninterrogated, while socioeconomic questions also go unanswered, reduced to the realm of affect à la identity politics. The political economy of power and discursive differentials—whether between the West and the non-West or between the majority and the minority within the West—is not to be neglected, but affect-induced cultural nationalist politics across the transnational and national terrains reductively transforms political economy into a war of cultures and ethnicities. This reactive culturalist and ethnicist reductionism, in conjunction with the condescending universalist reductionism of the West, has prevented the emergence of engaged discussions of multiply nuanced, ethical relationality among different contingents. Through a critique of both sets of reductionisms as products of affect-induced knowledges—such as the temporal coding of difference and the reaction to it ("when"), the ethnicization of nationality and culture and complicity with it ("Chinese"), the universalization of Western liberal feminism and resistance to it ("feminist") — this essay argues for modes of transnational relationality beyond scripted affect for subjects variously positioned in and outside the West. This ethical transnational relationality should be accountable not only for major-to-minor encounters, but also for minor-to-minor encounters, as subject positions shift and thereby multi-angulate their structuration by uneven operations of power.

"When," or the Value-Coding of Time

In the spring of 1988, I found myself sitting next to Zhang Jie, perhaps the most prominent woman writer in China at the time, at a reception in Beijing for American writers hosted by the Chinese Ministry of Culture. As the interpreter/translator for the American delegation, I had acquired the derivative power of proximity to prominent American and Chinese writers to enjoy a sumptuous banquet and to serve as the intermediary of conversation and cultural exchange. One of the questions that was frequently raised by the American delegation, especially by women writers during that reception and later during meetings in Beijing, Chengdu, and Shanghai, was whether Chinese women writers were keen on expressing feminist intent and exposing female oppression. Upon hearing the question thus posed and translated in my Taiwanese-inflected terminology, Zhang Jie appeared to be ill at ease. Despite the fact that she was then the most acclaimed writer of female sensibility, she replied after a short pause that there was no such thing as "feminism" (*nüxing zhuyi* or *nüquan zhuyi*) in China and that she would not call herself a "feminist" or a "feminist writer." This was my first trip to China as a Korean-born, Taiwan- and U.S.-educated Han Chinese residing in California, and, out of sheer ignorance, I understood her categorical rejection to be the expression of her care to avoid making any antiofficial statements at a state-sponsored event. Her statement, I assumed, hid other meanings and was therefore opaque to an outsider like me. As there were indeed many such moments of opacity regarding various issues during the entire trip, I did not probe any further.

Had I probed further, I would have found that Zhang Jie's refusal of the name, if not the substance, of something akin to "feminism" reflected a complex social and historical formation under Chinese socialism. Perhaps if I had had sufficient objectivity and a comparative perspective on her social and historical condition, I could have asked her to narrate the tale of Chinese socialism and its complex relationship to women's liberation over the previous decades, which I could have in turn translated for the American writers. It was, of course, not my place to interject my own questions, my role in these exchanges being that of a supposedly transparent medium without a subjectivity of my own. So when the Americans, out of a misplaced and misassumed politeness, did not follow up on that question, the opportunity for genuine exchange was dropped. The assumption shared by me and the American writers was that feminism was by definition a counterdiscourse to the state, the supreme embodiment of patriarchal power; thus, Zhang Jie's denial of the term betrayed to "us" a paranoia concerning the socialist state's regulatory presence. The moment of difference was thus explained away by a universalistic rationale that displaced the real intention to know and disguised sheer ignorance of the situation. In this case, my role as a transparent translator had ironically helped produce even more opacity. My positionality at that moment collapsed into that of the American writers, all of "us" lacking both the knowledge of the history of Chinese women's liberation in socialist China and the requisite curiosity and humility to learn. More importantly still, the presumptuousness and casualness with which the question was asked, passing the burden of explanation to the native woman Zhang Jie, was itself a high-handed gesture. Considering the complexity with which Zhang would have had to grapple to tell the story of the women's movement and socialism in China, Zhang's best answer could only have been "no" or silence; there would never have been enough *time* to tell such a long and complicated story.

This episode has since come back to me again and again, as I have begun to do research on Chinese women in socialist China and have become more sensitized to how easily cross-cultural encounters misfire, often simply because the Western subject refuses to acknowledge the historical substance that constitutes the other's supposed difference. The concept of cultural difference usually takes the form of one of two poles: reified absolutism or a been-there, done-that superiority complex. Either the other woman is frozen in absolute difference (too difficult and too time-consuming to understand fully) or she is trapped in the earlier phase of the development of feminism (too familiar and thus either dismissed or condescendingly told what to do next). In these scenarios, which often coexist, the other woman is readily dismissed as too different or too similar, or both, whichever works best at the time, the conceptual leap between difference and similarity being conveniently overlooked. It is not that the Western feminist has a mistaken notion of difference and similarity, which is the focus of much Third World feminist theory in its quarrel with Western feminism, but rather that the Western feminist enjoys the power of arbitrarily conferring difference and similarity on the non-Western woman. Elsewhere, I have charted the operation of an "asymmetrical cosmopolitanism" across the West/non-West divide: non-Western intellectuals need to be knowledgeable about Western cultures and speak one of the metropolitan languages to be considered "cosmopolitan," while Western intellectuals can be cosmopolitan without speaking any nonmetropolitan language.[6] The Western subject's strongest weapon in practicing asymmetrical cosmopolitanism is not that he or she denies the non-West access to cosmopolitanism, but that he or she has the power to assume sheer neglect or ignorance of the non-West. A politics of selective recognition — the non-Western other is recognized most readily through the modes of Orientalism and what I call "modernist ideology," with its attendant time-space value codings — cloaks the lack of desire to know the other. Orientalism is in this sense but an alibi for the lack of interest in comprehending the non-Western other in its own terms, reducing the other to the site of difference to explain away the need to attend to its opacity and complexity; modernist ideology, which sees history in linear terms as moving from the primitive to the developed, confers similarity on the other as the past of the self.

With the power to arbitrate difference and similarity in such reductive terms, the Western subject can thus simply *ignore* that which otherwise needs to be learned with time and effort, namely, the history, experience, and representation of the other woman in multiple contexts. If sheer ignorance and neglect are the more common basis of the West's misunderstanding of the non-West, then our critique of the West in terms of deconstructing Orientalism misses the larger target entirely. The discourse of anti-Orientalism, meant to deconstruct Western universalism, often ends up instead becoming an alibi for the West's resistance to looking elsewhere for paradigms of cross-cultural understanding that are able to attend to local contexts in more complicated and substantive ways. The deconstruction of Western universalist discourse in terms of its self-contradictions likewise ends up exercising the muscles of Western universalist discourse, rendering its chameleon-like flexibility more complex and better able to anticipate those latter-day deconstructive moves. Western discourse therefore becomes more and more complex, while non-Western discourse can be safely ignored — after all, if we want to study power and hegemony, we should study the West, right? While deconstructionism has recentered the West, an equally obsessive Foucauldianism has valorized the West as the site of power worthy of analysis and critique. The resulting disparity between the assumed methodological sophistication one takes to Western studies and the assumed naïveté of so-called area studies spells out this logic of narcissism and dismissal of the other, all marked by supposedly well-intentioned liberal soul-searching and guilt-induced critical self-reflection.

Troubling the West/non-West binarism evoked here, which I posit schematically for analytical purposes, is my own subject position as a translator in the episode narrated above. Due to my lack of knowledge of Chinese women's history in socialist China at that time, I was clearly aligned with the American writers. The alignment is troubling, to say the least, and is indicative of the kind of misuse of derivative power a Third World diasporic intellectual can wield to further mystify the Third World woman, thus constituting herself as another imperialist agent in the neocolonial production and circulation of knowledge. Gayatri Spivak's questions concerning the new diasporic women, "For whom do they work?" and "In what interest do they work?" are powerful ones. I was guilty of providing "uncaring translations that transcode in the interest of dominant feminist knowledge" (Spivak 260). Even though I am not from China, my recruitment as a translator for the trip was based on my ability to speak Chinese like a native, which was taken to be a good enough marker of my authenticity as a "Chinese" person, since I also "look" Chinese. One episode that exposes the paradox of the situation occurred while we were on the Three Gorges river cruise in first-class compartments. From our comfortable compartments, we had to walk through the third- and fourth-class communal bunks and seats of the locals to reach our very own dining room, where we were served eight-course lunches and dinners. We often saw some of the poorer locals eating their meals, which consisted of nothing but rice soaked in water mixed with hot pepper powder. I was asked innocently by one of the American writers, who seemed genuinely amazed by how different I looked from the locals, since she thought I was also Chinese: "Shu-mei, why are you so much fairer and healthier-looking than these people?" I answered humorlessly or humorously, depending on how one looks at it, "Well, I am well-fed!" To be sure, I myself was more than confused as to whether I was Chinese or not during that first trip to China, and questions such as this one brought out my identity conundrum even more. It did not matter to the writer that I was not Chinese in the way the locals on the boat were; she refused to acknowledge my statement that I was not from China. If an American person of German or French heritage speaks German or French fluently, it is considered a skill that adds to rather than undermines his/her American identity. But it was confusing to her that a Chinese-speaking, ethnic Han Chinese could be *not* from China. The ethnicity-language-nationality assumption here is clearly racialized. Besides my own small misfortune of being racialized, which bespeaks the paradox of being both the Americans' shadow (their translator) and the Chinese's shadow (their racial compatriot) at once, the graver issue is the ignorance of the person who asked me that obvious question.

My role as translator, thus determined by multiple axes of nationality, ethnicity, and diaspora, implicated me not merely because of the high-class food I shared with the American writers, but also because my translation was so helplessly dysfunctional in reducing obscurity and opacity. Without acknowledging or studying the history of socialist China, the American writers and I, feminist or not, turned the possibility of cultural translation and mutual understanding into an encounter of incommensurability. Incommensurability is thus the consequence not of difference made essential or absolute, but of ignorance. Even a cursory, schematic overview of Chinese women's history in the twentieth century will show multiple points of intersection with and divergence from Western feminism. In the following simple overview, a reversal of the value coding of time in the assumption of a supposedly "advanced" Western feminism vis-à-vis its "backward" "Third World sisters" will be analyzed as a way to rethink the theory of time in the representation of the other.

To be sure, Chinese women's liberation has traced a historically different path from that of the West. Scholars of China have traced this path from liberal, Western-style feminism in the 1920s to revolutionary feminism in the 1930s and after, most importantly to the socialist, state-sponsored official feminism established in 1949 and in place until the 1980s.[7] When it came to power in 1949, the socialist state legally instituted equality between men and women through the Marriage Law

(1950) and the Chinese Constitution (1954), guaranteeing women equal rights in all social and political spheres (Yang, "From Gender Erasure," 37). The Women's Federation, the intermediary institution between women and the socialist state that had capillary extensions to the village level, vigilantly safeguarded women's economic, political, cultural, and educational rights. Compared to that of women in the West, who still had not acquired many of the rights that Chinese women were granted by the state in the 1950s — such as "equal work/equal pay" for women — the condition of Chinese women's liberation could be seen as more "advanced." Since the state granted women equality, there had been no need for women to be situated against the state or against men in Maoist and post-Mao China, hence the presumed irrelevance of "feminism" as such in the Chinese context.

This attribution of an "advanced" character to Chinese women's liberation troubles the assignment of temporal value in Western feminist discourses through such time-charged terminologies as "first wave," "second wave," "third wave," or Kristeva's homologous three-stage theory of feminist consciousness in her celebrated essay "Women's Time," and the related assumption that non-Western feminism is stuck in the nationalist stage (Jayawardena).[8] Such discourses code temporal movement in terms of progress and development, always implying that what came *after* is superior to or an improvement over what came *before*. If we consider the fact that Chinese women were legally more equal to Chinese men than Western women to Western men in the 1950s and after, and thus more "advanced," the usual temporal hierarchy of the West over China is resoundingly subverted. Indeed, during Kristeva's Maoist phase, this advanced status was both the site of envy and anxiety, as her *Des chinoises* so uncomfortably shows. For Kristeva, Chinese women were both liberated under Mao and embodiments of the silent, primordial Orient.

Li Xiaojiang, the famous refuser of Western feminism and the protagonist of my second narrative, eloquently remarks on this contradiction:

> [American women's studies scholars] created two myths about Chinese women. One is the myth of women's liberation in the 1950s. After World War II, Western women, including American women, returned home while the Chinese women began to enter society. When in 1963 the publication of Betty Friedan's *The Feminine Mystique* inspired a new feminist movement, they saw that Chinese women [already] had equal rights and entered the work force equally

with men in society, and they thought Chinese women were the forerunners of women's liberation in the world. I call it the myth of "women's liberation" because there indeed exists an element of truth in saying that Chinese women underwent a dramatic transformation. But [these] Western women did not realize that we entered society in the condition of a very low productivity standard, and because of the heavy burden of labor, including social and domestic labor, Chinese women had not really achieved real liberation. You said we were liberated, and we said we were exhausted (loud laughter from the whole room).

After reform [since the death of Mao], many Western women's studies scholars went to China, noticed that numerous women's problems had emerged, and then returned and wrote many books, deconstructing the myth of the 1950s that they themselves had created and giving Chinese women another myth, which I call the myth of "double oppression" of the 1980s. One source of oppression is still tradition, as they see the continued oppression of Chinese women by the traditional family; the other source of oppression is seen to stem from the state and politics, since Chinese politics is undemocratic and the economy underdeveloped. Chinese women are thereby presented as living in hell amidst indescribable suffering. Several women's studies scholars in the United States, including those who wrote these books, told me that they felt comforted that, despite their own problems, Chinese women were worse off than they were! (Loud laughter from the whole room.) (*Challenge* 88–89)[9]

Addressing a German audience at the University of Heidelberg in 1991, Li humorously pointed out the misplaced perceptions of the Western scholars who were so quick to jump to conclusions about Chinese women and to turn them into myths. In these two diametrically opposed myths, there is an unquestioned, contradictory assignation of temporal value to Chinese women, first as "forerunners," thus ahead of Western women, and then as backward sisters living in an "underdeveloped" country under "double oppression." One wonders how Chinese women could reverse revolution so as to be at first so advanced, then suddenly so backward. The problem here is not so much that the temporal value is assigned wrongly, but that it is assigned *carelessly*, without an analysis of the complexity of local situations in both Maoist and post-Mao China. Li remarks that Western feminism tends to code Chinese women's movements in terms of what she calls "stagism" (*jieduan lun*) rather than contextualizing them (*Woman?ism* 264). The "stagism" imposed on Chinese women's situation is a form of decontextualization.

Li Xiaojiang's work in women's studies in China in the 1990s was in some part a critique of both of these myths, especially because the first myth — that Chinese women were fully liberated in socialist China — was upheld by the Western feminists as well as by the Chinese state. She argues that state-instituted equality between men and women hid an implicit male norm, according to which women were equal to men insofar as they were like men, thus degendering and "neutralizing" (*zhongxing hua*) women and depriving them of their difference and femininity. Li and Zhang put it this way:

> [Women's studies] scholars now recognize that the guiding principle of "whatever men do, women can do also," while inspirational, in fact helped to conceal a male standard for women's equality. In other words, women's equality meant that women were equated with men. A male standard, however, only creates an illusion of equality, since women ultimately have no distinct gender identity within the context of so-called liberation. Thus these scholars now conclude that the first task of women's liberation is to allow women themselves to discover who they are, where they come from, and how much they have been influenced by distorted, patriarchal images of their gender. This is the first step in breaking through the patriarchal line of dominant ideology. (146)

Here, state patriarchy is criticized not because of its obvious sexism, as in the West, but because its mode of liberating Chinese women ultimately prevented that liberation from being complete. As Li's Heidelberg lecture illustrates, it was women as laborers and workers who were equal to men, not women as "women" with their particular gender identity.[10] In other words, women were equal to men insofar as they were workers or the so-called socialist constructors deployable for the development of the nation-state, which instituted the hegemonic identity of women as gender-neutral. Li and others therefore emphasized self-discovery and the self-consciousness of women as women to search for the grounds of women's subjectivity (*zhutixing*) outside the dictates of the state. Consonant with such a critique of state-sponsored women's liberation as normatively male was the emergence of a strong refeminization drive among urban women, who were freshly incorporated into the politics of femininity in global capitalism, celebrating their newfound femininity with flair. After a detour in history through anti-imperialist socialism, China in the post-Mao era has seemingly reentered the global arena and been subjected to a renewed teleological narrative of capitalist development and modernity within which Western liberal feminism is situated.

Li's rhetoric of self-discovery and self-consciousness undoubtedly demonstrates a proximity to Western liberal feminism, although of course she would refuse such an interpretation. The moment of China's incorporation into global capitalism in the 1980s was also the moment of affinity between Western feminism and Chinese women's studies. Thus, when Western feminists expressed disapproval of such refeminization tendencies as reversing the advances Chinese women had achieved, the famed woman writer Wang Anyi, in an interview with Wang Zheng, defended refeminized Chinese women indignantly: "We have just encountered differences between men and women; we lived without such a difference for such a long time" (166). Li, likewise, emphasizes how, even with all the current problems in the "regendering" of women, such as women becoming capitalist consumers and objects of capitalist exploitation and commodification,[11] the current situation affords Chinese women more choices and subjectivity than under state-sponsored gender liberation. Indeed, if women were "liberated" or "freed from" gender under Maoism, they are now reconnected with their gender, albeit in problematic ways. Wang Anyi defends Chinese women's love of cosmetics, saying that it was only natural for them. She notes how it has become a "luxury" for women to demand that their sexual, biological, and other differences be recognized against the hegemony of the discourse of sameness and equality when in fact femininity was their natural right. For her, difference is the root of female identity and female empowerment (Wang Zheng 160–178).

This is easily perceived as a paradoxical situation. In the language of temporality, the more "advanced" condition of Chinese women's liberation has seemingly regressed overnight to an underdeveloped condition as China reenters the globe both materially and discursively. Chinese women's liberation thus appears to be caught in an earlier phase of Western feminism, when the celebration of essential difference was the prevailing agenda. This was what Elaine Showalter designated as the "female" phase that preceded the "feminist" phase, and what Kristeva termed the second generation of feminists, who celebrated difference and preceded the third generation, which theorized gender in nonessentialist and nonreified ways. It is therefore not surprising that several feminist scholars of China situated in the West would use the Kristevan scheme to designate whatever stage of Chinese feminism they happened to be studying at that moment as the supposed current stage of Chinese feminism (Z. Zhang 322–327). There may in fact be grounds for nostalgia for Maoist gender equality, especially from the materialist, postcapitalist feminist perspective emerging in the hypercapitalist West. Chandra Mohanty has recently argued, for instance, for the primacy of the identity of "worker" for Third World women who are producers and agents of history as well as the "potentially revolutionary basis for struggles against capitalist recolonization, and for feminist self-determination and autonomy" (29). Whether we agree with the truth-value of such a statement or not, one can imagine an extremely productive dialogue between someone like Li Xiaojiang, who is situated in a postsocialist society, and Chandra Mohanty, who wishes to take a postcapitalist position in which the pros and cons of the primacy of the "worker" identity for Third World women can be debated. In such an exchange, we would have to more dramatically confront the fault lines of Western-centric and (post)capitalogic postcolonial and diasporic theorizing in the United States.

When Johannes Fabian provided a workable solution for Western anthropology in its struggle to represent the non-Western other—the Western anthropologist must be vigilantly self-reflexive about his or her practice of othering and maintain a dialectical notion of cultural difference rather than a relativist or a taxonomist one[12]—he was theorizing a two-way interaction unmediated by diasporic and postcolonial intellectuals, who transform the dyadic interaction into a tripartite construct.[13] The tripartite construct does not merely add an intermediary to the interaction but dramatically reshapes that interaction. Diasporic and postcolonial intellectuals are positioned ambiguously vis-à-vis both native and metropolitan women, easily becoming spokespersons of Western feminism to Chinese women and spokespersons of Chinese women to Western feminists if they do not vigilantly guard against their "representative" function.[14] They are positioned ambiguously in the temporal plane as well, since they move between the "advanced" and the "backward" in their travel and migration. One can still discern, as Johannes Fabian has done so masterfully, the contradiction between actual encounters (coeval communication with the object of one's research in China and with Western women in the West) and representation (denial of coevality to the object of representation) as operating in diasporic intellectuals' work and thereby chart a complex web of coeval encounters and distancing narratives, in this case, mixing up the aporetic time-value even more due to the frequency of travel.

My evocation of Fabian is meant to show how the persistent value coding of time in representation and thought actually contributes to the mystification, rather than clarification, of the situations of Chinese women. Saying Chinese women are advanced or backward does not really say anything; the obsession with analyzing such a claim is itself a displacement of the need to attend to the substantive complexities of Chinese women's lived experience and history. It remains a narcissistic practice whereby *Western* constructs of Chinese women are tirelessly analyzed, the agent of representation being, still, unquestionably, Western women. The obsessive critique of temporalizing the other, Fabian's "chronopolitics," always already posits Chinese women as the perennial object of study and does not presume the necessity of equal and genuine dialogue and exchange. How can a self-reflexive anthropology that often ends up being narcissistic, then, "meet the other on the same ground, in the same Time" (Fabian 165)? Might it not just be a clever alibi, as I have suggested earlier, for Western scholars to resort either to temporalization and its critique, or Orientalism and its critique, whereby they absolve themselves from the obligation to understand the other better and to meet the other halfway in what is otherwise an asymmetrical landscape of discursive relations?

"Feminist," or Feminism and Ethnicization

From the perspective of historical and ideological difference from the West and Western feminism's imperialist and universalizing gesture, Li Xiaojiang's repudiation of Western feminism can be readily understood. But this clear-cut repudiation is complicated first of all by the recognizable similarity between some of Li Xiaojiang's views and those found in Western feminism. In the 1980s, when Li was almost single-handedly pioneering the academic field of women's studies (*funü yanjiu*) in China, the cultural zeitgeist of the decade was to "walk towards the world" (*zouxiang shijie*). This zeitgeist was variously called the "culture fever" (*wenhua re*) and the "new enlightenment" (*xin qimeng*) and consisted of a general fervor for Western-style modernism and cultural cosmopolitanism,[15] which were considered the logical consequences of strong humanist tendencies in the early 1980s. Like feudalism before it, socialism was repudiated as another "tradition" by the new generation of enlightenment intellectuals, who saw Chinese history as "a space of failure" (Dai 192). Li was cosmopolitan in her views, very much like the other new enlightenment intellectuals, freely appropriating Western ideas and theories, including Western feminism. In an early work entitled *An Exploration of Women's Aesthetic Consciousness*, we find extensive references to Western women writers such as the Brontë sisters, Dickinson, Mansfield, Plath, Woolf, and Oates, as well as frequent quotations (without much critical mediation) from feminist scholars and theorists including de Beauvoir, Showalter, Gilbert and Gubar, and de Lauretis. In another book written before her 1992 trip to the Harvard conference, *Women, A Distant and Beautiful Legend*, we are given a gallery of exemplary women figures who are fiercely independent and rebellious, culled from myths, literature, and history across the world (Greece, Australia, Russia, China, India, Germany, and so on). Although these cultures are juxtaposed without apparent hierarchy, the list of exemplary women is predominantly Western, and the book ends with a quote from Goethe's *Faust*, evoking the "eternal woman" as the universal source of inspiration and sublimation.

Although such frequent references to Western literature and feminism gradually disappeared in Li's work in the 1990s, Li's views on Chinese women remain very much the same, consistently positing the necessity for women to become subjects with independent wills and inviolable freedom of choice and judgment. She argues that Chinese women were the passive recipients of handouts of equality by the state and that only in the 1980s did women start coming out of "passivity" to determine their own subjectivity on their own terms ("Political Connotation of the 'Women's Issue'"). After the safety net of the socialist state was removed, women were finally awakened to "women's consciousness as subjects" (*nüxing zhuti yishi*) and "women's collective consciousness" (*nüxing qunti yishi*) and began to actively participate in China's social transformation, using their "progress and development" to actively propel the "progress and development" of Chinese society (*Woman* 7–9). The increase in the unemployment rate of women in the post-Mao era paradoxically initiated a necessary process by which women began to define themselves outside the state's problematic protection. The main task for women's liberation, in Li's view, is not the acquisition of equality, but the "independence of female character and self-worth," "the awakening of female self-consciousness and efforts towards self-improvement," and an "awakening of female subjectivity" ("Economic Reform" 380–382): "If the collective consciousness of Chinese women were awakened, then we would definitely see *enlightened* women actively involved in society, and would see *self-improvement* and consciousness-raising movements for women" (382; my emphasis).

A rhetoric of enlightenment, progressivism, individualism, and humanism punctuates Li's work even as she has vehemently repudiated Western feminism. The history of Chinese women who were "granted" equality by fiat by the state and thus were in need of a humanist, enlightened, self-conscious subjectivity of their own traces a reverse trajectory of Western women's pursuit of equality from the state. One could, however, still fruitfully examine the similarities between some of her views and those expounded by Western feminism. What prevents such a project from being a viable one to her and others, ironically, is not that it is wrong or impossible, but that it has been conducted with too much facility, failing to account for historical and cultural differences and often ending up being an imperialist gesture of the Western feminist who imposes her paradigm only to reproduce a neocolonial regime of knowledge. Having perceived this, Li rejects Western feminism's hegemony in the strongest terms possible and argues passionately for the particularity of Chinese women's situation, denouncing Western feminism as another imported discourse that will damage new women's movements in China. For her, Western feminism is another form of ideological domination, foreclosing "the possibility of our autonomous thinking" ("With What Discourse" 264) and undermining the "untranslatable history" of Chinese women (269). From the 1980s to the present, Chinese women have increasingly become "untranslatable" to the West because of the West's willful mistranslation of them and the subsequent reaction of Chinese women against such mistranslation.

Li would increasingly refrain from using Western women as examples of liberation or referencing Western classics in her writing, due to her awareness of the discursive imbalance between China and the West. Evolving from a Westernized intellectual into a vocal critic of Western feminism's pretense to universalism, Li Xiaojing's change is analogous to that of many intellectuals on the Chinese New Left, who had in the 1980s espoused the new enlightenment discourse of Westernization but in the 1990s became critical of the expanding Western cultural domination that came with the spread of global capitalism into China.[16] To the new generation of liberals (*ziyou zhuyi pai*), who advocate speedy and complete integration with global capitalism, the New Left represents old statist lines of anti-imperialism and is helplessly out of date. The irony is that now that the state itself has increasingly turned to economic liberalism as the balm to quell potential political dissent, the New Left's orientation is at odds both with the current policies of the state and with mainstream perceptions of how China should proceed, appearing to uphold the old ideological lines of the pre–Deng Xiaoping state. Such is the predicament of what may be called the postsocialist New Leftist position in China: its critique of Western cultural invasion is easily mistaken for a recuperation of old socialist, statist lines, whereas its agenda is in fact to keep alive the hope of a more accountable state that protects the working classes and local culture. The New Left's stance vis-à-vis the state is not unlike that of Spivak on the importance of the state in Third World nations as the "instrument of redistribution and redress" against the transnational financialization of the globe (263). This explains why Li Xiaojiang's position in recent years has become increasingly ambiguous and, one may say, posthumanist in regard to statist discourses such as the policy of population control through forced abortions (*Challenge* 215, 245). Herein lies the crux of the deep disagreement over "human rights" issues across the West and non-Western countries.

When encountering Western culture in China in the 1980s, prior to her visit to Harvard, Li's discursive construction of "the West" as such had been different. The West, so to speak, was very much the counter-discourse to what she had to write and argue against in those years. The encounter in 1992 and its aftermath could be seen as the time when the politics of sameness and difference, universalism and particularism, discursive colonization and resistance, surfaced in cross-cultural interactions for Li to the extent that she became a virulent critic of Western feminism and a defender of the irreducible differences between Chinese women and Western women in history, culture, and society. Li Xiaojiang would later half-jestingly write that "the disaster started at Harvard" (*Woman?ism* 1). So what exactly happened at Harvard? Over the years, Li wrote several essays reflecting critically upon this event. In all of these, the target of her most severe criticism was not the white feminist scholars of China but the diasporic Chinese women intellectuals who presented themselves as "feminists." This is another significant aspect of Li's famous repudiation of Western feminism — it is directed at both Western feminists and diasporic Chinese "feminists" and is differentially articulated against these two targets. The 1992 encounter was the moment the tripartite construct of the China/West encounter became more explicit, and a nativism articulated against Western feminism began to be mediated by a nativism against diasporic intellectuals. The diasporic intellectuals, rather than being simple intermediaries between the West and China, are implicated in complex and full-fledged relations with each of the others in this tripartite construct.[17]

Li was most offended by diasporic Chinese women scholars who called themselves "feminists" and presumed to speak on behalf of Western feminism to Chinese audiences and on behalf of Chinese women to Western audiences. On the third day of the conference, 8 February 1992, Li presented her lecture on how Western feminism should not be blindly applied to the Chinese context. According to her narrative, she was asked these three critical questions by a diasporic Chinese woman scholar named "P":

1. What is feminism in your understanding?
2. Why do you say it is "Western" feminism?
3. What do you think are the differences between what you call the "particularities of the Chinese women's movement" and feminism?

Behind these three questions, Li detected P's three hidden implications:

1. What you call *feminism* is not true feminism;
2. *Feminism* is universal, not "Western";
3. Therefore there is no so-called "Chinese" particularity outside *feminism*. (*Woman?ism* 2; original English words in italics)

Not having been present at the conference, I cannot determine whether Li's interpretation of what she calls P's hidden agenda is accurate. What can be discerned here clearly is that Li was offended by the condescension implied by the questions posed. This would later be developed into a general position regarding discursive rights:

> In the fields of humanities and sciences, scholars from developing or underdeveloped countries cannot but be "resistant" in their "dialogues" when facing Western-centric culture and its self-contained discursive system. If you don't raise your voice, there will always be those who will speak uninvited on our behalf as part of "us." It becomes clear to you that what they call "we" does not have a position for you. To clarify who you are, you must stand out and declare

"No." What you want back is not necessarily national sovereignty but another right intimately related to sovereignty: discursive right. (*Q and A* 51)

For Li, the "we" is assumed by diasporic intellectuals who speak on behalf of Chinese women and thus deprive women back in China of the right to discourse and utterance. While Western feminists make Li feel "exhausted" in their insistence on imposing Western standards to judge Chinese women and telling them what ought to be done and how (*Challenge* 211), these diasporic women leave her feeling indignant that her discursive rights are being usurped. In her perspective, she is thus doubly deprived. She contends, furthermore, that these diasporic women had not been involved with women's studies in China and "became feminists" only after their "education" in the West; hence they tend to speak in terms of Western feminist paradigms (interview). Li writes sarcastically that white Western intellectuals, who presumed to be "teacher-lords" (*jiaoshiye*) to the non-West, have become quite immobilized by the critique of their Orientalism and the suspicion of their identity. In response, they have retreated to a second line of defense, allowing native informant "assistant teachers" (*zujiao*) to speak for them as teacher-lords so long as the assistants use the teacher-lords' discourse as their "weapon" (*Q and A* 52). We are familiar with various criticisms directed toward postcolonial, diasporic intellectuals in Western academia who build their careers at the expense of native societies and are complicit with global capitalism (Dirlik 52–83; Spivak). The general assumption about the relationship between Orientalism and diasporic intellectuals is that the critique of Orientalism provided the opportunity for non-Western scholars to speak for themselves and participate in Western academia in a more clearly integrated and relational fashion. But Li Xiaojiang's critique here is even more unrelenting than that of Dirlik and Spivak: the critique of Orientalism, she contends, actually made Western discursive hegemony more indirect and hence more powerful, because it denied Western intellectuals their discursive hegemony only superficially. Western intellectuals could now leave it to the diasporic intellectuals from the non-West to do the work of upholding Western discursive universalism. As I argued above, this form of critique exercises the muscles of Western-centric universalism because it is articulated within the discursive limits of the West using the same paradigms and confined within the same parameters; there is supposedly no "outside" or externality to the West per se. The existence of the inside/

outside of the West as a discursive construct is a moot question, since all discourse is relational, but one can still easily discern whether a certain discursive practice pays more or less attention to the complexity of local contexts. Denying that there is any "outside" to Western discourse can serve as a strategy to gloss over a lack of research on the local and as an easy way to safeguard the primacy of the West as the source of methodological and theoretical paradigms. The diasporic intellectual, desiring to be recognized as fully in command of Western theory and eligible for admittance to the pantheon of theorists (since all theory is Western), contributes to the closed circuit of Western theory through his/her mimetic act of "doing theory."

If we consider coevality to be a lure that inspires the non-Western intellectual's mimetic desire for the West, the Foucauldian pessimism that there is no outside to Western discourse likewise traps the non-Western intellectual within the limits of Western discursive paradigms, thus regenerating and perpetuating Western discursive universalism and hegemony. One might reasonably ask: why do we not posit that there is no outside to Chinese discourse? What might it mean to say that? Shouldn't all American scholars take Chinese discursive paradigms into account? In this sense, one may argue that positing coevalness as the object of desire is a trap set by the Western subject for the other within the limits of Western discourse. For coevalness is premised first on assigning a primitive temporality to the other and then on arousing the other's mimetic desire to become like the Western subject by encoding temporality with value. And all this happens within the confines of Western discursive parameters. From this perspective, charging Li Xiaojiang's repudiation of Western feminism with naive or narrow-minded nationalism or nativism is too simple to have any explanatory power. Rather, her position can be interpreted as expressing the desire not to be contained within the trap of coevality that restricts the other to the universal claims of Western knowledge. Her refusal, then, is the refusal to be ethnicized by the global reach of Western feminism, whose mode of containing ethnic difference is by way of multiculturalism. Furthermore, since many of her views are similar to those of Western feminism, her refusal of the imposition of "feminism" can be chiefly interpreted as the rejection of its mode of incorporation and containment, which swings between the two extreme poles of treating the non-Western intellectual as the recalcitrant ethnicity (the embodiment of absolute difference and the other) or the assimilated ethnic minority (as is the case for diasporic feminists). In her most recent writings, Li has become less adamant about her rejection, saying that it was the discursive hegemony of Western feminism that she had been resisting, not its tenets per se, and she is no longer quick to deny "surprising similarities" between the conditions of Chinese women and American women in different historical periods (*Woman?ism* 32).

The itinerary of Li Xiaojiang, from a Westernized liberal humanist to a nativist resistant to Western feminism (with and without diasporic intellectuals' mediation), who sees through the politics of discursive power in Western assertions of hegemony, marks the reverse trajectory of many Chinese diasporic women. In the extreme versions of the diasporic trajectory, the diasporic woman exposes the darkness of China for Western consumption and writes narratives of liberation in the United States and her rebirth as a "feminist." The story of Anchee Min and her book *Red Azalea*, with which I began this paper, is an example of such a diasporic trajectory. By now, Min has become quite a celebrity, having published three books in English and been portrayed in many major journals and newspapers as an authentic voice from China. Her autobiography ends with these words:

> One day in 1983 an overseas letter came from a young friend whom I used to know in film school. She had left China three years before and was now living in Los Angeles. She asked me whether I had ever thought of coming to America. The idea was as foreign to me as being asked to live on the moon, the moon as my father described it—icy, airless and soundless. Yet my despair made me fearless. Though I spoke not a word of English, though I hated to leave my parents, my sisters, my brother, and to fight for permission to leave would take all my energy, I knew that escaping China would be the only solution.
>
> I fought for my way and I arrived in America on September 1, 1984. (336)

Here the autobiography comes to a close, implying the arrival in America as the escape from China, that is, the end of trauma. Described as an exposé of the "brutality and oppression" of the Cultural Revolution, a time and place "where the soul was secondary to the state" and "where beauty was mistrusted and love could be punishable by death" (jacket blurb), the autobiography takes a putatively "feminist" stance by criticizing state patriarchy, presenting the stereotypes of weak Chinese men and heroic Chinese women, and providing a feminist rereading of the fate of the Cultural Revolution's most scapegoated politician, Jiang Qing, Mao's wife. What is most sensational is how this putative "feminism" embellishes a seductive narrative of sex and violence with a tantalizing structure of voyeurism built into it. The American reader is invited to gaze at Cultural Revolution China framed by the Hollywood formula of eroticism tinged with brutality and violence.[18] What helps confirm the American reader's sense of self and self-righteousness is an underlying ethos of humanism and liberalism that pervades the whole book. This is the kind of humanism and liberalism that celebrates pet culture[19] and endorses the reading of Western children's stories such as "The Little Mermaid," "Snow White," and Hans Christian Andersen fairy tales (Min relates that a schoolteacher was tortured because she lent these books to the author) in order to solicit mainstream readers' disapproval of the Chinese past (how can anyone be tortured for the sake of innocent children's literature?). Clearly, Min's perspective is retrospective and strongly colored by her American experience and her knowledge of an American readership, and she accordingly renders her "past" experience in the "present" language of liberal humanism and feminism. In this rendering, China is the primitive, raw, and brutal arena whose representation has earned Min such accolades as "courageous," "honest," and "brave," while her work is praised as a book "of deep honesty and morality."[20] The virtues of honesty, courage, and morality attributed to the book reflect the assumption that Min is telling the truth in her autobiography. Her harrowing depiction of China under the Cultural Revolution coheres with the typical vilifications of China during the Cold War era, which a post–Cold War readership has continued to accept and even desire since the demise of the Soviet Union.[21]

The autobiography is clearly teleological, with the United States as destination and promise of liberation, where Min "becomes" a "feminist" and to which she frequently refers as "heaven" (Ni, E1). This narrative of becoming, like those of other diasporic intellectuals whom Li Xiaojiang criticizes, confirms the assimilationist narrative of freedom and the American dream in the anxious haste with which diasporic intellectuals claim to be part of Western feminism and the ease with which they feel entitled to represent their native sisters. This representative function has aided their/our arrival in the United States, enabling them/us to find a place of identity that is simultaneously sought after and imposed. If this identity as the representative Chinese woman is sought by Min, Li, and other diasporic women, it is also a function of the lack of other identity options in ethnicized transnational encounters in which the other always needs to be represented by a spokesperson so that the prolific heteroglossic voices of the other can be ignored or displaced. What further complicates this representative function of the diasporic Chinese woman is how she functions to displace the need for white feminists to engage with Asian American feminists, transnationality displacing the necessity to redistribute discourses and resources within the nation-state. Scholars have noted that postcolonial studies, promoted by diasporic intellectuals, unwittingly functions to displace ethnic studies, since now the white mainstream has another, more authentic other to deal with, one who decries the ills of colonialisms long gone in faraway places (and mostly British or French and not American) rather than the internal, racialized colonialism in the United States. Although the logic behind this reasoning is that there is only so much of the American pie allotted to different others, so that when one particular other takes a piece, the other others are displaced, one needs to be aware of the fault lines of transnational theorizing in regard to ethnic minorities within the nation.

One of the pernicious effects of transnationality is therefore the displacement of one ethnic other (domestic minority) with another (from another nation) through a globalizing multiculturalism: national cultures are ethnicized and commodified into different representatives of the global multicultural scene. That is why Li Xiaojiang and Anchee Min can so easily become and be reduced to "representatives" of Chinese women; their ethnicity is the clear outer limit of their identity. When Chinese women can be represented by one representative, the West needs only to listen to her summaries and conclusions. Ethnicization is that unspoken procedure that buttresses the West's willful reductionism and ignorance of non-Western and ethnicized others at home and abroad.

"Chinese," or the Limits of "Chineseness"

As "time" and "feminism" prove to be overdetermined codes of value within the West/non-West relation, "Chineseness" is likewise multiply encoded and has increasingly become the site of contention from peripheral, diasporic, and minority perspectives. This contention is importantly centered on the critique of the heavily political and ideological determinations of Chineseness in diaspora (Chun, "Fuck Chineseness," "Diasporas of Mind") and a two-pronged refutation of both the sinochauvinism of the Chinese in and from China and the racism against persons of Chinese descent in diaspora (Ang, "Can One"; Chow, "On Chineseness"). In both China and diasporic locations, two very different regimes reduce the complexity and multiplicity of Chineseness, one regime ascertaining its centrality and supremacy as the most authentic Chineseness to which all persons of Chinese descent in the world should pay homage, the other the racialized equation of all persons of Chinese descent, whether in Australia or the United States, with a reified and homogeneous notion of Chineseness as ethnicity and cultural identity. What further complicates this complicity between the two regimes that for very different reasons codify Chineseness in reductionist ways is the way in which national Chineseness has itself been ethnicized. By this I refer to a process of ethnicization of national cultures by Western-centric global multiculturalism in which the family of nations is reduced to the family of ethnic cultures, following the logic of domestic multiculturalism in the United States. Nation-bound U.S. multiculturalism has always ethnicized minority peoples as embodiments of ethnic cultures where ethnicity is displayed and commodified as the site of difference. With globalization, we increasingly see national cultures in geographical locations outside the United States being readily transformed into ethnic cultures, American multiculturalist logic doing the job of ethnicizing wherever it goes (see Shih, "Globalization"). Even before the current era of globalization, of course, management of national cultures as ethnic cultures that embody essential differences was prevalent in the imperialist discipline of anthropology; in the specific case of China, classical sinology in the West has been charged with being the ethnicity management mechanism that reduces Chineseness to essence and ethnicity (Chow, "On Chineseness").

In this reductive scene of Chineseness, Li Xiaojiang's and Anchee Min's assumptions of Chineseness in China, in travels, and in diaspora will have to be problematized. Three issues need to be dealt with: the inevitable reinscription of Chineseness through traveling and diaspora, Chineseness as ethnicity in racialist thinking, and the representative roles of Li Xiaojiang and Anchee Min as spokespersons of Chineseness. Anchee Min's becoming an ethnic minority as an immigrant in the United States, the most expedient means for which is submission to the majoritarian stereotype of the "strong Asian woman/evil Asian man,"[22] is also the moment when her Chineseness undergoes a process of destabilization. Even though she perceives herself to be as authentically Chinese as she had been in China, she is ineluctably implicated in the racialized logic of minoritization and ethnicization in the United States within which the game of authenticity is also the mark of the foreigner. It is commonly observed that first-generation immigrants often turn a blind eye to their minoritization, choosing instead to remain loyal to their nations of origin, if not politically, then culturally. This willful blindness could be a defensive posture adopted by a victim of racism (for first-generation immigrants), the result of an illusion that he or she will be accepted as an equal by whites due to his or her exceptional accomplishments (for the model minority), or any number of other reasons, but this blindness risks losing the political language of minority rights and becoming an obstacle to minority struggles for redistribution.[23] In the case of Min, her avoidance of her minority status and persistent presentation of herself as a Chinese person who speaks on behalf of Chinese culture, history, and women, is problematic in many ways: not only because she thereby remains aloof to minority causes in the United States (and is hence an easy target of Asian American cultural nationalist attacks on the immigrant generation as the exemplification of the stereotype that Asians are "perpetual foreigners"), but also because she becomes complicit with the mainstream's need to translate (read: reduce and simplify) minority and national cultures into shorthands and summaries provided by a handful of authentic representatives.

In contrast, Li Xiaojiang's journeys to the West in the 1990s can be seen as the moment of reactive affirmation of her Chineseness as a unique identity, even though during the 1980s her Chineseness was very much framed in Westernized cosmopolitan terms. Her repudiation of translatability between Chineseness and Westernness can be better understood as a rethinking of her own earlier cosmopolitan stance, which had taken translation for granted. This was the moment when Chineseness was solidly equated with and reduced to ethnicity, a comfortable zone of inviolable difference for both the nativists and the Eurocentrists, which readily shows us how nativism runs the danger of being the defensive flipside of Eurocentric racism in regard to the question of ethnicity. For Li, especially in the assumed/imposed role of spokesperson for Chinese women to Western audiences, to assert Chinese difference as absolute, even if for very understandable reasons, may thus be similar in effect and become complicit with Western sinology's management of Chineseness as ethnic difference, as Chow charges. Even when she deplores the diasporic women's usurpation of her discursive rights, one cannot help but wonder to what degree she is in fact asserting her higher degree of authenticity over the diasporic women, since she still lives in China. Whether, in other words, it is not a struggle over *who* gets to represent China, Chineseness, and Chinese women.

Furthermore, when Chineseness is reduced to ethnicity as represented by Li as spokesperson, the infinitely complex institutional, political, ethnic, class, and gender determinations of Chineseness within China appear by one stroke of the magic wand to be homogenized. The internal diversity of Chineseness is suppressed in the interest of simplifying it for external consumption, as if all Chinese are Chinese in the same way. The history of Chinese women that Li and other scholars construct ought to be self-reflexive about the conditions of possibility of such history writing, including certain gender, class, educational, and economic privileges. If Li's criticism of diasporic intellectuals is to be taken seriously, we should not lose sight of the old issue of the role of the intellectual in his or her representation of the "people" or the masses. What has changed in the reemergence of this issue since Marx and Gramsci is that now the intellectual has to reflect critically not only upon his or her representative function within his or her nation-state, but also cross-culturally and transnationally. Whether he or she is diasporic or not, he or she is equally implicated in overlapping fields of symbolic power.

It is therefore of great significance that in Li's most recent work she has moved away from a staunch nativist stance and has expressed a willingness to reengage with dialogues and translations. As she says plainly, "In situations without the pressure from imperialism and cultural imperialism, I am not a nativist" ("The Choice of a Feminist" 83). The question that remains, of course, is whether Western feminists are ready for her or not. In the end, what Li's trajectory tells us, then, is not that there is an ontological lack or wealth of translatability between Chineseness and Westernness, but that the conferral of translatability and opacity is itself a historically determined and *affective* act conducted in the field of unequal power relations.

Ethics, or beyond Scripted Affect and Recognition

I have tried to show above that translatability and opacity in transnational encounters through migration and traveling are not results of essential differences (as essential differences themselves are constructs)[24] but *affective* acts of conferral of difference and similarity through value codings of time, space, ethnicity, and gender subjectivity. For the stereotypical Western feminists, Orientalists, sinologists, and others situated in the West, the usual affective investments—such as fear of the other, condescension towards the other, or desire for the Orient's exoticism—dictate a politics of neglect and/or essentialism. These affective investments produce a complex set of cognitive procedures that value-code time, place, ethnicity, subjectivity, and so forth, which then comprise a self-consolidating epistemology that sets *the* standard of subjectivity to be imitated/affected by the non-Western other. These value codings give theoretical support to Western-centric knowledge production and circulation. The irony for Western feminists is that the feminist agenda in the domestic realm is in principle opposed to such knowledge, but becomes paradoxically supportive of it in transcultural situations. For instance, Western feminists may claim Western women's time to be cyclical in contradiction to Western men's time (Felski 18–20), but their time becomes linear in relation to that of non-Western women (advanced versus backward). The affective manipulation of the terms of transnational encounters ensures that Western-centric feminist discourses are viewed as universal objects of affectation/imitation and end up reconsolidating masculinist paradigms. In the final analysis, the (neo)colonialist value encoding of time in terms of backwardness and progress is contiguous with the capitalist measurement of time as value in economic terms. Indeed, in all forms of temporal management of the other, the value coding of time has always gone hand in hand with the universalization of capitalist modes of production, consumption, and exchange. Nothing is valuable unless it has use value; the value coding of time has been useful for material and discursive colonization of the non-West. Time as value is as material as it is discursive, and it has been known to have successfully produced surplus value for the West.

For non-Western others who willingly aspire to meet the standards of a Western-centric epistemology in the process of migration, traveling, or the neocolonial circulation of knowledge, assimilation and imitation are often primary goals; thus, they *affect* Western-centric values and join in the essentialization of the non-West. For immigrant subjects, this occurs in the fractured terrain of ethnic populations' critical struggles against the host nation-state as they attempt to move away from conforming assimilationism and thus can become the object of the critical minority's accusation of being naive assimilationists fresh off the boat (FOBS). This accusation needs to be examined properly, and I do not have space here to do so. Suffice it to say that being born in the United States is not the necessary condition of one's becoming a critical minority (many immigrants are of a critical mind-set as well), and that often such accusation is a subtle expression of internalized white racism (the logic that FOBS are making Asian Americans look bad).

For non-Western others who resist assimilation and incorporation, affective investments in a strong sense of injustice and anger trigger reactive desires of essentialized difference and forthright rejection. Indeed, it is not only the West that essentializes, but also the non-West (Chen; Sakai). Reactive affect is the expression of counteressentialization, and nativism is one of its expressive modes. Affect, which appears to be subjective emotion, is thus historically determined and leads to serious consequences in the cognitive and epistemological realms, which in turn yield political consequences; as one of the *American Heritage College Dictionary*'s definitions of "affect" indicates, it is a "strong feeling having active consequences." The challenge before us is how to imagine and construct a mode of transnational encounter that can be "ethical" in the Levinasian sense of nonreductive consideration of the other, for which the responsibility of the self (be it Chinese or Western) toward the other determines the ethicality of the relationship (*In the Time*). I do not agree with Levinas's philosophical emphasis on the irreducibility and absolute difference of the other, nor with his re–value coding of the time of the other as that of the future; both are unable to deal with the history of colonialism and imperialism that has irrevocably hybridized cultures and used temporal categories in highly value-ridden ways.[25] But his non-Hegelian insistence on "going out toward" the other, in which the other is not reduced to the object of knowledge and where subjectivity is defined not in terms of autonomy (through assimilation of the other to the self) but, rather, in terms of heteronomy (presented by the other), is instructive in rethinking a transnational politics of interaction, communication, and representation (Surber, 295–299).

What Levinas is arguing in the philosophical realm resonates with recent materialist rethinkings of identity politics that have focused on recognition as a means to subjectivity for minority populations. To demand recognition is to subscribe to the Hegelian notion that one's subjectivity exists only when recognized by another subject. Nancy Fraser argues that such emphasis on recognition — as in a minority's struggle for representation in metropolitan countries — has displaced the struggle for redistribution in economic and political realms, caused the reification of group identities, and perpetuated the status subordination of minorities. Enlarging the scope of Fraser's discussion to the transnational terrain of a self/other encounter in which a politics of recognition has likewise operated—the non-Western other desiring to be "recognized" whether through assimilation or nativism—we can see how the politics of recognition binds the terms of relationality to the very limited options determined by a Hegelian dialectic. The Hegelian dialectic incites affect in both terms of the subjective-subjectivization relationality. Ethics, then, may be defined as that relationality beyond affect and recognition.

A practical consideration of such an ethics of transnational encounter has been articulated by Li Xiaojiang in terms of what she calls "transpositionality" (*lichang de zhihuan*) and "transvaluations" (*jiazhi de zhihuan*). In a 2001 interview, she proposed a new epistemology and methodology for women's studies in China, which she has tried to institute in the new Center for Gender Studies she established at Dalian University. This practice includes three surprisingly simple methodological procedures: (1) the transposition of gender positions wherein men are also studied and male perspectives are considered; (2) the return of issues to their original contexts, that is, shifting the perspective of one moment and space to that of another moment and space; (3) an analysis of the simultaneity of loss and gain for all ideologies and paradigms in order to "multidimensionalize" them, that is, to include multiple and contradictory perspectives. As can be inferred from these procedures, the key to transnational communication is the ability and willingness to situate oneself in both one's own position and the other's position, whether on the plane of gender, historical contexts, or discursive paradigms. In practice, this could mean that the Western feminist is asked to speak about China's problems by shifting her position from Western universalism, returning Chinese women to their original contexts and using the multiple and contradictory discursive paradigms used there. This is not nativist, since the "there" is not a pure construct free of discursive contamination and influence from the West. According to Li, this will help reduce the two major problems of Western feminism in transnational encounters: "a monistic perspectival narrowness in scholarship" and "a political narrowness that uses moralistic perspectives to criticize any nonfeminist orientations" (interview). This is not unlike the calls of minority feminists in Australia and the United States for white feminism to practice a politics of partiality beyond the pretenses of universalism (Ang, "I'm a Feminist but . . ."), and of the Italian transversalists arguing for the need to root oneself in one's struggle and shift one's position to that of the other as a coalition-building strategy among different groups of women (Yuval-Davis). Li takes these insights to the transnational terrain and further demands that this politics of partiality be buttressed by a knowledge of other contexts and other genders as well as a historicized and critical view of all knowledge claims coming out of a certain location. "Transvaluation" is the result of such transpositionality, since to position oneself in the history of the other is to be given the opportunity to see how a given system of value production works and thus to be exposed to the mechanisms of value encoding and knowledge production as political, material, and affective acts.

Beyond the Hegelian logic of recognition that requires affect as the underlying mode of operation in encounters of differences, a transpositional and transvaluational relationality may be the definition of what ethics means in our increasingly globalized world. For minority populations, this does not mean foregoing struggles for representation but means emphasizing at the same time struggles for material redistribution; for those in the non-West, this means insisting on a nonreactive and nonaffective mode of relation with the West while contesting discursive asymmetry; for Western feminists, this means not positing themselves as the objects of mimesis or reducing the non-West to the object of knowledge — both of which are affective acts with colonial implications — but practicing partiality and shifting positions to local ones, with all the hard work that implies; for diasporic non-Western intellectuals living or working in the West, this means exploiting their transpositional potential to the fullest for critical purposes rather than self-enhancing purposes. There are basically two kinds of multiply situated subjects who shift and root in different positions: those who flaunt their multiple subjectivity as a strategy of flexibility for maximum accumulation of money or fame, and those who practice multiple subjectivity out of ethical, political, and historical necessity, with all the difficulty, contradiction, and confusion it implies. Attending to this necessity vigilantly, border-crossing intellectuals and scholars must use their radically multiple positions to destabilize the production and circulation of value from any one given locational standpoint as preparation for transpositional dialogues in transnational encounters.

Notes

This paper was shaped over conversations with many colleagues and friends at the Humanities Research Institute and the Transnational and Transcolonial Studies Multicampus Research Group at the University of California. My gratitude goes to Rey Chow, Chris Connerey, Ying-ying Chien, Gail Hershatter,

Françoise Lionnet, Ellen Rooney, Letti Volpp, Marguerite Waller, and Rob Wilson for their comments and suggestions. This is a revised version of the paper with a similar title that appeared in *differences*.

1   Anchee Min's name order is Anglicized with first name and last name in their Anglicized order, while Li Xiaojiang's follows the Chinese convention with the last name appearing first. Clearly, how one writes one's name order is an indication of one's location.

2   In the purist version of Asian American cultural nationalism, one is not granted "Asian American" status unless one was born in the United States. Those who continue to consider themselves Chinese "nationals" are discriminated against variously as unacculturated immigrants and diasporics who unfortunately continue to exemplify the "perpetual foreigner" status charged to Asian Americans by white America. However, those Chinese who came as "sojourners" in the nineteenth century and intended to return to China have been claimed as part of "Asian American history." Asian American cultural nationalist valorization of early immigration and unspoken bias against recent immigration is the consequence of a complex set of social and psychological conditions having partly to do with internalizing or rejecting white racism. Conversely, there has been prejudice by new Chinese immigrants that American-born Chinese (sarcastically termed ABCS) are not Chinese enough. The old "juk-sing" (empty bamboo heart) accusations to second-generation Chinese Americans by the immigrant generation in the late nineteenth and early twentieth centuries also live on in different guises.

3   This essay posits "identity" as a process within which moments of identification are arrested temporarily or strategically for political and other purposes.

4   For a rethinking of the uses of postcolonial theory for the study of an earlier moment in Chinese history, the early twentieth century, see Shih, *The Lure of the Modern*, esp. the introduction and conclusion.

5   Korean American poet Myung Mi Kim asks simply but powerfully, "How would it be possible to deliberate on the oppositional in a way that does not re-enact and replicate those very dynamics that are being 'opposed'?" (75).

6   See Shih, *The Lure*, chapter 6.

7   See Barlow, "Theorizing Woman"; Yang, *Spaces of Their Own*; Liu, and Rofel.

8   This is not unlike Fredric Jameson's totalistic designation of all Third World narratives as national allegories. For any Third World cultural production, be it feminism or literature, it is often assumed that it must be undergirded by nationalism and its related issues. This reductionist thinking effectively withholds from Third World cultural production a potential claim to redefine the universal, on the one hand, and denies it the palpable cosmopolitanism that is always already Westernized thanks to colonialism and neocolonialism, on the other.

9   Unless otherwise noted, all translations from the original Chinese are mine.

10 Li Xiaojiang offers an astute analysis of women's incorporation into labor in an earlier unpublished essay: "With the encouragement for women's employment and the lure of 'equal pay for equal work,' the government has incorporated women into the pattern of 'employment-work unit-state' and completed the transformation of the traditional family structure. Women are therefore mobi-

lized and integrated into the new polity of the state and are put under its direct control" ("Political Connotation" n.pag.).

11 We may note here the neglected underside of the conjunction of China's turn toward capitalism and assertions of femininity and difference: the resurgence of a masculinist critique of Maoist policy of gender equity. According to this perspective, the degendering of Chinese women in the Maoist era had gone hand in hand with the feminization of Chinese men. Men had been castrated by the state, as the state patriarchy had displaced male patriarchy within the family by empowering women. This castration ensured that both men and women were made submissive to the state; hence the family had come under the unmediated control of the state. As can be expected, the post-Mao remasculinization drive has taken on a blatant form for compensatory effect, emboldened by the rise of a new culture of masculinist entrepreneurship. This dovetailed perfectly with women's rediscovery of femininity, to generate a condition of increasing gender disparity and oppression based on essentialist conceptions of gender difference laden with terms of inferiority and superiority. Hence, the unfortunate emergence of problems that were branded capitalist vices in the Maoist idiom: widespread commodification of women's images and bodies, the devaluation of women's labor, resulting in their widespread unemployment, and the reinstitution of gender discrimination in all aspects of society. In other words, the unavoidable other side of the coin for Chinese women's search for femininity is Chinese men's reassertion of their masculinity. The market economy has provided the perfect arena for such reassertions. See also Yang, "From Gender Erasure."

12 See especially chapter 5.

13 The aftereffect of the influence of Fabian's critique of Western anthropology and call for self-reflexivity is well known: there has been a prevailing sense of paralysis as well as a strong apprehension that anthropology cannot be revived as a respectable discipline except as a form of self-critique. This paradoxically resulted in the overflowing of obligatory self-reflexive narratives, with anthropologists reporting their minute emotions and perceptions in their writing of ethnography. These narratives cannot help but come through as plainly narcissistic sometimes. For an analysis of this "deadlock," see Chow, *Primitive Passions*, part 3.

14 I will deal with Li Xiaojiang's critique of Chinese diasporic feminists working in the United States later in the essay.

15 See Jing Wang, *High Culture Fever*.

16 For an overview of the New Left movement in China by one of its leading voices, see Wang Hui.

17 Wang Anyi also implicated Chinese diasporic women in an interview: "Foreigners and people in Hong Kong have often asked me if I am a feminist. When I say no, they get angry. Have you any idea what feminism is, they say? Perhaps they thought that I was denying point-blank because I did not actually know that I was a feminist. It appears that they would very much like me to be a feminist. . . . I found it scary" (Wang Zheng 164–167).

18 Min was reportedly asked by her editor to add lesbianism to the text in order to make the narrative more titillating (Yin 171).

19 The problematic of American pet culture is not unlike that of the highly contentious human rights problematic. American pet culture selectively humanizes or anthropomorphizes animals, so that Chinese or Vietnamese eating dog meat is considered barbarous. In *Red Azalea*, the author depicts a chicken that the family raised and describes how it became a pet for the author, who thus denounces those who ate the chicken. A diametrically opposed, critical analysis of American pet culture can be found in Glen Cao's novel about Chinese immigrants in New York, entitled *Beijinger in New York*.

20 Reviews on the jacket cover of *Red Azalea*.

21 This is not meant to suggest that the Cultural Revolution was not violent and brutal, but to question *what* and *whose* interests are being served by Min's sensational exposé of the atrocities of the Cultural Revolution. Also telling is the different fate of this autobiography in the United States and China: even though the book is a huge success in the United States, Min's own father in China has refused to read it and has forbidden his daughter from translating it into Chinese (Ni).

22 I analyze this domestic stereotypical race/gender formation expanding to the transnational terrain in the management of global multiculturalism in "Globalization and Minoritization."

23 Many first-generation immigrants who have experienced police brutality motivated by racism are unwilling or unable to articulate their predicament in the language of minority rights. One of my acquaintances was a victim of such brutality with clear racialized motivations, but he would rather see it as an unrelated, unfortunate incident than risk losing his fiercely defended sense of masculinity. Since Asian masculinity in the United States is constantly under threat by racism, linking police brutality with racism is equivalent to admitting one's emasculated status. For members of the professional class, the unwillingness to admit their minority status under the illusion that upper-middle-class Asians can be accepted as whites deprives them of the language to name the violence done to them. See Susan Koshy's "The Postmodern Subaltern," in this volume, for an analysis of such a legal case.

24 I am referring, here, to Diana Fuss's argument that essentialism itself depends on the construction of an essence and thus cannot be posited in an oppositional dynamic with constructivism. Repudiating neither essentialism nor constructivism, Fuss would rather analyze the causes, processes, and contexts in which these two assumptions are mobilized (1–21).

25 See Levinas, *Time and the Other*, and the translator, Richard A. Cohen's, informative introduction to this work. E. San Juan Jr. places Levinasian philosophy in the phenomenological tradition and criticizes it thus: "One can raise the question here whether or not the fusion of hermeneutic horizons proposed by Gadamer and Heidegger, an orientation informing Levinas's transcendence through the other, has been able to illuminate the historical complicity of Western powers in exploiting the hermeneutic circle for its benefit" (214).

Works Cited

Ang, Ien. "Can One Say No to Chineseness? Pushing the Limits of the Diasporic Paradigm." *boundary 2* 25.3 (fall 1998): 223–242.

———. "I'm a Feminist but . . . 'Other' Women and Postnational Feminism." *Transitions: New Australian Feminisms*. Ed. Barbara Caine and Rosemary Pringle. New York: St. Martin's, 1995. 57–73.

Barlow, Tani, ed. *Gender Politics in Modern China: Writing and Feminism*. Durham: Duke University Press, 1993.

———. 1994. "Theorizing Woman: Funu, Guojia, Jiating [Chinese woman, Chinese state, Chinese family]." *Genders* 10 (spring 1991): 133–160.

Cao, Glen. *Beijinger in New York*. Trans. Ted Wang. San Francisco: Cypress, 1993.

Chen, Xiaomei. *Occidentalism: A Theory of Counter-Discourse in Post-Mao China*. New York: Oxford University Press 1995.

Chow, Rey. Introduction. "On Chineseness as a Theoretical Issue." *boundary 2* 25.3 (fall 1998): 1–24.

———. *Primitive Passions: Visuality, Sexuality, Ethnography, and Contemporary Chinese Cinema*. New York: Columbia University Press 1995.

Chun, Allen. "Diasporas of Mind, or Why There Ain't No Black Atlantic in Cultural China." Cultural Studies, Ethnicity and Race Relations Working Papers Series 14. Pullman: Washington State University, 2000.

———. "Fuck Chineseness: On the Ambiguities of Ethnicity as Culture as Identity." *boundary 2* 23.2 (summer 1996): 111–138.

Dai, Jinhua. "Rewriting Chinese Women: Gender Production and Cultural Space in the Eighties and Nineties." Yang, *Spaces* 191–206.

Dirlik, Arif. *The Postcolonial Aura: Third World Criticism in the Age of Global Capitalism*. Boulder: Westview, 1997.

Fabian, Johannes. *Time and the Other: How Anthropology Makes Its Object*. New York: Columbia University Press, 1983.

Felski, Rita. *Doing Time*. New York: New York University Press, 2000.

Fraser, Nancy. "Rethinking Recognition." *New Left Review* 3 (May/June 2000): 107–120.

Fuss, Diana. *Essentially Speaking: Feminism, Nature and Difference*. London: Routledge, 1989.

Kim, Myung Mi. "Generosity as Method: Excerpts from a Conversation with Myung Mi Kim." With Yedda Morrison. *Tripwire: A Journal of Poetics* (spring 1998): 75–85.

Kristeva, Julia. "Women's Time." *The Kristeva Reader*. Ed. Toril Moi. New York: Columbia University Press, 1986. 187–213.

Jayawardena, Kumari. 1986. *Feminism and Nationalism in the Third World*. London: Zed.

Levinas, Emmanuel. *In the Time of the Nations*. Trans. Michael B. Smith. London: Athlone, 1994.

———. *Time and the Other*. Trans. Richard A. Cohen. Pittsburgh: Duquesne University Press, 1998.

Li Xiaojiang. *Challenge and Response: Lectures on Women's Studies in the New Period* (*Tiaozhan yu huiying: Xin shiqi funü yanjiu jiangxuelu*). Zhengzhou: Henan People's Press, 1996.

——. "The Choice of a Feminist: The Creator of the First Chinese Women's College Refuses to Join World Women's Congress" (*Nüquan zhuyi zhe de jueze: Zhongguo dalu xiujian nüzi xueyuan chuangbanren jüjue chuxi shifuhui*). *Ming Bao Monthly* (Oct. 1995): 81–83.

——. "Economic Reform and the Awakening of Chinese Women's Collective Consciousness." *Engendering China: Women, Culture and the State*. Ed. Christina K. Gilmartin, et al. Cambridge: Harvard University Press, 1994. 360–382.

——. *An Exploration of Women's Aesthetic Consciousness* (*Nuxing shenmei yishi tan wei*). Zhengzhou: Henan People's Press, 1989.

——. Interview with Shu-mei Shih. Beijing, China. 30 Jan. 2001.

——. "Political Connotation of the 'Women's Issue' in Modern China: The Status and Role of Chinese Women in Modern Social Transformation." Unpublished typed and handwritten script, 1992.

——. *Q and A about Women* (*Guanyu nuren de dawen*). Nanjing: Jiangsu People's Press, 1997.

——. "With What Discourse Do We Reflect on Chinese Women? Thoughts on Transnational Feminism in China." Yang, *Spaces* 261–277.

——. *Woman, A Distant and Beautiful Legend* (*Nuren yige youyuan meili de chuanshuo*). Taipei: Awakening Foundation, 1992.

——. *Woman?ism: On Cultural Conflict and Identity* (*Nuxing? zhuyi: Wenhua congtu yu shenfen rentong*). Nanjing: Jiangsu People's Press, 2000.

Li, Xiaojiang, and Xiaodan Zhang. "Creating a Space for Women: Women's Studies in China in the 1980s." *Signs: Journal of Women in Culture and Society* 20.1 (autumn 1994): 137–151.

Liu, Lydia. "Invention and Intervention: The Female Tradition in Modern Chinese Literature." Barlow, *Gender Politics* 33–57.

Min, Anchee. *Red Azalea*. New York: Berkeley Group, 1995.

Mohanty, Chandra. "Women Workers and Capitalist Scripts: Ideologies of Domination, Common Interests, and the Politics of Solidarity." *Feminist Genealogies, Colonial Legacies, Democratic Futures*. Ed. Chandra Mohanty and M. Jacqui Alexander. London: Routledge, 1997.

Ni, Ching Ching. "Confronting the Ghosts of Shanghai." *Los Angeles Times* 10 Sep. 2000: E1+.

Rofel, Lisa. "Museum as Women's Space: Displays of Gender in Post-Mao China." Yang, *Spaces* 116–131.

Sakai, Naoki. *Translation and Subjectivity: On "Japan" and Cultural Nationalism*. Minneapolis: University of Minnesota Press, 1997.

San Juan, E., Jr. *Hegemony and Strategies of Transgression*. Albany: State University of New York Press, 1995.

Shih, Shu-mei. "Globalization and Minoritization: Ang Lee and the Politics of Flexibility." *New Formations* 40 (spring 2000): 86–101.

———. *The Lure of the Modern: Writing Modernism in Semicolonial China, 1917–1937.* Berkeley: University of California Press, 2001.

Showalter, Elaine. "Toward a Feminist Poetics." *Women's Writing and Writing about Women.* Ed. Mary Jacobs. London: Croom Helm, 1979.

Spivak, Gayatri. "Diasporas Old and New: Women in the Transnational World." *Textual Practice* 10.2 (1996): 245–269.

Surber, Jere Paul. "Kant, Levinas, and the Thought of the Other." *Philosophy Today* 38:3 (Fall 1994): 294–316.

Wang, Hui. "Fire at the Castle Gate." *New Left Review* 6 (Nov.–Dec. 2000): 69–99.

Wang, Jing. *High Culture Fever.* Berkeley: University of California Press, 1996.

Wang, Zheng. "Three Interviews: Wang Anyi, Zhu Lin, Dai Qing." Barlow, *Gender Politics* 158–208.

Yang, Mayfair. "From Gender Erasure to Gender Difference: State Feminism, Consumer Sexuality, and Women's Public Sphere in China." Yang, *Spaces* 35–67.

———, ed. *Spaces of Their Own: Women's Public Sphere in Transnational China.* Minneapolis: University of Minnesota Press, 1999.

Yin, Xiao-huang. *Chinese American Literature since the 1850s.* Urbana: University of Illinois Press, 2000.

Yuval-Davis, Nira. *Gender and Nation.* London: Sage, 1997.

Zhang, Zhen. "The World Map of Haunting Dreams: Reading post-1989 Chinese Women's Diaspora Writings." Yang, *Spaces* 308–336.

The Postmodern Subaltern

Globalization Theory and the Subject of Ethnic,

Area, and Postcolonial Studies

Studies of globalization have announced their significance in terms of a paradigmatic break from the constraints of ethnic, postcolonial, and area studies in identifying and defining the nature, forms, and meanings of inequality in the contemporary world. It is argued that the conceptual limitations of these other fields derive from a spatial and a temporal problem; they have failed to adequately comprehend the new geographies created by the accelerating and mutating mobility of global capital and have remained temporally preoccupied with understandings of power based on colonial or modern rather than postmodern models (see Hardt and Negri, 137–156). The temporal and spatial misconceptions in these fields are said to be reflected in their overvaluation of the nation-state as the explanatory framework for analyses of power and inequality. By contrast, scholars of globalization foreground the central problematic of the eroding sovereignty of the nation-state that they see reflected in the changing spatialities and reterritorializations induced by capital; they also point to the emergence of new networks of economic and political forces institutionalized in supranational governance mechanisms, transnational corporations, transnational legal regimes, and global civil society (see Harvey; Sassen). The emergence of these new sites of normativity that exceed the nation-state are linked to a marked shift in the operations of capital dating from the late 1970s. This change in the determination of capital has been driven by the dramatic reductions in the time and cost of movements of goods and people, the information revolution, and accelerating scientific and technological innovation.

Certainly, globalization theorists are right in pointing to the serious limitations in the way in which postcolonial studies has conceptualized its subject thus far and in its inability to offer models for understanding contemporary modes of power. Postcolonial studies has focused primarily on critiquing colonial and nationalist historiography and discourse, on highlighting the invention of traditions and communities in the colonial period, and on emphasizing the strategic mimicry and ambivalence that characterized the encounter between the colonizer and the colonized. Discussions of the contemporary context, when they have been undertaken, have been largely pursued through the study of diasporic formations and narratives. Ironically, I would note, the preoccupation with European colonial hegemony has led to a striking neglect of alternative cartographies of exchange and contact, or of non-Eurocentric comparative frameworks for understanding inequality and social conflict, especially in the present. I would argue that although these matters are of the utmost political urgency in understanding the present global order and in engaging the forces of global capitalism, there has been little sustained comparative analysis of the differential failures and successes of decolonization, the contemporary linkages between various sectors of the former Third World (South Asia and the Arab world, East Asia and Southeast Asia, East Asia and Latin America, Africa and South Asia), or of the complex politics of issues like human rights, trade regulations, biotechnology, intellectual property rights, consumerism, and human trafficking.

Political and economic power is no longer ordered into a tripartite division of the world; geopolitical realignments, global capital movements, and population transfers are creating new local and transnational communities. I contend that it is crucial to understand and engage these structures and identities because the opposition to global capitalism will be articulated through these emergent formations. However, I should point out that simply announcing that area, postcolonial, or ethnic studies is obsolete and switching from micro- to macrosystems in the way that globalization theory does will not aid us in the political task at hand. Indeed, I would argue that it is symptomatic of work in globalization theory that a major work like Michael Hardt and Antonio Negri's *Empire* can declare the birth of "the Multitude" but can neither offer evidence to support its existence as an embryonic political formation nor provide specifics on how the opposition to global capitalism will crystallize.[1] In fact, most studies of the new social movements reiterate what David Harvey indicates is a major challenge to a new oppositional politics: the global proletariat may be larger than ever, but it is also more diverse, dispersed, divided by national competition, weaker, and harder to organize (71).

Instead, I argue that if the challenge of forging a new politics is to be met, globalization studies, area studies, ethnic studies, and postcolonial studies will need to work synergistically together to locate the "spaces of hope" on the global terrain, instead of insisting on the vanguardism of globalization theory. The relationship between postcolonial, ethnic, and area studies and globalization is usually addressed through the rhetoric of globalization theory as moving "beyond" any one of the putatively particularistic frames of area, ethnic, or postcolonial studies. In my view, the critical discourse of the "beyond" draws its rhetorical force from the cache attached to the "post-" in current critical formulations and the status of the "post-" as a marker of the new. However, the terminology of "beyond" doesn't adequately engage the need for new paradigms in each of these areas, nor does it confront the reality that understanding the interconnections between these areas requires constituting new objects of knowledge. Finally, as I will show, the linear temporality of the "beyond" fails to capture the cross-hatching of multiple temporalities that is one of the defining features of global capitalism. In other words, I argue that it is less a matter of ethnic, area, postcolonial, or globalization studies superceding each other than of these fields analyzing the new and shifting relationships between them. Ethnicity, regional formations, and empire have not been rendered obsolete by the advent of the "global," but they have been profoundly transformed, and the critical task at hand is to understand the nature and implications of this transformation. It is only through an inter-articulation of these fields that we can shape a transnational literacy that will enable us to read the multiple sites of resistance and transformation in the new global order.

A recent example of the limitations of formulations of the global that subsume rather than engage the minor is Michael Hardt's and Antonio Negri's study *Empire*. Hardt and Negri rehearse the advent of globalization at two levels: first, as a long genealogy of Western philosophical dialogues on governance, juridical authority, and constitutionality, and second, as a long historical narrative of ever-expanding spheres of Western capitalist activity. The primary focus on *Western* texts and actors, while coinciding with the disciplinary specialization of both authors, is, however, explained as deriving from the imperative of examining the philosophical texts that exercised a determining force on the emergence of the global order. Third World nations, intellectuals, and political movements make cameo appearances as combatants pitted in heroically noble or heroically misguided struggles against Western imperialism and capitalism. What we are left to infer from this world-historical account of empire is that Third World figures and events have lacked *transformative agency* and *theoretical comprehensiveness* in engaging, resisting, evading, or colluding with Western expansionism and that, hence, the narrative of the emergence of a global order can be told without reference to non-Western temporalities or modernities. Hardt and Negri are certainly not the first to divide the world into the haves and have-nots of originality and agency in their metanarratives of world-historical developments. The debate between Benedict Anderson and Partha Chatterjee on the mimicry attributed to Third World nationalisms is too familiar to require rehearsal. I will simply cite Chatterjee's eloquent response to Anderson's *Imagined Communities* to signal the colonizing impetus implicit in Anderson's undoubtedly progressive intellectual project:

> If nationalisms in the rest of the world have to choose their imagined community from certain 'modular' forms already made available to them by Europe and the Americas, what do they have left to imagine? History, it would seem, has decreed that we in the postcolonial world shall only be perpetual consumers of modernity. Europe and the Americas, the only true subjects of history, have thought out on our behalf not only the script of colonial enlightenment and exploitation, but also that of our anti-colonial resistance and postcolonial misery. Even our imaginations must remain forever colonized. (216)

In Hardt's and Negri's book, we have yet another Euro-American hookup that locates originary forms in the West while tracing their impact on the rest of the world. The underlying methodological problem here and in other similar projects is their need to recover pure genealogies of European and American continuity in the undeniably promiscuous and miscegenous encounter between the West and the rest of the world. *Euro-American dominance is mistaken for sole authorship of the global order.* In the protracted struggles that have shaped the last five centuries the advantage has largely been held by the Western powers, but the multiple resistances they have encountered have irrevocably shaped the world birthed by those struggles. Surely, this is the heart of Foucault's insistence that power is not repressive but productive: "Faced with a relationship of power, a whole field of responses, reactions, results, and possible inventions may open up" (220). Furthermore, since the end of the Cold War, major geopolitical realignments have led to the ascendancy of new national and regional powers like China and the Asian Newly Industrialized Countries, while eroding the power of former dominant nations like the Soviet Union, or of ideological blocs like the Non-Aligned Movement and the Eastern-bloc powers.

Within this global terrain, Western philosophical genealogies can only partially illuminate the forms of governance and emergent normative regimes. If the Multitude that is posited as the revolutionary subject of the contemporary struggles for a new economic order is largely constituted by women and the poor of non-Western countries, how can a narrative that evacuates their contributions to globalization or reads them largely through the lens of Western philosophical traditions hope to enable and elucidate the forms of this struggle?

On the one hand, the structure and policies of supranational organizations like the UN and the WTO may reflect the hegemony of Western interests and norms, but on the other hand, these entities have also been the arena of sustained contestation by developing nations. It is worth keeping in mind that the WTO summit in Seattle in 1999, which initiated the global wave of protests against supranational financial agencies, was disrupted by the opposition and protests from developing nations more than by the highly publicized protests on the streets. Subsequently, another two-day meeting had to be organized in Geneva in 2001 to help bring developed and developing nations closer together so that the next round of trade talks would not collapse in failure as it did in Seattle. Since the WTO operates by consensus, developed nations were forced to offer some, albeit limited, concessions to developing nations, which were united by a groundswell of feeling that they had been shortchanged by the international agreements they had entered into during the Uruguay round of talks (Olson). This is not to suggest at all that a mathematical adjustment be made to Hardt's and Negri's thesis so that influence is equally attributed to both. On the contrary, it is to suggest that inequality of power does not warrant erasing historical agency in the name of establishing philosophical continuities. Institutions of governance exist as philosophical texts but also as politicohistorical projects contaminated by their worldliness. To clarify this point, it might be useful to introduce the analytic distinction Etienne Balibar makes between a *theoretical* humanism and a *practical* humanism:

This does not . . . mean that practical humanism is necessarily founded on theoretical humanism (that is, on a doctrine that makes man as a species the origin and end of declared and established rights). It can also be founded on a theology, on a non-religious form of wisdom subordinating the idea of man to the idea of nature, or which is decidedly different, on an analysis of social conflict and liberation movements which substitutes specific social relations for the general notions of man and the human race. (63)

I would argue that the focus on a practical humanism will enable a different representation of the agency of dominated groups in narratives of globalization that excavate the genealogy of universalism.

The methodological limitations of Hardt's and Negri's approach are clearly evident in their discussion of the constitution of the UN. For instance, in their extended discussion of the gap between the initial aspirations surrounding the genesis of the United Nations — that it would emerge as a supranational governing body that could implement a form of global order that could override national jurisdiction — and the political reality — that it helped found an interstate system in which national sovereignty remained preeminent — they focus primarily on the idealistic plans of one of the architects of the UN, Hans Kelsen (1–8). Here again, the UN and the international human rights regime associated with it is conceived as a Western brainchild. What is missing from this account is the pivotal role played by representatives from the Soviet Union and the developing nations in arguing for the need to use human rights protections to override state jurisdiction in cases of human rights violations. At this stage in the constitution of the UN, Western nations, led by the United States, maneuvered for and eventually won the battle to preserve national sovereignty as a foundational principle in the new international order, thereby undercutting the scope and force of an international human rights regime. Furthermore, when we look at the present-day international human rights instruments, which are almost ubiquitously and erroneously identified as authored by the West, we see that they encode what Stephen Marks has identified as three generations of rights deriving from three different revolutions and political traditions. According to Marks, the first generation of civil and political rights, associated with Western liberal democracies, developed out of the bourgeois revolutions in France and America in the late eighteenth century; the second generation of social and economic rights were the product of socialist revolutions in the early decades of the twentieth century; and the third generation of solidarity rights, like the right to development and the rights of peoples, emerged from the post–World War II anticolonial revolutions. Thus to identify the project of universalism embedded in human rights norms as Western, whether as an act of genealogical valorization by globalization theorists or as an act of repudiation by radical scholars, is mistaken and short-sighted, because it surrenders a crucial arena of struggle in the current global conjuncture. The project of universalism encoded in human rights documents has been the site of unequal struggle, but it is a historicopolitical project that has been shaped by the West and the non-West, although its multinational provenance would not be visible if one insisted on focusing a narrow genealogy of its constitution.

I have undertaken an extended critique of the parameters of Hardt's and Negri's *Empire* not because I seek to replace the putative Western progenitors of the global order with non-Western ones or to argue that the West played only a limited role in shaping the contemporary global order. Rather, my interest is in examining the strategic sites and necessary conditions for the creation of a transnational literacy adequate to comprehending the new world order.

Such a literacy can only emerge by combining an analysis of macrosystems with a close study of the histories, traditions, and struggles of the disadvantaged, whether defined by race, gender, language, religion, sexuality, or class. And such a literacy seems even more urgent at a time when disparate protest movements are erupting across the globe, "a veritable ferment of opposition," but remain in large part disconnected from each other (Harvey 71). The recent protests against the WTO, IMF, and the G-8 have brought together a tenuous but growing coalition of anarchists, environmentalists, labor unions, religious organizations, pacifists, feminists, gay activists, the unemployed, and the homeless against supranational agencies that exercise inordinate power over their lives. No compelling paradigm for organizing and articulating the terms of the resistance has yet emerged from these protests. In the shift that I have elsewhere defined as a shift from the Cold War to the Trade War, it has become increasingly apparent that national civil societies that have historically provided the mechanisms for petition, redress, social transformation, and social support against the downturns and shock-cycles of interstate trade have become less and less able to buffer their populations against the depredations of a capitalism that, while conjuring images and opportunities for incredible wealth and consumption, has ravaged the security, predictability, and existence of a vast majority of humankind across the globe. The targeting of the WTO, IMF, and G-8 clearly reveals that the engines of global capitalism have been identified as the object of popular resistance and hence that the protest, although not uniformly identified as socialist, is nevertheless clearly anticapitalist in nature.

Although these highly publicized protests are commonly labeled antiglobalization protests by the media, I would argue that this rubric completely misconceives the dynamics of these multiple, disparate, and convergent resistances and obscures the depth and scope of other ongoing resistances worldwide to which they are related. I suggest that the term "minor transnationalism" offers us a conceptual framework for aggregating numerous movements, groups, and discourses that, whether local, regional, or multinational in organizational structure, are fighting a guerrilla war against the colossal forces of the major transnationalism represented by an unleashed global capitalism. While the minor has typically been imagined in opposition to and in tension with hegemony at the level of the nation-state, the processes of globalization have resulted in the production of the minor in transnational forms. The framework of minor transnationalism also allows us to connect numerous transnationalized communities and identities that may not yet be explicitly linked at this time, but in relation to which a global civil society is being constructed. Thus, minor transnationalism offers strategic sites for analysis within the larger project of constructing a transnational literacy that can enable and elucidate the oppositional movements that are coming to define our time. The examination of minor transnationalism can thus further the political task of creating a *sustainable universalism* adequate to representing the diverse constituencies of the new global order.

In the following section, I analyze a particular instance of minor transnationalism that highlights the differential erosion of boundaries to the movement of people and goods in a global capitalist regime. I focus on the understudied phenomenon of sex trafficking, its relationship to globalization, and the transnational legal regimes and rights discourses that have emerged to address this postindustrial global problem. My interest is in identifying the normative subject of these rights discourses — whether framed as human rights, women's rights, immigrant rights, or civil rights — and in showing how the subaltern subject (the trafficked person) renders visible the limitations of these available modes and discourses of redress in dealing with the problem of sex trafficking. I move from a discussion of the historical debates among feminists about how to frame the problem of sex trafficking and seek redress for it in UN human rights documents to a consideration of a specific case involving sex trafficking which was tried in the United States and in which the perpetrator and victims were both of Indian origin and, in fact, came from the same village in India.

This analysis focuses on the subject of sex trafficking that has been neglected in theorizations about globalization and challenges the axiomatics of the retreat of the state. As Richard Friman and Peter Andreas note, "The illicit global economy reveals even greater fluidity in state power in relation to transnational economic forces than that suggested by prominent scholarly debates. The illegal global economy also suggests extensive variation in the challenges to state power and, in turn, the retreat, persistence, and reassertion of the state" (8). In the following section, I examine a case of human trafficking involving a businessman of Indian origin, Lakireddy Balireddy, whose real estate empire in the United States was subsidized by the labor of men, women, and minors who were smuggled into the United States and used as menial workers and sex slaves. The analysis points to the differential mobility of labor in contrast to the mobility of information, capital, and goods in the "borderless economy" ushered in by globalization.

The specific legal case that I examine exemplifies powerfully the larger theoretical questions that this analysis seeks to examine, namely, the transformation of the subject of ethnic, area and postcolonial studies under globalization. Ethnicity, as historically formulated in ethnic studies, has offered a ground for defining a common experience of oppression among minority subjects in the United States; however, in this instance, ethnicity functions as a source of oppression because (1) ethnic circuits facilitate efficient access to trafficked persons; (2) it can be mobilized to secure their trust; (3) it becomes a weapon for ensuring the compliance of trafficked persons by threatening reprisals against family members in the home country; and (4) it creates a dependence on the perpetrator in alien surroundings. Within such a context, and given the scope of the problem of trafficking in the postindustrial world, it is imperative that the transformed meanings of the ethnic subject in transnationality be reexamined. Similarly, the scale of the movements of people in illegal transnational circuits has created new cartographies that cut across the traditionally recognized areas. In the case I examine, the transnational circuits linked Velvadam, a small village in South India, with a real estate empire in Berkeley. This circuit cut across two areas which have until the last few decades been seen as sharing few historical, cultural, political, and economic connections.

That these two historically distinct areas are now closely and increasingly intermeshed is itself testimony to the rapidity of the transformations inaugurated by globalization. It is also evidence that the very concept of an "area" has been rendered more dynamic and must be recognized as such, if we are to understand the import of globalization in transforming our lives and creating new forms of subjection. Finally, while postcolonial studies has initiated the study of the old and new diasporas and distinguished between the various types of diaspora produced by colonialism, in most studies, the postmodern diasporic subject is primarily theorized as an economic migrant or a cosmopolitan subject. Other forms of displacement, mobility, and transience in which diaspora is constituted as a sign of violence and in which, for instance, the practice of bonded labor has been recast under transnationalism have been overlooked. Therefore, I would contend that, on the one hand, transformations in the subject of ethnic, area, and postcolonial studies call for new paradigms to understand changes in power and inequality in the contemporary world, but that on the other hand, the new understandings produced by these fields are critical to the creation of a "thick" globalization theory, because these epistemologies in conjunction with the insights of globalization theory can lay the groundwork for the creation of transnational literacy. As I will show in my analysis of the Balireddy Lakireddy case, the strategies for representing the victims in the case were formulated by a fortuitous coalition between the ACLU, a nationally based organization, and identity-based minority groups and diasporic South Asian feminist and women's groups. I read the responses of these diverse constituencies and their coalitional efforts as an instance of transnational literacy.

Paper Daughters and Transnational Godfathers

In November 1999, eighteen-year-old Lakshmi Patati returned to her Berkeley apartment to find her two Indian female roommates, both minors, unconscious from carbon monoxide fumes. Soon after, a passing motorist, Marcia Poole, spotted several Indian men hurriedly carrying out what appeared to be a heavy rug from an apartment building. Noticing the nervousness of the men carrying the rug, the small crowd of Indian bystanders that had gathered around them, and a sobbing Indian girl in their midst, Poole became suspicious and stopped to find out what was happening. When she got closer, she realized the men were carrying not a rug but a body, which they were hastily loading into a van belonging to

Reddy Realty Company. After they put the body in the van, the men tried to drag the weeping girl into the van with them. Poole immediately attempted to intervene, but was told brusquely that it was none of her business. Undeterred, she quickly stopped a passing motorist and told him to call 911.

Within a few hours, the young girl whose body had been loaded into the Reddy van, and whose name was given as Sitha Vemireddy, was pronounced dead. Her sister, Lalitha, was treated for smoke inhalation and survived. News reports stated that the parents of the two girls lived in another apartment in the same building. Their apartment building was owned by Lakireddy Balireddy, the richest landlord in Berkeley, who was reputed to be worth $50 million in real estate holdings and was the owner of 1,000 apartment units and two restaurants.

As the investigation opened, news of the girl's death rapidly reached Velvadam in India, home to all the young girls involved in the case and to their landlord Balireddy. Anonymous letters sent from Balireddy's village to the U.S. consulate in Chennai (Madras) opened up a completely different dimension to what appeared, till then, to be a case of accidental death caused by a blocked heater vent. The young girls, who as minors had been taken into protective custody, had also begun to talk to the authorities. According to their statements, the dead girl's real name was not Sitha Vemireddy but Chanti Prattipatti, and Chanti and her sister were not upper-caste Reddys as their fake papers indicated, but were Dalit Christians, who belonged to the lowest caste in Velvadam. The man and woman who had claimed to be the girls' parents were, in fact, a brother and sister who had made a deal with Balireddy to bring the girls into the country as their daughters in exchange for fraudulent visas and money. The paper father had posed as a computer programmer working for a Reddy company. The girls stated that they had been sold by their real parents to Balireddy, thus joining the numbers of the more than 15 million children sold into bonded labor in India. Balireddy had sexually exploited the girls and also put them to work cleaning his restaurants and apartment buildings.

In January 2001, Balireddy was charged on nine counts including importing minors for the purpose of illegal sexual activity and conspiracy to commit immigration fraud. Subsequent investigations uncovered a well-established scheme orchestrated by Balireddy and his family members over several years to illegally bring in Indian women, men, and children to be used as sex slaves and menial workers in his real estate empire, using the trafficking to cut costs in his U.S. businesses and to finance philanthropic projects in his hometown, building temples, schools, and engineering colleges that bolstered his reputation as a demigod in Velvadam. His reputation in his hometown, where he recruited his workers, was that of a native son who would remake Velvadam into a "little America." Reports in Indian newspapers noted that journalists' inquiries about Balireddy's activities and reputation were met with resentment, silence, or hyperbolic testimonials from villagers. The *Indian Express* reported that "wherever reporters went, a group of villagers followed and kept listing out Bali Reddy's philanthropic activities" ("Velvadam" 2). According to this report, the dead girl's parents refused to talk to the press and "disowned" her. Then, a few days after the arrival of reporters, the parents left the village and their neighbors refused to discuss their whereabouts. When the parents of the sisters' roommate Lakshmi were questioned, they maintained that Lakshmi had been sent to work in the hotel on their request, ending with the indignant question, "How can we sell our only girl?"

A year later, however, the picture changed when Balireddy entered into a plea bargain. He pleaded guilty to four felony counts including two counts of smuggling minor girls in foreign commerce for illegal sexual activity and one count of conspiracy to commit immigration fraud. He was sentenced to eight years in prison and ordered to pay $2 million in restitution to his victims. Immediately after he pleaded guilty, public opinion about him in Velvadam seemingly underwent a dramatic reversal. The banners and hoardings posted outside his school buildings proclaiming, "Balireddy is God's gift to Velvadam" and "Balireddy is our Mother Teresa" were taken down. His once-respected family members lived in fear of being assaulted by villagers, and some of them publicly denounced him as "a shame to the family." The local correspondent for *Andhra Prabha*, D. Ramaiah, reported that dozens of families who had sent their daughters to the United States through Balireddy left the village because of the stigma attached to their daughters' being used as sex slaves. The parents of Chanti and Lalitha, an old Dalit couple, never returned to the village (Iype, "The End of an American Dream," "He Is a Shame"). Meanwhile, the two surviving girls, Lalitha and Lakshmi, are being represented in a class-action lawsuit filed by the Immigrants' Rights Project of the ACLU against Balireddy. In addition, South Asian women's groups in the Bay Area like Narika and Maitri offered support services to the girls, and their plight led to the creation of activist groups in Berkeley like ASATA (Alliance for South Asians Taking Action).

My interest in this issue is the way in which the position of the female subaltern subject is made legible, recognized, and addressed by the existing national and transnational legal regimes in a period that has witnessed a significant increase in sex trafficking globally. What processes and barriers regulate or impede the movement of sex workers across national borders, and how does the functioning of these mechanisms transform our understanding of the strength and meaning of national sovereignty within globalization?

Phil Williams links the proliferation of organized criminal activity in human trafficking to the emergence of a borderless global economy: "Criminal organizations carry on their activities in what for them is, in effect, a borderless world, while law enforcement is significantly constrained by having to operate in what is still a bordered world" (ix). The changes in the global economy have coincided with the proliferation of criminal networks that fund, control, and facilitate this traffic while generating huge profits in the process. Next to drugs and guns, human trafficking is the most profitable sphere of international criminal activity; it is also the fastest growing. Moreover, Laura J. Lederer points out, "unlike drugs, which are sold only once, a human being . . . can be sold over and over again" (qtd. in Branigin). Thus, on a fundamental level we see that while transnational legal regimes have emerged to facilitate the movement and accumulation of global capital, transnational legal regimes that protect the interests of transnationalized labor have been much slower to emerge, and the gap between the two has been advantageous to capital (whether for criminal organizations or for legal corporations). Indeed, the existence of national jurisdiction over immigration as a central tenet of the interstate system and the inadequacy of transnational legal regimes that protect the rights of migrant sex and other workers have been enormously conducive to global capital. Furthermore, economic prosperity in developed nations has made it possible for sex tourists to purchase sexual services in other countries that would be illegal in their own, thus allowing them to use the uneven development and enforcement of legal protections within diverse national jurisdictions to fuel the global sex trade. What we see here is the marriage of national sovereignty and global capitalism.

Globalization has signaled a new shift in the modes and scale of prostitution worldwide. At present, prostitution comprises the largest segment of the global market in women, followed by the mail-order bride industry and the export of domestic workers. The flow of trafficked women is from the developing to the developed world, while the flow of primarily male sex consumers operates in the reverse direction. The consumers of the global sex trade are primarily from Europe, North America, Japan, Australia, and the Middle East. UN reports estimate that 1 to 2 million women and children are trafficked each year, and a 1991 conference of Southeast Asian women's organizations estimated that 30 million women had been sold worldwide since the mid-1970s (Mirkinson 30).

The growth in the global sex trade can be traced back to the growth of sex industries around U.S. military bases in Asia during the Vietnam War, and after the closing of the military bases, to the aid and pressure applied by international financial institutions like the World Bank and the IMF to utilize the existing infrastructure for promoting tourism as a development strategy, and the policies and regulations developed by complicitous governments and law enforcement in developing nations to profit from this lucrative trade (see Bishop and Robinson). A 1996 International Labor Organization report points to the "feminization" of international labor migration as one of the most striking economic and social phenomena of recent times.[2] This shift, most pronounced in Asian countries, is largely a result of the growth of the sex industry. In addition, the economic and political changes following the collapse of the Soviet Union have led to a massive increase in the numbers of Russian and Eastern European women entering the sex trade.

Feminism, Sex Trafficking, and the Subject of Human Rights

Given the scope of the problems, what human rights instruments have been formed to tackle global sex trafficking and how have divergent feminist responses to the problem shaped these norms? The international norms on combating prostitution have evolved over time so that, as Jo Doezema points out, UN declarations have gone from "focusing on repressive measures to eliminate the practice of prostitution" to a concern with "the prostitute as a subject whose rights can be violated" (41). From the time of the first such document, the 1949 Convention for the Suppression of Traffic in Persons and of the Exploitation of the Prostitution of Others to the 1979 Convention on the Elimination of All Forms of Discrimination against Women (CEDAW), prostitution was viewed as inimical to human dignity and personhood. However, a major shift was effected in the General Recommendation 19 of CEDAW (1992), which reaffirmed the need to "suppress all forms of traffic in women and the exploitation of the prostitution of others" while stipulating that "prostitutes are especially vulnerable to violence because their status, which may be unlawful, tends to marginalize them. They need the equal protection of laws against rape and other forms of violence." This last document focuses on the prostitute as a worker whose illegal status requires protections against violence and exploitation (Doezema 35–40).[3] The distinction between forced and voluntary prostitution, implicit in the earlier document, is fully and explicitly articulated in the Declaration on the Elimination of Violence against Women (1993). Since the adoption of the resolution, the declaration has represented the international standard for international agreements on violence against women and has served to institutionalize the difference between voluntary and forced prostitution.

The shifting discourse of international agreements and human rights documents reflects the ideological differences among feminists and between sex-worker groups and some feminists about how to conceptualize prostitution. The modern antitrafficking campaign is ideologically divided into two main groups. First are the radical feminists who have articulated an abolitionist approach to dealing with prostitution and sexual slavery and see all forms of prostitution as a violation of women's human rights and as being responsible for women's subordination as a group. Second is the position that developed from the prostitutes' rights movement. The prostitutes' rights movement, a response to the feminist opposition to all forms of prostitution, insisted upon a distinction between voluntary and forced prostitution and on rejecting the notion of the prostitute as a victim to be saved. Instead, the prostitutes' rights movement has called for a recognition of the self-determining subject who can choose to work as a prostitute. The prostitutes' rights movement also called for the recognition of prostitution as a form of work and for the need to address the abuses and exploitation in prostitution as a question of labor rights and standards. The 1985 World Charter for Prostitutes' Rights calls on governments to "decriminalize all aspects of adult prostitution resulting from individual decision." The prostitutes' rights movement originated in the West, and its primary spokespersons were sex workers and advocates based in the West. Subsequently, however, sex-worker groups have organized in many developing countries, and the concerns with decriminalizing sex work, improving working conditions, and protecting the human rights of sex workers have been formulated in conjunction with some sex-worker groups in the developed countries.

Recently, however, sex-worker activists like Allison Murray and Jo

Doezema have begun to argue that the distinction between forced and voluntary prostitution that had been articulated by the prostitutes' rights movement has come to serve as an alibi for abolitionist feminists, who, while accepting the distinction between the two forms of prostitution, have concentrated their energies on campaigning against forced prostitution while largely ignoring the struggle for the rights of voluntary prostitutes, an issue they remain deeply ambivalent about. Furthermore, they argue that the forced/voluntary dichotomy produces an East/West dichotomy that views the economic situation of sex workers from developing nations as different from that of their Western counterparts and hence reinforces stereotypes of the passive, helpless Third World woman versus her emancipated Western counterpart (Murray 60).

What this conflict between the two main factions in the international debate on prostitution and trafficking reveals is the way in which both groups have sought to deploy the figure of the Third World female sex worker to bolster their claims to addressing the "real" problems of global prostitution and to validate their status as globally representative organizations. Thus, ironically, the female subaltern subject of prostitution emerges as a figure in a debate between hegemonic feminisms about the very agency that is denied her through this discursive move. I would argue that despite the potential pitfalls of the distinction between forced and voluntary prostitution that have been raised by critics like Murray and Doezema, given the political, legal, cultural, and economic differences in the position of sex workers in developed and developing nations, it would be highly problematic to reject the distinction in the interests of formulating a "common" platform for sex workers aimed at preempting feminist avoidance of voluntary sex-worker rights issues. The distinction between forced and voluntary prostitution allows for a prioritization of concerns without abandoning the need to address a broader agenda. In addition, it acknowledges that the self-determining subject of individual rights, the universalist subject of the prostitutes' rights movement, is inadequate to address the way in which women's entry into sex work is shaped by uneven development. To limit the concern with forced prostitution to a protection of the labor rights of prostitutes fails to address the structural problems of gender, economic, and other types of inequality that drive women into prostitution. The cooptation of the forced/voluntary dichotomy by segments of the feminist movement should not be the determining factor in jettisoning the terms; in other words, the universalist subject of the movement may have to retain for the present a recognition of the structural differences in women's experiences of sex work. Preserving the distinction between the forms of sex work also recognizes the large-scale increase in human trafficking over the last decade and the growing reality of sex work as a form of involuntary servitude.

How can one understand the trafficking of the female subaltern subject Chanti Pratipatti within the existing feminist and prostitutes' rights discourses that posit her as either the exploited victim of Indian patriarchal practice or as a self-determining subject whose choice of sex work should be decriminalized and whose labor rights as a sex worker should be protected? Chanti's and her parents' relationship to Balireddy is determined not only by her gender but also by her family's lower-caste status. Her servitude to Balireddy cannot be absorbed within the notion of the self-determining subject. Rather, the terms of her servitude assume a complex and shifting form that is transformed by her later status as an undocumented worker in the United States and her parents' dependence on her earnings. Balireddy first noticed her when she worked as a maid in his Velvadam mansion during one of his frequent visits to India: he approached her parents with the promise of a job and immigration to the United States for her and her sister. Her "choice" is linked to the need to support her parents, their desire to translate a gendered economic liability (the necessity to pay for the daughters' marriages) in the local context into an economic asset through migration (work that pays in dollars). The complex interdependence between the aging Dalit parents, the commodification of their daughters' labor, and the power wielded by Balireddy over all their lives as the richest man in Velvadam, as an upper-caste landlord, and as a nonresident Indian (the gatekeeper to American dreams), renders the construction of the autonomous self-determining sex worker inherently problematic even as one can stipulate the possibility of conceptualizing her/their agency within these constraints. The mode of that agency, however, is not that of the individualist subject. I should add that this form of locating and recruiting workers was by then an established pattern for Balireddy, whose contacts with and donations to local police, politicians, and fake passport suppliers had created an efficient, smooth, and profitable transnational conduit. It is crucial to note that the sexual exploitation of the young women was intensified by their underground existence as non–English speaking undocumented workers, economically dependent on Balireddy, and in ever-present danger of the exposure of their illegal status and of reprisals to family members in Velvadam. Within this context, "sex slavery" rather than "sex work" describes their status; in this case, neither the emphasis on decriminalizing sex work or abolishing prostitution addresses the conditions of servitude endured by the young women. Their situation here is comparable to the exploitation of other undocumented workers in sweatshops, restaurants, and small businesses — a stream of labor that is fed by human trafficking and includes sex workers but extends beyond them. Decriminalizing sex work fails to address the broader problem of human trafficking that in turn emerges from dramatic geopolitical economic inequalities. The problem of human trafficking is fed by the need for cheap labor in the developed world and the enormous profits to be made from the illegal transportation of migrants. Existing feminist and sex-worker discourses have paid insufficient attention to the problem of sex work in developing nations as a matter of labor migration and uneven development.

The Postmodern Subaltern Subject and National and Transnational Legal Regimes

The double bind of the girls' predicament is that as undocumented migrants and sex slaves they are simultaneously victims of the limitations of national laws in addressing these problems and of the power of underground transnational circuits of capital accumulation that, in placing them outside the legal mechanisms and informal social controls of their home environments, render them exposed to unchecked exploitation. Thus, they inhabit a legal void that highlights the unevenness in the development of transnational legal regimes in their recognition of capital and labor as transnational actors and subjects of international law. As Saskia Sassen comments, "The production of new forms of legality and of a new transnational legal regime privilege the reconstitution of capital as a global actor and the denationalized spaces necessary for its operation. At the same time there is a lack of new legal forms and regimes to encompass another crucial aspect of this transnationalization . . . the transnationalization of labor" (xxx).

However, an important distinction needs to be made in speaking of the transnationalization of labor since the movement across national borders assumes very different trajectories for highly skilled as opposed to unskilled workers. The immigration of highly skilled workers (especially in the high-tech and healthcare sectors) has been expanded and kept open in many developed nations, while the mobility of unskilled workers has been criminalized and consequently rendered vulnerable to superexploitation.

For instance, in the Balireddy case, Balireddy's wealth was generated by the terms of his transnational mobility just as Chanti's, Lakshmi's, and Lalitha's servitude was secured by the terms of theirs. As undocumented workers they exist in a global system where redress is largely channeled through national laws that call for their exclusion as aliens, and as low-caste girls they inhabit a local context where Balireddy's upper-caste status and wealth can buy the law enforcement officials. Thus, they are doubly "outlawed."

The illegal status of the girls and their precarious economic and political position in the United States rendered their condition inaccessible to mechanisms of redress and recompense while Chanti was alive. As in many such situations, a catastrophe (the burning of factories, brothels) or death exposes the criminal networks that support human trafficking. The illegal status of the victims makes it nearly impossible for them to prosecute their oppressors or claim sanctuary or protection because of the threat of deportation or of death. The self-determining subject in this context is a moot issue.

Chanti's death, however, precipitated the transformation of the status of her sister and friend to "minors" held in the protective custody of the law. In exchange for the testimony of the girls and because of the wide publicity drawn by the case, the authorities helped them to legalize their status as immigrants, an unusual move in cases of this nature. Meanwhile, the mobilization of South Asian women's groups and feminist organizations around the girls allowed for the public construction of the girls as the subjects of women's rights. While attorneys for Balireddy claimed a "cultural defense" for his actions by stating that the judge "consider that Lakireddy Balireddy is a product of a society" in which "the norms of his society were amenable to conduct which is clearly offensive in the U.S.," South Asian women's groups rejected the framing of the problem as one of cultural practices: "It is not a cultural practice to molest minors" ("Cultural Defense"), and to insist on its framing as an issue of sexual and labor exploitation. In addition, the Immigrants' Rights Project of the ACLU undertook to file a class-action lawsuit on behalf of the young girls, positing them through this action as the immigrant subject of civil rights.

This part of their story reveals the accessibility of mechanisms of redress at the state level in the United States because of the violation of national laws criminalizing trafficking and sex with minors. Under normal circumstances, the defendants in a case like this would be subject to deportation since the restitution attained through national laws only strengthens the principle of the inviolability of national boundaries rather than addressing or framing the issue of trafficking as a transnational problem. As such the status of the victims of trafficking remains that of aliens who must in accordance with this logic be returned to their own country.

It is precisely here that one of the difficulties of dealing with the problem of trafficking lies, the problem of extending claims to place or entitlements that do not derive from national citizenship. Some globalization theorists like Saskia Sassen see possibilities for productive openings created by the new global economy for rethinking the idea of citizenship. She points to the copresence of diverse, conflicted, and proximate constituencies in the "global cities" which have become central to the new global economy as creating "a transnational economic and political opening in the formation of new claims and hence in the constitution of entitlements, notably rights to place, and more radically, in the constitution of 'citizenship'" (xx). Sassen is particularly hopeful about the prospect that international human rights, which bases rights not on national membership but on individuals *as persons* rather than *as citizens*, has the force to "impinge on the principle of nation-based citizenship and the boundaries of the nation" (95). She points to the pivotal role of refugees and undocumented immigrants as key claimants and "mechanisms for the expansion of the human rights regime."

Sassen's hypothesis is certainly plausible, but it tends to overstate the scope, significance, and efficacy of international human rights instruments in advancing new claims to place and entitlements that override national sovereignty. International human rights instruments are primarily invoked to ensure the fair and humane treatment of undocumented immigrants and to guarantee their nondiscriminatory treatment by national laws. These documents also posit the right to asylum and the right to freedom of movement as universal human rights. But, in practice, the right to asylum has often been given in the United States for political rather than humanitarian reasons. Moreover, although the right to freedom of movement is recognized in the International Covenant on Civil and Political Rights, this right to movement is subordinated to the foundational principle of national sovereignty except in certain limited, exceptional instances: "The Covenant does not recognize the right of aliens to enter or reside in the territory of a State party, but, in certain circumstances, an alien may enjoy the protection of the Covenant even in relation to entry and residence, for example, when considerations of nondiscrimination, prohibition of inhuman treatment and respect for family life arise" (UN Economic and Social Council 8). The instances in which international human rights documents can override national sovereignty are extremely limited, and thus the proposition that they can form the basis of new claims to place and entitlements, as Sassen asserts, is overstated. In fact, Liisa H. Malkki points out that despite the grounding of international refugee law within the framework of the international code of human rights, "in practice, this legal apparatus tends to take the contemporary order of sovereign nation-states as given" (502).

Furthermore, anti-immigrant sentiments in many developing nations, among them European nations and Australia, have resulted in intensified efforts and legislation to restrict the entry of refugees and undocumented immigrants (see Perlez; Lyall, "In a British Election," "When Asylum Seekers Knock"). At the recent European summit meeting, one of the major items on the agenda was immigration control, an issue that has galvanized the public and politicians across the continent (Erlanger). In the Balireddy case, we can see that the case against Balireddy turned on his violation of national laws. Even the entry of a national civil society institution like the ACLU, which advanced claims on behalf of the young girls, did so on the basis of their rights as workers.[4]

Interestingly enough, in this case, the emergence of and pivotal role played by identity-based activist groups undercuts the thesis common in globalization theory that identity-based movements are inadequate to the challenges of globalization. The role of local women's groups and South Asian American activist groups was crucial in interpreting and publicizing the meanings of this case and in offering support services to the victims. They foregrounded the global scope of the problem of labor and sexual exploitation along with the caste and gender specificities through which it is articulated in this particular instance. Thus, a transnational literacy formulated around gender, caste, ethnicity, and migration was crucial to shaping the outcome of the proceedings, as were the national laws prosecuting trafficking.

Finally, while restitution was provided to the girls through the existing legal mechanisms and the exceptional circumstances surrounding the event, the story of the young girls was never to begin with just the story of the young girls' exploitation. If we follow the trail back to Velvadam, the other part of their story that cannot be recognized by the existing formulations of their condition and the available mechanisms of redress becomes visible. The parents of Chanti Prattipatti and the families of dozens of other young women who had been sent to the United States with Balireddy disappeared from Velvadam. For the time being, the U.S. consulate in Chennai has refused to grant visas to any applicants from Velvadam and neighboring villages. This part of the story and the violence it encodes marks a kind of limit to available discourses of rights and redress that have emerged around issues of trafficking and sex and labor exploitation.

Notes

1 Hardt and Negri use the term "the Multitude" to refer to the revolutionary subject of the new era of globalization. The Multitude includes the new transnational proletariat, whom they define amorphously as "all those whose labor is directly or indirectly exploited by and subjected to capitalist norms of production and reproduction" (52).

2 Lin Lean Lim, ed. *The Sex Sector: The Economic and Social Bases of Prostitution in Southeast Asia*. Geneva: International Labor Organization, 1998.

3 The following account draws on Doezema's summary.

4 A look at the five priority areas targeted by the Immigrants' Rights Project of the ACLU, one of the leading organizations advancing the rights of asylum seekers, undocumented immigrants, and legal residents, shows the following: unconstitutional restrictions on the right to judicial review; the grossly unfair expedited removal process; new indefinite and mandatory detention rules; and workers' rights. These priority areas do not suggest that "immigrants' rights" become a vehicle for substantively revising ideas of national sovereignty. See http://www.ac lu.org/issues/immigrant/hmir.html.

Works Cited

Balibar, Etienne. "Racism and Nationalism." *Race, Nation, Class: Ambiguous Identities.* Etienne Balibar and Immanuel Wallerstein. Trans. of Etienne Balibar by Chris Turner. London: Verso, 1991. 37–67.

Bishop, Ryan, and Lillian Robinson. *Night Market: Sexual Cultures and the Thai Economic Miracle.* New York: Routledge, 1998.

Branigin, William. "A Different Kind of Trade War." *Washington Post* 20 March 1999, K7.

Chatterjee, Partha. "Whose Imagined Community." *Mapping the Nation.* Ed. Gopal Balakrishnan. London: Verso, 1996. 214–225.

"Cultural Defense for Importing Girls Cited." *Los Angeles Times* 16 June 2001, B10.

Doezema, Jo. "Forced to Cho*ose: Beyond the Voluntary v. Forced Prostitution Dichotomy." *Global Sex Workers: Rights, Resistance, and Redefinition.* Ed. Kamala Kempadoo and Jo Doezema. New York: Routledge, 1998. 34–50.

Enloe, Cynthia. *Bananas, Beaches and Bases: Making Feminist Sense of International Politics.* London: Pandora, 1989.

Erlanger, Steven. "European Summit Talks Open Today: Focus Is Immigration Control." *New York Times* 21 June 2002, A8.

Foucault, Michel. "The Subject and Power." Afterword to *Michel Foucault: Beyond Structuralism and Hermeneutics*. Ed. Hubert Dreyfus and Paul Rabinow. 2nd ed. Chicago: University of Chicago Press, 1983.

Friman, H. Richard, and Peter Andreas. "Introduction: International Relations and the Illicit Global Economy." *The Illicit Global Economy and State Power*. Ed. Friman and Andreas. Lanham: Rowman & Littlefield, 1999. 1–23.

Hardt, Michael, and Antonio Negri. *Empire*. Cambridge: Harvard University Press, 2000.

Harvey, David. *Spaces of Hope*. Berkeley: U of California P, 2000.

Immigrants' Rights Project of the ACLU. http://www.aclu.org/issues/immigrant/hmir.html.

Iype, George. "The End of an American Dream." 8 Feb. 2000 http://www.rediff.com/news.

———. "He Is a Shame to Our Family." 13 Mar. 2001 http://www.rediff.com/news.

Koshy, Susan. "From Cold War to Trade War: Neocolonialism and Human Rights." *Social Text* 58 (1999): 1–32.

Lim, Lin Lean, ed. *The Sex Sector: The Economic and Social Bases of Prostitution in Southeast Asia*. Geneva: International Labor Organization, 1998.

Lyall, Sarah. "In a British Election, the Alienated vs. the Aliens." *New York Times* 2 May 2002, A4.

———. "When Asylum Seekers Knock: Europe Is Deaf." *New York Times* 20 June 2002, A3.

Malkki, Liisa H. "Refugees and Exile: From 'Refugee Studies' to the National Order of Things." *Annual Review of Anthropology* 24 (1995): 495–523.

Marks, Stephen P. "Emerging Human Rights: A New Generation for the 1980s?" *Rutgers Law Review* 33 (winter 1981): 235–252.

Mirkinson, Judith. "The Global Trade in Women." *Earth Island Journal* 13.1 (1997): 30–32.

Murray, Allison. "Debt-Bondage and Trafficking: Don't Believe the Hype." *Global Sex Workers: Rights, Resistance, and Redefinition*. Ed. Kempadoo and Doezema. 51–64.

Olson, Elizabeth. "Two Camps at W.T.O. Said to Be a Bit Closer." *New York Times* 1 August 2001, W1.

Perlez, Jane. "Deep Fears Behind Australia's Immigration Policy." *New York Times* 8 May 2002, A3.

Sassen, Saskia. *Globalization and Its Discontents: Essays on the New Mobility of People and Money*. New York: New, 1998.

Truong, Thanh-Dam. *Sex, Money and Morality: Prostitution and Tourism in Southeast Asia*. London: Zed, 1990.

UN Economic and Social Council, *Report of the Special Rapporteur on the Human Rights of Migrants*. January 2001.

"Velvadam, Accused's Village Labels Him a Philanthropist." *Indian Express* 24 January 2000, 2.

Williams, Phil. "Introduction." *Combating Transnational Crime: Concepts, Activities, and Responses*. Ed. Phil Williams and Dimitri Vlassis. London: Frank Cass, 2001.

PART II
HISTORICIZING

Murder in Montmartre

Race, Sex, and Crime in Jazz Age Paris

The 1940 film *The Letter*, one of Hollywood's great melodramas, opens with an arresting scene. Set on a rubber plantation in British Malaya, the film starts with a trailer shot setting the story's colonial context: native men are shown sleeping, gambling, and passing the time in general. Suddenly from the main house a series of shots rings out, and a white man stumbles out of the front door onto the veranda. A white woman strides behind him in close pursuit, determinedly emptying her revolver into her victim. He collapses, and she lets the gun slip from her hand to the ground, all in view of the horrified natives.

At first glance little would seem to link this scene from a classic Bette Davis potboiler with a murder case that occurred in Paris in the 1920s. On closer inspection, however, the film and the crime have much in common. *The Letter*'s graphic portrayal of white female violence, its colonial context, and its fascinatingly hybrid character as a Hollywood movie derived from a British short story set in Malaya,[1] parallel the untimely demise of Mr. Leon Crutcher, an African American jazz pianist murdered by his wife in the French capital during the Jazz Age.[2] This essay explores the 1926 Crutcher murder case as a window onto intersecting dynamics of race, gender, and violence in interwar France. It considers the ways in which transnationalism operated at the level of everyday life, far removed from elite political strategies or high intellectual and theoretical production. This crime provides an intriguing demonstration of how perspectives from different national traditions and histories can alter the meanings of a specific event, so that transnational history becomes significantly more than the sum of various national narratives.

On the face of it, the Crutcher case seemed no different from many other humdrum domestic tragedies that afflicted the human condition from then until now, and in part the Crutcher case derives its importance from its common quality. Yet at the same time this tale of a white French woman murdering her black American husband involved distinctions in ways that cast light upon important fault lines in contemporary French society. More generally, by considering this event from the standpoint of French, francophone, and African American studies, this essay considers the ways in which issues of social and cultural difference can both shift from one context to another and also have the power to change pre-established contextual frameworks.

France during the 1920s struggled with the challenges posed by the Great War, challenges which included adapting to the new roles of a variety of groups within and without French society. The unprecedented use of French women in previously masculine jobs during the war, and the postwar specter of the New Woman, was perhaps the most obvious of shifts underlying the increased sense of instability after 1918.[3] The war had also brought a new relationship between the metropole and the Empire, as the colonies contributed manpower and materiel to the war effort, in the process becoming more tightly integrated into the economy and culture of France. In particular, the importation of hundreds of thousands of colonial soldiers and workers to the metropole during the war produced the first large population of color on French soil in the modern era and began to undermine the divisions between the European nation and the overseas Empire.[4] Moreover, these various levels of alterity interacted with each other: for example, gendered concerns about France's declining birthrate and wartime losses of young men intensified fears for the future of the French race, which fuelled debates about immigration in the metropole and miscegenation in the colonies.[5] Finally, the fact that France won the war in part thanks to a friendly American "invasion" which proved not just military but financial, economic, and cultural as well set forth another series of challenges to the French way of life.[6] In short, modernity wore many different faces in the France of the *années folles*.

The murder of Leon Crutcher touched upon all of these facets of France's era of anxiety. This essay will proceed first by giving a brief history of the case, then by considering it from three different geographical and theoretical perspectives: the tradition of the crime of passion in French law and society; questions of race, gender, and violence in the colonies; and racial violence in the United States. I will argue that although the Crutcher case has much in common with all three types of crime, ultimately it does not fit neatly into any of these categories. Rather, one should consider it a new, postcolonial example of criminality, one that reflected shifts in gender and racial discourses after the Great War. Given that jazz constituted the theme music of modernity in early-twentieth-century France, this murder mystery in jazz will hopefully both amplify and enlighten our appreciation of that nation's conflicted journey into the modern age.[7]

Death in the Afternoon

In the early 1920s a unique community of musicians formed in the storied Parisian neighborhood of Montmartre. Composed for the most part of black jazz performers from the United States, the community developed an array of cheap hotels, restaurants and cafés, and above all nightclubs centered around the Rues Pigalle, Fontaine, and Douai, south of the Place Pigalle and the boulevards. Many factors combined to produce the black Montmartre of the interwar years. Montmartre had of course a long tradition of popular entertainment dating back to the wine shops of the early nineteenth century and, more recently, to celebrated music halls like the Moulin Rouge and the Chat Noir.[8] However, the creation of a specific black jazz culture in Montmartre arose from more specific causes, including the postwar employment crisis of musicians in America; the presence of blacks from both the United States and the French Empire in the metropole during the war; the impact of American mass culture; American tourism and the Lost Generation; the French fascination with blackness that had its roots in the Belle Epoque but reached its zenith during the 1920s; and the widespread belief among African Americans that France offered both better financial opportunities and more tolerance than their own country.[9] By 1925, the year of Josephine Baker's debut in the *Revue nègre*, this small section of Montmartre had been transformed into a transatlantic version of Jazz Age Harlem, with black jazz bands and a wide variety of nightclubs that provided a cosmopolitan population with hot dance music and overpriced champagne until the sun came up.[10] Chief among these night spots was Bricktop's, owned by a black woman from West Virginia who quickly became the reigning queen of Montmartre's jazz culture after her arrival from New York in 1924 (Bricktop).

Into this world came the tragic couple, Leon and Marie Crutcher, in

1925. Leon Crutcher was a young light-skinned black man from Philadelphia, twenty-four years old, who was fortunate to possess both good looks and a talent for playing the piano. He came to Europe with the first postwar wave of African American jazz musicians and by 1925 was playing at a nightclub in Nice where, according to one account, he "overjoyed the lovers of the Charleston."[11] There he met Marie-Léonie Boyard, a French woman a year younger than him. Boyard's background is equally obscure, but press accounts from her trial hinted at a troubled and hardly respectable past. She had grown up in poverty on a provincial farm, as a ward of public assistance. Boyard left home at the age of fifteen "in the company of a gentleman," and gradually made her way into the world of nightclubs and dancehalls, where she found work as an *entraineuse* or dancehall hostess, a woman paid by nightclubs to dance with the male patrons and get them to buy as much alcohol as possible.[12] Boyard was attracted by Crutcher's handsome face and high spirits, and the two became lovers. Soon after that they moved to Paris, where they married on Christmas Day, 1925. They settled into an apartment at 11, rue Joubert, a few blocks behind the Paris Opéra and about five blocks from the center of black Montmartre. Leon Crutcher easily found a job as a bandleader at a local nightclub, the Abbaye de Thélème; Bricktop herself called him the best piano player in Paris. Marie Crutcher also secured employment as a dancehall hostess; by the beginning of 1926 they had become a classic couple of the Montmartre *demi-monde*.[13]

Stable wedded bliss was not a central theme of Parisian modernity, and it certainly seems to have escaped the Crutchers. Neither paid much attention to his or her marriage vows. At her trial Marie Crutcher pointed out, when asked about her lifestyle as a dancehall hostess, "J'ai eu des amis, mais je ne suis pas une fille." Leon Crutcher became known as the "Don Juan of Montmartre," a man whose attractive appearance and talent for dancing did not pass unnoticed in the nightclubs where he performed, and who at times bragged of his sexual exploits to his wife's face. The relationship quickly turned stormy, neighbors reporting frequent loud fights at their apartment. This discord culminated in the tragic events of February 26, 1926. The Crutchers had spent the previous evening working, as usual, then gone out for drinks until 5 A.M. At that point Marie decided to go home and to bed, but Leon refused to accompany her, preferring to stay out. When he finally did return home at three in the afternoon a quarrel immediately erupted. Exclaimed Marie, "You've come home late, have you been cheating on me?" Leon responded by saying "Yes, as often as possible! I've only paid you back for what you've done to me!" At that Marie picked up a large military revolver and threatened Leon with it, saying "What if I killed you?" "Go ahead if you want," was Leon's fatal response. Marie fired one shot, which pierced Leon's lungs, killing him immediately. Another musician who lived in the same building heard the sound of the gunshot and came running, then called the authorities. When the police arrived they found Marie Crutcher in tears, proclaiming she didn't know how the gun had gone off, that she never wanted to kill her husband. They arrested her and took her to prison.[14]

One account of the murder and the immediate reaction to it is provided by the white American writer Robert McAlmon in his memoir of the Lost Generation, modestly titled *Being Geniuses Together*. McAlmon had spent that evening at Bricktop's in the company of Man Ray, Kiki of Montparnasse, and several others, lingering into the morning as black musicians gathered from other nightclubs to chat and play for each other. Leon Crutcher played piano for a while, then left to go outside and argue with his wife, prompting worried looks from Bricktop. McAlmon and his friends left Bricktop's for another restaurant, stayed there for a while, and were preparing to leave when Bricktop came in with a huge bunch of flowers. " 'Knock on wood,' she said hoarsely. 'Crutcher's shot dead.' " She then went on to explain, "He was fighting with that French chippy outside my place . . . They went home and she threatened to shoot him if he cut up with other women. He asked her how about her with other men, and when she pointed a gun at him he dared her to shoot. She shot, and she shot straight. I got these flowers for him. There ain't going to be no sleeping for me this day. I'm getting to think Paris is hoodooed" (51).[15]

Marie Crutcher went on trial for murder on October 7, 1926, in the Assize Court of the Department of the Seine. A parade of witnesses from Montmartre testified to the ongoing conflicts between the Crutchers, at the same time providing the court's spectators a glimpse into the exotic world of Paris's black jazz culture. Several musicians appeared, as did a young black woman who claimed to have been married to Leon Crutcher, but was able to furnish only an insurance policy as proof. Marie Crutcher herself steadfastly maintained her innocence, every bit the grieving widow who had made a tragic mistake, wiping her eyes with a handkerchief when the prosecutor described her husband's death. "I loved him," she exclaimed, "I wanted to frighten him . . . I picked up a revolver, and I don't know how it went off! No, really!"[16] She also described their lives in

Montmartre, defending her profession as honorable and in fact competitive. Under questioning she revealed that her husband had been quite well paid, earning some 2,000 francs a week, and that he never paid taxes, a revelation which prompted the judge to comment, "Charming! . . . People like him play tunes, while we are made to dance!" Marie Crutcher was defended by a team of women lawyers, who pleaded eloquently and effectively for her acquittal. That, plus a lackluster speech by the prosecuting attorney, was enough to win a vote of not guilty from the jury, and Madame Crutcher walked out of the Assize Court a free woman.[17]

If the Crutcher case can be seen as a murder mystery, the mystery is not who killed Leon Crutcher, or even why. Rather, the key question is why did the Assize Court vote to acquit Marie Crutcher of the crime? More generally, what did this acquittal reveal about issues of gender, race, and crime in interwar Paris, and their complex interactions? Although the Assize Court made the decision to acquit, others in Paris had their own opinions about the trial and the verdict. How did various constituencies, including French women and men, local African Americans, and others, perceive the Crutcher case? I will consider the case from a variety of different perspectives in order to arrive at some conclusions about its historical significance.

A Crime of Passion?

The most obvious context in which to consider the murder of Leon Crutcher is the French tradition of the crime of passion. The concept of the crime of passion, briefly defined as murder or grave physical assault committed against a victim by a spouse or lover, has a history in French jurisprudence that goes back well before the Revolution. Although lacking a specific legal designation, crimes of passion emerged as a social and cultural reality during the nineteenth century, distinguished by juries and the general population from other violent crimes. Although the nature of these crimes varied significantly, they usually involved an outraged person killing his or her spouse for infidelity; the classic prototype was the man who caught his wife in bed with another man, and in a fit of rage killed him, her, or both. Such perpetrators were frequently acquitted by French courts, due to popular beliefs that they had been overcome by their emotions and were therefore not responsible for their acts, or that their victims deserved their fates.[18]

Both men and women committed these crimes: although by the late nineteenth century the majority of these criminals were men, crimes of passion constituted a greater percentage of crimes committed by women, so that the phenomenon became perceived as a female one. Women portrayed themselves as victims of husbands or lovers, men who betrayed promises to marry them, engaged in infidelity, or otherwise treated them dishonorably, and were regularly acquitted for in effect taking the law into their own hands. Public attention tended to focus on middle-class women with no criminal history, suddenly seized by violent and irresistible murderous rage. Such trials frequently became major public spectacles during the *Belle Epoque*. The most famous was that of Madame Henriette Caillaux, who in 1914 murdered the editor of the leading daily newspaper *Le Figaro* for having besmirched the reputation of her husband, former prime minister Joseph Caillaux. Madame Caillaux portrayed her act as one of love for her husband, and was duly set free (Berenson).

Although husbands and wives continued to murder each other in France after World War I, the social and cultural context of such crimes shifted. The rise of the phenomenon of the New Woman, suggesting a more aggressive posture of France's female population and the threatened emasculation of the nation, cast the specter of violence by women in a different, more sinister, light. Instead of exemplifying the emotional, hysterical, even childlike simplicity of women in general, female murders took on a new symbolism as subversive acts that threatened society as a whole. In this context, the crime of passion receded in significance before other murders by women seen as directed more against authority. Two of the most notorious cases of female violence in interwar France differed sharply from traditional crimes of passion. In 1933 two servants, the sisters Christine and Lea Papin, were arrested for beating their employer and her daughter to death in their home. A year later Violette Nozières went on trial for poisoning her parents. All three women were convicted (Flanner [Genêt] 98–104, 158–164). Compared to such outrages, the crime of passion seemed almost Victorian in its innocence. In commenting on the Nozières case, American journalist Janet Flanner made this parallel explicit:

> Maybe our grandmothers were right and female standards are, on all sides, not so high as they used to be. Certainly an eclectic comparison between the mediocre murder recently committed by the 19-year-old Parisian flapper Mlle. Violette Nozière and the stylish assassination achieved by the consummate Mme. Germaine d'Anglemont,

aged forty-eight, indicates a deplorable decline of the younger generation. Mme. d'Anglemont shot her lover like a lady, because she was jealous; Violette Nozière killed her father like a cannibal, because she wanted to eat and drink up the savings that were his French life and blood. (158)

Certainly much about the murder of Leon Crutcher corresponds to the classic pattern of the crime of passion. Marie Crutcher killed her husband in a violent rage after he defiantly admitted an affair with another woman. Her tearful expressions of confusion and regret at her deed, along with her protestations at the trial that she still loved her victim, had all been seen before in trials and investigations of such crimes. Observers of the trial concluded as much. In commenting on the case, the English writer Ralph Nevill argued, "It may be remarked that the Jury of the Seine is ridiculously lenient towards murderers and murderesses provided their crime is in some way connected with love" (197). The correspondent for *Le Figaro*, whose own editor had fallen victim to a similar crime twelve years earlier, acidly concluded that "Prosecutor Lémant gave an excellent summation, but the jurors, as is usually the case, acquitted this nervous woman, since her victim was only her husband."[19] The Crutcher jury's speedy decision for acquittal reinforces a view of the case as merely yet another crime of passion.

Yet certain aspects of the Crutcher case tend to undermine that conclusion. Most of these centered around the perceived character of Marie Crutcher. Key to the tradition of the female crime of passion was the idea of a virtuous woman defending her honor against a man who had wronged her. However, in general commentators on the case portrayed Madame Crutcher as a woman with little honor and less virtue. The press made much of her profession, labeling her as little better than a prostitute, and suggested that she had slept around at least as much as her husband.[20] More generally, her association with Montmartre, famed not just for jazz but for drugs, crime, and sex for sale in general, made it hard to argue that Marie Crutcher had "shot her lover like a lady." Instead, her association with modernity at its sleaziest suggests a lot more in common with Violette Nozières.[21] Finally, the color of her husband and victim introduced a new racial dimension into this murder case. Accounts of the Crutcher affair did not fail to note the victim's race, usually in stereotypical terms. Leon Crutcher was handsome, charming, seductive, amoral: in short, if Marie was little better than a prostitute, he was essentially a pimp.[22] The interracial aspect of the case presents the possibility that in acquitting Marie Crutcher the jurors saw the question of her honor in racial, not sexual terms; she was pardoned in effect for defending the honor of the white race, not her own.

The coverage of the Crutcher case in the newspaper *Le Petit Parisien* provides an interesting example of this. The *Petit Parisien* was Paris's reigning scandal sheet during the 1920s, the kind of newspaper that routinely featured the photographs of murderers on its front page. Crimes of passion were its bread and butter, and not surprisingly it devoted more coverage to the Crutcher case than did any other newspaper.[23] In the version of the case offered by the *Petit Parisien*, Marie Crutcher emerged as the clear victim. The newspaper emphasized her youth and vulnerability, downplaying the suggestions of prostitution evident in other accounts. It also gave an exceptionally harsh portrait of Leon Crutcher: "Crutcher was both fickle and jealous. He drank, he gambled, and frequently Léonie Boyard's body showed traces of his violent temper."[24] Finally, the newspaper highlighted Mme. Crutcher's claim that she never cheated on her husband, and in general portrayed her action as that of an abused but loving woman whose nerves finally gave way.[25] In short, it was a classic crime of passion. But the *Petit Parisien* could only convincingly make the crime of passion argument by demonizing Leon Crutcher in the most stereotypical terms; for example, no other newspaper alleged he beat his wife. In effect, therefore, Marie Crutcher's abuse by a black man restored her to a state of virginal whiteness.

In order to explore the racial dimensions of the Crutcher case more fully, it is necessary to explore the interaction of race, sex, and violence in two other contexts: the United States and the French Empire.

Miscegenation and Retribution

Throughout the history of African Americans in twentieth-century Paris, the theme of love across the color line, especially between black men and white women, has been a constant of the community's life. This was certainly true of blacks in interwar Montmartre, a neighborhood with a cosmopolitan attitude toward sexuality.[26] As Bricktop herself commented, "Everybody was sleeping around. It was the thing to do . . . I slept with white men and black men" (Bricktop 131). For American blacks, and black men in particular, opportunities for relationships with white women represented the ultimate proof of French racial tolerance, a phenomenon so

graphically different from customs in their homeland.[27] Such relationships varied widely, from fleeting commercial encounters to marriage and
long-term associations, but they seem to have been a central aspect of
black life in Montmartre. As a French musician remembered in an interview years later, "To the blacks, life in Europe was like heaven, I can tell
you. One good reason was the white women . . . A lot of French guys
resented the blacks going off with their women. But every guy I knew
found himself a white broad — Montmartre women mostly, not necessarily whores. They met them as hostesses who danced with them and
they got a tip as an escort" (Leo Vauchant, qtd. in Goddard 262).[28]

The image of Jazz Age Montmartre as a paradise of miscegenation and
racial tolerance derived of course from the contrast with racial realities
in the contemporary United States. In America the war for democracy
abroad that many blacks had hoped would bring greater acceptance at
home gave way instead to the Red Summer, an era of massive race riots in
1919 that usually featured assaults by white vigilantes on black communities.[29] The aftermath of the war also saw an upsurge in lynchings: 60
blacks were lynched in 1919, more than in any year between 1908 and
1930 (Tolnay and Beck 272). This rise in vigilante murders of African
Americans is doubly relevant to our story. First, black men who had served
in the U.S. armed forces in France were particularly targeted; a number of
the victims were actually demobilized soldiers in uniform. Many southerners feared that the kind reception of blacks overseas had led them to
forget their place at the bottom of America's racial hierarchy. Fears of
sexual transgression ran particularly sharp, as one Mississippi senator's
reference to "French-women-ruined negro soldiers" made clear (qtd. in
Stovall, *Paris Noir* 27).[30] Second, as American historians have demonstrated, lynching in the United States had clear ties to perceived sexual
violations of the color line. A large percentage of lynching victims in the
late-ninteenth- and early-twentieth-century American South were black
men accused of raping white women, and southern justifications of lynchings overwhelmingly emphasized the need to protect white female virtue.
The graphic images of nude, at times castrated, black male bodies dancing
at the end of ropes underlined the sexual nature of lynching. For African
American men in interwar Montmartre, therefore, sex and love with a
French woman illustrated the radically different level of acceptance af-
forded by Parisian exile.[31]

Did the Crutcher case appear to these individuals as a kind of transatlantic lynching? In this instance, as in Southern lynchings, the anger of a white woman meant destruction for a black man, or to put it another way, the penalty for miscegenation was death. Moreover, Marie Crutcher's acquittal, on the flimsiest of excuses, of the crime by a presumably white jury must have recalled American parallels for the blacks of Montmartre. If a pointed reference to "high-tech lynching" in 1991 could assure the confirmation of an American Supreme Court Justice, then surely African Americans living during the era of the rope and faggot could not have failed to see the analogy.[32] The fact that white southern women who cried rape by black men were often perceived (by blacks) as women of low morals highlights the significance of Bricktop's reference to Marie Crutcher as a "French chippy," and her concerns about the consequences of that relationship for Leon Crutcher. Certainly the blacks of Montmartre considered the Crutcher murder more significant than the ordinary crime of passion. As Robert McAlmon observed immediately after hearing the news, "All these Negro boys looked pale around the gills, and they said they were 'superstitious' about French girls. Several of them had white mistresses, but now they felt cowed, and they agreed among themselves that the French girl would not be sentenced" (51). And of course they were right.

However, one can be right for the wrong reasons; just as the Crutcher case differed significantly from the traditional French crime of passion, it also did not conform in some important ways to the normative racial and sexual dynamics of lynching. The American image of the black rapist (and to a large extent the rapist in general) has usually been that of the stranger in the night, rather than an acquaintance of the victim; any personal interracial relationship would not be acceptable in contemporary American society.[33] The fact that Marie Crutcher was not only married to her black victim, but cried infidelity rather than assault, underlined her differences with the prototypical outraged Southern white woman. Also, the prospect of a white woman herself killing a black man departs significantly from the classic lynching script, in which the victim of sexual assault was supposed to target and accuse her aggressor, but leave to the men of her community the bloody work of vengeance.[34] Such a pattern, which reestablished both racial and gender norms, was sharply contradicted by Marie Crutcher; after all, Desdemona was not supposed to kill Othello.[35] Crutcher's display of agency suggests that, whereas race clearly factored into this case, it did not do so in the same way as it might have on the other side of the Atlantic.

Finally, it is important to consider the Crutcher case in the context of French colonial life, an area in which race, sex, and violence interacted regularly and dramatically. As Frantz Fanon and others have pointed out, violence suffused all aspects of the colonial encounter.[36] The nature of this violence was not only racially structured, pitting white soldiers and masters against nonwhite rebels and servants, but also frequently sexually encoded, from the widespread violation of indigenous women to the telling use of phraseology like "the penetration of virgin interiors" to characterize colonial conquest (McClintock 24–31). Although the black members of Montmartre's jazz bands came from the United States and lived in France, they were typically viewed by the French as Africans rather than Americans, and integrated into the interwar vogue for the colonial and exotic.[37] For example, in virtually all of Josephine Baker's performances on the French stage and screen she played a native of the French colonies, not an African American.[38]

The murder of Leon Crutcher has some interesting parallels with imperial themes as well. As the case of Josephine Baker so dramatically demonstrates, one aspect of the exotic that found particular favor in interwar Paris was colonial sexuality, building upon a long tradition of French male fantasies about lust in the tropics.[39] At the same time, official circles devoted increased attention to the role of French women in the Empire.[40] Prewar efforts to promote the migration of white women to the colonies gained force, and the interwar years in general saw increased settlement of both French women and men in overseas France.[41] Whereas black and brown women in the metropole appeared as embodiments of primitive, uninhibited sexuality, by contrast the image of French women in the colonies as virtuous vessels of decorum and civilized values gained in significance.[42] The new emphasis on eugenics in interwar France reinforced this racial polarity. This belief in preserving and improving the quality of the French race saw white women as the key to creating racially pure white families in the tropics, so that the settlement of French women in the interwar Empire took place in the context of increased hostility to *concubinage* with indigenous women and the creation of a mixed-race population.[43] More than in the nineteenth century, therefore, interwar colonial ideology gave French women a central role in the creation of Empire.

Marie Crutcher's murder of her husband symbolically replicated these tensions surrounding race and gender in the colonies after World War I.

Her low moral status and association with the exotic underworld of black Montmartre certainly underlined French stereotypes of primitivism and female sexuality. Sander Gilman has pointed to the similarity between representations of the black woman and the white prostitute in nineteenth-century European medical discourses, and Marie Crutcher's lack of sexual inhibition and marriage to a black man fit neatly into that perspective. At the same time, in a colonial context she could be seen as an example of white decadence in the tropics, surrounded by the classic symbols of such decay, alcohol and miscegenation. In murdering her husband, however, Crutcher moved from an earlier stereotype of white women in the colonies as adventuresses, to the new model of woman as paragon of racial identity. In addition, the jury's acquittal of Madame Crutcher parallels the tendency of colonial courts and administrators to excuse or punish lightly white acts of violence against the natives. Nonetheless, Marie Crutcher certainly did not correspond to the imperial ideal of the French female settler in the colonies. She was much closer to the image of the New Woman, against whom this ideal was in part directed. She may have ended her foray across the sexual color line, but in the views of commentators on the trial Crutcher remained very much a part of the Montmartre *demimonde*, far removed from any respectable society.

This last comparison leads me most directly to my conclusion, that the Crutcher murder case offers a glimpse of emerging postcolonial relations of race and gender in early-twentieth-century France. The term "postcolonial" has been used more often by proponents of literary and cultural studies than by historians, but I would argue that it has relevance here, if defined as the development of new relations between empire and metropole caused by the increased interaction of the two in both the late imperial and postimperial periods.[44] One aspect of the Crutcher case that suggests this perspective is its central relationship between a white woman and a man of color. Whereas the dominant form of interracial relationship in the French colonies has been white men and women of color, the prevailing pattern in postcolonial France has been the reverse, largely due to patterns of military and labor recruitment which have tended to bring black and brown men rather than women to the metropole. In the colonial pattern racial and gender hierarchies operate in the same direction, whereas the postcolonial model is much more complex, bringing together individuals who combine both high and low social status. The fact that in this case a woman murdered a man also acted to destabilize colonial and gender relations. Marie Crutcher exhibited a level of agency that called into question not only relations between men and women at home, but also the imperial ideology of white femininity. Her low moral standing and her connections to black Montmartre suggested a kind of New Woman in the tropics, blending metropolitan anxieties and colonial racial practices.

In addition, the American dimension of this case supports a postcolonial characterization. Kristin Ross has argued that in the 1950s French life was doubly colonial, concerned both with retaining the nation's own empire and with warding off colonization by the United States. The murder of Leon Crutcher provides an interwar example of the same phenomenon. Its resemblance to southern lynchings, at a time when some Parisian hotels and restaurants were beginning to exclude blacks in deference to white American tourists, sets forth the possibility of new, American-style patterns of race relations in France. At the same time, Marie Crutcher may have won acquittal precisely because her victim was an American, and a relatively wealthy one at that. The 1920s witnessed not only a massive increase in the number of American tourists visiting France, but also a protracted dispute between Paris and Washington over French war debts, as well as the precipitous decline of the French franc against the dollar. The resulting transatlantic tensions culminated in the summer of 1926, producing a spasm of hostility and even violence against Yankee tourists in the French capital. As the franc hit an interwar low of 50 to the dollar in July, 20,000 French veterans staged a silent protest in Paris against American pressures for repayment of wartime loans. More alarming were the attacks on American tour buses that occurred in the city two weeks later (Levenstein). In this context, the insinuations that the Crutcher jurors absolved the accused out of hostility to a foreigner whose weekly salary was at least ten times that of the average French worker must be taken seriously.[45] Just as African American jazz combined the attractions of both primitivism and American mass culture for interwar Parisians, so too did Leon Crutcher represent at the same time the exotic man of color and the rich American.

One cannot solve definitively the mystery of Marie Crutcher's acquittal for the murder of her husband. Many factors entered into this decision, and each juror may have acted on different grounds. Nonetheless, this sordid domestic drama does provide some interesting insights into the larger dynamics of race, sex, and violence in Jazz Age Paris. It shows how a crime involving these elements could both resemble other contexts, yet at the same time transform them. It provides one example of how new racial realities in metropolitan France could add another dimension to social patterns and conflicts based upon gender, while at the same time being altered by changing relations between men and women. Finally, it offers a glimpse of new patterns of social difference in a nascent postcolonial France. If improvisation is the soul of jazz, then one can say that Leon Crutcher's life fulfilled the promise of his music, bringing forth new patterns with its last dying note.

Notes

1 The film is based upon the short story by W. Somerset Maugham.

2 *The Letter* involves a British woman on a plantation in colonial Malaya murdering her British lover out of jealousy at his marriage to a Eurasian woman. She lies about the crime and is exonerated by a colonial court yet ultimately dies for her sins. The interracial dimension of the case, the theme of female agency, and the outcome of the trial all parallel the Crutcher case, as this essay will demonstrate.

3 On the question of the New Woman in interwar France, see Roberts; McMillan; and Downs. For a comparison with previous incarnations of the cultural phenomenon of the New Woman, see Silverman.

4 On French colonial soldiers in the Great War, see Michel; Lunn; Nogaro and Lucien Weil; Meynier; Horne; Vidalenc; Favre; and Stovall, "Colour-blind France?" and "The Color Line."

5 On the crisis of natality in late-nineteenth- and early-twentieth-century France, see Ronsin.

6 See, in particular, Kaspi.

7 On jazz and French culture in interwar France, see Jackson.

8 See Chevalier. See also the many informative memoirs on Montmartre during the age of impressionism, including Yaki; Warnod; MacOrlan; and the many fiction and nonfiction works of Francis Carco.

9 See Cowley; Fitch; and Fabre.

10 See Stovall, *Paris Noir*; and Blake.

11 *La gazette des tribunaux*, 8–9 October 1926, 535.

12 *Le Figaro*, 8 October 1926, 2.

13 See on this point Chevalier 374–396.

14 All the quotations in this paragraph are from *Le Figaro*, 8 October 1926, 2. They were taken from testimony by Mme. Crutcher herself to the police immediately after the incident. It is of course impossible to verify the accuracy of these words, since there were only two people present at that encounter and one of them definitely could not tell his side of the story. Therefore, these words should be viewed less as an objective account, and more as indications of Mme. Crutcher's state of mind.

15 It is notable that McAlmon gets the date of this incident wrong by several years, ascribing it to July 1923. See also Carpenter 107.

16 *Le Figaro*, 8 October 1926, 2.

17 Ibid.; see Nevill 198.

18 On the history of the crime of passion in France, see Guillais; Martin; and Harris.

19 *Le Figaro*, 8 October 1926, 2.

20 For example, in the words of Ruth Harris, "the *criminelle passionnelle* was placed at the opposite end from the prostitute" (240–241).

21 In fact, one of Nozières's lovers was also a black American jazz musician from Montmartre.

22 It is interesting to note a certain amount of confusion about Leon Crutcher's racial identity. Crutcher, who was light-skinned, was described as a mulatto by *La gazette des tribunaux* and a Negro by *Le Figaro*. Both agreed on his good looks and attractiveness to women: *Le Figaro* observed that "Les petites parisiennes blondes se laissent souvent séduire par les hommes de couleur," 2.

23 *Le petit Parisien*, 27 February 1926, 1, 3; 6 October 1926, 2; 7 October 1926, 1, 2.

24 6 October 1926, 2.

25 It is interesting to note that the *Petit Parisien* always referred to Mme. Crutcher by her maiden name, and called her Leon Crutcher's "companion," not his wife.

26 See, for example, Bennett; Cunard; and Crowder.

27 This phenomenon was much more pronounced in the years after World War II for African American men in Paris.

28 In contrast, Elliot Carpenter, one of the first jazz band leaders in interwar Paris, commented: "The Negroes would go into them cafes up in Montmartre and they'd throw their money away as soon as they got it. Drinking wine and spending it on those whores they had up there" (Goddard 302).

29 On the history of America's Red Summer, see Rudwick; Tuttle; and Haynes.

30 See also Barbeau and Henri.

31 On the history of lynching in America, see Williamson; Brundage; Litwack 280–325; and Harris.

32 For example, this reference and the Clarence Thomas/Anita Hill drama in general inspired Jacquelyn Dowd Hall to write her study of the antilynching campaign launched by white Southern women in the early twentieth century (Hall xv–xxxviii).

33 See Brownmiller; Tabori; and Vigarello.

34 See, for example, Litwack's discussion of Rebecca Felton, a white southerner who demanded that southern white men assert their masculinity by defending white women against black male attackers (304–305).

35 There were of course instances of white women crying rape in order to cover up their consensual (but socially unacceptable) sexual relations with black men. See Ware 167–224, especially 181.

36 See Fanon; Scully; and Vann.

37 See, for example, the short story "Congo" in Morand.

38 See Rose and Sharpley-Whiting.

39 See Blachère; Martinkus-Zemp.

40 Studies of European women in the colonies during the modern era include Chaudhuri and Strobel; Midgley; Clancy-Smith and Gouda; and MacMillan.

41 See Renucci; and see Knibiehler and Goutalier.
42 See Stovall, "Love, Labor, and Race."
43 See Schneider and Conklin.
44 For recent overviews of the concept of postcolonialism, see Xie; McCallum; and Parker.
45 In 1924 Jacques Valdour cited working class hourly wages in the Paris area of 2.2 to 4.25 francs per hour, or a maximum of roughly 200 francs per week.

Works Cited

Barbeau, Arthur E., and Florette Henri. *The Unknown Soldiers: Black American Troops in World War I.* Philadelphia: Temple University Press, 1974.

Bennett, Gwendolyn. "Wedding Day." *The Sleeper Awakes: Harlem Renaissance Stories by Women.* Ed. Marcy Knopf. New Brunswick: Rutgers University Press, 1993. 48–54.

Berenson, Edward. *The Trial of Madame Caillaux.* Berkeley: University of California Press, 1992.

Blachère, Jean-Claude. *Le modèle nègre: Aspects littéraires du mythe primitiviste au Xxe siècle chez Apollinaire, Cendras, Tzara.* Dakar: Nouvelles Éditions Africaines, 1981.

Blake, Jody. *Le tumulte noir: Modernist Art and Popular Entertainment in Jazz-Age Paris.* University Park: Pennsylvania State University Press, 1999.

Bricktop, with James Haskins. *Bricktop.* New York: Atheneum, 1983.

Brownmiller, Susan. *Against Our Will: Men, Women, and Rape.* New York: Simon and Schuster, 1975.

Brundage, W. Fitzhugh. *Lynching in the New South: Georgia and Virginia, 1880–1930.* Urbana: University of Illinois Press, 1993.

Carpenter, Humphrey. *Geniuses Together: American Writers in Paris in the 1920s.* London: Unwin Hyman, 1987.

Chaudhuri, Nupur, and Margaret Strobel, eds. *Western Women and Imperialism.* Bloomington: Indiana University Press, 1992.

Chevalier, Louis. *Montmartre du plaisir et du crime.* Paris: Éditions Robert Laffont, 1980.

Clancy-Smith, Julia, and Frances Gouda. *Domesticating the Empire: Race, Gender, and Family Life in French and Dutch Colonialism.* Charlottesville: University of Virginia Press, 1998.

Conklin, Alice L. "Redefining 'Frenchness': Citizenship, Race Regeneration, and Imperial Motherhood in France and West Africa, 1914–1940." In Clancy-Smith and Gouda 65–83.

Cowley, Malcolm. *Exile's Return: A Literary Odyssey of the 1920s.* New York: W. W. Norton & Co, 1934.

Crowder, Henry. *As Wonderful as All That?* Navarro, CA: Wild Trees Press, 1987.

Cunard, Nancy. *Black Man and White Ladyship: An Anniversary.* London: Utopia, 1931.

Downs, Laura Lee. *Manufacturing Inequality: Gender Division in the French and British Metalworking Industries, 1914–1939*. Ithaca: Cornell University Press, 1995.

Fabre, Michel. *From Harlem to Paris: Black American Writers in France, 1840–1980*. Urbana: University of Illinois Press, 1991.

Fanon, Frantz. *The Wretched of the Earth*. New York: Grove Press, 1963.

Favre, Mireille. "Un milieu porteur de modernisation: Travailleurs et tirailleurs vietnamiens en France pendant la première guerre mondiale." Thèse, 2 vols. École nationale des Chartes, Paris, 1986.

Fitch, Noel Riley. *Sylvia Beach and the Lost Generation: A History of Literary Paris in the Twenties and Thirties*. New York: Norton, 1983.

Flanner, Janet. *Paris Was Yesterday, 1925–1939*. New York: Penguin, 1981.

Gilman, Sander L. "Black Bodies, White Bodies: Toward an Iconography of Female Sexuality in Late Nineteenth-Century Art, Medicine, and Literature." *"Race," Writing, and Difference*. Ed. Henry Louis Gates Jr. Chicago: University of Chicago Press, 1985.

Goddard, Chris. *Jazz away from Home*. New York: Paddington Press, 1972.

Guillais, Joëlle. *Crimes of Passion: Dramas of Private Life in Nineteenth-Century France*. Cambridge: Polity, 1990.

Hall, Jacquelyn Dowd. *Revolt against Chivalry: Jessie Daniel Ames and the Women's Campaign against Lynching*. New York: Columbia University Press, 1993.

Harris, J. William. "Etiquette, Lynching, and Racial Boundaries in Southern History: A Mississippi Example." *American Historical Review* (April 1995): 387–410.

Harris, Ruth. *Murders and Madness: Medicine, Law, and Society in the* Fin de Siècle. Oxford: Clarendon, 1989.

Haynes, Robert V. *A Night of Violence: The Houston Riot of 1917*. Baton Rouge: Louisiana State University Press, 1976.

Horne, John. "Immigrant Workers in France during World War I." *French Historical Studies* 14 (1985): 57–88.

Jackson, Jeffrey. *Making Jazz French*. Durham: Duke University Press, 2003.

Kaspi, Andre. *Le temps des Américains: Le concours américain à la France en 1917–1918*. Paris: Publications de la Sorbonne, 1976.

Knibiehler, Yvonne, and Régine Goutalier. *La femme au temps des colonies*. Paris: Stock, 1985.

Levenstein, Harvey. *Seductive Journey: American Tourists in France from Jefferson to the Jazz Age*. Chicago: University of Chicago Press, 1998.

Litwack, Leon F. *Trouble in Mind: Black Southerners in the Age of Jim Crow*. New York: Knopf, 1998.

Lunn, Joe Harris. "Kande Kamara Speaks: An Oral History of the West African Experience in France 1914–1918." In Melvin E. Page, ed., *Africa and the First World War*. London, 1987.

MacMillan, Margaret. *Women of the Raj*. New York: Thames and Hudson, 1988.

MacOrlan, Pierre. *Montmartre: Souvenirs*. Brussels: Les Éditions de Chabassol, 1946.

Martin, Benjamin F. *The Hypocrisy of Justice in the Belle Epoque*. Baton Rouge: Louisiana State University Press, 1984.

Martinkus-Zemp, Ada. *Le blanc et le Noir*. Paris: A-G. Nizet, 1975.

Maugham, W. Somerset. "The Letter." In *The Complete Short Stories of W. Somerset Maugham, vol. 1, East and West*. Garden City, New York: Doubleday and Company, 1934.

McAlmon, Robert. *Being Geniuses Together, 1920–1930*. San Francisco: North Point Press, 1984.

McCallum, Pamela. "Introductory Notes: Postcolonialism and its Discontents." *Ariel*, vol. 26, no.1. January, 1995.

McClintock, Anne. *Imperial Leather: Race, Gender and Sexuality in the Colonial Conquest*. New York: Routledge, 1995.

McMillan, James F. *Housewife or Harlot: The Position of Women in French Society, 1870–1940*. New York: St. Martin's Press, 1980.

Michel, Marc. *L'appel à l'Afrique*. Paris, 1982.

Midgley, Claire, ed. *Gender and Imperialism*. Manchester: Manchester University Press, 1998.

Morand, Paul. *Magie Noire*. Paris: Ferenczi, 1936.

Nevill, Ralph. *Days and Nights in Montmartre and the Latin Quarter*. New York: George H. Doran Company, 1927.

Nogaro, Bertrand, and Lucien Weil. *La main-d'oeuvre étrangère et colonial pendant la guerre*. Paris: Les Universitaires de France, 1926.

Parker, Ken. "Very Like a White: Postcolonialism between Canonicities and Ethnicities." *Social Identities* 1 (spring 1995): 155–174.

Renucci, France. *Souvenirs de femmes au temps des colonies*. Paris: Balland, 1988.

Roberts, Mary Louise. *Civilization without Sexes: Reconstructing Gender in Postwar France, 1917–1927*. Chicago: University of Chicago Press, 1994.

Ronsin, Francis. *La grève des ventres: Propagande néo-malthusienne et baisse de la natalité française*. Poitiers: Aubier, 1980.

Rose, Phyllis. *Jazz Cleopatra: Josephine Baker in Her Time*. New York: Doubleday, 1989.

Ross, Kristin. *Fast Cars, Clean Bodies: Decolonization and the Reordering of French Culture*. Cambridge: MIT Press, 1995.

Rudwick, Elliott M. *Race Riot at East St. Louis*. Carbondale: 1964.

Schneider, William H. *Quality and Quantity: The Quest for Biological Regeneration in Twentieth-Century France*. Cambridge: Cambridge University Press, 1990.

Scully, Pamela. "Rape, Race, and Colonial Culture: The Sexual Politics of Identity in Nineteenth-Century Cape Colony, South Africa." *American Historical Review* (April 1995): 335–359.

Sharpley-Whiting, T. Denean. *Black Venus: Sexualized Savages, Primal Fears, and Primitive Narratives in French*. Durham: Duke University Press, 1999.

Silverman, Debora. *Art Nouveau in Fin-de-Siècle France: Politics, Psychology and Style*. Berkeley: University of California Press, 1989.

Stovall, Tyler. "The Color Line behind the Lines: Racial Violence in France during the Great War." *American Historical Review*, vol. 103, no.3. June, 1998.

——. "Colour-blind France? Colonial Workers during the First World War." *Race and Class* 35.2 (1993): 35–55.

——. "Love, Labor, and Race: Colonial Men and White Women in France during the Great War." *French Civilization and Its Discontents: Nationalism, Colonialism, and Race*. Ed. Tyler Stovall and Georges Van Den Abbeele. Lanham: Rowman and Littlefield, 2003.

——. *Paris Noir: African Americans in the City of Light*. Boston: Houghton-Mifflin, 1996.

Tabori, Paul. *The Social History of Rape*. London: New English Library, 1971.

Thobie, Jacques, Gilbert Meynier, Catherine Coquery-Vidrovitch, and Charles-Robert Ageron, eds. *Histoire de la France coloniale*, vol. 2, *1914–1990*. Paris: Armand Colin, 1990.

Tolnay, Stewart E., and E. M. Beck. *A Festival of Violence: An Analysis of Southern Lynchings, 1882–1930*. Urbana: University of Illinois Press, 1995.

Tuttle, William M., Jr. *Race Riot: Chicago in the Red Summer of 1919*. New York: 1970.

Vann, Michael G. "White City on the Red River: Race, Power, and Culture in Colonial Hanoi, 1870–1954." Ph.D. diss., University of California, Santa Cruz, 1999.

Valdour, Jacques. *De la Popinqu'à la Ménilmuch*. Paris: Éditions Spés, 1924.

Vidalenc, Jean. "La main d'oeuvre étrangère en france et la première guerre mondiale, 1901–1926." *Francia* 2 (1974): 524–550.

Vigarello, Paul Georges. *Histoire du viol: XVIe–XXe siècle*. Paris: Seuil, 1998.

Ware, Vron. *Beyond the Pale: White Women, Racism, and History*. London: Verso, 1992.

Warnod, André. *Fils de Montmartre: Souvenirs*. Paris: Librarie Arthème Fayard, 1955.

Williamson, Joel. *The Crucible of Race: Black/White Relations in the American South since Emancipation*. New York: 1984.

Xie, Shaobo. "Rethinking the Problem of Postcolonialism." *New Literary History* 28.1 (1997): 7–19.

Yaki, Paul. *Le Montmartre de nos vingt ans*. Paris: Éditions Tallamdoer, 1933.

Giving "Minor" Pasts a Future

Narrating History in Transnational Cinematic Autobiography

What happens when contemporary feminist and minoritarian filmmakers pick up the camera to self-narrate aspects of their lives and experiences? Cheryl Dunye offers one answer at the end of her debut feature film *The Watermelon Woman* (1996). Looking directly into the camera, she tells the spectator what her search for the Watermelon Woman, an obscure African American actress from the 1930s, has meant to her: "What she means to me, a twenty-five-year-old black woman, means something else: it means hope, it means inspiration, it means possibility, it means *history*!" Dunye's emphatic statement gives voice to one of the problems facing minority experimental filmmakers in the United States, a problem not overtly confronted by their precursors in the classical American avant-garde (1943–1972). Though earlier experimental filmmakers championed autobiographical and personal cinema as an alternative to industry cinema, they generally avoided historical reference, locating the difference of their autobiographical texts in idiosyncratic aesthetic formal innovation.[1] As the urgency in Dunye's "it means history" suggests, contemporary minoritarian filmmakers would appear to face an involuntary conscription to the cause and expression of history. Confronting historical frameworks where they are not represented or imagined, where there is no place for them, they instead innovate, invent, and improvise. As Dunye concludes, "Sometimes you have to create your own history. The Watermelon Woman is a fiction."

When the autobiographical filmmaker hails from a transnational minority group, the problem of history is compounded with that of geography, of origin, of home. In transnational cinematic autobiography, the conventional coordinates of narrative and of self-narration — orientation in (national) space and (historical) time — become multiple, fragmented, contradictory. In this, these narratives provide an inverted mirror of the assertions of the nation-state, particularly those of an imperial character.[2] This essay will consider representations of history in two contemporary transnational cinematic autobiographies, focusing on how they undo or challenge the presumptive coherence of time and space underlying histories articulated by and through nation-states. They do so by drawing on the subjective enunciation of autobiography and the paradoxical status of the cinematic image — its potential for both evidential certitude and illusionist rapture.

By cinematic autobiography, I mean film texts in which the director employs strategies of self-narration and takes him or herself as subject matter, usually serving as narrator and protagonist of the resulting narrative. Though this definition includes films that investigate the thoughts, feelings, and experiences of supposedly coherent selves, the work I will discuss employs experimental, self-reflexive form that calls such a self into question. Significantly, contemporary transnational minority and feminist filmmakers frequently use autobiography and self-narration to undermine the coherence of their own voice and identity.[3] The autobiographical form foregrounds the speaker's voice and experiences, while the use of self-reflexive formal and narrative strategies allows the filmmaker concretely yet paradoxically to register "the nonidentity experienced by minorities as the oppressive effects of Western philosophies of identity" (JanMohamed and Lloyd 16). However, these autobiographers have been mindful of the conclusion subsequently outlined by Abdul JanMohamed and David Lloyd to the effect that this nonidentity "is the strongest reason that a rigorously critical minority discourse, in its positive transformation of the discourses emerging from that nonidentity, should not merely fall back on the oppositional affirmation of an essential ethnic or gender identity" (16).

Thus these films perform and embody different encounters between the rhetorics of modernity and postmodernity (the end of master narratives, the death of the subject and of history, etc.) and the self-narration of transnational minority subjects. That is, the discursive, postmodern innovation of these texts arises from the narrational instability and the material disadvantages of the lives they ultimately cannot envision by means of conventional representation. Yet, the self-reflexive autobiographical form also enables these filmmakers to document aspects of transnational minoritarian experience while also certifying the differences and complexity riddling this experience, thereby precluding any essentialist expression or understanding of it.

In choosing film as their medium, these artists avail themselves of the temporally and spatially concrete and specific quality of the cinematic image (Nichols 176). By also putting their bodies in front of the camera, the "histories" they recount are necessarily "embodied, corporeal" (174). But these filmmakers use the specificity and corporeality of the cinematic image to register a material feature of their lives—the representational absence and invisibility integral to transnational minority experience. Using the eloquence and compression of images, these filmmakers solicit spectators' affect in relation to historical negations and absences while never submitting to their reification.

Autobiography provides an apt vehicle for such complex expression. A substantial tradition exists within autobiography that highlights the necessary presence of the subject in knowledge and underscores the consequent instability of both in relation to truth. These filmmakers adapt this tradition to their concerns with historical representation. They draw from an array of histories and sources—the history of Euro-American experimental cinema, of ethnic and transnational autobiography and biography across media, of experimental autobiography—and make use of their transnational minoritarian experience to transform aspects of their personal lives or their culture into imaginative, political and/or analytical tropes that are exteriorized and/or formalized in their narratives. In so doing, they explicitly relate presumably private, subjective concerns— interiority, affect, and any individuated sense of self—to the material world, its apparatuses, and its social relations.

In effect, by inventing, innovating, and sometimes fictionalizing their autobiographies in this way, the filmmakers also localize and historicize them, transgressing the usual affective, personal conventions that contain self-representation and instead invoking public rhetorics and institutions to which the self is subject. For example, Cheryl Dunye's film documents, historicizes, and critiques the relationship between Hollywood film and its spectators' desire by using this industry's visual and narrative conventions to compel the spectators of her film to want the Watermelon Woman, want her to have existed, as much as she does. By thereby appropriating and remotivating this visual and narrational rhetoric, another story emerges that provides a critical perspective on this institution, its conventions, and the profoundly historical character of desire and its relationship to media. Dunye skillfully blends the cinema's capacity to document and to elicit desire, such that the spectators of her film feel the pain of the absence she (falsely) documents.

The filmmakers that I will focus on in this essay also appropriate and remotivate the filmic representation of coherent national histories: they either make manifest their nonidentity in such histories or they invert the conventional relationship between autobiography and history. Rather than history being the overarching and tacit narrative in which autobiography takes place, autobiography serves as the overarching framework within which history is explicitly narrated, situated, and embodied. In this respect, these films can be seen as transforming the tradition of experimental autobiography in the United States. Filmmakers of the classical avant-garde originally used self-narration and autobiography to contest the imaginary mystification and "universalism" of Hollywood storytelling. Critically, this challenge was understood and canonized exclusively in formalist terms.

Transnational minoritarian film nuances experimental autobiographical films' conventional identification with formalist aesthetics and their tacit generic location within discrete national cinemas. Refusing formal self-reflexivity in and of itself, these filmmakers instead make use of self-reflexive rhetorical strategies to situate their subjectivity and vision within and in some instances as deriving from historical, political, and cultural circumstances and discourses.[4] Thus instead of rarified aesthetic creations expressive of their own idiosyncratic points of view, these filmmakers appropriate historical modes of visual documentation, incorporating newsreels, photos, and documentary and industry film footage within their autobiographies. They therefore materially register the absence of or misrepresentation of transnational minorities, their "nonidentity" in hegemonic media, as a condition of their own self-narration.

From among many possible choices, I would like to consider the work of three filmmakers, Rea Tajiri, Guillermo Verdecchia, and Ramiro Puerta, who directly but in very different ways mobilize questions concerning the representation and narration of history within a transnational — and thereby spatially ambiguous — framework. These filmmakers each articulate their films around tropes, images, and stereotypes associated with their respective transnational cultures, but they refashion and remotivate them, such that these representations serve an inventive and critical rather than a stereotypic function.[5] Tajiri invokes the temporal, genealogical tropes of generations, ancestors, and spirits to elaborate upon the Japanese American experience of internment during World War II in *History and Memory* (1991). The internment constituted an attempt by the United States to create an internal border, to spatially sequester and differentiate Japanese Americans from the larger U.S. population.[6] Tajiri's video focuses on the internment's effects on different generations of Japanese Americans, using narratives of this trauma to undermine the structures of credibility supporting the U.S. media's account of this event.[7] Verdecchia and Puerta look at the recurring and persistent historical and subjective disturbances provoked by borders in their film *Crucero* (1994). Borders, in creating nations, also create the transnational, both within and outside the nation. Indeed the border is nothing if not a transnational space. Verdecchia and Puerta's film explores the cost exacted on individuals by the fantasy of nation and belonging, by the collusion between geopolitical space and identity perpetuated by the idea of the coherent nation. They problematize the conjunction of space, identity, and history, using the figures of the border, the Pachuco, and the Latin lover.

Spectacles and Specters: Rea Tajiri's History and Memory

The opening to Rea Tajiri's video *History and Memory* is significant for what it withholds: the image. Instead, a lengthy scroll of text, white letters on black background headed by the date "December 7, 1961," describes an aerial shot of a man and woman that is *not* there as an image. This scroll is followed by another, in parentheses and italics, that grounds this absent shot, absent image in a very specific historical context: "The spirit of my grandfather witnesses my father and mother as they have an argument about the unexplained nightmares their daughter has been having on the twentieth anniversary of the bombing of Pearl Harbor, the day that changed the lives of 110,000 Japanese Americans who shortly after were forced by the U.S. Government to sell their property, homes, cars, possessions, leave their communities and relocate to internment camps." In this sequence, history is conjoined with an impossible perception, an event and a location for which there is no image; a visual framing (overhead — a crane shot? A zoom?) is wedded to, explicated by a metaphysical conceit. We are going to hear a ghost story, a horror story, a history lesson filtered through, haunted by generations of family and of images.

As we read this scroll, we are compelled to imagine three very different scenes: the point of view of an ancestral spirit, the grandfather, who has passed; the argument in the present between the parents; and the nightmares and psychic trauma of their daughter whose future includes the making of *History and Memory*. Three generations of Japanese Americans stand in very different relation to Pearl Harbor and the subsequent internment. The grandfather, dead before the war, witnesses his son and daughter-in-law, who experienced the war and internment directly, grapple with its deleterious effects on their daughter, born after it was over. The transnational marks those in each generation and their difference from one another: the grandfather is an Issei or immigrant; the parents, Nisei or first generation American-born; their daughter, the filmmaker, a Sansei or second-generation Japanese-American (Yamamoto xiii; Feng 127 n. 29). From the outset mobilizing the very different experiences of these three generations, Tajiri avoids making a film in which Japanese Americans are reified as a unified group while also underscoring a significant cultural and transnational feature of all of their lives: that the distinction between generations in the United States is named and formalized.

Near the end of this scroll, we hear Tajiri's voice-over talking about a fragment, an image she has always had in her mind. The image, of her mother standing at a faucet filling a canteen with very cold water, appears on the screen for a couple of seconds, as Tajiri says, "The sun's just so hot, it's just beating down and there's this dust that gets in everywhere and they're always sweeping the floors." The image Tajiri shows us, an image that haunts her, is her invention, her reenactment of a memory she could not possibly have had. Acting the part of her mother, impersonating her (experience) and also filming this impersonation, Tajiri remembers and reenacts an experience her mother had before she was born, a memory her mother has repressed almost completely. Though the image, presented as Tajiri's own memory, is referentially and logically false, her video will articulate a context in which its lack of a referent will document the historical truth of memories that do not exist for a history that *did* happen.

Tajiri's film draws from both prose and cinematic autobiographical, fiction, and documentary traditions to underscore the profoundly mediated character of that context. Literary theorist Traise Yamamoto notes that Japanese American autobiography, until recently almost exclusively produced by the Nisei, emerged after World War II, a direct if paradoxical consequence of the war and the experience of the internment (112–113). She writes:

Japanese American autobiography exists between two impulses: historical motive and cultural reticence. On the one hand, Nisei autobiographies are the written record of a community betrayed by the dark side of democracy — majority rule or . . . majority racist hysteria. On the other hand, the autobiographical form is fundamentally at odds with the Nisei tendency to downplay the individual self, a behavioral adaptation largely shaped by the desire to "fit in" and thus avoid racist discrimination. (105)

Consequently, the theme of a split or bifurcated self "runs throughout all Nisei autobiographies" (114). In choosing the internment and how it has affected her, Tajiri locates her film within a tradition springing from her mother's generation, but in Tajiri's autobiography, the splits or bifurcations running through it divide her generation from her mother's. As we learn later in the film, Tajiri feels betrayed by and angry with what she perceives to be her mother's reticence and refusal to tell her about the camps.

To compensate for her mother's silence, Tajiri decides she will tell the story from her perspective. She searches the National Archives and film archives for films, documentaries, written accounts, and documents from the camps and she interviews family, relatives, and other internees and their families. But Tajiri is also a filmmaker and she synthesizes the concerns animating her research with those of avant-garde self-reflexive filmmaking, thereby enhancing and transforming the scope of both.[8] Though some criticized her for doing so (see Hansen, Higashi, and Hulser), other critics and theorists have found Tajiri's work exemplary of "the fragmented consciousness" of feminist minoritarian experimental autobiographers (Lesage 310) and of those ethnic filmmakers whose approach is "changing the entire landscape of media representations" (Ginsburg 8).

In its opening minutes, Tajiri's film refers to complicated relationships involving history, witnessing, dreaming, memory, representation, and different modes of visual documentation based on her family's and many other Japanese Americans' experience of trauma in the aftermath of Pearl Harbor. In its representational structure, the film implements provocative relationships among its signal concerns: Tajiri's familial genealogy, her parents, her ancestors, and their memories and witness, living or dead, of Pearl Harbor and the subsequent Japanese American internment; the genealogy and range of public and popular images, photographs, documentary, and fiction film footage mediating these same events; and finally the various media within which these images are conveyed to us. Significantly, Tajiri shot *History and Memory* on video, not film, a format in which the "generation" of the recording poses both possibilities and concerns. Much of the visual footage in *History and Memory* is dubbed from other filmic sources, much of it from the 1940s and 1950s, interspersed with live video footage Tajiri shot during the making of the film in the early 1990s. The diverse generations and resulting historicity of the images brought into relation and conflict by the video's montage thereby reflexively echoes the conflicts and differences in perspective among different generations and members of Tajiri's family.[9]

In addition, as Lucy Fischer notes in her discussion of this film, Tajiri generally avoids synchronous sound, layering images with voice-overs and commentary (202). In this, the construction of the video and its relationship to the historical events with which it is concerned allegorize Tajiri and her generation's experience of the camps — it is not "live" nor synchronous but is nevertheless recorded or "dubbed" in their psyches, as her "unexplained nightmares" as a child attest. At the level of the images represented, Tajiri uses the documentation she has amassed to systematically reference and retell the official story of the camps through the spectacular modes (Department of War Information documentaries, newsreel and Army Signal Corps footage, Hollywood films from then and now, etc.) in which it was represented. And she just as systematically underscores the partial and flawed character of the visual historical record by aligning its images and accounts with the personal testimonies and material fragments (ID cards, a wooden bird, a piece of tar paper from the camps) she gathers from her family and other former internees, stories and images that the official record either withholds or that do not exist.[10]

Tajiri is led to unearth these stories by puzzling and logically inexplicable behaviors in her own generation. What of her memory of her mother at the faucet in the camp where she was interred years before Tajiri was born? And what of the nightmares she began having as a young girl on the anniversary of Pearl Harbor? And what of her sister's curious behavior, the visual rendering of which opens the film proper, of following a boy on whom she had a crush through the park every day after school? Tajiri's voice-over tells us this was a phase her sister went through in high school and notes: "Rather than talk to him, she told me, she preferred to take his picture." Intercut with film stills of famous couples (Elizabeth Taylor and Montgomery Clift, Rock Hudson and Dorothy Malone, Jack and Jackie) and seemingly anomalously, from *Gulliver's Travels*, black-

and-white video footage depicts Tajiri's sister attempting to pose her re-luctant subject. Tajiri explains that her sister had a box full of pictures of Hollywood movie stars, inherited from an aunt, that she would pore over. She wonders "where my sister's habit of observing others from a distance came from." We see the stills. Her sister craves images but they are all of white people. Her desire is not for the Japanese American boy but for his image.

Subsequently, under a caption titled "History," Tajiri shows us footage from a 1941 newsreel titled "Attack on Pearl Harbor." On the sound track she muses, "There are things which have happened in the world while there were cameras watching, things we have images for." A clip from *From Here to Eternity* (1953) follows, under the caption "History," as Tajiri continues: "There are other things that happened while there were no cameras watching which we re-stage to have images of." Two more clips, one taken from captured Japanese footage from *Hawai Mare Okino Senjo Eigwa* (1942) and the last from the John Ford documentary *December 7th* (1943), illustrate Tajiri's final observations on images and events: "There are things which have happened for which the only images that exist are in the minds of the observers present at the time, while there are things that have happened for which there are no observers save for the spirits of the dead." These meditations, aligned with the anecdote about her sister, subtly confound "private" issues of desire and sexuality with "public" concerns of history, documentation, and witnessing. Narrative and docu-mentary film, photographs, and film stills solicit and suture private desires and identities within public imaginings, as in the instance of Tajiri's sister, but extend beyond entertainment to world-historical events.[11] Yet what Tajiri's film is concerned with are the images, both fictional and documen-tary, which are withheld, whose effects — on her sister's desires, on her own dreams — are registered and interconnected by their absence.

Tajiri renders this concern by contrasting publicly recorded and dis-seminated historical accounts of Pearl Harbor and the subsequent intern-ment of Japanese Americans with the memories and records of those American citizens whose lives were uprooted, their constitutional rights abrogated, their homes and possessions lost.[12] She represents these dif-ferent perspectives in the sound, image, and text tracks of her film. A clip from Curtiz's *Yankee Doodle Dandy* (1942) featuring the song lyric "We're one for all, all for one" in the war effort prefaces Tajiri's narrative of her mother's and father's entire families being interned while her father was serving in the U.S. Army. Tajiri's ongoing voice-over and the voices of her aunts, her father, her brother, and her mother radically alter the meaning of what we are seeing on the screen. Later in the text, for example, over rare camp film footage, we see smiling Japanese Americans digging ditches and performing other daily activities as Tajiri remembers "living in a family full of ghosts. I could remember a time of great sadness before I was born." The lie of the smiles, of the "home movies" in the camp is revealed by an impossible memory whose assertion we nevertheless immediately recognize as the truth. Tajiri continually documents the effects of an intergenerational memory whose temporality completely eludes the logical, contemporaneous, and subject-bound relationship we take to exist between an event and its experience. She begins her film with the puzzling memories and behaviors of her generation, only to trace their causes to the experiences of her parents, experiences they have not told her about and, in the case of Tajiri's mother, do not remember.[13]

Tajiri's script inverts the usual hierarchy between a public national history and private memories in relation to truth. But she enacts this inversion in a film that consistently undercuts or qualifies its own referential function and locates the truth in what we are not seeing, in images that exist not as documentation but as fiction, and finally in experiences of which there is no recollection. She articulates these referential enigmas primarily through the relations she constructs between the image and the sound tracks. Save for one brief clip of her looking at images and stills and her impersonation of her mother at the faucet, Tajiri's presence in the film consists entirely of her disembodied voice-over — a "voice of god" technique that mimics the authoritarian voice-over of traditional documentary. Yet rather than recounting "just the facts," Tajiri's narration is intimate, personal, autobiographical. Though the experiences she and other members of her family detail in voice-over are articulated as their own, in some instances they are inconsistent with each other, as if Tajiri derived her script from an amalgam of survivors' testimonies and delivered them as her family's own. In contradistinction, on the image track, Tajiri's family does not appear live on the screen, save for two very brief moments, but rather in old photos and in various identification cards intercut with footage of other, usually anonymous internees. Tajiri also uses text of questions ("Who chose what stories to tell?") and of family anecdotes and stories superimposed on documentary images to interrogate, question, and undercut what they depict.

Thus, for the most part, Tajiri and her family remain invisible, heard but not seen. Sumiko Higashi argues that, in this, "Tajiri's representa-

tional strategy mirrors . . . the dominant discourse it engages in debate"
and effectively erases the "subjectivity of Japanese internees" (1182). Yet
Higashi herself opens her review by observing that Japanese Americans
are "stereotyped as the 'quiet Americans' " (1181), a stereotype that Tajiri
emphatically refutes in the multiple voices and testimonies that animate
her soundtrack and the multiple texts superimposed on the image track.
More importantly, in refusing to match familial voices with familial bodies, Tajiri maintains the film's intimate and concrete connection with
its audience, while also disengaging these stories, these voices from specific bodies, specific individuals. The testimonies that we hear are consequently both concrete and generalized. Thus Tajiri cultivates identification and empathy with her family's plight while also never allowing the
trauma documented by the video to be limited to what happened to them.

Tajiri uses documentary and entertainment imagery to certify its limits, its lacunae. Rather than make a film that fills in what was historically
left out, she creates an image (of her mother at the faucet) to demonstrate
the evidentiary capacity of absence.[14] The end of the video consists of
footage depicting Tajiri literally re-searching her mother's lost memory
of the camps — that is, she visually retraces her mother's journey there,
videotaping the landscape rushing by, as we hear her mother's voice on the
sound track saying, "I don't remember this. I don't remember how we got
there." Here Tajiri uses the image to assert the truth of memory over that
which we understand as history by documenting the traumatic memories
her mother *does not* have.

In the official historical records whose documentation Tajiri visually
cites throughout her film, the United States represents itself to its citizens
as homogenous, coherent, all for one and one for all. Yet the specters and
traumatized silence that haunt this representation of a national history
depict its coherence as utterly illusory, testifying to what the (idea of the)
nation both depends upon and cannot possibly realize — its foundational
fantasy of an abstract citizen that every body can inhabit equally. Against
the idealism of this abstraction, Tajiri musters the ghosts, the absences,
the gaps in the national history to which this abstraction gives rise. The
notion of the transnational thereby emerges in the paradox documented
by her film: that the nation cannot contain or adequately represent the
very people who constitute it precisely because the "people" exist not as
an unmarked unity but through their differences, differences that traverse
the nation and its histories.

Tajiri then ends the video, having explicated the elusive image with which she began it—that of her mother filling a canteen with water at a faucet. She has been living with this image and now she has given it a story. Taking up the stereotypic conceit of ghosts and ancestors, Tajiri fashions a research trope around which to articulate the impossibility of a representative national history in relation to the transnational body(ies) of its (minority) citizenry. Her ghosts, her specters take shape from the suppression of historical atrocities and the memories they have obliterated.

Finally, she made this image for her mother, made a memory neither of them had in a history that was stolen from them. Tajiri brings a ghost into the world of representation, placing it into struggle with the official story by giving it epistemological status that ultimately outweighs its (false) ontological one.

Crucero: "The Border Is You!"

In their film *Crucero/Crossroads* (1994), filmmaker Ramiro Puerta and writer/performance artist/actor Guillermo Verdecchia take up and foreground the trope of the border, consciously positioning themselves in relation to theoretical and narrative considerations of it in Chicana/o border autobiographies. This relation is signaled in the title of Verdecchia's autobiographical performance piece, *Fronteras Americanas (American Borders)*, from which the film is taken, which gestures to Gloria Anzaldúa's foundational autobiographical/theoretical work, *Borderlands/La Frontera* (1987). As subsequent critics have noted, Anzaldúa's text unleashed a "flood" of work in "border studies."[15] While her articulation specifies the United States–Mexico border, "the birthplace, really, of border studies and its methods of analysis"(Michaelson and Johnson 1) the border quickly comes to represent in a metaphorical sense all interstitial or liminal spaces or identities precipitated by a boundary or norm.[16] While *Crucero's* narrative locates itself in relation to an actual border, it does so with a twist. The film features Verdecchia narrating, acting out, and commenting on aspects of his life and identity. In life, as in the film, Verdecchia is a Latino, a Toronto-based actor, who identifies as a Chicano even though he was born in Argentina and has only ever felt at home living in Paris as an illegal with a perfect French accent. The borders he contends with in *Crucero* are those between Canada and Mexico, a contention that thereby renders the entire United States as a border zone between these two countries with the Chicano as its archetypal subject. In this geopolitical reimagining of nations and the transnational space that separates them, *Crucero* exposes the normative relationships between individual and nation, narrative and history underpinning autobiography by refusing to conflate them in the way they usually are. If films in the mode of Tajiri's offer a transnational critique of the nation and the media and the adequacy of their representation of all of their subjects on a temporal axis, *Crucero* uses the spatial figure of the border to fracture the coherence of the subject, nation, and history. Thus the film conceives of borders not according to the physical contiguity of nations, but rather in relation to autobiographical subjectivity. But Verdecchia confronts structural and internalized borders or schisms as well.

Conforming to some of the generic markers of the autobiographical film (Verdecchia the writer is also Verdecchia the narrator and one of the two main characters), *Crucero/Crossroads* also confounds the fundamental impulse of the genre (a narrative about the self written, told, and filmed by the self in question) by being a collaborative venture, with Ramiro Puerta behind the camera, real-izing Verdecchia's autobiographical performance. This doubling in the production of the film is mirrored in its narrative. On screen, Verdecchia's confusion about his complex identity is acted out by two different dramatic personae, both played by him, but each inhabiting completely different responses and orientations to his immigrant experience and cultural difference. While as Guillermo Verdecchia, he acts out an interiorized personal and psychological position, while his alter ego Facundo Morales Secundo inhabits Latino stereotypes with a vengeance to publicly and politically challenge culturally racist representations.

Verdecchia's alter ego's name, "Facundo," directly alludes to sources in Latin American literature and autobiography whose structure and characters appear to have influenced the schismatic subjectivity at the heart of *Crucero*. *Facundo* is the title of a famous novel by the exiled Argentine writer Sarmiento, who also wrote several autobiographies. Sylvia Malloy observes: "The books where [Sarmiento] seems to strive the most for personal figuration [are] *Recuerdos de provincia*, his own autobiography, and *Facundo*, the biography of his enemy and mirror image Quiroga and, it might be argued, an oblique portrait of himself" (29). Verdecchia borrows the figure of the antagonistic double to make manifest contradictory subjective responses to immigration and transnational difference, allowing them to interact in his embodiments of them.

In the film, Verdecchia shifts languages (Spanish, English, and French), accents, and affects as he brushes his teeth, walks down the street, irons his clothes, has coffee, goes to a club to dance, and performs any number of everyday activities. His affective and linguistic shifts are dictated by the actor's movement back and forth between his two different personae — his own, Guillermo Verdecchia, and that of Facundo, a man who wears a bolero, a costume native to Argentina, and identifies himself as a *pachuco*, a term referring to a particular Mexican American youth culture in the 1940s. In his own embodiment, Guillermo is confused about his identity, about where he fits in. He has strange physical maladies that doctors cannot diagnose and for which he sees both a therapist and a *curandero* or healer. Guillermo, whose dialogue is rendered in the film strictly in voice-over, remembers with pain and embarrassment the contortions his grade school teacher Miss Wiseman went through on the first day of class when she tried to pronounce his name. As he narrates this memory, we see a close-up of a woman's lips, twisted and distorted, as she tries to pronounce "Guillermo Verdecchia." The film emphatically registers through the personae of Guillermo what Abdul JanMohamed and David Lloyd identify as the "damage more or less systematically inflicted on cultures produced as minorities by the dominant culture" (4). The film then counterposes this effect with another, embodied in the persona of Facundo.

Earlier in the film, we have seen that Facundo has a completely different approach to these kinds of problems. As he sashays down the street, speaking directly to the camera as he does throughout the film, he says in accented English: "When I moved here, people would say to me "Sorry? What's the name?" I would tell them "Fac un do/Facundo." They would say, "Wow, that's a new one. Mind if I call you Fac?" "No, not at all — mind if I call you 'shithead'?" Because of the problems with his name, Facundo had to come up with a Saxonical name: "I go by the name Wideload McKenna now." Wideload/Facundo is a mover and a shaker. He wants to move out of the barrio because it is going to the dogs — yuppies are moving in, renovating, and making a lot of noise. Because Latinos are a hot commodity, he talks to a Saxon developer about starting a Third World theme park in a toxic waste dump because "you people love that kind of shit." His theme park will undersell travel agents who are making lots of money selling package tours to Brazilian slums.

The film's interplay between Guillermo and Facundo transforms the spatial boundary of the "border" into the dilemma of the crossroads — which way to go, which way to be — constituted by the very different ways in which these two "identities" react to the social and political circumstances that situate them as belonging or alienated. These circumstances are what we understand as history. Guillermo suffers; there is no secure, unified place for him in his multiple and liminal identities. Facundo aggressively appropriates multiple Latino stereotypes and fashions to represent and act out the logic of ethnic discrimination and racism. Through them, the film asks: What does one do when knowledge, identity, history, and nationality, like one's public, private, sexual, professional, and emotional selves, are fissured and fragmented by what are generally represented as irreconcilable differences? How does one live or narrate such a conflicted self, self-knowledge, and national identity? In what language? With what kind of cinematic or narrative devices? How does one trace a history, a genealogy from the standpoint of many nations, many origins whose stories and histories contest one another? The genre of autobiography, especially in its Latin American variant, provides the perfect vehicle, as Malloy observes: "A strong testimonial stance informs autobiographical writing in Spanish America. If not always perceiving themselves as historians, autobiographers will continue to see themselves as witnesses . . . capturing a tension between self and other, . . . generating a reflection on the fluctuating place of the subject within its community, allowing for other voices, besides that of the 'I' to be heard in the text" (8–9).

While Guillermo testifies to his experiences, focuses on his alienation from the many communities with which he has been involved but does not feel he belongs, Facundo/Wideload turns the tables. While Guillermo resorts to history and historical explanation to resolve the mystery of his disparate selves, Facundo/Wideload becomes an ethnographer of Saxon rituals and culture.

As we watch Guillermo go to a café, we hear his voice-over recounting such a history:

Maybe it starts with Columbus. Maybe it starts with the genius Arab engineer who invented the rudder. Maybe a little history is required to put this all in order. Our history begins approximately 200 million years ago in the Triassic period of the Mesozoic Era when the original supercontinent broke up and the continents of the earth assumed the shapes we now recognize.

5000 B.C.: The first settlements appear in the highlands of Mexico and in the Andes mountains.

Early 1400s A.D.: Joan of Arc is born and shortly thereafter, burned. At the same time, the Incas in Peru develop a highly efficient political system.

1492: Catholic Spain is very busy integrating the Moors.

Guillermo continues, blending references to Velazquez, Beethoven, and Goya with U.S. and French attacks on Mexico in the nineteenth century, the U.S. acquisition of the Panama Canal, alluding to Beatrix Potter and the U.S. attack on Cuba in the twentieth century. His history culminates in 1969: "1969: Richard Nixon is inaugurated as president of the U.S., Samuel Beckett is awarded the Nobel Prize for literature, the Montreal Canadiens win the Stanley Cup for hockey, and I attend my first day of classes at Anne Hathaway Public School."

The history that Guillermo recounts begins with geology, geography, and genealogy initially merged, then fragmenting.[17] A civilization develops in the Americas and Verdecchia then gives a "world" history patched together from events whose temporality is similar or whose occurrence brings different people together. In the first instance, he contrasts the barbarism of France (the burning of Joan of Arc) with the political efficiency of the Incas. In the second, he recounts the exploits of the Spanish very busily integrating the Moors, an assimilation illustrated by Verdecchia stirring sugar in his coffee, trade items that were the economic cornerstone of colonialism. In the modern period, Mexico becomes the object of U.S. and European aggression, a history that is not new. What is new is the parallel Guillermo makes between Beatrix Potter (of Peter Rabbit fame) and the U.S. control of the Panama Canal, and, by extension, the Americas. His grand historical narrative becomes idiosyncratic in its treatment of the twentieth century, culminating not in another historical event, but in the symbolic nationalism of sport and the personal banality of his first day of school: "My name is next. Minutes, hours, a century passes as the teacher forces her mouth into shapes hitherto unknown to the human race as she attempts to pronounce my name. 'Gwillyou-ree-moo . . . Verdeek-cheea?' I put my hand up. I am a minuscule boy with ungovernable black hair, antennae, and gills where everyone else has a mouth. 'You can call me Willie,' I say. The antennae and gills disappear." The teacher's mangling of his name signals the crisis of this entire history — his difference is monstrous, he has gills and antennae instead of a mouth. He accedes to assimilation — "You can call me Willie" and as he does, his difference disappears, but so does he.

What is significant about the history Guillermo recounts is not only its idiosyncrasy but that it exemplifies the seemingly arbitrary character of (any transnational) historical narration divorced from the perspective of a distinct location or nation. While Guillermo tells this history to explain his abjection and lack of a sense of a distinct self and place, his account also reveals the dependency of historical narration on a coherent sense of space. Guillermo's history also explains the emergence of his alter ego, Facundo, who embodies an entirely different relation to history, that of hyperidentification.

Facundo is the "trickster at the crossroads who is always the master of possibility."[18] He facetiously assimilates by taking the name of Wideload McKenna and counters the tragedy of Guillermo's history with ethnographic comedy, specifying and historicizing whiteness. In nominally tolerant and patronizing tones, he describes Saxonian identity and mating rituals. "I like you Saxons," he says, "I have the greatest respect for your culture." He spends some time commenting on Saxonic dancing, which he finds "so free that nothing gets in the way, not even the rhythm." In true anthropological fashion, he even provides an ethnographic film that depicts "the morris dance," a Saxon mating ritual "of sexual joy." The footage we see is of a group of white men dressed in Bavarian shorts, knee socks, suspenders, and bells, hopping around to the high-pitched sound of a flute. Wideload observes: "You have the morris dance and we have de mambo, de rumba, de cumbia, de son, son-guarijo, son-changui, de charanga, de merengue, de tango, de samba, salsa . . . shall I continue?"

Facundo inhabits Anglo projections (of, for example, the "Latin lover") in a definitive charismatic identity, while the "real" Guillermo seems diffident and diffuse. Each embodies a different maneuvering or positioning toward history: the one abject, the other that of hyperidentification. The two are formally differentiated by two different narrational modes—while Guillermo's internal monologues are rendered in voice-over narration, Facundo/Wideload speaks to the camera, directly addressing the film's audience. If, as Charles Ramirez Berg has observed, "Who speaks the narration speaks History" (89), *Crucero* bifurcates the narration of its history into two voices—that of the individual who suffers the history he tries to narrate and that of mimetic performativity, the stereotype, the colonialist hallucination talking back to, striking back at the imaginary that precipitated him.[19] Finally, *Crucero* uses the split subjectivity at the center of its autobiography to disarticulate the coherence of individual and nation, history and narrative. While the response of neither persona—Verdecchia nor Facundo—is adequate in and of itself, both together suggest that subjectivity is never simply private nor completely within or outside of the myths and machinations of the nation and the state.

Conclusion: Giving Minor Pasts a Future

Stories are for joining the past to the future.
— Sharon O'Brien

Both Rea Tajiri's *History and Memory* and Guillermo Verdecchia and Ramiro Puerta's *Crucero* amply demonstrate the cogent synthesis of theory, material evidence, and narrative pleasure that can be attained in the autobiographical video and film. Though the narrative for both films comes from the transnational minoritarian experience of the filmmakers and that material elicits affect and identification from the films' audiences, the rhetorical construction of each film insures that this identification take place within transnational historical narration, a narration that gives the lie to any uncomplicated, "essential" identity and any coherent national history. Thus these films exploit the pleasure of narrative, of humor, of identification, while also emphasizing that "becoming minor" is not a question of essence (as the stereotypes of minorities in dominant ideology would want us to believe) but a question of position: a subject position that in the final analysis can be defined only in "political" terms — that is, in terms of the effects of economic exploitation, political disenfranchisement, social manipulation, and ideological domination on the cultural formation of minority subjects and discourses (JanMohamed and Lloyd 9).

In each of these films, the autobiographer's transnational experience cannot be narrated within a history predicated on the collapse/coherence of space and time characteristic of the historicity of nation-states. Rather, the internment of Tajiri's mother and other Japanese Americans effected an internal border, a non-American America where their otherness, their threat could be contained. The trauma of this splitting off, this division, rent the psyches of those who experienced it and then sundered this generation from their children in a silence that only seemed protective. Tajiri probes the disturbances in temporality, in generation, and in history of the public and private silences surrounding the internment. In imposing spatial boundaries on Japanese Americans, the nation's ability to historically account for this event was fissured as well.

Puerta and Verdecchia address a similar problematic but from a perspective at once more specific—the psyche of the autobiographer—and more general, in Verdecchia's attempt to narrate his life and his history from a transnational Latino perspective. Using the figure of the double, *Crucero* attempts to apprehend the contradictory but related logics of the multiple and the fragment, the transnational and the personal, concluding in the end that they are inextricable. As *Crucero* ends, Guillermo recalls hearing his curandero saying to him as he is passing out, "The border, the border is *you!*" The fissures and the inadequacies of the nation and the state locate themselves in the body of the transnational minority subject. In giving this elusive body a past, these transnational autobiographies give a different historical body to the future.

Notes

1 In 1978, P. Adams Sitney, then the preeminent theorist of the American avant-garde, argued that "true cinematic autobiography" resulted from the self-reflexive equation experimental filmmakers developed between the cinematic apparatus and their own perceptions. Sitney asserted that, rather in the spirit of the romantic artist, the filmic autobiographer composes his film from what and how he sees (100). Despite the fact that the 1970s saw a creative explosion of autobiographical filmmaking by minority and feminist filmmakers, Sitney drew all of his examples from the films of white men. Perhaps even more significantly, his formalist definition excluded any consideration of history, context, or diverse identities in its definition of legitimate autobiographical film.

2 Writing on the United States, Robert Carr analyzes the features of the "interested representation" of history promoted by primary imperialist powers. He notes: "Narratives of geography collapse into narratives of history to create an understanding of, at first, the Anglo-European's right to any land they stumbled across or took by force."

3 Examples include Cheryl Dunye's *Watermelon Woman*, Su Friedrich's *The Ties That Bind* and *Sink or Swim*, Bill Jone's *Massillon* and *Finished*, Marlon Rigg's *Tongues Untied*; *Black Is, Black Ain't*; and *Kidlat Tahimik's Perfumed Nightmare*; Janice Tanaka's *Who's Going to Pay for These Donuts Anyway*, Rea Tajiri's *History and Memory*, and Guillermo Verdecchia and Ramiro Puerta's *Crucero*.

4 Julia Lesage cogently theorizes this relationship—between oppressive material circumstances and the formal make-up of women's experimental autobiographical film—in "Women's Fragmented Consciousness in Feminist Experimental Autobiographical Video," an article which has influenced my approach here.

5 For a summary of the scholarship on stereotypes and racialization in film, see Wiegman 158–168. On diverse uses of the stereotype, see Rosello. Mimura describes Tajri's work, among others, as having to do with invention (156).

6 Thanks to Carole-Anne Tyler for pointing this out to me.

7   See Nornes and Xing for their views of how Tajiri uses memory to challenge
    official accounts of history.

8   For an excellent overview of the tradition of independent Asian American film-
    making within which internment documentaries were made, see Tajima 10–33.
    Tajiri can also be seen as implementing in film what Michael M. J. Fischer argued
    was being accomplished in postmodern ethnic autobiography in the eighties, "a
    (re-)invention and discovery of a vision, both ethical and future-oriented," to-
    gether with an insistence on "a pluralist, multidimensional, or multifaceted con-
    cept of self" (196).

9   See Feng's astute discussion of Tajiri's montage as an example of Bakhtinian
    dialogism (76–79, 93–98).

10 In an impressive article that provides crucial contextual information on this video,
    Kent Ono argues that Tajiri uses the visual track to discredit "that which has been
    orally given, rendering the image superior to the oral" (137). My reading does not
    see the visual track of this film as dominant. I am more in agreement with Feng on
    the "aura of indeterminancy" provoked by the interplay of visual and aural tracks,
    though I find the aural track to carry more of the tape's truth value. Feng, 92.

11 Note Feng's different emphasis on the interrelation between public and private
    constructed by this film.

12 For detailed accounts of the injustices suffered by Japanese Americans, see Roger
    Daniels, *Prisoners without Trial: Japanese Americans in World War II* (New York:
    Hill and Wang, 1993).

13 Her narrative is very similar to the temporally displaced experiences characteris-
    tic of trauma victims, but in Tajiri's video, traumatic effects are imprinted upon a
    subsequent generation from whom the story of the traumatic experience has
    been withheld. Tajiri's film is also in some respects an example of what Hirsch
    calls "postmemory," an imaginative and creative investment in the past experi-
    enced by children of Holocaust survivors or survivors of other kinds of world-
    historical trauma whose lives are shaped by stories of events that occurred before
    their birth. These stories, of the previous generation, overwhelm those of the
    second generation (22). Tajiri quite clearly has an imaginative and creative invest-
    ment in her mother's story, but again Tajiri's account differs from the phenome-
    non that Hirsch describes in that her parents withheld the stories of the in-
    ternment and what they experienced. On trauma and its effects, see Caruth,
    Unclaimed Experience and *Trauma*; and LaCapra. On postmemory, see Hirsch.
    See Sturken's use of this concept in her analysis of why the Japanese internment
    never attained "certain kinds of direct cultural representation," an analysis occa-
    sioned by Tajiri's *History and Memory*.

14 Tajiri is also very careful to put the story she is telling in relation to other
    minorities and the constitutional inequities they have suffered. *History and Mem-
    ory* includes a savagely ironic segment of Paul Robeson singing "*The Battle Hymn
    of the Republic*" in front of the Lincoln memorial, and Tajiri points out that the
    camp in which her family was interred was built on land taken from an Indian
    Reservation.

15 See Michaelsen and Johnson 1. While they attest to Anzaldúa's influence in their

opening remarks, Michaelson and Johnson quickly lose sight of the necessary foundation she provides for their own work in their harsh (and very gendered) critique of her.

16 Claire Fox critiques the metaphorization of the border in the introduction to her book *The Fence and the River*.

17 This focus on geology and geography as the foundation for a genealogy also informs the opening chapters of *Facundo*.

18 George Lipsitz, talk delivered at University of California, Riverside, May 2000.

19 See Taussig's theory of the hallucinatory character of the colonial relation in *Shamanism, Colonialism and the Wild Man* and his argument about the mimetic character of this relationship in *Mimesis and Alterity*.

Works Cited

Anzaldúa, Gloria. *Borderlands/La Frontera: The New Mestiza*. San Francisco: Aunt Lute, 1987.

Berg, Charles Ramirez. "El Geneo del Genaro: Mexican American Border Documentaries and Postmodernism." *Reflexiones: New Directions in Mexican American Studies*. Ed. Yolanda C. Padilla. Austin: Center for Mexican American Studies, University of Texas, 1999. 69–101.

Carr, Robert. "Crossing the First World/Third World Divides: Testimonial, Transnational Feminisms, and the Postmodern Condition." *Scattered Hegemonies: Postmodernity and Transnational Feminist Practices*. Ed. Inderpal Grewal and Caren Kaplan. Minneapolis: University of Minnesota Press, 1994. 153–172.

Cathy Caruth. *Unclaimed Experience: Trauma, Narrative, and History*. Baltimore: Johns Hopkins University Press, 1996.

——, ed. *Trauma: Explorations in Memory*. Baltimore: Johns Hopkins University Press, 1995.

Daniels, Roger. *Prisoners without Trial: Japanese Americans in World War II*. New York: Hill and Wang, 1993.

Feng, Peter. *Identities in Motion: Asian American Film and Video*. Durham: Duke University Press, 2002.

Fischer, Lucy. *Cinematernity: Film, Motherhood, Genre*. Princeton: Princeton University Press, 1996.

Fischer, Michael M.J. "Ethnicity and the Post-Modern Arts of Memory." *Writing Culture: The Poetics and Politics of Ethnography*. Ed. James Clifford and George E. Marcus. Berkeley: University of California Press, 1989: 194–233.

Fox, Claire. *The Fence and the River: Culture and Politics at the U.S.-Mexico Border*. Minneapolis: University of Minnesota Press, 1999.

Ginsburg, Faye. "Culture/Media: A (Mild) Polemic." *Anthropology Today* 10.2 (April 1994): 8.

Hansen, Arthur A. "Oral History and the Japanese American Evacuation." *Journal of American History* 82.2 (September 1995): 625–639.

Higashi, Sumiko. "Who's Going to Pay for These Donuts Anyway?" Film review, *American Historical Review* (October 1993): 1181–1184.

Hirsch, Marianne. *Family Frames: Photography, Narrative and Postmemory*. Cambridge: Harvard University Press, 1997.

Hulser, Kathleen. "*History and Memory* (For Akiko and Takashige)." Film review, *American Historical Review* (October 1991): 1142–1143.

JanMohamed, Abdul, and David Lloyd. "Introduction: Toward a Theory of Minority Discourse: What Is to Be Done?" *The Nature and Context of Minority Discourse*. Ed. Abdul JanMohamed and David Lloyd. *Cultural Critique* 6 (spring 1987): 5–12.

LaCapra, Dominick. *Representing the Holocaust: History, Theory, Trauma*. Ithaca: Cornell University Press, 1994.

Lesage, Julia. "Women's Fragmented Consciousness in Feminist Experimental Autobiography." *Feminism and Documentary*. Ed. Diane Waldman and Janet Walker. Minneapolis: University of Minnesota Press, 1999. 309–338.

Malloy, Sylvia. *At Face Value: Autobiographical Writing in Spanish America*. Cambridge: Cambridge University Press, 1991.

Michaelsen, Scott, and David E. Johnson, eds. *Border Theory*. Minneapolis: University of Minnesota Press, 1997.

Mimura, Glen Masato. "Antidote for Collective Amnesia? Rea Tajiri's Germinal Image." *Countervisions: Asian American Film Criticism*. Ed. Darryl P. Hamamoto and Sandra Lui. Philadelphia: Temple University Press, 2000.

Nichols, Bill. "Getting to Know You . . ." *Theorizing Documentary*. Ed. Michael Renov. New York: Routledge, 1993. 174–191.

Nornes, Abe Mark. "Our Presence Is Our Absence: History and Memory." *Asian America: Journal of Culture and the Arts* 2 (winter 1993): 167–171.

Ono, Kent A. "Re/membering Spectators: Meditations on Japanese American Cinema." *Countervisions: Asian American Film Criticism*. Ed. Darrell Y. Hamamoto and Sandra Liu. Philadelpia: Temple University Press, 2000.

Rosello, Mireille. *Declining the Stereotype: Ethnicity and Representation in Contemporary French Culture*. Dartmouth: Dartmouth University Press, 1998.

Sarmiento, Domingo F. 1845. *Facundo or Civilization and Barbarism*. Trans. Mary Mann. New York: Penguin, 1998.

Sitney, P. Adams. "Autobiography in the Avant-Garde Film." *The Avant-Garde Film: A Reader of Theory and Criticism*. Ed. P. Adams Sitney. New York: New York University Press, 1978. 199–246.

Sturken, Marita. "Absent Images of Memory: Remembering and Reenacting the Japanese Internment." *positions* 5.3 (1997): 687–707.

Tajima, Renee. "Moving the Image: Asian American Independent Filmmaking, 1970–1990." *Moving the Image: Independent Asian Pacific American Media Arts*. Ed. Russell Leong. Los Angeles: UCLA Asian American Studies Center and Visual Communications, Southern California Asian American Studies Central, Inc., 1991. 10–33.

Taussig, Michael. *Mimesis and Alterity: A Particular History of the Senses*. New York: Routledge, 1993.

———. *Shamanism, Colonialism and the Wild Man: A Study in Terror and Healing*. Chicago: University of Chicago Press, 1987.

Verdecchia, Guillermo. *Fronteras Americanas (American Borders)*. Toronto: Coach House Press, 1993.

Wiegman, Robyn. "Race, Ethnicity, and Film." *The Oxford Guide to Film Studies*. Ed. John Hill and Pamela Church Gibson. Oxford: Oxford University Press, 1998.

Xing, Jun. "Imagery, Counter-Memory, and the Re-visioning of Asian American History: Rea Tajiri's *History and Memory: For Akiko and Takashige*." *A Gathering of Voices on the Asian American Experience*. Ed. Annette White-Parks. Fort Atkinson: Highsmith, 1994.

Yamamoto, Traise. *Masking Selves, Making Subjects: Japanese American Women, Identity, and the Body*. Berkeley: University of California Press, 1999.

Filmography

Crucero. Prod. and dir. Ramiro Puerta. Written and perf. Guillermo Verdecchia. Snake Cinema, 1994. Ramiro Puerta, 5, Palmerston Ave., Toronto, Ontario, M6J 2H8-Canada. International sales: Laura Ruiz, LATINA S.A. DE C.V., Atletas No. 2 A-301, Col. Country Club, 04220 Mexico D.F., tel. 525-689-3850, fax 525-549-1820.

History and Memory: For Akiko and Takashige. Written, prod., and dir. Rea Tajiri, 1991. Sales and Rental: Women Make Movies, Inc. Film and Video Department, 462 Broadway, Suite 500Q, New York, NY 10013, tel. 212-925-0606, fax 212-925-2052, www.wmm.com

Major and Minor Discourses of the Vernacular

Discrepant African Histories

Language has been and remains one of the most potent symbols of ethnicity and group identity in human community. In Joshua Fishman's opinion (32), language is the "quintessential symbol" of ethnicity. To wit, there have been an increasing number of mobilizations around questions of language and identity in different parts of the world. From the language-based nationalisms of Eastern Europe in the nineteenth century to the more recent language movements of the post–Soviet Union, from the struggles over Afrikaans in apartheid South Africa to the conflicts over bilingual education and the English Only movement in the United States, language seems poised to become, even more than in previous centuries, a convenient flashpoint and battleground for resolving disagreements over identity, nation, migrancy, and territory. This essay will focus specifically on discourses of the vernacular, but because there is a tendency to speak of dissimilar mobilizations around language in terms that obfuscate different types of responses to dominant cultures, I find it useful to start by explaining what exactly I mean by a discourse of the vernacular. I define a discourse of the vernacular here as the organized activity of concerned individuals undertaken with a view to making mother tongues the officially recognized medium of communication in the major institutions of the society.

Given the well-documented attitudes of diverse colonizers and dominant groups toward the languages of the colonized and the marginalized, it has become commonplace to read every instance of advocacy on behalf of the vernacular and vernacular writing as intrinsic and unproblematic exemplars of minority politics. Abdul JanMohamed's and David Lloyd's essay on a theory of minority discourse, for example, is replete with such assumptions about the politics of language. When the authors conclude, as have many others before them and since their essay, that members of a minority population who write in a dominant European language "pay homage to Western intellectual and political hegemony" (JanMohamed and Lloyd 2), the unstated corollary is that those who write in vernacular languages have somehow succeeded in evading such hegemony.

My argument, however, is that texts written in vernacular languages in these contexts are not necessarily and inherently less complicit in character than those produced in the languages of former colonizers. Indeed, as will become evident in the particular instance of the British African colonies, the entire complex that emerged to service a vernacular literature—including advocacy on behalf of vernacular writing and education, transcription and translation work, the establishment of printing presses and translation bureaus, the selection of texts for publication—represents one of the early examples of active European intervention in the production of what was being presented as indigenous and local African culture. But defining local culture is, we need to keep in mind, always a matter of strategic functionality for different groups positioned in different ways at different points in time in relation to the local culture in question.

Likewise, as JanMohamed and Lloyd (9) have also argued, "becoming minor" is a question of a positioning best conceptualized in political terms. Intellectuals committed to defending the agenda of both majority and minority groups will often pursue dissimilar goals relating to the political order but may deploy similar dialectical strategies toward the accomplishment of these divergent ends, as is often the case with discourses of the vernacular. Discourses of the vernacular, as I will attempt to demonstrate here, are neither inherently nor invariably aligned with the radical politics of any minority. On the contrary, they are only one of many available discourses that have become truly transnational in scope and whose appeal largely cuts across ideological lines. Because these discourses easily lend themselves to the production of the kinds of oppositions described by Nancy Hartsock (25) as "radical dichotomies," they serve the interests of majorities just as well as they serve the interests of minorities. From this perspective minor forms of such discourses are to be distinguished from the major versions not so much by the logic of their deductions, but mostly insofar as they have been specifically mobilized to disrupt existing configurations of power.

I should point out that my concern with issues of language and identity here derives mainly from a desire to explain the emergence of African literatures in European languages and their continued resiliency in comparison to African literatures in indigenous languages. Scholars of African and postcolonial literatures are generally familiar with narratives recounting the imposition of European languages in the educational systems of colonial Africa. While such narratives provide invaluable insight into the intellectual climate of an age from the viewpoint of those who actually suffered through such experiences of imposition, it is worth noting that the majority of these narratives have nonetheless been recorded in texts produced in European languages. In other words, to the extent that they continue to use the imposed languages and have not become involved in movements to change the language policies of the communities to which they belong, their condemnation of colonial educational policy cannot yet be considered a discourse of the vernacular. It is the failure of most African writers to transform concerns about language into active discourses of the vernacular that I find particularly intriguing, and which leads me to some of the following reflections on major and minor discourses of the vernacular in the contemporary world.

In response to a tradition of criticism that largely overlooked writing in indigenous languages, there has been considerable effort in recent years to prove that African literature written in indigenous languages was as significant as writing in European languages. Accounts of this neglect of indigenous language literatures in the canon of African literature generally deploy a vocabulary replete with the well-known oppositions between colonizer and colonized, foreign and native, center and periphery. While the fact of colonialism is absolutely central to any discussion of the marginalization of indigenous language literatures in Africa, discussions of the language situation that move rapidly from the fact of colonialism to the colonized mentality of the educated elite in explaining the continued dominance of European languages in literary writing confuse the historical setting with the response to the setting. Like Philip Zachernuk (*Colonial Subjects* 183), I suspect that "colonial intellectuals are [not] predictable simply by virtue of being colonial," and as such, responses to the colonial encounter are preferably studied as distinct from, and not as extensions of a particular administrative system.

In order to come to a more precise understanding of the response of educated Africans to questions of language choice in the colonial period, I have chosen to concentrate on an instance where the colonizing authorities did in fact support the idea of vernacular literacy for the colonized, as happened with the British authorities in several of their West African colonies. Where colonizers systematically imposed their own language, it is easy to conclude that the colonized elite had little choice but to acquiesce to the policy of imposition. But where colonizing officials embraced a discourse of the vernacular, we may have to consider other possibilities in explaining the failure of a colonized elite to take advantage of the opportunity that was being offered them. All colonizers no doubt considered their culture superior to the cultures of the colonized, but all colonizers did not develop a discourse around the vernacular. Most colonized groups sought to defend and safeguard their culture in some way, but all such groups did not develop a discourse of the vernacular as part of their resistance to colonialism. And perhaps for these reasons, the ambivalence of African nationalist figures and writers toward discourses of the vernacular ought to be considered not so much as an aberration to be deplored, but as a fruitful illustration of the circumstances in which discourses of the vernacular become unattractive to those who have been designated as its intended beneficiaries.

To start with in advancing our understanding of these circumstances, I propose to consider "major" discourses of the vernacular, or discourses developed by those in a position of power, and the kinds of reactions that such major discourses engender on the part of designated beneficiaries who are usually excluded from positions of power. The activity of British authorities in the colony of Nigeria in the late nineteenth and early twentieth century is instructive in this regard. Here, as elsewhere, the question of vernacular literacy most frequently surfaced in relation to educational policy. In southern Nigeria, the first policy statements on educational matters by the British authorities were made public in 1882. The fact that the 1882 Ordinance, as it was called, made no provision for the teaching of the local languages or instruction in the vernacular within the formal school system provoked an immediate outcry from missionaries who prepared a memorandum of protest, and from many educated Africans whose reactions were recorded in the lively Lagos press (Fajana 50–55, Omu 107–108, Awoniyi 62–67). The vigorous protests addressed to the British authorities on the matter are often identified with the onset of a larger wave of cultural nationalism among educated Africans in Lagos, which lasted from the 1880s roughly until the second decade of the twentieth century. But for a host of reasons, which have been adequately discussed elsewhere (Zachernuk, *Colonial Subjects* 56–57; Ajayi 234–264; Ayandele 246–251), and which included the increasing institutionalization of racism in the colony, disagreements with the British authorities were increasingly played out in the political rather than cultural arena after the 1920s.

The 1882 Ordinance was apparently the foremost occasion when the colonial authorities disregarded the role of indigenous languages in educational policy in colonial Nigeria. The 1882 incident was also the main instance when politically active educated Africans made a discourse of the vernacular a significant part of their political agenda. However, subsequent ordinances passed into law from 1887 reversed the provisions of the 1882 Ordinance regarding the place of indigenous languages in native education. In fact, the 1926 Education Ordinance stated that "among infants and younger children, all instruction should as far as possible be given in the vernacular," and it was responsible for such a turnabout in the language policies of the colony that Awoniyi (99, 127) credits it with generating renewed interest in the work done on at least one of the indigenous languages, Yoruba, as from the 1920s onward. Special memoranda were also issued in 1927 and 1943 by the British authorities stating preference for the use of vernacular, at least in the early years of schooling in the colonies.

Support for vernacular literacy in southern Nigeria started long before the 1882 Ordinance. Earlier in the nineteenth century, Protestant missionaries had begun complaining about the use of English in schools. Reverend Buhler, the German director of the Training Institution established in 1859 by the Christian Missionary Society, complained about the confusion caused by instruction in English and recommended instruction in Yoruba (Awoniyi 50–51). Among the missionaries, the initial impetus for supporting vernacular literacy arose from the desire to provide scriptures to African converts in their own language (Ajayi 131). But with time, evangelization took a back seat, and the discourse on vernacular literacy was increasingly realized within the context of concerns related directly or indirectly to the form of the education to be provided for colonized Africans. Those who spoke most frequently on the need for vernacular literacy often spoke in the same breath of these other issues, so that they gradually became integral components of the discourse on vernacular literacy.

The European advocates of vernacular literacy in Africa during the colonial period made their views known in books, journal articles, and at international conferences linked to specific interest groups, namely missionaries, education officials, linguists, and anthropologists. The international conference on Christian Missions in Africa, which took place at

Le Zoute, Belgium, in 1926, was one such forum which brought together missionaries and therefore those largely responsible for educational instruction in colonial Africa. Opinions on language and education were also to be found in journals dealing with educational questions in the colonies, such as the journal *Overseas Education*, published by the British colonial government, and in publications linked to Protestant missionary organizations such as the *International Review of Missions*, or the *Bible Translator*.

In my opinion, some of the most interesting articles on vernacular literacy and literature were featured in anthropological journals that specialized in African studies, including, for example, the journal *Africa* and the *Journal of the African Society*, later renamed *African Affairs*. *Africa* deserves special attention because it featured more articles on the structure of African languages, on vernacular writing, and on native education than other Africanist publications such as the *Journal of the African Society*. *Africa* made its first appearance in 1928 in Britain as the main publication of an organization called the International Institute of African Languages and Cultures, which later became the International African Institute. The IALC intended to differentiate itself from other anthropological bodies working on Africa by giving special consideration to African languages and literature in the vernacular in a time of social change.

The founding editor of *Africa* was Professor Diedrich Westermann, who had earlier served as a missionary in Togo, before becoming a professor at the University of Berlin. Professor Westermann was a staunch supporter of African vernacular literacy and widely recognized as a foundational figure in West African linguistics. The editorial inclinations of *Africa* under Westermann's direction and his many publications on the subject of vernacular literacy provide numerous instances of the cultural entrepreneur at work. It was no surprise, given his predilections and those of the IALC, that the first three articles in the inaugural issue of *Africa* dealt either in passing or extensively with the role of the vernacular in colonial Africa. The IALC further established an annual competition for African vernacular literature in December 1928 to act as a stimulus for authors writing in indigenous African languages (Westermann 497).

There were a number of related concerns linked to this campaign on behalf of the African vernaculars. In the first place, and looking through several articles on vernacular literacy and education in the early editions of *Africa*, it is soon apparent that distrust of the highly educated and therefore Europeanized or "denationalized" African served as the major premise for much of this discourse. Proposing a system of education based on respect for African tradition and the use of the vernacular in one of the early editions of *Africa*, Bryant Mumford, the superintendent of education in Tanganyika in East Africa, declared without hesitation: "The semi-Europeanized Native, everyone agrees is a product to be avoided" (156). Frederick Lugard, chief architect of the policy of "indirect rule" in British Africa, and variously high commissioner and governor-general in the colony and protectorates established in Nigeria between 1905 and 1919, was one of those who strongly agreed. His dislike of educated Africans was legendary and is well documented (Zachernuk, *Colonial Subjects* 105; Omu 188; Perham 593; Fajana 121). He favored the development of what he considered suitable education for the natives, which would include instruction in the vernacular.

Concern for African cultural integrity and distrust of the lingua franca were other components of this discourse. Though there was disagreement about whether or not to promote vernacular literacy at the Le Zoute conference, the participants were apparently able to come to agreement on at least one point: "No attempt . . . should be made to impose upon larger language units any African so-called lingua franca" (Smith 113).

In the third place, support for African vernacular literacy was closely linked to statements acknowledging the value of real African culture — that is, traditional culture — and of the African past in particular. On the surface, the discourse appeared driven by a kind of teleological purpose that would eventually lead Africans to modernity. But at the heart of the discourse on vernacular literacy was the postulation of a gap between the African and the European that was both cultural and temporal. As individual cultures and peoples were called to individual destinies, so also they were assigned to their own temporal vocations. The vocation of Europe was modernity, that of the African, the past. It was not the past of antiquity, which too was European; rather it was some kind of intermediate stage, subsequent to European antiquity and prior to European modernity. In an article on vernacular language literature in 1932, E. R. Hussey explained the connection between the vernacular and the African past for readers of *Africa*. The advocates of vernacular literacy, he said, dedicated themselves to this cause because "they believe that African languages form an essential link between the people and their past" (174).

Fourth, it was understood that where higher education was offered to Africans, proficiency in European languages would play a significant role in such education. But it was also implied that only a small minority of

Africans would have access to higher education. Thus, the vast majority would have no need to acquire literacy in European languages (Westermann, "Linguistic Situation" 350). In the Lagos colony, for example, the missionaries vigorously opposed the idea of education beyond the elementary level for Africans (Fajana 34–36, Ajayi 152–153, Ayandele 286–289), and if secondary schools were eventually established, it was mainly in response to overwhelming pressure from African parents who demanded higher education and also raised the finances to support the schools.

If colonial administrators and missionaries who were responsible for most of the education available in the British colonies up till the 1950s were so committed to providing instruction in the vernacular, how then did the use of English as a language of instruction ever become so widespread, not only in secondary schools, but also in elementary classes in many British colonies in Africa? The answer in part is that African parents demanded it, particularly in those places where a previous tradition of literacy had not taken root before the arrival of the Europeans.[1] The missionaries knew that most communities were uninterested, if not hostile to the message they brought, and would tolerate their presence only if they accepted to offer education, which had to include teaching literacy skills in English. For the first half of the twentieth century, the missionaries in southern Nigeria were dependent on education as their main tool of evangelization, and thus had no choice but to oblige African parents and communities by teaching English or lose the opportunity to make potential converts.

These developments came as no surprise to European supporters of vernacular literacy who were well aware of the possible reactions that their proposals might generate among both literate and illiterate Africans. In anticipation of the expected reaction, W. Schmidt (139) proposed in a paper delivered to the Executive Council of the IALC that African feelings on the matter be disregarded: "It would be undesirable," he wrote, "to comply with any unwise wishes the natives themselves may express in favor of adding European languages to the school curriculum." The political repercussions of implementing all the components of the discourse of vernacular literacy for Africans were equally evident to those Europeans who embraced it. Bryant Mumford, who worked in Tanganyika, remarked: "Attempts to preserve the old methods may be interpreted by many Africans as an attempt to keep them a subject race and to withhold the benefits of civilization" (154). Nonetheless, British officials continued to offer support for vernacular literacy, and a tradition of writing in the vernacular did begin to emerge in many of the British colonies, making writing in several indigenous languages a viable option in southern Nigeria. Indeed, both Yoruba and Igbo, with the highest number of native speakers and literates, had produced winning entries for the IALC competitions in the 1930s.[2] But it is not enough to know that a tradition of creative writing developed in a particular language. To get a sense of its significance for both its producers and audience, we must also map out the ways in which this practice aligns itself with various other cultural and political forces within the society.

And when we consider writing in English in southern Nigeria, we quickly realize that once historical, then journalistic, and later creative African writing began to appear in English, it often took positions that were at odds with those promoted in European discourses on African vernacular literacy. The attempts to discourage Africans from seeking higher education, the condemnation of literary education and preference for technical and agricultural education, the emphasis on providing an education that would make the African fit for his or her subordinate status in colonial society—these were all aims that incurred the suspicion of educated Africans.[3] If educated Africans were particularly hostile to Lugard during his tenure as governor of Lagos, it was not only because of the many repressive policies that he authored, but also because of an awareness that he opposed everything that the educated African stood for (Fajana 121, Omu 219–220).

In general, scholars of African language literatures have tended to extend grudging approval to the relative respect accorded to African languages and cultures by the British colonial authorities and Protestant missionaries, in contrast to the apparent disregard for the African cultural heritage embodied in the French preference for assimilation in their African colonies. Such opinions represent a fundamental misunderstanding of the premises underlying the cultural politics practiced by European colonizers since the eighteenth century. Whether the preferred ideal was assimilation as with the French or indirect rule as with the British, the goal of these modern large-scale colonialisms was to establish the other, the native, the Negro, the Indian as unworthy of the privileges, rights, and protection enjoyed by citizens of the mother country under metropolitan law. Even where assimilation was the stated goal, it was rarely pursued as an end in itself and in a manner consonant with the eventual transformation of all natives into Europeans. A consistent application of assimilation was possible mainly in colonies where a majority of the indigenous population had already been exterminated, so that the ongoing suppression of indigenous culture in policies of assimilation served to remind disempowered survivors of their fundamental otherness, manifested in their need for "civilization."[4] Such policies also had the advantage of providing a posteriori justification for the violence visited upon earlier generations of indigenous inhabitants of the colony. They were killed, not because it was their land, but because they were barbarians.

In African colonies where a majority of the indigenous inhabitants survived the rigors of conquest and colonization, and where the colonial administration claimed to favor assimilation, only a handful of the local population ever acquired enough of European culture to warrant bestowment of French or Portuguese citizenship in half a century and more of active colonialism and contact with Europeans.[5] If the intent of assimilation was truly to transform most natives into Europeans, one can only infer extreme administrative lethargy in view of the unimpressive results obtained over several decades of activity designed to achieve this very result. Talk about assimilation in the African colonies, we must understand, was intended to maintain and reinforce cultural boundaries, and not to dissolve them.

Similar conclusions can be drawn about Britain's policy of indirect rule as it was practiced in the African colonies. These were policies devised to fortify cultural, and by extension legal, boundaries rather than policies inspired by an acceptance of African cultures as equals with European civilizations in the Western ratings of world cultures. If European culture and languages represented a higher stage of civilization, as assumed by many European Africanists at the time, there was no need to insist on total African reliance on indigenous languages, except as a strategy for preserving the presumed disparity between civilizations and cultures.[6] As articulated in the British colonies, the discourse on vernacular literacy was a natural extension of the assumptions which informed the policy of indirect rule, and thus it comes as no surprise that one of the most ardent British defenders of the principle of vernacular literacy, Frederick Lugard, was also the main inspiration behind the policy of indirect rule.

The discourse on vernacular literacy developed by British colonial officials and Africanists involved with the journal *Africa* is, to my mind, a perfect example of a major discourse of the vernacular, a discourse generated by scholars and administrators occupying positions of power in relation to the intended beneficiaries of the discourse. In its variable formulations, a major discourse on the vernacular is produced on behalf of subordinated groups and advocates the use of the mother tongue in formal educational systems as a way of protecting such subordinated groups from experiences of cultural alienation that have been precipitated in the first place by the violent intrusion within communities of new power structures dominated by foreigners. The fact is, the authority exercised by the advocates of the vernacular over diverse natives is often in itself emblematic of the root causes of the condition for which a remedy is being proposed.

There is invariably in major discourses of the vernacular a kind of territorial logic at work, with the result that where vernacular literacy becomes government policy some type of fracturing of territory and administration is ultimately contemplated. Thus, when colonizers and other dominant groups develop a discourse of the vernacular on behalf of subjugated populations, it is usually because they envision these subjugated populations as residing in a place distinct from their home, and where the laws governing life at home have no longer any application. The process of elaborating a discourse of the vernacular in such circumstances inevitably implies a certain conception of space requiring that those who speak separate languages inhabit separate spaces, where they are subject to distinct laws and administrative procedures. In twentieth-century Africa, the country that gave the most consistent support to the idea of vernacular literacy for subordinated groups was undoubtedly apartheid South Africa.[7] It was also a country that increasingly moved in the same period toward excising the designated beneficiaries of this policy, blacks, from the South African polity, first denying them legal rights and ultimately relocating them into homelands that were supposedly separate from white South Africa.

James Crawford has argued that the visibility of the English Only movement in the United States during the 1990s did more than reflect concerns about language; the discourse also enabled diverse groups in American society to articulate their fears about a number of issues, including immigration, welfare, civil rights, and multiculturalism (22). Major discourses of the vernacular are similarly indicators of political trends and conceptions about foreignness and localness within a community. On the whole, these discourses are useful where some members of a dominant group derive benefit in making distinctions between home and abroad, between fellow compatriots and diverse foreigners. In addition, these discourses satisfy the need of professionals like missionaries and colonial administrators, whose vocations are realized through travel to find difference at the endpoint of their journeys, thus justifying their own career choices. Major discourses of the vernacular likewise accommodate the fissiparous tendencies of Protestant missionary organizations and their proclivity for establishing distinct religious structures, supported by missionaries working independently of each other around individual language units and people groups as they are now more frequently known in contemporary Evangelical and Pentecostal circles.

I am by no means implying here that Protestant missionary organizations were or are insincere in their dedication to providing transcriptions and translations of the Bible into local languages, which is the main reason for their involvement in the production of discourses of the vernacular. Rather I wish to suggest that the investment in mother-tongue literacy almost always requires as a corollary acceptance of the idea of separate administrative arrangements for separate language groups residing in separate territories. Little wonder, then, that highly centralized religious organizations like the Catholic Church and centralized political systems like the French colonial administration showed such little interest in discourses of the vernacular in colonial Africa. Certainly in the French African colonies, there was a tendency to see *métropole* and *outre-mer* as part of an unbroken continuum in relation to administrative structuring and urban planning.[8] And though French colonial officials did begin to adopt policies showing greater respect for local cultures in the twentieth century, this did not generally translate into the development of distinctive administrative structures for different ethnic groups and territories. At the same time, the monadic principle continued to hold sway in formal educational systems, with French remaining the sole language of instruction admitted in most French African colonies.

Organizations that deploy a uniform administrative structure over all the territories under their control, making no distinction between the metropolis and the periphery or between different areas of the periphery in terms of administrative structures, appear to obtain minimal gain from pursuing a project of mother-tongue literacy, since to do so would amount to an acknowledgement of cultural particularities and provide a basis for questioning the universality claimed for the colonizer's culture, embodied inter alia in the practice of administrative uniformity for all colonized territories. In other words, major discourses of the vernacular have the greatest appeal where acknowledgement of cultural particularity can be used to justify asymmetries of power and administrative arrangement, especially in relation to marginalized populations residing in territories clearly demarcated from those identified as home by the articulators of the discourse.

By contrast, individuals belonging to subordinated groups develop what I would like to describe here as minor discourses of the vernacular in instances where their place of origin and residence has already been incorporated as an integral element into the territory and home of a dominant group.[9] The discourse on vernacular literacy then becomes part of a larger program to win political autonomy and possibly even territorial separation for the subordinated group. However, even in such instances, the proponents of vernacular literacy are usually those members of the subordinated community who are at the forefront of interaction with the dominant foreign culture.[10] They are frequently better educated than the norm, have lived longer periods outside their home community, have had more extensive contact with the dominant cultures. In consequence, they also have a more acute sense of impending cultural loss for the society that they hope to avert by advocating aggressive implementation of policies promoting mother-tongue literacy. But the interesting fact in relation to many British colonies in Africa is that the bulk of discourses of the vernacular produced during the colonial period emanated from European officials, and not from educated Africans. Even where Africans chose to write in indigenous languages, they rarely promoted vernacular literacy as essential to anticolonial agitation. Educated Africans may have spoken their own mother tongues as a matter of course, but the usefulness of encouraging writing in all the vernaculars spoken in each colony as part of a program of resisting colonial rule was not evident to all. In consequence, discourses of the vernacular in colonial Africa, as an explicitly articulated project, were almost always the work of European administrators, missionaries, linguists, and other professionals of education.

Given this situation, it is useful at this point to make a distinction between discourses of the vernacular and the natural state of affairs in any community. Members of a country, of an ethnic group, of a religious community, will speak a first language, which may or may not be the language spoken by their immediate forebears.[11] In contexts of migration, prolonged contact with other cultures and especially of foreign domination, some kind of language shift is as much the norm as is language maintenance. Even though it may present itself as such, a discourse of the vernacular is in this situation more than simply a description of a natural state of affairs. On the contrary, it is an active intervention calculated to precipitate change or to preempt changes that are already occurring in terms of language use in a given community. In any case, minor discourses of the vernacular often have less appeal for those segments of the subordinated population who, though they speak a mother tongue, have minimal contact with cultural outsiders and thus no consciousness of impending cultural alienation. Furthermore, those who do become advocates of minor discourses of the vernacular embrace this position only when it becomes part of a larger program to deliver tangible political results.

Educated Africans in the British West African colonies began turning to English partly because they could perceive no such political benefit in endorsing discourses of the vernacular. The Nigerian writer Chinua Achebe has provided the best explanation yet of the attitudes at work among some of the early English-language writers:

> Some of my colleagues . . . have tried to rewrite their history into a straightforward case of oppression by presenting a happy monolingual childhood brusquely disrupted by the imposition of a domineering foreign language. . . . My position is that anyone who feels unable to write in English should follow their desires. But they must not take liberties with our history. It is not simply true that the English forced us to learn their language. . . . We chose English not because the English desired it, but because having tacitly accepted the nationalities into which colonialism had grouped us, we needed its language to transact our business, including the business of overthrowing colonialism itself. (32)

The few African leaders, like those in North Africa, and Julius Nyerere of Tanzania, who made an African language the national language of their countries after independence, were not, as is widely believed, unproblematic advocates of mother-tongue literacy. Kiswahili was no doubt widely understood particularly in Tanzania in the 1960s, but it was not the mother tongue of most Tanzanians at the time when Nyerere made it the national and official language of the country. Arabization policies pursued in North Africa similarly entailed disregarding the form of Arabic recognized by most North Africans as their mother tongue, and further marginalizing the mother tongue of linguistic minorities such as the Berbers. The intent, in other words, was neither to institutionalize instruction in mother tongues for the majority of the local population nor to practice vernacular literacy as I have defined it here.

In formulating their language policies, the leaders of these countries invoked the principle of the lingua franca, rather than that of the mother tongue, the demands of that emblem of modernity, the nation-state, rather than loyalty to traditional heritage and precolonial polities, the need to build anew rather than to preserve the past. By contrast, the colonial discourses on the vernacular placed emphasis on the construction of a supposedly authentic African culture from which educated Africans, nationalists and other dissenters were naturally excluded. The focus in such discourses on the role of indigenous languages as essential components in preserving a valuable premodern African reality is especially significant. Johannes Fabian's contention that anthropology originated as a discipline using temporal categories to articulate otherness is relevant here, since the colonial discourses of the vernacular enabled concerned Europeans to translate cultural difference into a temporal distance that needed to be noted in adjudging how all Africans were to be treated in the twentieth century (16).

Educated Africans, on the other hand, increasingly perceived their role in colonial society as one of moving the community beyond the legacies of the past. The early forms of resistance to colonial rule directed by the traditional authorities had failed to dislodge the foreigners; it was now up to the educated to provide a new and hopefully more viable form of resistance. In varying degrees, their commitment then, as political leaders, as journalists, as creative writers and other educated artists, was to modernity and not to tradition. In this connection, Zachernuk ("Lagos Elite" 147) remarks, for example, that one of the foremost concerns of the Lagos intelligentsia from the middle of the nineteenth century onward was the idea of progress, which by the end of colonial rule was largely defined by Western standards and conflated with the quest for modernity. Ironically, those African writers and critics who favored African-language literatures continued to frame the language debate with the very same tropes used by colonial advocates of vernacular literacy, decrying the alienation of educated Africans, advocating respect for the past, preservation of cultural heritage, and the need to speak to each community in its own language. The continuing emphasis on language as vernacular rather than on language as lingua franca accounts in my opinion for the widespread ambivalence toward writing in indigenous languages on the part of an African artistic community largely committed to various forms of territorial integration and to the construction of modernity.[12]

Where cultural distinctiveness supplied the main argument used in demanding political autonomy, local elites in subordinated communities have thrown their support behind discourses of the vernacular. However, where cultural distinctiveness provided the basis for denying civic rights to communities located beyond the home envisioned by the colonizer, local elites have been much less enthusiastic about discourses of the vernacular. In any case, since most states are multilingual and multiethnic in composition, it is likely that the idea of a judiciously applied vernacular literacy will become at some point incompatible with the standardizing agenda pursued by many contemporary nation-states. Sooner or later, in seeking to reconcile the reality of linguistic diversity with the desire to develop economies of scale, rulers in nation-states become, on matters of language, defenders of the ideal of the lingua franca. African elites after independence were no exception. Whether they were able to find an indigenous language to play this role as happened in Tanzania or eventually turned to European languages, as happened in the majority of African states, political leaders have declined in practically every instance to implement a systematic policy of vernacular literacy.

Notes

1 To consider a few examples from southern Nigeria, chiefs in Bonny sent a letter to missionaries in Liverpool as far back as 1848 requesting teachers to provide instruction in English for their children (Ajayi 56). Parents in such communities had minimal interest in either the religious instruction or the vernacular literacy that the missionaries proposed. And so when missionaries began providing instruction in the vernacular in Efik communities also in the southeast, school attendance actually suffered a decline (Zachernuk, *Colonial Subjects* 25). The situation was not much different in Yoruba-speaking territory, also in southern Nigeria, once schools began to be established. Much against the desire of the missionaries, the parents demanded the teaching of English (Awoniyi 50). Parents who consented to receive adult literacy lessons in Yoruba insisted on English-language instruction for their own children (Awoniyi 54). And in Fajana's words, the desire to learn English may have been the sole incentive for even attending school in this period (55).

2 *Omenuko*, written by the Igbo writer Pita Nwana and published in 1933, won the competition, as did *Ogboju Ode ninu Igbo Irunmale*, published in 1938 and written by the Yoruba author Daniel Fagunwa. Both novels were widely read within their respective language communities and reissued several times over. See Lindfors (3) and Emenyonu (xiv, 33) for information on both works. Such was the popularity of Fagunwa's novels among the Yoruba that Lindfors claims that he may have been "the author with the largest reading audience in Africa" (13). The success of these novels certainly confirms the existence of a viable readership for creative writing in some of the indigenous languages of southern Nigeria, particularly during the colonial period. But, notwithstanding the popularity of these

early and subsequent texts in Igbo and Yoruba, a tradition of writing in English did develop among these very same language communities. The objective of this essay is to explain why such a development ever occurred against the background of considerable official support for vernacular literacy in southern Nigeria.

3 Literary histories of southern Nigeria will often mention, for example, the founding of the first Yoruba newspaper, *Iwe Irohin*, founded by the British CMS missionary Henry Townsend in 1849 in the city of Abeokuta. But literary scholars usually fail to locate Townsend in the context of his politics. Such omissions undermine our full understanding of the context of his activities on behalf of vernacular writing. In Townsend's case, the context does include his relentless opposition to the promotion of educated Africans to positions of leadership in the church hierarchy. His lengthy battle against the promotion of Samuel Crowther, an African, to the position of bishop of the Niger, which eventually translated into a lifelong battle against the Crowther family and children, is well documented (see, for example, Ajayi 180–196). In such circumstances, it is easy to see why educated Africans could not always readily associate themselves with the vernacular initiatives of the missionaries in the colonial period.

4 I am thinking here in particular of colonization in the Americas.

5 In the early twentieth century, associationism, which was partly inspired by British policies of indirect rule, tended to supplant assimilation as the preferred mode of operation among French colonial administrators. The impracticability of implementing assimilation where a large proportion of the indigenous population had survived may be one reason among others for this shift in thinking.

6 For example, Westermann (*African Today* 259), like many other Africanists writing about native education, admitted that a small class of Africans would need to acquire advanced Western education and mastery of English in order to become the vanguard for developing the entire community. At the same time, because instruction in European languages "constituted one of the powerful disintegrating factors in African life" (260), the teaching of European languages was to be discouraged, particularly at the elementary level, which Westermann considered adequate education for most Africans. In other words, the gap between civilizations would be maintained to the extent that his African contemporaries remained faithful to their vernacular languages.

7 Apartheid South Africa's support for vernacular literacy for blacks is not incompatible with the legislation requiring instruction in Afrikaans that sparked the Soweto uprising of 1976. In South Africa as defined by the apartheid authorities, instruction was to be in Afrikaans, while in the black homelands, education would continue to be provided in the black vernaculars. The problem of course was that townships like Soweto were not located in homelands.

8 Gwendolyn Wright notes, for example, how in the French colonies in the early decades of the century, policies for colonial cities provided French architects and urban planners with an opportunity to find solutions for problems that afflicted French cities (54). She further observes: "Between the two world wars Morocco provided a foil to architecture and urbanism in France. One textbook on urban design compared Casablanca, Paris, and Marseille on the same terms, without

suggesting that the North African example was in any way distinct" (135). This to my mind represents a way of conceptualizing space in both the metropolis and the colony that does not highlight the disjunctions between these spaces to the same extent that we find in British colonial policies.

9 I think here for example of the connections between Czech-language movements and the development of Czech nationalism (see Seton-Watson 150–154) or the symbolic importance of the Irish language for Irish nationalists (see Edwards 53–65).

10 In the Irish case, John Edwards notes, for example, that members of the organizations founded to revive and protect Irish were often "upper-middle-class individuals" (55). The same observation would be valid for Africa, where advocates of vernacular literacy are often highly educated scholars and other professionals.

11 John Edwards provides useful summaries of many instances of language shift where communities no longer speak the language of their forbears, but retain a sense of distinct identity (47–98).

12 But since the colonial period, advocacy on behalf of indigenous languages has been most appealing to local intelligentsias in Africa when it was linked to projects for modernization. I think here, for example, of the Vy Vato Sakelika movement in colonial Madagascar, which supported writing in Malagasy and looked to Japan as a model for modernization that did not require giving up local identity. See Adejunmobi for further details on this movement.

Works Cited

Achebe, Chinua. "New Songs of Ourselves." *New Statesman and Society* 9 Feb. 1990: 30–32.

Adejunmobi, Moradewun. *JJ Rabearivelo, Literature and Lingua Franca in Colonial Madagascar.* New York: Peter Lang, 1996.

Ajayi, Ade. *Christian Missions in Nigeria, 1841–1891: The Making of a New Elite.* Evanston: Northwestern University Press, 1965.

Awoniyi, T. *Yoruba Language in Education, 1846–1974, A Historical Survey.* Ibadan: Ibadan University Press, 1975.

Ayandele, E. A. *The Missionary Impact on Modern Nigeria, 1842–1914.* London: Longmans, 1966.

The Council. "Textbooks for African Schools: A Preliminary Memorandum." *Africa* 1.1 (1928): 13–21.

Crawford, James. *At War with Diversity, U.S. Language Policy in an Age of Anxiety.* Buffalo: Multilingual Matters, 2000.

Emenyonu, Ernest. *The Rise of the Igbo Novel.* Oxford: Oxford University Press, 1978.

Edwards, John. *Language, Society and Identity.* Oxford: Basil Blackwell, 1985.

Fabian, Johannes. *Language and Colonial Power: The Appropriation of Swahili in the former Belgian Congo, 1880–1938.* Cambridge: Cambridge University Press, 1986.

Fagunwa, Daniel. *Ogboju Ode ninu Igbo Irunmale.* London: Thomas Nelson, 1950.

Fajana, Adewunmi. *Education in Nigeria, 1842–1939: An Historical Analysis.* Lagos: Longman Nigeria, 1982.

Fishman, Joshua. *Language and Ethnicity in Minority Sociolinguistic Perspective.* Philadelphia: Multilingual Matters, 1989.

Hartsock, Nancy. "Rethinking Modernism: Minority vs. Majority Theories." *The Nature and Context of Minority Discourse.* Ed. Abdul JanMohamed and David Lloyd. New York: Oxford University Press, 1990. 17–36.

Hussey, E. R. "The Languages of Literature in Africa." *Africa* 5. 2 (1932): 169–175.

JanMohamed, Abdul, and David Lloyd. "Toward a Theory of Minority Discourse: What Is to Be Done?" *The Nature and Context of Minority Discourse.* Ed. Abdul JanMohamed and David Lloyd. New York: Oxford University Press, 1990. 1–16.

Lindfors, Bernth. *Early Nigerian Literature.* New York: Africana Publishing Company, 1982.

Lugard, Frederick. "The International Institute of African Languages and Cultures." *Africa* 1.1 (1928): 1–12.

Mumford, Bryant. "Education and the Social Adjustment of the Primitive Peoples of Africa to European Culture." *Africa* 2.2 (1929): 138–159.

Nwana, Pita. *Omenuko.* London: Longman, 1963.

Omu, Fred. *Press and Politics in Nigeria, 1880–1937.* London: Longman, 1978.

Perham, Margery. *Lugard, The Years of Authority, 1898–1945.* London: Collins, 1960.

Schmidt, W. "The Use of the Vernacular in Education in Africa." *Africa* 3.2 (1930): 137–149.

Seton-Watson, Hugh. *Nations and States: An Enquiry into the Origins of Nations and the Politics of Nationalism.* Boulder: Westview, 1977.

Smith, Edwin. *The Christian Mission in Africa.* London: The International Missionary Council, 1926.

Westermann, Diedrich. "The Linguistic Situation and Vernacular Literature in British West Africa." *Africa* 2.4 (1929): 337–351.

———. *The African Today.* London: Oxford University Press, 1934.

———. "The Work of the International Institute of African Languages and Cultures." *International Review of Missions* 27.104 (1937): 493–499.

Wright, Gwendolyn. *The Politics of Design in French Colonial Urbanism.* Chicago: University of Chicago Press, 1991.

Zachernuk, Philip. "The Lagos Elite and the Idea of Progress." *Yoruba Historiography.* Ed. Toyin Falola. Madison: University of Wisconsin Press, 1991. 147–165.

———. *Colonial Subjects, an African Intelligentsia and Atlantic Ideas.* Charlottesville: University Press of Virginia, 2000.

PART III

READING, WRITING, PERFORMING

Transcolonial Translations

Shakespeare in Mauritius

Koumadir enn lepok finn tingn ek enn lepok pe ne (III.1)
[Seems like an era's been switched off and a new one's being born]
— Dev Virahsawmy, *Toufann* (1991, trans. 1999)

[. . .] one day
My bare fist, my bare fist alone
will be enough to crush your world!
The old world is falling apart!
— Aimé Césaire, *Une tempête* (1969; trans. 1998)

Things fall apart; the center cannot hold [. . .]
A shape with lion body and the head of a man,
A gaze blank and pitiless as the sun,

....
And what rough beast, its hour come round at last
Slouches towards Bethlehem to be born?
— William Butler Yeats, "The Second Coming" (1921)

In their essay on Ameridian literacies, Walter Mignolo and Freya Schiwy write about the traditional academic distinction between literature, which belongs to the category "culture," and knowledge, which tends to come under the rubric of "theory." They draw attention to the problem of uneven development between the institutional production of what counts as "knowledge" and the diversity of perspectives and languages that get subsumed under a quasi-anthropological approach to forms of thought and literacies emerging from the peripheries. They argue that only those documents that can easily be used as case studies of existing theories acquire scholarly value and thus end up meriting "translation" into Western languages and concepts: "What gets translated is literature, but literature, we know, falls within the intellectual distribution of labor within the [modern world] system: Third World or Third World–like countries produce culture, not knowledge" (267). Setting aside the vexed debates surrounding the conditions under which the category "literature" itself becomes defined and incorporated into a canon of texts from the peripheral cultures of the world, I want to focus here on the *logic* of translation and its role in reinforcing the standard academic distinction between form and matter or method and archive. As the two critics go on to add: "The future of theories and practices of translation . . . will come from the perspective of coloniality and the colonial difference. . . . The possibility of going beyond dichotomies presupposes an-other logic, not . . . a reconfiguration of the content." (279). Creole-language literatures from the Caribbean and the Indian Ocean generally fall into two broad categories: "content" or source of knowledge about the local culture for existing academic disciplines (literature or sociology), and mimetic or pedagogical activity aimed at transposing European classics into local languages. Because they have a relatively short history, Creole literatures are not usually studied as technically innovative interventions capable of pushing the existing boundaries of genre and the parameters of literary analysis. Their self-referential questionings about their own conditions of possibility and the kinds of knowledge, concepts, or theories that they might produce are rarely discussed. The fact that they have their own internal logic that destabilizes the convenient but simplistic institutional dichotomies of academic research is hardly ever recognized.

Mignolo and Schiwy point out that in order to go beyond these familiar binary categories, we need to adopt "an-other logic." How might we theorize this other logic of writing without simply seeing it as "a reconfiguration of the content"? What might "an-other logic" be for Creole-speaking writers and critics? How do subaltern Creole cultures become translated into a global context of understanding and, more importantly, what gets lost in the process? In this essay, I want to focus on what writing in Creole means today in colonial and postcolonial cultures of orality and orature that have made the leap from the spoken to the new technologies of visuality and performance.[1] What can writers from the Indian Ocean tell us about these issues? How do we highlight the transcultural dimensions of their work and their intellectual contributions to the shaping of new contexts of understanding in which the familiar questions of theory and practice, form and content, knowledge and understanding, politics and culture, are brought to the fore? Many contemporary discussions about "minor literature" (Ahmed, JanMohamed and Lloyd) or the cultural "politics of recognition" (Taylor) continue to stumble on those issues. Finding useful ways of articulating Creole texts (oral, written, or visual), not just with their European generic "models" but also with postcolonial creative texts and performances, is an important step in the process of conceptualizing the links among the varied cultures of the so-called peripheries. More lateral comparisons among "minor" texts and genres or marginalized artistic productions and languages will eventually allow us to bypass altogether the mediation by a center, and the usual comparison of the margin with its hierarchical other that becomes inevitable in studies of intertextuality, literary influence, and cross-pollinations. My goal here will be to try to outline as comprehensive a context as possible with regard to the Mauritian poet and dramatist Dev Virahsawmy's Creole theater.

Translations in/of Creole Theater: Alternative Literacies

In an essay called "*Créolité* in the Indian Ocean: Two Models of Cultural Diversity" for the *Yale French Studies* volumes that assessed the state of the field ten years ago (1993), I argued that multiculturalism in the island of Mauritius differs significantly from the kind of "créolité" prevalent in the French Departments d'Outre-Mer (or DOM: Guadeloupe, Guyana, Martinique, Reunion). I pointed out that in Mauritius (unlike the French DOM), there is no single dominant, hegemonic, or standard language to contend with. Rather, French and English are both known and spoken, as they are the "residues" of colonial histories, whereas Hindi, Urdu, Tamil, or Hakka are also present as part of the legacies of the same histories. Mauritian Creole, though basically a French-based language, incorporates words and turns of phrase from many other tongues. This affords writers and speakers the opportunity to integrate many forms of thought and many languages within their use of Creole. They can do so without having to oppose Creole to a single dominant language, since different contexts of enunciation will determine different dynamics. The dominant language will vary according to each of these contexts.[2] A real sense of multiplicity can thus be exploited to great effect, as in the work of Dev Virahsawmy, whose play *Toufann* will be my primary focus.

Virahsawmy's pioneering work first received international recognition when his play *Li*, initially published in Creole in 1977 and translated as *The Prisoner of Conscience* in 1982, won first prize in the Radio France Internationale's *Concours Théâtral Inter-Africain* in 1981. Ten years later, Virahsawmy published *Toufann: Enn fantezi antrwa ak* (1991), a very loosely adapted Shakespearean *Tempest*, thus joining the "club" of postcolonial writers, such as George Lamming, Aimé Césaire, and Edward Kamau Brathwaite, who have engaged with the Bard's influential evocation of colonialism and resistance. *Toufann* premiered in Creole at the Rose Hill Plaza Theatre in Mauritius in 1995. On 12 December 1999, its London premiere on the stage of the Africa Center led to broad critical acclaim and further strengthened the author's renown. As Martin Banham declared: "This production rightly serves to bring his enterprising and astonishing theatre to a wider audience and to remind us that Virahsawmy ranks alongside the major figures in contemporary African drama."[3]

Virahsawmy is an important public intellectual figure in Mauritius. He has been a tireless advocate of cultural and ethnic diversity and has maintained a strong commitment to social justice and human rights. After Mauritian independence in 1968, he was active in the radical socialist party, the Mouvement Militant Mauricien (MMM), running for office and winning a seat in Parliament. But he eventually found himself in disagreement with the cultural and political agenda of the party and became disillusioned with the political expediency and predictable pragmatism of those who accede to power and must engage in shifting alliances to maintain it. He left electoral politics to devote himself entirely to writing and teaching. His plays are creative riffs on literary history. They are also disguised critiques of well-known public figures and effective means of satirizing authority. Staunchly opposed to all forms of communalism or divisive identity politics, he creates multiethnic casts of characters and deploys themes from literary history as well as everyday life. He represents contemporary conditions on the island with humor, affection, and an unerring talent for conveying the vernacular sounds, inflections, and specificities of diverse Creole voices.

Using his academic training as a linguist to further the development of Mauritian Creole as a written language, he has been the country's main proponent of its lingua franca as a *national* language. His commitment to diversity and his ecumenical and multicultural stance have led him to transpose into Creole not just British literature, but also French and Indian classics, including the musical adaptation of *Les Misérables*, Molière's *Tartuffe* (*Tartif Froder*), and the *Mahabharata*. He aspires to show that Mauritian Creole "is capable of expressing 'great thoughts' (Wilkinson interview 111), that it is a fit "symbol of . . . supra-ethnic identity in a plural society" (110), and that it has real aesthetic value, since it is also a way for him to share with others "things I find beautiful" (111), as he puts it.

Translated into English by Nisha and Michael Walling, and produced in England by Michael Walling, the artistic director of the London-based Border Crossings theater company, *Toufann* has received serious critical attention from Mauritian (Mooneeram, Toorawa, Tranquille), British (Banham, Walling), and Belgian (Zabus) critics. It is a comedy—and a very serious "fantasy"—that allegorizes the problematic potential of electronic media and the dangerous political uses of global technology. Combining these concerns with a postmodern interest in the simulacrum and a postcolonial attention to issues of race, gender, sexuality, and linguistic license, he achieves a radically original reworking of conventional Shakespearean topics within a context where Renaissance magic is represented as science fiction and technical know-how. *Toufann* has received much critical praise for its innovative recombinations of several Shakespearean characters from both *The Tempest* and *King Lear*, and for its denunciation of the new technologies of knowledge as aggressive forms of social control and surveillance.

The creative retitling of the play has been noted (Toorawa, Tranquille) and taken to be an explicit gesture of the dramatist in favor of his own ancestral ethnic tradition as an "Indo-Mauritian." Indeed, the word "toufann" exists in both Farsi and Hindi for "tempest." It is not the local vernacular word for "cyclone" or "hurricane," the tropical zone's destructive summer storms known in Mauritian Creole as *siklonn*. Michael Walling speculates that the use of the Hindi title must therefore be "a way for [Virahsawmy] to say 'I'm sticking to my past'" ("Staging Shakespeare" 119) even as he defends and promotes the use of Creole in his creative work. Walling thus seems to suggest that this loyal and firm advocate of the emerging literary language of his creolophone nation is also an author who remains bound to history and memory, that he feels rooted in the past, and that he understands the paradoxical situation of the postcolonial subject's need, on the one hand, to establish or maintain a filiation by means of a "communal" linguistic practice, and his desire, on the other hand, for a new political, cultural, or national identity mediated by the use of the island's lingua franca. Such paradoxes and heteroglossic practices are not uncommon in multilingual areas. Changes of registers are also normal for monolingual speakers, as pointed out by Mikhaïl Bakhtin. Indeed, multiple allegiances, code switchings, and the performance of plural and hyphenated selves are quotidian occurrences in an urbanized and globalized world.

The problem with Walling's statement, however, is that Virahsawmy's personal familial background is South Indian and Tamil-speaking, not linked to Hindi or the other languages and customs of northern India. Furthermore, Virahsawmy himself does not speak Tamil and has made it clear that he is more interested in the development of situated knowledges, preferring to focus on where he is "at" rather than on where his ancestors might be "from," to paraphrase the formula made famous by Paul Gilroy. Virahsawmy is solidly grounded in the present and less interested in reconnecting the broken threads of his family's diasporic past. His choice of the term "toufann" is thus not meant to hark back to a source or an identity located upstream from the linguistic shores of Creole. It is rather his way of *performing* the language's fluidity and its openness to new idioms (such as Hindi) — in other words, its ability to welcome, absorb, and fold into its current or flow terms that may not yet have passed into common usage but can give a new direction to its adaptable stream. In keeping with the open-ended processes of creolization that generate change, Virahsawmy's use of words makes visible all the layers of cultural influence that enrich his practice of linguistic defamiliarization. His playful verbal inventions and strategies of erudite borrowings are quite proper to poetic discourse and indicate a sophisticated creative talent.

Virahsawmy weaves together different textual and performative threads by means of the multiple meanings of "toufann." In keeping with his practice, I read *Toufann* against the grain of existing postcolonial critical theory. Instead of focusing solely on the rewriting and rereading of the Shakespearean canon as a form of counterdiscourse that has punctuated the literary and cultural history of the twentieth century, I would like to suggest that Virahsawmy engages with what I have called elsewhere a "transcolonial" form of solidarity with the subversive aspects of the "original," *The Tempest*, and *also* with the preoccupations of other African writers and public intellectuals living in countries where politics, culture, and the public sphere are contested sites of power between bourgeois elites and the ordinary people.[4] To read *Toufann* by highlighting its transcolonial cultural echoes is a way to underscore the regional similarities in the social and artistic agendas of some Mauritian and African writers, especially those who have had a fraught relationship with politics and power. Virahsawmy's work brings dramatic passion and comic relief to these debates while critically taking up his own long historical legacies of colonialism.[5]

Baroque Modernities

The institutional "centrality" of Shakespeare's *Tempest* still makes it hard to bypass its influence, and Virahsawmy dedicates his play to the writer, foregrounding the usefulness of the source as a starting point for serious, comic, and indeed political insights. By ostensibly bringing the intensity of Shakespeare's popular theater within modes of address that situate its global reach in a very specific form of local knowledge, Virahsawmy opens paths that connect with a multilayered network of allusions and references requiring complex levels of reading as well as different degrees of literacy. A typical Mauritian audience would be comprised of readers of Shakespeare (a curriculum requirement in a nation where education is now universal) who can find in the performance of *Toufann* a renewed contemporaneity as well as the mass appeal that echoes the original purpose of the play as "popular" entertainment in Shakespeare's own time. As long as the legacies of colonial education continue to construct a center and a canon through which certain literary and critical ideals are promoted, that center will inevitably mediate some of the readers' or the audiences' responses. The classic aspects or intertexts of the play thus call for further analysis.

The Tempest is Shakespeare's last play, and one of his shortest and most elliptical. The gaps in this work have been open invitations to many writers (such as those mentioned above) and filmmakers (namely Peter Greenaway, Derek Jarman, and Paul Mazursky; see Zabus 243–264) to engage in creative adaptations and interpretations of their own (Hulme and Sherman, Zabus). It is hardly surprising that a writer's explicit involvement with the substance of the early modern play would lead critics to focus primarily on that announced intertext and its long history, and to try to unravel the "contrapuntal" (Said) meanings of the original in relation to its adaptation or translation. Such a critical approach, however, remains for some simply "reactive," "still caught up . . . with the canonicity of the given metropolitan text," thus participating in "strategies of ex-orbitation and supplementation" that reveal a theorist's inability to formulate his or her "own autonomous teleology," as Radhakrishnan has argued.

But the mixture of genres, the gaps, and the bricolage of modes and registers in *Toufann*, as in *The Tempest*, imply important similarities and echoes that must be addressed. Virahsawmy combines characters from *The Tempest* (Prospero, Kalibann, Aryel, Ferdjinan) with those of the tragedy *King Lear*, replacing Miranda with the much more assertive Kordelia (Tranquille), Alonso with Lerwa Lir, and adding to the mix a Poloniouss, an Edmon, and a Yago, self-conscious about his stereotypical image as a villain, who bemoans the way authors and critics fix his sinister identity into a cliché that he cannot shake: "Mo pa gagn droi sanze moi?" [Ain't I allowed to change too?] (III.1). Such an authorial strategy provides a comic commentary on the very notion of the canon as something fixed and unchanging. Virahsawmy daringly rearranges Shakespeare's original scenarios, and the way *Toufann* brings together European and non-European traditions and realities is precisely what makes the play a creative statement about the openness of Creole cultures to an infinite array of cultural transpositions. Engaging with those is another way of "provincializing" the classic, as Dipesh Chakrabarty might put it, of subsuming it into the local knowledges of the Mauritian landscape with its various interlocking cultural spheres. José Antonio Maravall has drawn attention to *The Tempest's* affinities with "the technique of incompleteness" or the aporias of a baroque aesthetics, a topic studied at length by Dominique Chancé (*Poétique baroque*, "De *Chronique*"). As Chancé states, "the mélange of styles, the satire and parody of media interviews and public speeches, . . . the presence of the marvelous and the actual rudiments of a project in-the-making are all elements of the baroque genre" ("De *Chronique*", 886, my translation). In *Toufann*, Virahsawmy activates such a baroque aesthetics by using creative mélanges and parodying the original as well as contemporary cultural scenarios.

In a note to the British director who had asked for casting advice about the racial mix of the characters, Virahsawmy wrote back to Walling: "Imagine we're on a sort of asteroid somewhere. Prospero's Indian, King Lir's white, Kalibann's black and white mix" or a "batar" ("Staging Shakespeare" 118–19). The stage directions in the body of the play are very precise about Aryel's ethnicity — "enn kolos blon ar lizie ble" (a big guy with blue eyes) — and his machinelike abilities. He is "enn robo ki preske kouma enn dimoun" [an almost but not quite human robot] evoking, for me, the affectless and ultrarational Dr. Spock of *Star Trek*, an entirely plausible comparison, given Virahsawmy's explicit allusion to the world of science fiction ("a sort of asteroid"). With his innovative take on Kalibann and Aryel, who have become more central characters here, paired up with Kordelia and Ferdjinan, respectively, Virahsawmy further emphasizes the ambiguities of hybrid identities and the nonbiological components to ethnicity.[6]

Some of the characters are also veiled references to political figures (Walling, Interview 118). Mauritian audiences easily decode these hints, and they will "get" the hilarious nature of the caricatures. The Indian Prospero suggests Ramgoolam, the first Prime Minister of the nation after Independence (Wallling, "Staging Shakespeare" 118). King Lir represents the Franco-Mauritian elite, and his son, Ferdjinan, makes a zany final remark alluding to the play's respect for the classical rule of three unities, especially those of place and time: "Zame pa pou dir ki tousa finn arrive dan enn lazourne" [Impossible to say that all this happened in the course of one day] (III.1). His ironic nod toward the classical tradition (also alluded to in Shakespeare) is an echo of Aryel's earlier wry comment in II.4: "Dapre Aristot, pa plis ki 24 er" [According to Aristotle, no more than twenty-four hours]. Ferdjinan then adds, "Koumadir enn lepok finn tingn ek enn lepok pe ne" [Seems like an era's been switched off and a new one's being born] (III.1), a remark that situates him even more firmly as the ironic figure or mouthpiece of the European tradition in its now more British or Yeatsian echoes, as my epigraphs make clear: "What rough beast/Slouches towards Bethlehem to be born."

The multiplication of references and the proliferation of allusions build up the baroque qualities of the play. A magical universe is sustained by Prospero's technological know-how and the control he thinks he has on his puppetlike subjects ("mo diriz zot kouma enn mazisien," I.7; "bann maryonet," III.1 [I direct them as a magician would; a bunch of marionettes]). When the practical Kordelia points out to her father that there is a real risk that victims will become torturers, and that his error as a ruler was to confuse the need for justice with the desire for vengeance — "avegle par to pouvoir to nepli ti fer diferans ant lazistis ek vanzans" [blinded by your power, you were unable to discern between justice and vengeance] (III.1) — her comments resonate with the broad political contexts of Mauritian and African independences. The surprises of history and the public disillusionment with new rulers who become tyrants in the image of their former colonizers have been constant themes in postindependence

African literatures. Here, as Prospero's reign comes to a conclusion, the Kordelia-Kalibann couple (instead of the Miranda-Ferdinand one of the Renaissance play) takes over as the new queen and king of the island. But nothing is resolved; only more questions surface: the ship's sailors start a mutiny, the virtual harbor ("por miraz," I.2) in the middle of the virtual island disappears, as other subjects suddenly risk being excluded from a history based on the simulacra of democratic rule. The farcical Kaspalto-Dammarro couple, a drunk and a druggie, respectively, come to embody the potential for a repetition of colonial scripts. In keeping with Marx's famous statement in the *18th Brumaire*, there is now a risk that with them history will repeat itself, but as farce.

The pairing off of characters, however, does not lead to the "fundamental and inalterable opposition . . . that between good and evil" (886, my translation), which, according to Chancé's reading of Chamoiseau's *Biblique*, is the reverse of baroque ambiguity. In Virahsawmy (as in Shakespeare), ambiguity reigns and the coupling of characters does not lead to a binary impasse in which opposites collapse into one another and discrete identities become fused into a bland postcolonial brew. By creating extraneous spaces and using "strategies of ex-orbitation" that defamiliarize and ironize the real, Virahsawmy bypasses both the dangers of identitarian fusion and the hardening of local communal and political boundaries. Characters pair up across human, ethnic, and "posthuman" lines in rather unexpected ways, and in so doing, they focus our attention on the meaning of affective behavior, and on the conditions of possibility for freedom of thought and feeling in a social environment where the few are trying (in vain) to control the rest. Sentiments take center stage, especially in relation to Aryel and Kordelia, whose happiness with their respective partners, Ferdjinan and Kalibann, becomes the emotional core of the play.

The sexual ambiguities of Aryel and Ferdjinan work to reinforce the generic elements of the baroque. Chantal Zabus has argued that in *Toufann* queerness is censored and homosexuality sanitized. She suggests that "Virahsawmy's portrayal of Aryel as blond and blue-eyed . . . intimates that homosexuality is believed to be an Aryan phenomenon unlikely to contaminate 'wholesome' Mauritian society" (242). It is true that the play seems coy about its apparently asexual characters, who are called "zimo" or "twin brothers." Virahsawmy seems to make a troubling link between homosexuality and impotence, as Ferdjinan announces that he is betrothed to Aryel ("mo'nn fianse"), that the latter has "no sex" ("li peyna sex"), and that that's all right, since plastic or reconstructive surgery after his car accident has failed to give Ferdjinan a fully functional sexual organ: "Mo inpwisan . . . Dezir ou plezir sexiel pa inateres moi" [I am impotent . . . Desire or sexual pleasure does not interest me] (III.1). In Walling's staging of the play in London, the performances of Aryel and Ferdjinan were very physical, serving to accentuate the difference between corporality and words, gestures and speech, and the tension between the physical acts of touching and kissing and the verbal denials pronounced by both male characters. There is no question that in Mauritius homosexuality has yet to be fully accepted: if gay males have become more visible in public life and gay politicians no longer need to hide their sexual preference, lesbians still do not "exist" as a category nor are they visible in everyday life. The play's ambivalence about these issues reflects a local mentality in process, one that is evolving slowly. It seems to me, however, that Virahsawmy's pairing of Aryel, the "posthuman" robot, with Ferdjinan, the surgically imperfect human, underscores evolving technologies of identity, in keeping with the overall, but indeed imperfect, deconstruction of fixed identities promoted by his script.

The play does not shy away from explicit references to other forms of sexuality or metaphoric understandings of pleasure and *jouissance* that raise questions about both power and potency. In Poloniouss's and Edmon's exchange about the former's use of "metaphors" (II.6), Edmon puns: "To meta ti tro for," literally "your meta was too strong." The Wallings translate this as: "I don't care what you were using metal for." This formulation tries to replicate the wordplay of the Creole line, and the miscommunication between the two characters, but it fails to get at the true meaning of the exchange.[7] It thus eliminates from the English version another clever self-referential quality of the play. Edmon's pun immediately precedes a hilarious sexual moment full of double entendres. He emerges from behind the throne, where, it is implied, he has just masturbated after watching the staged performance of an "erotic" dance with "belidansing" and "striptiz." Yago, who has come to look for him, shouts: "Vot Mazesté? Kot ou? Beze! Zot finn kidnap nou leroi. . . . Edmon, Edmon, kot toi?" [Your majesty? Where are you? Fuck! They've kidnapped the king. . . . Edmon, Edmon, where are you?], to which Edmon replies from behind the throne "Ataaaann!" [Waaaait!] and Yago exclaims: "Ki to per fer laba?" [What are you doing over there?], and Edmon sighs: "Aaaa! Sa ki apel zwisanss . . . E Yago! To'nn trouv mo pouvoir" [Aaaa! That's what's called jouissance . . .

Hey Yago! You've discovered my power]. The Wallings politely render "Beze!" as "Oh no . . ." (241), and do not translate the first part of the retort ("Sa ki apel zwisanss"), thus completely eliminating the sexual edge present in the Creole. It is unclear to me whether they did not know what to make of the Creole or decided to avoid both dealing with an instance of masturbation and using the swear word that wittily concretizes that instance. Furthermore, the script's implied critique of the link between jouissance and power, as in the French phrases "jouir du pouvoir" or "jouir d'un bien" (which means to have legitimate power or to be the owner or beneficiary of a privilege), is completely erased. The Creole dialogue between the two characters suggests a clear link between sexual pleasure or potency and authority; but this is purged from what I would now call a "sanitized" (Zabus) English translation in which much of the play's political philosophy has been lost, and its implicit questionings of what constitutes legitimacy, eliminated.[8]

In an uncanny way, the censoring of queerness in *Toufann* is a revealing metaphor for the political problems of postcolonial societies in which neither freedom of speech nor sexual freedom is the norm, and the stereotypical demonizing of individuals (to which Yago calls attention) is an all too frequent occurrence. It is common knowledge, in Mauritius, that the sexual escapades of the powerful are tolerated — regardless of their preferences. Power *is* sexual freedom and potency. If Ferdjinan is compelled to represent himself as "impotent" and uninterested in sexual satisfaction, this is a subtle tactic for the playwright, a way to allude to Ferdjinan's abdication and his willingness to hand over the crown to Kalibann and Kordelia, in short to his disinterest in power and *its* pleasures. Ferdjinan's statement reflects, metonymically, a conscious disengagement with the realm of realpolitik.

One can argue, like Zabus, that the play remains somewhat uncertain about its own means of either understanding sexual diversity or incorporating it into its orbit, since the script makes fun of and normalizes an act of sexual self-gratification but appears to shy away from a straightforward representation of homosexuality. But I would suggest that the real issue is the broader question of the possible uses (metaphorical and metonymical) of all forms of sexuality within the postcolony (Mbembe). Thus, in his new play, *Prezidan Otello* (2003), Virahsawmy deals openly and directly with the issue of gay marriage. Otello is a gay president who wishes to marry and adopt children, and who thus embarks on the project of changing the laws that prevent same-sex marriages in his nation.[9]

Transcolonial Networks: Language and Politics

If the repression of nonnormative sexuality can be read metaphorically against a background of political problems, the way to bring forward those issues is through the kind of "lateral" or transcolonial comparisons to which I have referred above. Francophone African playwrights, notably Sony Labou Tansi, have made explicit the link between sexual prowess and political authority (Thomas 66–71). Such lateral comparisons become even more crucial when we push the investigation of the polysemic nature of the play's title. The term *toufann* points to the colonial French origins of Mauritian Creole as well as to its creative articulation with another major contact language spoken by a large proportion of the Mauritian population, Hindi. It is thus rather remarkable that no critic seems to have noticed that the common Creole phrase "tou fan" or "tou fané" meaning "it's a mess" or "everything's falling apart" is perhaps the most immediate popular connotation of the play's title. "Fann" or "fané" derives from the French "faner," meaning to wilt or to disperse, disintegrate, and crumble. Heard and understood in this way (without the interference or background noise that the explicit reference to, and translation of, Shakespeare's "tempest" suggest), the title challenges the Creolophone reader and critic to dive first of all into local Creole literacies before searching for additional and possibly extraneous (if totally legitimate) meanings and interpretations. When the familiar popular denotation of "tou fann" is transposed into English, the phrase suddenly resonates with the famous first line of Yeats's "Second Coming": "Things fall apart; the center cannot hold."

This line has elicited a rich set of signifying practices from postcolonial writers who have contested Yeats's views on the impending collapse of civilization, and his apparent belief that a tide of barbarians, monstrous hybrids, creatures "with lion body and the head of a man," announces the passing of the civilized Christian world as he knows it. Notable among those is the loud and dissident echo from Chinua Achebe's canonical postcolonial novel, *Things Fall Apart* (1958). This book is one of the Nigerian author's many responses to the stereotypical representations of Africa in British literature. His title is a challenge to Yeats's lament about the transformations of culture in the "center" of civilization as well as a sustained critique of colonial and native excesses, of the systems of thought that have led to independence in Africa but are now in the process of disintegration. Likewise, Virahsawmy's play is an internal critique of (post)colonial culture and the excesses of new rulers. It emphasizes the alterations and contaminations of earlier — purer or more committed — ideological paradigms of resistance, the fact that those are now "wilting" and crumbling, decomposing under "the suns of independence," to use the title of a 1968 novel by Ahmadou Kourouma, the Ivory Coast writer who has eloquently portrayed the corruptions of both colonial and post-independence regimes. Virahsawmy thus appears to be in a productive, if only implicit, dialogue with several African writers whose political and aesthetic concerns intersect with his own.[10]

Several lines from Aimé Césaire's *Une tempête* were also translated in a way that evokes Yeats, as in Philip Crispin's remarkable 1998 rendering of the play that had its English premiere in Notting Hill at the Gate Theatre in October 1998 (Hulme and Sherman, 149). Césaire's Caliban is a rebellious voice that accuses Propero, in the final scene, of being "a great illusionist" who imposed an erroneous and "incompetent" identity on his slave. In his last speech, Caliban announces the crushing of "the old world" with a "bare fist" while Prospero roars that he will "defend civilization." Even more than Achebe or Virahsawmy, Césaire echoes Yeats's "Second Coming," creating a rebel who wants to appropriate the master's power the better to reveal the "boomerang effect" of oppression, "the phenomenon by which colonialism poisons and dehumanizes both sides" (Rix 249). Césaire remains rooted in the lordship-bondage binary dialectic first conceptualized and criticized in Hegel's *Phenomenology*. As Joan Dayan states, Césaire "*recognizes* the force of mutuality, the knot of *reciprocity* between master and slave, between a prior 'classic' and his response to it . . . a labor that defies any simple opposition between black and white, . . . original and adaptation, authentic and fake" (140, my emphases).[11]

But the phenomenon of reciprocity that a politics of recognition presupposes (since within such a politics, the master recognizes that the slave is human like him and vice versa, and that one can take the other's place) is entirely foreign to the multiplicities of language and identity present in Virahsawmy. Césaire's Caliban seems to *become* the other, whereas Virahsawmy's Kalibann becomes *an-other*, free without having had to rebel, and transformed by Kordelia's feminine understanding of true autonomy as a way of being in-dependence, not independent but interdependent, co-existing in a state of confident mutual relation and reconciliation, not unlike the poetics of relation developed by Edouard Glissant. Virahsawmy wants Creole to find *a* place, its own place, in relation to all the other languages that have nourished it, not in order to replace them, but to interlace them on its own terms, and within *its* own generative matrix.

Unlike Glissant, who never granted any credit to feminism, Virahsawmy creates a conscious and interesting echo of the main intellectual and political tenets of the last wave of twentieth-century feminist theorizing. For him, the "feminine" principle is the one that enables the deconstruction or "dispersal" (*fann*) of the oppositional logic of role reversals. He has developed this view in several poems, in particular in the volume *Labouzi dan labriz* (*Candle in the Wind*). He calls for a future in which it is "Pa repiblik maskilin singilie / Me feminin pliryel" [Not the republic of the masculine singular / But that of the feminine plural] that will prevail. The conception and dramatization of the feminine in all of his oeuvre is an important topic to which I cannot do justice here, since it raises many other issues concerning power and sexuality, strength and weakness. Suffice it to say that Virahsawmy's Kalibann has little in common with Césaire's rebel. He is neither a mirror nor a foil for Prospero, and he comes across as the rightful "partner" of a resisting, dissident, and feminist Kordelia.

If the epistemological frameworks created by the Caribbean and Mauritian authors exist in tension with broad concepts of freedom and civilization, and the distortions to which these terms have been subjected throughout the course of colonial history, the concrete political questions they raise and the tensions between identity and language that they foreground do diverge significantly and dramatically. Virahsawmy works to promote the use of a previously devalued idiom, often described as a dialect or "patois." This does not just mean giving written form to, and normalizing the orthography of, that idiom. His purpose is to infuse this hybrid language with the capabilities and the range integral to other "pedigreed" or "literary" languages, and to use it to express abstract concepts, complex thoughts, affective modes of being, and aesthetic possibilities. In short, it is to make it into an instrument of poetic playfulness, intellectual reflection, and creative dialogue that does not patronize the speakers of this marginalized language. Unlike the Caribbean, Reunionais, or African writers who develop a creative "regional" or "creolized" French and can thus publish with the major Parisian houses, Virahsawmy has never published in French. His work appears in the literary pages of respected Mauritian weeklies or dailies, and with the Creole press of the organization Ledikasyon pu Travayer (Education for the Workers). He started his own (now defunct) small publishing company,

Boukie Banane, and has not shown any interest in "crossing over" to the other languages that are available to him in Mauritius. He finds it more democratic to publish on the World Wide Web, and he has made his works freely accessible to all. He leaves the translation of his plays to native speakers of English and writes only in Creole, creatively stretching the language to reveal its poetic, narrative, and performative aspects and to make it express his own philosophy.

His linguistic choices thus set him apart from the (post)colonial writers who translate their works into French, such as Raphaël Confiant, or who write in Kikuyu and translate into English, such as Ngugì Wa Tiongo. Césaire famously stated in a 1969 interview with François Beloux:

> There is a language problem in the Antilles; that problem is less acute for an African than for a Martinican. Which language to use? An African can at least use his own dialect . . . but we do not have a language. . . . French started out like Creole, then acquired its canonical status. Creole will eventually become a real language in the course of history. . . . French needs to be inflected by black genius. . . . My aim has been to give it the color of Creole [my translation].

Of course, Césaire was grossly oversimplifying the differences between Martinicans and Africans: colonial education created the same conditions under which francophone or anglophone literature emerged in Africa. If Césaire was interested in bending or coloring French to fit his own purposes, as were African writers, he appears, in 1969, as the uncontested precursor of the Martinican Créolistes, even if his statements about the "poverty" of Creole have incurred the wrath of Confiant, whose critique of the poet of *négritude* has been widely commented.

Virahsawmy does not publicly engage with these Caribbean debates, and he has not made statements about African writers and their use of language. Nonetheless, the political and epistemological questions raised by Achebe and Césaire in their engagement with the "great books" of the European tradition resonate with Virahsawmy's treatment of the same politics of knowledge. As a vehicle for philosophical discussions of knowledge and freedom, reason and feelings, *Toufann* is in the best tradition of the theater of ideas, or the *littérature engagée* of a Sartre or a de Beauvoir (whose name is mentioned in II.7 by Kalibann when he comments on Kordelia's free-spirited critique of masculinist authority, on her ironic: "Zot tou matcho" [All of you, machos]).

Toufann foregrounds the use of technologies of representation (maps) and detection (radars, cameras, and TV monitors), contrasting those with eyewitness accounts of truth and reality. Prospero is the all-knowing and powerful sovereign subject whose access to instruments of authority and knowledge gives him control over nature as well as the other characters in a world that can best be described as a virtual realization of Michel Foucault's description of the panopticon. In his "kontrol roum" (I.7), Prospero is the magician, the "author," who "diriz tou ar so baget mazik" [directs everyone with his magic wand] and whose computer-generated images conjure up a Mauritian *Truman Show* (Zabus): "En bann kamera ek mikro partou lor lil la" [There are cameras and microphones everywhere on this island]. There is no room for improvisation, and the actors, like Prospero's subjects, must follow the plan and the script. The first scenes are filled with comments that echo early modern as well as contemporary crises of perception and perspective or belief and understanding: "sakenn get listoir dan so manier" (I.6) [each understands the story from his/her own point of view], and the deferral to power and dominance that a paternalist Prospero encourages: "Pli tard to pou konpran" [You'll understand later] (I.2), "Mo pe fer tousa pou toi, pou to boner" [I'm doing all this for your future happiness] (I.7). Exchanges between Lir and Poloniouss articulate a contrast between speculative knowledge and pragmatic understanding, theory and practice, as Poloniouss asserts that "sipozision li enn fason reflesi" [speculation is a way of thinking] (I.3), whereas Lir only wants a quick way to find "sime pou sorti depi isi" [the way out].

The play thus generates its own set of open-ended questions about epistemology. It goes "beyond dichotomies" (Mudimbe-Boyi, Mignolo and Schiwy) to enunciate a new logic of relational understanding that breaks apart, decomposes, disarticulates, and indeed, *fanns* the symptomatic oppositions set up in the knowledge-making contexts of the academy between Creole-language "literatures" as suitable case studies and the theoretical instruments by which they can be deciphered and categorized. This new logic does not erase the specificities of those literatures, but rearticulates them "transcolonially," and with a new "accent," so that they become echoes of the other "minor" literatures with which the playwright is in implicit dialogue, beyond the obvious European and Shakespearean intertexts. As Edouard Glissant asks in "The Unforseeable Diversity of the World": "What might writing mean today? It is not just writing stories/histories to amuse or move people; it may be, above all, a matter of looking for the frail but trustworthy link between the wild diversity of the world and the balance and knowledge we desire to have" (295).

Dev Virahsawmy has achieved this remarkable balance of entertainment and theory. He has succeeded in creating a subtle reconfiguration of a Mauritian "ideoscape" (Appadurai), one so completely and deeply heterogeneous that the layers of languages and practices present within it point toward multiplicities of content and identity that are also modes of understanding and theorizing the real. His plays provide examples of cultural "content" that will continue to require rigorous elucidation, but more importantly, they do so while questioning the epistemological foundations of the *means* by which stories can get told, understood, translated, and disseminated, both internally within their culture of origin, and globally in the contemporary market of ideas.

Notes

I thank the Committee on Research and the Dean of Humanities at UCLA, Pauline Yu, for funding support and a research leave that allowed me to complete work on this project. I also thank the Rockefeller Foundation and the Bellagio Center in Italy for a blissful residency. My conversations with Danielle Tranquille and Dominic Thomas have been enlightening. Any errors that remain are of course my own.

1 The term "orature" is commonly used in anglophone African criticism; in Haitian literary criticism, the term "oraliture" is preferred. See Malena 116 n. 2.

2 I am not suggesting that Caribbean Creoles do not serve as vehicles for a multiplicity of cultural and linguistic influences. But I am contrasting the "official" policy of diversity in Mauritius with the more integrative or universalizing use of Francophone paradigms within the DOM.

3 The circulation and reception of his theater in European contexts thus duplicates the history of metropolitan successes bestowed upon other similar texts and the enduring Franco-British colonial interest in that region of the Indian Ocean. Francophone African dramatists such as Sony Labou Tansi were also crowned by Radio France Internationale.

4 For a discussion of the term "transcolonial," see Lionnet, "Transnationalism . . ."

5 There would be much to say in a comparative study focused solely on Virahsawmy and African and Caribbean writers, and space constraints do not allow me to develop these points here. Further study of regional theatrical practices in the sub-Saharan areas would be a source of productive "minor" to "minor" comparisons.

6 For a discussion of the way African writers such as Henri Lopes and Bessie Head complicate the binary between insider and outsider, colonizer and colonized, see Thomas. For an elaboration of the concept of *métissage* as an implicit deconstruc-

tion of biological and racial categories, and as a "tissage" of textualized selves, see the introduction to Lionnet, *Autobiographical Voices*. For a related approach to nonbiological technologies of identities in the era of global networks, see Amselle's theory of "branchements."

7 The translation seems to want to echo Gonzalo's "No use of metal, corn, or wine, or oil" (*Tempest* II.1.153), which is itself an echo of Montaigne essay on cannibals.

8 For other treatments of power and (im)potency in African literature, see Sembène, Labou Tansi, *La vie et demie* and *Qui a mangé*, and Thomas.

9 Virahsawmy's new play is available only on his Web site.

10 Other productive comparisons could be made with Tierne Monénembo, Were-were Liking, and Kossi Efoui.

11 For an important discussion of the philosophical concepts of recognition in Western philosophy and Heidegger's challenge to the metaphysics of oppression, see McCumber, to whom, as usual, I owe much more than can be expressed here.

Works Cited

Achebe, Chinua. *Things Fall Apart*. New York: Anchor Books. 1994.

Ahmed, Sara. *Strange Encounters: Embodied Others in Post-Coloniality*. London: Routledge, 2000.

Amselle, Jean-Loup. *Branchements: Anthropologie de l'université des cultures*. Paris: Flammarion, 2001.

Appadurai, Arjun. *Modernity at Large: Cultural Dimensions of Globalization*. Minneapolis: University of Minnesota Press. 1996.

Bakhtin, Mikhaïl. *The Dialogic Imagination*. Ed. and trans. Michael Holquist. University of Texas Press. 1981.

Banham, Martin, ed. *The Cambridge Guide to Theatre*. Cambridge: Cambridge UP, 1995.

———. "Dev Virahsawmy: Catching the Mood of Mauritius." http://www.border crossings.org.uk/ToufMaur.html.

Banham, Martin, James Gibbs, and Femi Osofisan, eds. *African Theatre in Development*. Oxford: James Currey, 1999.

———., eds. *African Theater: Playwrights and Politics*. Oxford: James Currey, 2001.

Beloux, Francois. Interview. "Un poète politique: Aimé Césaire" *Magazine littéraire* 34 (Nov. 1969). http://www.magazine litteraire.com/archives/ar_cesai.htm.

Césaire, Aimé. *A Tempest*. Trans. Philip Crispin. London: Oberon, 1998.

Chakrabarty, Dipesh. *Provincializing Europe: Postcolonial Thought and Historical Difference*. Princeton: Princeton University Press. 2000.

Chancé, Dominique. "De *Chronique des sept misères* à *Biblique des derniers gestes*, Patrick Chamoiseau est-il baroque?" *MLN* 118: 4 (fall 2003): 867–894.

———. *Poétique baroque de la Caraibe*. Paris: Khartala, 2000.

Confiant, Raphael. *Aimé Césaire: Une traversée paradoxale du siècle*. Paris: Stock, 1994.

Dayan, Joan. "Playing Caliban: Césaire's *Tempest*." *Arizona Quarterly* 48 (1992): 125–145.

Gilroy, Paul. "It Ain't Where You're From, It's Where You Are At . . . The Dialectics of Diasporic Identification." *Third Text* 13 (1990–1991): 3–16.

Glissant, Edouard. *Le discours antillais*. Paris: Seuil, 1981. *Caribbean Discourse: Selected Essays*. Trans. with an introduction by J. Michael Dash. Charlottesville: University Press of Virginia, 1989.

———. *Poétique de la relation*. Paris: Gallimard, 1990. *Poetics of Relation*. Trans. Betsy Wing. Ann Arbor: University of Michigan Press, 1997.

———. "The Unforseeable Diversity of the World." Mudimbe-Boyi 287–295.

Greenblatt, Stephen, et al. eds., *The Norton Shakespeare*. New York: W. W. Norton & Company, 1997.

Hulme, Peter, and William H. Sherman, eds. *'The Tempest' and Its Travels*. London: Reaktion, 2000.

Kourouma, Ahmadou. *Les soleils des indépendences*. Paris: Coll. Points, Le Seuil, 1995.

———. *The Suns of Independence*. Trans. Adrian Adams. Ann Arbor: University of Michigan Press, 1994.

JanMohamed, Abdul, and David Lloyd, eds. *The Nature and Context of Minority Discourse*. Oxford: Oxford University Press, 1990.

Labou Tansi, Sony. *La vie et demie*. Paris: Seuil, 1979.

———. *Qui a mangé Madame d'Avoine Bergotha?* Bruxelles: Éditions Promotion Théâtre, 1989.

Lionnet, Françoise. *Autobiographical Voices: Race, Gender, Self-Portraiture*. Ithaca: Cornell University Press, 1989.

———. "*Créolité* in the Indian Ocean: Two Models of Cultural Diversity." *Post/Colonial Conditions: Exiles, Migrations, Nomadisms*. Spec. issue of Yale *French Studies* 82 (1993): 101–112.

———. "Transnationalism, Postcolonialism, or Transcolonialism? Reflections on Los Angeles, Geography, and the Uses of Theory." *Emergences: Journal for the Study of Media and Composite Cultures* 10.1 (2000): 25–35.

Malena, Anna. *The Negotiated Self: The Dynamics of Identity in Francophone Caribbean Narrative*. New York: Peter Lang, 1999.

Maravall, José Antonio. *Culture of the Baroque: Analysis of a Historical Structure*. Trans. Terry Cochran. Minneapolis: University of Minnesota Press, 1986.

Mbembe, Achille. *De la postcolonie: Essai sur l'imagination politique dans l'Afrique contemporaine*. Paris: Khartala, 2000. *On the Postcolony*. Berkeley: University of California Press. 2001.

McCumber, John. *Metaphysics and Oppression: Heidegger's Challenge to Western Philosophy*. Bloomington: Indiana University Press. 1999.

Mignolo, Walter, and Freya Schiwy. "Beyond Dichotomies: Translation/Transculturation and Colonial Difference." Mudimbe-Boyi 251–286.

Mooneeram, Roshni. "Theatre in Development in Mauritius: From a Theatre of Protest to a Theatre of Cultural Miscegenation." Banham, Gibbs, and Osofisan 1999, 24–37.

Mudimbe-Boyi, Elizabeth, ed. *Beyond Dichotomies: Histories, Identities, Cultures, and the Challenge of Globalization*. Albany: SUNY Press, 2002.

Said, Edward. *Culture and Imperialism*. New York: Knopf, 1993.

Radhakrishnan, R. "Globalization, Desire, and the Politics of Representation." *Globalization and the Humanities*. Spec. issue of *Comparative Literature* 53.4 (2001): 315–332.

Rix, Lucy. "Maintaining the State of Emergence/y: Aimé Césaire's *Une tempête*." Hulme and Sherman 236–249.

Sembène, Ousmane. *Xala*. Paris: Présence Africaine, 1973.

Taylor, Charles. *Multiculturalism and "The Politics of Recognition": An Essay*. Princeton: Princeton University Press, 1992.

Thomas, Dominic. *Nation-Building, Propaganda, and Literature in Francophone Africa*. Bloomington: Indiana University Press, 2002.

Toorawa, Shawkat. "Strange Bedfellows? Mauritian Writers and Shakespeare." *Wasafari* 30 (autumn 1999): 27–31.

——. "Translating *The Tempest*: Dev Virahsawmy's *Toufann*, Cultural Creolisation, and the Rise of Mauritian Creole." Banham, Gibbs, and Osofisan 125–138.

Tranquille, Danielle. "Translator: Trans Alter. A Reflection on Dev Virahsawmy's *Toufann*." *Revi Kiltir Kreol* 2 (2003): 34–45.

Virahsawmy, Dev. *Boukie Banane*. http://pages.intnet.mu/develog.

——. Interview with Danielle Tranquille. "Translation into Creole. A New Strategy to Promote the Language." *Rencontres: The Journal of Mauritian Studies* (2000): 92–103.

——. Interview with Jane Wilkinson. "Staging Shakespeare across Borders." Banham, Gibbs, and Osofisan 109–114.

——. *Labouzi dan labriz*. Poems. 2002. http://pages.intnet.mu/develog.

——. *Li*. Rose Hill: MMMSP, 1977. *Li/The prisoner of conscience*. Trans. Ramesh Ramdoyal. Moka: Éditions de l'Océan Indien, 1982.

——. *Prezidan Otello*. 2003. http://pages.intnet.mu/develog.

——. *Tartif Froder*. Port Louis: Boukie Banane, 1999.

——. *Toufann: Enn fantezi entrwa ak*. Rose-Hill: Boukie Banane. 1991. *Toufann: A Mauritian Fantasy*. Trans. Nisha and Michael Walling. Banham, Gibbs, and Osofisan 217–254.

Walling, Michael. Interview with Jane Wilkinson. "Staging Shakespeare across Borders." Banham, Gibbs, and Osofisan 115–124.

——, and Nisha Walling. "*Toufann* and Translations: Presenting Virahsawmy's Play in London." *Rencontres: The Journal of Mauritian Studies* (2000): 38–46.

Zabus, Chantal. *Tempests after Shakespeare*. New York: Palgrave, 2002.

Postcolonial Theory and the

Predicament of "Minor Literature"

In spite of the presumptuously general title of this essay, in what follows I offer a specific, albeit meditative, rereading of a francophone novel, Driss Chraïbi's *Les boucs* (*The Butts*), by way of reflecting on the broader question of how we, as postcolonial critics in the American academy today, read and teach the works of "minority" writers. What are the theoretical aims and pedagogic implications of reading a body of literary works by "minorities" about the condition of being "minor" in Western metropolises through general postcolonial theory in the American academy? What is culturally and politically at stake in teaching, say, a francophone novel in a transnational context? Do we teach such a novel in the same way we would teach a more canonical text? And how do we negotiate the boundaries of the aesthetic and the political, the cultural, and the historical in teaching these texts to our students? To be sure, several postcolonial theorists have already answered some of these general questions by arguing that since all minorities "share the common experience of domination and exclusion by the majority," the general goal of reading and teaching "minority" literature is to fashion a critical structure that connects these "other" cultures by way of empowering minorities against the dominant cultures that work to marginalize them.[1] Generally defining the condition of being "minor" in terms of political (dis)empowerment and geographical displacement, postcolonial critics tend to assume a binary relationship between power and opposition, hegemony and resistance, and nationalism and exile in describing the relationship between "majority" and "minority" discourses. Through such binaries, minorities and their discourses are defined as necessarily oppositional, always working collectively against oppressive power relations and cultural hegemony while displacing nationalist forms of identification with diasporic subjectivities. Following Gilles Deleuze and Félix Guattari's characterization of "minor" literature, postcolonial critics have consistently viewed aesthetic works by Third World authors as products of "deterritorialization" whose contents are always and necessarily collective, political, and oppositional. "The theoretical project of 'minority' discourse," Abdul JanMohamed and David Lloyd maintain, "involves drawing out solidarities in the form of similarities between modes of repression and struggle that minorities experience separately but experience precisely as minorities" (9). What has therefore been emphasized in the postcolonial readings of "minority" literature are "the political and cultural structures that connect different minority cultures in their subjection and opposition to the dominant culture," and their "strategies of resistance" (JanMohamed and Lloyd ix).

In this essay, I wish to revisit the above-mentioned questions by way of proposing the need for a more situated and historicized approach to studying and teaching this literature than those offered by postcolonial critics such as Lloyd and JanMohamed, calling into question the critical value of *general* and *generalizing* theories of colonial oppression and post-colonial resistance in reading and teaching "minority" literature. My critical aim in other words is twofold: on the one hand, I wish to draw attention to the problematic tendency to lump together a broad range of aesthetic and cultural practices under the rubric of "minority" that, as "product of damage," connotes automatic resistance to "pathos of hegemony" (Lloyd and JanMohamed 4, 5); on the other, I hope to demonstrate that general theories of postcoloniality, including those of such canonical figures as Franz Fanon and Albert Memmi, may not yield adequate critical and pedagogical results in their applications to "minority" texts. In what follows, I will first contextualize the ways in which the "minority" text is traditionally read and taught by postcolonial critics, and then I will reflect critically on my own earlier postcolonial reading of *Les boucs* to demonstrate the pitfalls of using general theories of postcoloniality in studying and teaching "minority" literature.

Exile Intellectuals and Immigrant Communities

Edward Said begins his seminal essay "Reflections on Exile" with a statement that strikes me as symptomatic of the split discourse of displacement among postcolonial intellectuals through which postcolonial critics read "minority" literature: "Exile is strangely compelling to think about but terrible to experience" (159). Said's distinction between thought and experience, between intellectual reflection on the question of deterritorialization and the actual, empirical experience of being dislocated from one's "home," speaks to the split ways in which postcolonial intellectuals have broached the issue of how the "minor" literature represents a variety of political and cultural practices, *and* the relationship between displacement and intellectual/aesthetic works by "minorities" in various cosmopolitan contexts — such as Paris, London, Amsterdam, and New York. There is, in other words, a fundamental split between a tendency to consider the state of being "minor" an essential experience that is disempowering and a consideration of it as a matter of critical positionality that is intellectually empowering.

Interestingly, postcolonial intellectuals have for the most part valorized, if not romanticized, the seductive power of geographical displacement by following in some ways Victor Hugo's celebrated claim that exile is life. From Caribbean intellectuals (like C. L. R. James and George Lamming) to postcolonial writers (like Bharati Mukherjee, Salman Rushdie, Assia Djebar, and Driss Chraïbi), the move away from one's homeland has been described in salutary and celebratory terms, as the experience of deterritorialization considered central to the act of writing in a cosmopolitan context, a critical position that is intellectually indebted to "both Euro-American modernist exile formulations and postmodern theories of location," as Caren Kaplan aptly observes (112). They view the decision to live in exile, without the security of one's culture, as a redemptive movement, one that mediates a dialogic awareness, thus enabling the creative process of writing and critical thinking. Although these intellectuals have spoken of the psychological losses and political disenfranchisement that dislocation entails, not to mention the predicaments of race relations in the Western context, they have nonetheless claimed to transform their senses of displacement into a cosmopolitan vision that makes them worldly and revolutionary intellectuals. Said himself speaks of displacement as at once a "crippling" or "unhealable rift forced between a human being and a native place," and a heroic, creative, and triumphant trope in literature and culture (159). In several of his works, he has used the words of a thirteenth-century monk, Hugo of Saint Victor, to argue that total exile is the most complete form of identity. Distance and alienation caused by exile, according to Said, enable critical insight and discursive originality, since deterritorialization, whether through travel or migration, forces the writer to abandon fixed positions of identity as well as ideologies of mastery and nationalistic attachments.

Valorizing the redemptive possibilities of dislocation is also common in the fields of postcolonialism and cultural studies on the other side of the Atlantic. In the European context, Stuart Hall has persistently argued, "diaspora identities are those which are constantly producing and reproducing themselves anew, through transformation and difference" (235). Homi K. Bhabha has further claimed that postcolonial people, as deterritorialized subjects, "displace some of the great metropolitan narratives of progress and law and order, and question the authority and authenticity of those narratives" ("Third Space" 218). I have discussed elsewhere the problematic consequences of postcolonial critics' valorization of deterritorialization's redemptive power,[2] but suffice it to restate here that such a perception of displacement not only fails to historicize the particular predicaments of racial "othering" in various cosmopolitan contexts but also mystifies the redemptive qualities and oppositional possibilities of exilic consciousness. Moreover, as Inderpal Grewal and Caren Kaplan also have remarked, such celebratory theories of diaspora fail to acknowledge that "location is still an important category that influences the specific manifestations of transnational formations" (16).

In contrast to these intellectuals and writers are those theoreticians and critics who focus on the actual experiences of displacement, experiences that often entail a horrendous sense of homelessness, political and economic disenfranchisement, and even physical and psychological abuse. Outnumbered by celebratory theoreticians of postcoloniality, these scholars tend to be in ethnic studies and social sciences, especially sociology, history, and political science — I have in mind here scholars such as Kitty Calavita (*Inside the State: The Bracero Program, Immigration, and the* INS, 1992), Maxim Silverman (*Deconstructing the Nation: Immigration, Racism and Citizenship in Modern France*, 1992), William Barbieri (*Ethics of Citizenship: Immigration and Group Rights in Germany*, 1998), and Paul Gilroy (*"There Ain't No Black in the Union Jack": The Cultural Politics of Race and Nation*, 1987). As in their titles, in the works of these critics, situated terms (like "immigration," "citizenship," "race," and "racism") displace abstract notions (like "diaspora," "deterritorialization," "exile," and "hybridity"). In contrast to celebratory theoreticians of postcolonialism, these critics show how identifying the nation with an exclusive notion of race or ethnicity has led to restrictive immigration and discriminatory citizenship laws. Even a cursory glance at various immigrant communities confirms these critics' view that immigrants continue to be more politically disenfranchised and the target of nativist attacks, both in cases where they have socially and economically succeeded (for example, Southeast Asians in Africa, Asians in California, or Chinese in Malaysia) and where they have held the least desirable and low-income jobs (such as Turks in Germany, North Africans in France, and Latin American immigrants in Southern California). Even when successful immigrants have been valorized as "model minorities," their acceptance has been less a matter of national hospitality than a political trope to reaffirm the patriotic norms and dominant cultural values of host societies.[3]

The opposing views of displacement suggest a discrepancy between what the political scientist John Armstrong calls "mobilized" and "proletarian" diasporas that distinguish exile intellectuals from disempowered minorities whom they often claim to represent. Armstrong acknowledges the vagueness of the term "diaspora," used to describe every kind of geographical displacement. But he attempts to make this term more useful by introducing what I consider to be a very helpful, albeit insufficient, distinction between the proletarian class of immigrants (who are a "disadvantaged product of modernized polities") and the mobilized class ("an ethnic group which does not have a general status advantage, yet which enjoys many material and cultural advantages compared to other groups in the multiethnic polity") (393). Armstrong not only raises the issue of social class or even symbolic capital here, but he also discusses a broad range of other factors (such as religion, language, labor, cultural myth, family networks, and personal relationships) to schematize the critical differences that exist between various communities of immigrants. Obviously, no diasporic community fits neatly into these categories, because immigrants occupy a plurality of social and economic positions, but this sort of distinction is critically necessary, because it calls into question the unmoored metaphors of border crossing, travel, deterritorialization, and hybridity so prevalent among postcolonial intellectuals and cultural critics. The various distinctions introduced by Armstrong, on the one hand, are useful in accounting for the particular ways in which "location" and context inform the various manifestations of transnational movements. On the other hand, the distinction between mobilized and proletariat diasporas can be useful in understanding why émigré writers of privileged diasporas — privileged by virtue of access to discourse and representation — view displacement in celebratory terms while representing the everyday struggles of ordinary immigrants in Western metropolises in their aesthetic and critical discourses.

Contrapuntal Criticism

The situated and concrete discussions of displacement by sociologists, political scientists, and historians may seem on the surface less relevant than general theories of postcoloniality to the study of literary texts written by immigrant authors (Salman Rushdie et al.). This is perhaps what has made them less popular among postcolonial critics. I want to argue, however, that, read contrapuntally against these social science works, "minority" literature can be interpreted more accurately and taught more effectively to students because such a reading will allow us to account for the specific manifestations of displacement while avoiding the pitfalls of ahistoricism and depoliticization. Let me elaborate my point with a personal experience of teaching *Les boucs*, Driss Chraïbi's second novel, published in 1955. Let me summarize the plot before discussing how I initially read it and taught it through the logic of colonial identification I borrowed from Fanon and Bhabha. Then I will suggest how a political historian's work like *Deconstructing the Nation* may actually give us better theoretical tools to read and explicate the novel to our students.

Les boucs is a straightforward account of the inhumane condition of the Maghrebi immigrants in France. The story is narrated for the most part by an aspiring Algerian writer, Yalaan Waldik, who, like the cosmopolitan Moroccan author himself, comes to France full of hopeful illusions about living an artistic and productive life away from the strictures of his society only to encounter alienation, disenfranchisement, and racism. Waldik is at once an organic intellectual, living with and being part of the disempowered Maghrebi community, and a self-appointed spokesperson for his people, a contradictory position that splits the narrator between an egotistical ambition to transcend the limitations of his displaced condition and the social responsibility of representing the suffering and disillusionment of North African immigrants. Embittered by racism, economic disempowerment, and cultural alienation, Waldik seeks redemption through his representation of the immigrant community's misery — a search that ends, not surprisingly, in recognizing the very impossibility of salvation as he abandons his project of representation.

When I first taught and wrote about the novel several years ago, at a time when I was heavily influenced by emerging postcolonial theory, I viewed it as a hybrid text that experimented with the limits of diasporic identity by articulating an ambivalent form of consciousness through doubling and dissembling. I claimed that the violent language of the text pulverizes and subverts the dominant notions of self, home, and national belonging in order to account for the complexity of postcolonial displacement. Following Bhabha's discussion of postcolonial subjectivity, I claimed that the novel was a testimonial bearing "witness to the unequal and uneven forces of cultural representation involved in the contest for political and social authority within the modern world order" (Bhabha, "The Postcolonial and the Postmodern" 171). I went on to read the novel in relation to Fanon's psychoanalytic model of colonial identity to speak of the relation between the immigrant and the French. Comparing the ideology of assimilation to that of the French colonizers' "civilizing mission," I considered the dehumanizing treatment of North Africans in France as an extension of colonial oppression into postcolonial space. The ideology of assimilation, I suggested, forces cultural differences into a binary relation that privileges the French by identifying his/her Maghrebi "other" as inferior. This complex mode of differential identification is eventually internalized by the immigrant, just as Fanon's colonized internalized the colonizer's racial superiority. The choices available to immigrants like Waldik or Rauss (his friend and alter ego in the novel) is either the dissolution of their cultural differences through assimilation or marginalization to the point of negation.

My discussion of Waldik's resistance in the novel was also tinged with traces of postcolonial appropriations of the Gramscian model of political opposition. I viewed the character of Waldik as an organic intellectual who, recognizing his ability to speak the language of the master, considers his duty to translate and transmit what would otherwise remain unspoken — speaking the words of the subaltern who cannot speak. Having experienced rejection and alienation, he aligns himself, as an organic intellectual, with oppressed North Africans to mediate the possibility of "disalienation." Working within the binary opposition of power/resistance and colonizer/colonized, I considered both the writer and the novel's protagonist as oppositional figures struggling against the hegemonic and assimilative power of colonial and majority domination by writing a "counterhistory" that problematizes the normative history of modernity and Western imperialism. My argument then was that Waldik enables what Fanon called a "collective catharsis," a rearticulation of the collective unconscious that has constructed the North African as the inferior other of the French. Let me cite the conclusion of my reading of the novel by way of highlighting the problematic postcolonial logic of my argument:

> Driss Chraïbi's *Les boucs* has often been read as a realistic account of the dehumanizing treatment of North Africans in France. But to equate the novelist's narrative with that of Waldik seems a naïve, if not an imperceptive, understanding of the novel's *mise-en-abyme*. The novel's self-reflective uses of Waldik's writing practice ought to be viewed more accurately as a complex mode of representation that experiments with the limits of postcolonial identity, agency, and alterity. Exposing the split between the diasporic intellectual and the immigrant community, Chraïbi problematizes the unreflected claims to representation that remain within the boundaries of the oppressive logic they wish to transcend. Unlike Waldik's discourse of resentment, Chraïbi's novel recognizes the complexities of postcolonial relations of power as well as those of oppositional practices, a recognition that allows for a polylogical, polyvalent narrative in which the very limits of such dichotomies as identity and alterity, home and exile, self and other are exposed. (Behdad, "Exile Intellectual")

Even now, revisiting these lines critically a decade later, I find they sound good, even convincing — ironically they make me wonder why I am "deconstructing" my earlier reading! And yet, having worked further on legal, cultural, economic, and political aspects of immigration in France, I really cannot stand behind my earlier postcolonial discussion of *Les boucs*, let alone the hyperinflationary rhetoric of my argument, just as I find the postcolonial theories too general and too celebratory to be useful in reading the "minor" text.

Maxim Silverman locates three major problems in postcolonial/post-structuralist strategies of reading and resistance that partly explain why general theories of postcolonial identity are insufficient as critical tools: (1) a postcolonial "identity" politics "pays insufficient attention to the wider historical determinations of 'identities' "; (2) it "occasionally loses sight of power relations altogether in the effort to break the monolithic dualism of the master/slave model"; and (3) it "slips towards a liberal notion of a 'free' space of contestation outside the national/social complex" (125). Given these reasons, Silverman questions "how effective new identity theories can be as a politics of contestation of racialised discourse." Silverman's critique of the postcolonial is echoed by Ella Shohat and Anne McClintock, who also argue that the dubious temporality and spatiality of postcolonial theory have rendered it critically ineffective as a reading strategy and politically insignificant as an oppositional tactic.

Following these critics' observations, I wish to discuss four interrelated problems that render postcolonial discussions of displacement as a global and common phenomenon politically ineffective and discursively problematic in reading the "minor" text. First, as Edouard Glissant has cogently argued, "the permutations of cultural contact change more quickly than any one theory could account for. No theory of cultural contact is [thus] conducive to generalization" (19). In other words, one cannot claim a monolithic notion of postcolonial identity to describe every form of displacement in the West or elsewhere. Transnational formations are always interpolated by the politics of location, and as such their manifestations can be quite varied. There are indeed obvious and major differences between the experiences of various displaced communities — for example, while some communities, such as Armenians in Glendale, California, have been able to maintain a sense of collectivity and cultural particularity in the United States, Caribbean immigrants in New York City have fashioned a creolized identity with blacks and Latinos, an identity that is less nationalistically rigid and more culturally fluid. In addition, as Armstrong points out, there can be radical permutations even within a single immigrant community, permutations that are overdetermined by class, gender, religion, and language. Such differences within and across immigrant communities demand an understanding of interculturality that is attentive to the specificity of their historical formations and geographical locations.

Second, the metaphoric use of spatial tropes in postcolonial theory has led to a problematic discourse of utopian mobility that often conflates the privileged experiences of writers and intellectuals with those of the less fortunate immigrants — we can see this lack of attention to economic and cultural differences even in the case of a politicized and worldly critic like Said or Bhabha. One of the most disturbing aspects of global deterritorialization, as Pico Iyer insightfully observes, "is that the so-called linking of the planet has, in fact, intensified the distance between people: the richest 358 people in the world, by UN calculations, have a financial worth as great as that of 2.3 billion others, and even in the United States, the prosperous home of egalitarianism, the most wired man in the land (Bill Gates) has a net worth larger than that of 40 percent of the country's households, or perhaps 100 million of his compatriots combined" (25 – 26). In privileging theories of displacement over location, postcolonial critics have failed to address the contingent and uneven nature of transnational flows of capital, commodities, and people.

Third, it is not empirically evident that geographical or cultural displacement leads to originality of vision, to the breaking of intellectual and social barriers, and to solidarity in opposing hegemonic power of the majority, as postcolonial intellectuals from Lamming to Bhabha have suggested. For even the most superficial acquaintance with the ethnic politics of a city like Los Angeles reveals how stratified and conflicted Third World–origin and minority communities are in this city.[4] Issues of class and racism, gender and sexuality, language and religion splinter immigrant communities, making hostility, not solidarity, the rule in racial dynamics. The automatic association of "minorities" with solidarity and oppositionality thus fails to account for the complex ways in which they have been positioned in relation to the "white majority" and with each other.

Fourth, postcolonial critics' theoretical project of "minority" discourse relies too heavily, and problematically, on colonialism's Manichaean allegory of the colonizer and colonized and on the imperial model of center and periphery, both of which fail to account for the complex configurations of translational relations of power. As many cultural critics have already pointed out, inequalities and differences today are not necessarily the function of mechanisms of exclusion imposed by a hegemonic center as globalization has radically diminished the absolute spatial and racial division.[5] Today, as Kenneth Surin observes, "the exploiters are everywhere and so are the exploited" (1188). Given such a motley configuration of power, it is increasingly difficult to maintain the Manichaean opposition between "majority" and "minority" in explicating the complex web of cultural and economic determinants that produce social and epistemological asymmetries. To unpack transnational mechanisms of exclusion and opposition, we therefore need to locate new critical models to understand the interdependent and overdetermined processes that unequally articulate cultural, economic, and social relations across racial and geographical boundaries.

These are some of the reasons why I have found postcolonial discussions of displacement unhelpful in reading and teaching postcolonial novels. Instead, I have recently tried to read works like Chraïbi's *Les boucs* contrapuntally with the works of social scientists like Max Silverman or Gérard Noiriel. Obviously, my aim here is not to be prescriptive or generalizing about the uses of such social theories in studying and teaching minor literature; rather I wish to offer a specific example of how, in particular, such works can be pedagogically and theoretically helpful in reading and teaching this novel. Above all, in reading a work like Silverman's *Deconstructing the Nation*, I became aware of a crucial distinction between patterns of migration in France that are mostly linked to the country's colonial history and patterns of "integration" that are closely linked to France's Republican national history. In other words, in my earlier reading I conflated France's histories of immigration and colonialism, theorizing the condition of Maghrebi immigrants through the semiotics of colonization. So, for example, while I was correct in claiming that Waldik was in France precisely because the French had been in Algeria as colonizers, I was wrong to read the issue of assimilation in the novel, or what is referred to in France as *integration*, in terms of France's assimilationist colonial policy in Algeria. In my first reading I was also inattentive to the organization of labor and capital in France that had necessitated the policy of temporary immigration at the time, a policy that spoke to an economic, and not sociocultural, perspective on immigration.

Moreover, Silverman's perceptive discussion of the state, demography, and the economy of postwar immigration to France gave me a much better understanding of how immigrant characters like Rauss and Waldik were situated in the novel, what forces were against them, and how they expressed their resistance to racism in France. I began to understand, for instance, why the discourse of assimilation was at odds with the dominant economic policy at the time, which favored short-term immigration to fulfill specific labor needs. Instead of reading France's immigration policy solely in terms of its colonial discourse of race, I now became cognizant of the economic factors that led the state to pursue a policy of short-term immigration. The word *boucs* also gained a whole new meaning once I understood how the failure of the National Immigration Office to regulate the level of immigration after 1945 led the state to revert its immigration policy to the unfettered and exploitative practices of the 1920s in France.

My aim in rereading Chraïbi's *Les boucs* as a "minor" text has been to provide a counterexample to consider the theoretical, political, and pedagogic implications of a "horizontal approach" to the minority discourse, an approach that aims to provide a "theoretical articulation of the political and cultural structures that connect different minority cultures in their subjugation and opposition to the dominant culture," to use the words of JanMohamed and Lloyd again (ix). The horizontal approach to cultural formations echoes the claims of globalization theorists about the waning of nation-states and the emergence of cosmopolitan "minority" cultures that share a common structure of oppression and a common goal to displace hegemonic powers. Timely and appropriate though the horizontal approach may seem in the context of transnational cultural formations today, such a generalizing mode of cultural analysis can risk overlooking what one may call "vertical contingencies" of the "minor" text, by which I mean both the historical condition and the cultural context that define its subject as well as its reception. General concepts of deterritorialization and displacement can function as useful reading strategies only to the extent to which their specific manifestations are historicized, for without such contextualization they become new universal categories that homogenize minority identities and cultures. Surely a "minor" text such as *Les boucs* embodies the traces of different national cultures because of its inscription within colonial and transnational relations of power, but its formation remains always singular, a singularity marked by a particular set of historical and contextual contingencies. A "minor" text like Chraïbi's novel is a product of (post)colonial transculturation, and as such it may bear aesthetic and thematic resemblances with other "minor" texts, but, as my rereading of the novel suggests, the dynamic of its interculturality and the politics of its aesthetic representation can be mapped only by unpacking the particular histories and cultural formations in which the novel is inscribed and by which its subject matter is mediated.

Notes

1 I quote here Abdul R. JanMohamed and David Lloyd from their introduction to *The Nature and Context of Minority Discourse* (ix), but the theoretical point they make is shared by many postcolonial and "minority" critics.
2 See my essay "Global Disjunctures, Diasporic Differences, and the New World (Dis-)order."
3 For an insightful discussion of how successful immigrants are strategically deployed as "supercitizens" in the service of national renewal, see Honig 77–106.
4 I have elaborated this point in my essay with Laura E. Pérez, "Reflections and Confessions on the 'Minority' and Immigrant I.D. Tour."
5 See, for example, Canclini.

Works Cited

Armstrong, John. "Mobilized and Proletarian Diasporas." *American Political Science Review* 70.2 (1979): 393–408.

Behdad, Ali. "Exile Intellectual, Immigrant Community: Driss Chraïbi and the Maghrebis in France." Unpublished paper presented at the Annual Meeting of the Modern Language Association, San Diego, December 1994.

———. "Global Disjunctures, Diasporic Differences, and the New World (Dis-)Order." *A Companion to Postcolonial Studies*. Ed. Henry Schwarz and Sangeeta Ray. London: Blackwell, 2000. 396–409.

———, and Laura E. Pérez. "Reflections and Confessions on the 'Minority' and Immigrant I.D. Tour." *Paragraph: A Journal of Modern Critical Theory* 18.1 (March 1995): 64–74.

Bhabha, Homi. "The Postcolonial and the Postmodern: The Question of Agency." *The Location of Culture*. London: Routledge, 1994. 171–197.

———. "The Third Space." *Identity, Community, Culture, Difference*. Ed. Jonathan Rutherford. London: Lawrence and Wishart, 1990. 207–221.

Canclini, Néstor García. *Hybrid Cultures: Strategies for Entering and Leaving Modernity*. Trans. Christopher L. Chippari and Silvia L. López. Minneapolis: University of Minnesota Press, 1995.

Chraïbi, Driss. *Les boucs*. Paris: Denoël, 1955.

Deleuze, Gilles, and Félix Guattari. *Kafka: Toward a Minor Literature*. Trans. Dana Polan. Minneapolis: University of Minnesota Press, 1986.

Fanon, Franz. *Peau noire, masques blancs*. Paris: Seuil, 1952.

Glissant, Edouard. *Caribbean Discourse: Selected Essays*. Trans. Michael Dash. Charlottesville: University of Virginia Press, 1989.

Grewal, Inderpal, and Caren Kaplan. *Scattered Hegemonies: Postmodernity and Transnational Practices*. Minneapolis: University of Minnesota Press, 1994.

Hall, Stuart. "Cultural Identity and Diaspora." *Identity, Community, Culture, Difference*. Ed. Jonathan Rutherford. London: Lawrence and Wishart, 1990. 222–237.

Honig, Bonnie. *Democracy and the Foreigner*. Princeton: Princeton University Press, 2001.

Iyer, Pico. *The Global Soul: Jet Lag, Shopping Malls, and the Search for Home*. New York: Vintage, 2000.

JanMohamed, Abdul R., and David Lloyd, eds. *The Nature and Context of Minority Discourse*. Oxford: Oxford University Press, 1990.

Kaplan, Caren. *Questions of Travel: Postmodern Discourses of Displacement*. Durham: Duke University Press, 1996.

Lamming, George. *The Pleasures of Exile*. Ann Arbor: U of Michigan P, 1992.

McClintock, Anne. "The Angel of Progress: Pitfalls of the Term 'Postcolonialism.'" *Social Text* 31/32 (1992): 84–98.

Memmi, Albert. *Portrait du colonisé*. Paris: Gallimard, 1985.

Noiriel, Gérard. *Le creuset français: Histoire de l'immigration XIXe–XXe siècles*. Paris: Seuil, 1988.

Said, Edward W. "Reflections on Exile." *Granta* 13 (1984): 159–172.

Shohat, Ella. "Notes on the 'Postcolonial.'" *Social Text* 31/32 (1992): 99–113.

Silverman, Maxim. *Deconstructing the Nation: Immigration, Racism and Citizenship in Modern France.* London: Routledge, 1992.

Surin, Kenneth. "On Producing the Concept of a Global Culture." *South Atlantic Quarterly* 94.4 (1995): 1179–1200.

The Calm Beauty of Japan at Almost the Speed of Sound

Sakamoto Kyū and the Translations of Rockabilly

I'm only going to be there for a very short time, but I still want to introduce properly, in my own way, "Japan." For example, for my appearance on *The Steve Allen Show*, my costume hasn't been decided on yet, but if they tell me to wear a *chonmage* [a topknot hairstyle] or something, I plan to turn them down flat. Because I want to show them me just as I am, a completely ordinary visitor. In a foreign country where all they know about Japan is Fujiyama, geisha, and sukiyaki, I'd like to use this chance to get as many people as possible to change their way of thinking, even if it's just a little bit.

— Sakamoto Kyū on the eve of his departure for America, 1963 (Ishioka 246–247)

When Greil Marcus wrote his classic study *Mystery Train: Images of America in Rock 'n' Roll Music*, he borrowed his title not only from Elvis Presley's last single for Sun Records, but also from a whole tradition of American studies that saw in the train a leitmotif of national imagination. The train motif bolsters Marcus's thesis that popular music forms — blues, country, rockabilly, and others — fit the mainstream narrative of American studies as well as, perhaps even better than, the literary texts conventionally used in the field. He supplies new contents for the classic liberal narrative of democratic cultural nationalism but leaves unaltered its basic structure and dominant motifs, even its pontificating tone. In a sense, that was the whole point: Marcus was appropriating the authority of the national narrative in order to elevate the work of artists he admired.

While *Mystery Train* remains a fundamental text in popular music criticism, this narrative framework now seems problematic. Marcus's desire to judge "authenticity" against the touchstone of national culture, along with his eagerness to assimilate widely variant cultural strains into a single homogeneous whole, and his presumption of American exceptionalism all seem suspect. Moreover, when Marcus describes what he sees as the unique characteristics of America, his language suggests not so much the singularity of national culture as it does the leveling force of global capitalism. The struggles of musicians he depicts as battles with the contradictions of American culture are more persuasively explained as resistance against commodification in an increasingly global market, and they are hardly the exclusive birthright of artists who carry U.S. passports.

Paul Gilroy does not cite Marcus in his critique of the nationalism that pervades recent cultural studies. But in his attempt to address the historical reality of racism without conceiving of the culture produced in response to that history as an unchanging national essence, Gilroy suggests a productive way to refigure the music of the African diaspora. Although he notes the importance of trains, in particular Pullmans, to African American culture, he chooses an alternative central image in his desire to construct "a theory that was less intimidated by and respectful of the boundaries and integrity of modern nation states":

> I have settled on the image of ships in motion across the spaces between Europe, America, Africa, and the Caribbean as a central organizing symbol for this enterprise and as my starting point. . . . Ships immediately focus attention on the middle passage, on the various projects for redemptive return to an African homeland, on the circulation of ideas and activists as well as the movement of key cultural and political artifacts: tracts, books, gramophone records, and choirs. (Gilroy 4)

This image launches Gilroy's rereading of black music as an ever-changing "tradition," one that performs into existence a transatlantic cultural network linking up those who live simultaneously inside and outside of Western modernity.

Likewise, if we want to understand rockabilly — the short-lived but influential 1950s genre that combined rhythm and blues, rock 'n' roll, and hillbilly country music — as a (potentially) transnational minor culture, it seems that yet another switch in vehicles is in order. If we want to understand how this genre, so central to Marcus's work, crossed racial boundaries and yet was simultaneously defined as white, how it rode the transnational flows of commodity culture to become a global phenomenon even as it was defined as essentially American, we need a faster, more intensely capitalized vehicle. Transnational rockabilly provides us with an avenue to explore one of the central features of modern capitalism: the way it redraws the very lines it promises to erase. We can't rely on just trains or ships if we want to understand how capitalism reproduces boundaries of nation, race, gender, and class even as it claims to render them meaningless, or how it captures revolutionary desires to transgress boundaries and transforms them into an engine of social reproduction. To catch up with this problem, we need to ride an airplane — preferably a supersonic jet.[1]

Planes, of course, are as much a part of the rock 'n' roll legacy as are trains. Think of the crash that killed Buddy Holly in 1959, or the opening notes of the Beatles' "Back in the USSR." Or Japan Airlines (JAL) Flight 123, a Boeing 747SR that crashed in rural Japan on August 12, 1985, killing 520 persons, including the singer Sakamoto Kyū. The rise of rock 'n' roll and rockabilly — the two were synonymous in late 1950s Japan — as global phenomena is unthinkable in the absence of increasingly multinational record companies like Capitol (American corporate home to both Sakamoto and the Beatles) or RCA (corporate home to Elvis), able to place their product in the hands of teenagers around the globe with unprecedented speed. But rock 'n' roll as a global phenomenon also required air transport and the corporate networks and capital investment that made it possible: from the Pan American jet that delivered Sakamoto Kyū to several thousand screaming fans at Los Angeles International Airport in August 1963 for his first (and only) appearance on *The Steve Allen Show*, to the other Pan American jet that five months later would deliver the Beatles to their hysterical fans at Kennedy Airport in New York City for their appearance on *The Ed Sullivan Show*. Or, for that matter, the JAL jet that delivered the Beatles to Tokyo's Haneda Airport in the summer of 1966.

At the dawn of its invention, it was widely believed that the airplane would once and for all liberate the human race from its shackles: spatial distance, national boundaries, class conflict, even — as the Italian futurist poet F. T. Marinetti declared in 1912 — the constraints of syntax (Schnapp). And yet the rise of air travel led not to the erasure of national boundaries, but rather to their intensification. The first decades of the twentieth century gave birth to both the airplane and the modern passport-visa system, a new technology by which nation-states regulated border crossings. Under the latter, a temporary wartime measure that became permanent in the 1920s, the relatively porous borders and informal paperwork of mid-nineteenth-century migration were replaced with a highly systematic bureaucratic procedure. The spatial boundaries that commercial air travel deterritorialized were simultaneously reterritorialized by the nation-state, with its penchant for "monopolizing the legitimate means of movement" (Torpey). Although the rockabilly music of Elvis Presley traveled around the world at nearly the speed of sound in the 1950s, Elvis himself never appeared in concert overseas, both because he was apparently afraid to fly and because his manager, Colonel Tom Parker, was an illegal immigrant. Parker did not have a passport and hence could not leave U.S. territory for fear that he would not be permitted to return (Guralnick, *Careless Love* 91–119).

The airplane also made war between nations possible on a scale previously unimaginable. The attack on Pearl Harbor (two days before the birth of Sakamoto Kyū) and the atomic bombings of Hiroshima and Nagasaki are prominent examples of how air power simultaneously linked and divided nations. Sakamoto belonged to a generation of Japanese who grew up during the war, able to distinguish B-29 bombers and other makes of aircraft as they flew overhead. Later, during the Cold War, air power provided the strategic key to U.S. hegemony in Asia, a strategy that centered largely on U.S. air bases in Japan and Okinawa. It was at an enlisted men's club on one such base in Tachikawa, a suburb of Tokyo, in April 1958 that a sixteen-year-old Sakamoto Kyū made his public debut, singing a cover version of Elvis's "Hound Dog," apparently to great response from the American GIs in his audience (Ei, *Sakamoto Kyū monogatari*, 165–168). Without air power, that audience in Tachikawa would not have existed; without air power, Armed Forces Radio could not have provided Sakamoto's generation of Japanese teenagers with up-to-the-minute access to the latest in American pop. Without air power, Sakamoto's career would likely never have taken place.

Sakamoto is frequently cited as a symbol of Japan's postwar recovery. But air travel and air cargo made that economic growth possible. In civilian aviation, JAL became both a symbol of and a key player in Japan's postwar prosperity. Founded in 1951 as a private corporation, two years later it became part of the wave of post-Occupation counterreforms, in which the central government, no longer inhibited by U.S. Occupation reform policies, reasserted its authority. The Japan Air Lines Law of 1953 made JAL a semigovernmental corporation with a monopoly on international flights among Japanese carriers. JAL began transpacific service to

San Francisco in 1954 and in 1959 added a Tokyo–Los Angeles route; by the mid-1960s it was recognized as one of the world's leading airlines (Davies 425–514). It became a centerpiece in the government-industry cooperative relationship that came to be known as "Japan, Inc." The corrupt underbelly of that alliance surfaced to view in 1976, when former prime minister Tanaka Kakuei was arrested for accepting bribes to influence All Nippon Airways, Japan's second largest carrier, to purchase Lockheed jets.

Despite the scandal and the sporadic crashes that bedeviled the Japanese airline industry in the 1950s and 1960s, positions as pilots or flight attendants were among the most glamorous jobs to which young Japanese could aspire. It is hardly surprising that a sixth-grader Sakamoto, when asked to record his dream for the future, wrote that he hoped to become a pilot someday (Ei, *Sakamoto Kyū monogatari* 121). By 1963, the peak of Sakamoto's global fame, JAL had developed an international reputation for offering top-class service to its globe-trotting clientele — the transnational jet set. Yet the border-crossing commodity JAL offered for sale was, at least in part, national culture in a highly feminized form. JAL ads in American media from the early 1960s, for example, invariably feature kimono-clad women and frequently present biographical sketches of female flight attendants, identified primarily by their given names and their embodiment of Japanese "tradition." The copy in these ads repeatedly stresses both deterritorialization and reterritorialization, the overlapping of transnational and national spaces. The point is made explicitly in an ad from the 13 March 1961 issue of *Newsweek*:

> You inhabit two different worlds at the same time on the DC-8C Jet Couriers of Japan Air Lines. On the one hand, you're reclining at ease in a sleek giant of a jet, flying high over the Pacific at almost ten miles a minute. Then there's your other world, the restful, tranquil world of Japan. Aboard your new Jet Courier you're surrounded by an atmosphere which is delightfully Japanese. There are shoji screens, tatami carpets, chrysanthemum designs . . . everywhere the taste and restraint of Japan.

The air passenger transcends all national boundaries — only to find himself back in "traditional" Japan.

The emergence of the flight attendant as a sex symbol in the 1950s and 1960s in Japan and elsewhere was an ironic instance of reterritorialization in another sense, as well. Whereas in the 1930s, women in the United

States and Europe had to fight to cross the gender line and win positions in the previously all-male world of flight attendants, by the 1950s the gender line had been redrawn to fulfill a new function: stewardesses were now sex symbols, as well as icons of corporate and national identity (Love-grove). Commodity culture found a way to recreate the very gender line that had supposedly been erased.

The global circulation of rockabilly is also a problem of translation, another modern technology that promises to transcend boundaries. Naoki Sakai argues that in the eighteenth century, intellectuals in Japan reached a previously unknown epistemological relation to the language they used: they discovered that they were using a hybrid language, one composed of Chinese and Japanese elements (Sakai, *Voices of the Past*). With this discovery, a movement arose to separate the elements of the newly discovered hybridity into distinct national languages. It was no longer legitimate to read Chinese texts in Japanese; one should read Chinese texts in Chinese, and — if there was a need to read them to a Japanese-speaking audience — they should be properly translated into Japanese first. That is to say, what now appears as a heterogeneous linguistic realm was separated into two distinct realms; what Sakai calls "the schema of cofiguration" was introduced, in which the discovery of a stable image of an other — in this case, China — enabled the simultaneous discovery of an image of the self, Japan.

When two languages are separated in this way, the only permissible contact between them occurs by way of a certain representation of translation. Translation in this guise claims to serve as a technique for crossing a boundary, for linking two previously distinct realms, but in fact what this representation of translation actually achieves is the establishment of that boundary, a reterritorialization of heteroglossic reality into distinct national languages. "Strictly speaking, it is not because two different language unities are given that we have to translate (or interpret) one text into another; it is because translation *articulates* languages so that we may postulate the two unities of the translating and the translated languages as if they were autonomous and closed entities through *a certain representation of translation*" (Sakai, *Translation & Subjectivity* 2). The new discourse of translation installed the notion of a homogeneous national language shared by all the members of the national community as a medium for supposedly transparent communication.

Such a representation of translation obscured the fact that all communication occurs by way of translation; no linguistic community enjoys transparent language. The schema of cofiguration produced the fantasy of a national community grounded in a single homogeneous language and untroubled by internal difference. And yet the shared national language that all Japanese supposedly spoke did not exist: as Sakai notes, the newly discovered language arrived stillborn. Ueda Kazutoshi and other scholars in late-nineteenth-century Japan bemoaned the diversity of dialects — based on such factors as region, class, profession, and gender — that threatened the very possibility of the nationwide communication they thought was essential to the process of building a modern nation. Massive institutional and ideological policies were enacted to bring into existence the national language that was supposedly already the birthright of every Japanese citizen. As a result, a standardized language did emerge and became the basis for the national education system, industrial publishing, and the other commercial and bureaucratic institutions of the modern capitalist nation. In the first half of the twentieth century, it also became the lingua franca in Japan's growing overseas empire: in Taiwan, Korea, and elsewhere (Lee).

Other existing forms of speech simultaneously became nonstandard dialects: they were different from the hegemonic standard, and yet they were not foreign to the Japanese language. They became a kind of domesticated otherness that had to be regulated but did not pose the same kind of foreignness that a competing national language such as Chinese did. They might even prove a beneficial resource to the nation. Although a Tokyo speaker might not understand all the words spoken by a rural farmer, nonetheless no translation was needed: they were both speaking Japanese, after all.

Accordingly, to understand Sakamoto's rockabilly, I will explore the role translation plays in producing two kinds of otherness: first, the way translation according to the schema of cofiguration establishes a boundary between two supposedly distinct languages, and second, the way that the supposedly homogeneous language community produced through this translation includes various marginalized dialects, forms of language that are exotic yet belong to the interior of the speech community — the otherness, for example, of Korea and Taiwan on the one hand, and of Okinawa and Hokkaido on the other, as they have been conceptualized in Japan since 1945, as Seiji Lippit argues elsewhere in this volume. In the first instance, interlingual translation represents a certain text as belonging to a foreign language (and simultaneously establishes the translator and his or her readers as belonging to a single homogeneous linguistic community, thereby erasing the failures of communication within that community). If that is so, what techniques are used in the second instance, to establish a dialect as a kind of peripheral culture, but one that is still located within the boundaries of the speech community? What is the relationship between these two sets of techniques? How and when does the boundary between foreign and peripheral shift? And, most importantly, what opportunities are created within this fluidity for minor literature in the sense that Gilles Deleuze and Félix Guattari propose, of a literature that undermines existing power relationships?

Sakamoto Kyū's translation of rockabilly music presents a good field for exploring this problematic because as we trace through it, we see repeated instances of the processes by which minority discourses are both rendered peripheral and brought to the center of the social imaginary. We see the boundary between foreign and peripheral undergo fluid permutations. We also see repeated instances of translation, deliberate decisions made not to translate, and other instances that challenge the possibility of defining what translation is. In Sakamoto's music, we encounter a "blur of languages, and not at all a system of languages" (Deleuze and Guattari 24).

As I map out connections between airplanes, translation, and rockabilly, I will deal primarily with two songs that were central to Sakamoto's career. The first is an Elvis Presley song, "GI Blues." Released in late 1960, shortly after Presley's stint as a U.S. GI stationed in Germany, it was the theme song for a film of the same name. It was an enormous hit in the United States and around the world — including Japan. The song, written for Elvis by Sid Tepper and Roy C. Bennet, is a sort of translation, as was all of rockabilly.[2] It claims in its title to reproduce an African American musical genre, and it in fact does follow the traditional twelve-bar blues format, with lyrics structured around the usual call-and-response pattern. Yet the song is clearly a hybrid, mixing a variety of musical genres into its blues framework, most notably military march cadences. The film sound track as a whole is similarly hybrid, including lullabies, romantic ballads, straight-ahead rockabilly numbers (including another train song, "Frankfort Special"), and even a song adapted from German folk music ("Wooden Heart") that includes lyrics sung in German by Elvis.

The translation that Elvis achieved in "GI Blues" and earlier singles seemed to erase a preexisting boundary: a minority cultural form, the blues, was brought to the center of mainstream popular culture. In the words of producer Sam Phillips, "I went out into this no-man's-land, and I knocked the shit out of the color line," a crossing that he credited at least in part to Presley himself, since "Elvis Presley knew what it was like to be poor, but that damn sure didn't make him prejudiced. *He didn't draw any lines*" (qtd. in Guralnick, *Last Train* 134–135; original emphasis). Elvis's performances in fact did blur boundaries — not just racial ones, but also those of class, gender, and sexuality. It was these transgressions that provoked the sharply negative reactions to his early television appearances, accusations of vulgarity, of grinding like a striptease artist, of simulating sex acts on stage.

When Elvis appeared on Steve Allen's television program, the host attempted to defuse these criticisms by dressing Elvis in formal evening attire and having him perform "Hound Dog" (a song originally made famous by the female R&B singer, Big Mama Thornton) in the face of a real live basset hound. The incident is usually interpreted as a ridiculing of Presley, and perhaps this caused the wariness that Sakamoto Kyū expresses in the epigraph to this article. But what strikes me as particularly interesting here is the tactic used to marginalize Presley and the song. We find here not translation, at least in the ordinary sense, but rather a completely literal reading of the song's lyrics. The poetics of metaphor are denied to the song: it is ridiculed by making it literally into a song about a hound dog. There is an insistence that no translation is necessary. Literal reading is used here to elicit the otherness of the song, even as it is undeniably sung in the shared language of English.[3]

This was how mainstream society reacted to Elvis's crossing of boundaries. And yet we cannot ignore how Elvis's various crossings also redrew lines. More precisely, they showed that the crossing could occur only in certain directions. To get Elvis's early singles played on the radio and to secure concert bookings across the South, Phillips repeatedly had to assure skeptical music industry figures that his new singing sensation was in fact white.

In early 1961, Sakamoto Kyū released a cover version of "GI Blues" with the lyrics translated into Japanese by Minami Kazumi. The song was one of the last gasps in the rockabilly boom that had begun in Japan in 1958, with the First Nichigeki Western Carnival — the first in a series of concerts that caused a nationwide sensation, featuring local artists playing music in various genres of American teen pop (Kurosawa; Kitanaka 93–101). Later that year, the Third Nichigeki Western Carnival provided Sakamoto with his first taste of the national spotlight. In his performance there, as well as throughout his early career, Sakamoto was closely identified with Elvis. Sakamoto had already enjoyed several hits in Japan before "GI Blues," but this was the first released under his own name rather than that of Danny Iida and the Paradise Kings (although they continued to back him on the record), the band he had joined in 1958 at the behest of his management. "GI Blues" seems to have had a special impact on its Japanese audience. A feature on recent "Music Fashions" in the May 1961 issue of *Heibon*, a popular magazine, included a full-page spread on the "GI Blues" look. At least three other Japanese rockabilly singers — Kamayatsu Hiroshi, Sasaki Isao, and Mickey Curtis — also released cover versions of the song (photographs of the latter two in military uniforms were featured in the fashion article). But it was Sakamoto's version of the song that became the definitive Japanese-language version: it entered the *Music Life* domestic hit chart at number three in January 1961 (in fact, four of the eight songs listed that month are by Sakamoto) and remained in the charts until May.

In his version, Sakamoto adopts many of Presley's vocal mannerisms, including the slurring and hiccupy flourishes characteristic of American rockabilly. The singing style is quite distinct from that which Sakamoto had used on his previous hit singles but is likely closer to what he had used in his early live performances. The band behind Sakamoto plays a swinging arrangement by Danny Iida, a tight rockabilly weave accented with jazz-influenced drumming and dueling guitar and piano fills; it runs circles around the fairly staid arrangement on Elvis's original. The lyrics are translated into Japanese, except for a refrain that remains in English: "Hop, two, three, four, occupation GI blues" (somehow, "hup" has become "hop" in translation). Although Elvis's version is clearly sung from the perspective of a GI stationed in Germany, including references to the Rhine River, German food, and pretty fräuleins, these local references are erased from Sakamoto's version. In fact, Sakamoto's translation seems to relocate the speaker to Japan, so that the relevant occupation is the U.S. occupation of Japan.

Sakamoto's "GI Blues" raises a number of questions. First of all, what did it mean, at the dawn of America's Vietnam War and so soon after the massive anti-American protests that accompanied the 1960 renewal of the U.S.-Japan Security Pact, for a Japanese singer to sing lyrics mostly in Japanese but adopting the enunciative position of an American GI, complaining of homesickness and the squalor of barracks life — but also suggesting himself as an object of desire to local (Japanese) residents? The problem becomes more complex when we note that up through the mid-1960s, Japanese rock 'n' roll musicians — including the early Sakamoto —

found their most stable source of income in performances at clubs on U.S. military bases.

We should also consider the question of whether Sakamoto's version of the song — or any of his earlier translated covers of American pop music (including songs by Paul Anka, Bobby Darrin, and others) — could have been hits in the United States. I suspect the answer is no.[4] A Japanese singing American pop "straight" was certainly acceptable in Japan, but in the United States, it could be viewed only as an exotic joke, one that would elicit appeals to the supposed "authenticity" of Elvis's original. In the United States, Sakamoto the Japanese rockabilly singer of "GI Blues" could only produce laughter — laughter in the Bergsonian sense of a technique for the violent disciplining of materiality that jams up the smooth functioning of the social machinery. But if that was so, why was there no resistance to the idea of Elvis singing in German, or, for that matter, to his singing a song that claimed to be an African American blues number? Elvis, singing from the supposedly universal position of an American white man, could cite the particular of German folk music without raising eyebrows. Likewise, Sakamoto as a particular Japanese could invoke the universal of American rockabilly within the context of Japan. But Sakamoto singing rockabilly in America would result in cognitive dissonance, a discomforting confusion of hierarchies between universal and particular, one that might even suggest that the universal was simply another particular.

As Marcus notes, rockabilly in the United States was, above all, a white genre. But as Gilroy reminds us, "gender is the modality in which race is lived" (85). American rockabilly wasn't only racially exclusive, it was also almost exclusively male. Despite the presence of many well-known female voices in both country and blues, virtually all of the successful rockabilly singers were men.[5] Within the Japanese market, Sakamoto was able to perform the masculine role of an American soldier. But to achieve success in the West, as we will see, he had to take on a more feminized, nonthreatening "cute" role, more like a JAL stewardess than an American GI. Sakamoto's translations of rockabilly showed that borders could be crossed, but only in certain directions, at certain times, and by persons carrying the proper cultural passports.

On the second song I will deal with here, Sakamoto was backed by the Toshiba Recording Orchestra (the stable of studio musicians under contract to Sakamoto's Japanese record label). The single version of "Ue wo muite arukō"was released in Japan in late 1961, after Sakamoto performed the song to great acclaim on nationwide television. The song's title might be translated as "I will keep my head up as I walk." The music was composed by Nakamura Hachidai, the lyrics by Ei Rokusuke, a duo that composed many hit songs for Sakamoto and others. "Ue wo muite arukō" immediately became an enormous domestic hit. The single sold more than 300,000 copies in Japan, but did not win the coveted "Nippon Record Taishō" award because, in the mind of at least one member of the prize jury, the song sounded too American (Take 54–65).

This is the same song that under the title "Sukiyaki" became a number-one hit in the summer of 1963 when it was released by Capitol Records in the United States, the first Japanese-produced record to sell a million copies worldwide. The origin of the "Sukiyaki" title remains obscure; according to a 1981 interview with Sakamoto, a British DJ who liked the song but knew only three words of Japanese — *Fujiyama, geisha,* and *sukiyaki* — was responsible for the song's title in the English-speaking world (Aikura). The song had already become a hit in a number of European countries in 1962, either as "Sukiyaki" or under a number of other titles — in Belgium, for example, it was known as "Unforgettable Geisha Baby." It was originally introduced in England through an instrumental version by the Kenny Ball Orchestra, recorded after Pye Records president Louis Benjamin heard Sakamoto's original while on a trip to Japan. The popularity of the cover version prompted Pye to issue Sakamoto's original version in the United Kingdom, also under the title "Sukiyaki." In early 1963, DJs at West Coast stations in the United States began playing the Sakamoto version to great response, and another cover version by Billy Vaughn and His Orchestra began to enjoy chart success. These developments led Capitol Records to release the original Sakamoto version in the United States. The single entered the *Cashbox* hit charts on May 4, 1963, and reached number one seven weeks later; it remained at number one for four consecutive weeks. Numerous cover versions were also released, some with English lyrics. By July 1963 the song had been released in twenty-three different versions in thirteen different countries, including one by Masako, a Japanese American singer from Hawaii (Kurosawa 237; Schilling 215–217; Hogan).

The song's success abroad and the Gold Record award presented to Sakamoto the following year (again, the first ever to a Japanese performer) were widely reported in the Japanese media. One critic was quoted as saying that the song's breakthrough in the West shows that "our eighteen years of struggle in the postwar have not been in vain" ("Kyō-chan hoshi wo mitsuketa"). As we have already seen, when Sakamoto arrived at Los Angeles International Airport in August 1963 to perform the song live on *The Steve Allen Show*, he was met by thousands of screaming teenagers, foreshadowing what would happen the following February when the Beatles arrived in New York City. Incidentally, while in Los Angeles, Sakamoto asked to meet his idol, but was told that Elvis was too busy filming his latest movie.[6]

Ei Rokusuke's lyrics in the original Japanese version of "Ue wo muite arukō" present a man who is determined not to allow sadness and loneliness to overcome him; he vows to fight back tears, keep his chin up, and walk forward. The melancholic lyrics stand in odd contrast to the cheerful melody, which (particularly in the passages whistled by the singer) seems to take an active role in buoying his spirits. But most American listeners could not know this, because when Sakamoto's single was released in the United States, the lyrics were left in the original Japanese, with no translation. Yet as I have already noted, the song was given a new title.

"Sukiyaki," then, is not a translation of the original title — yet in another sense it might be the ultimate translation. Sakamoto himself was quoted at the time as saying, "At least 'Sukiyaki' is a Japanese word" ("Rising Son"), and of course that was the whole point. "Sukiyaki" was chosen because the word included a strong sense of Japaneseness or foreignness — an effect that literal translation would have spoiled. Somewhat incredibly (or predictably?), the single Sakamoto released in the United States to follow up "Sukiyaki" was a cover version of the old warhorse "China Nights (Shina no yoru)," an Orientalist fantasy about romance between a Japanese man and a Chinese woman that had first scored as a hit in Japan in 1939, during the heyday of the Japanese empire.[7] An article from a 1963 Japanese magazine retracing Sakamoto's August trip to Los Angeles quotes him on board the Pan American jet carrying him to America: "Next we'll see if I can get 'Shina no yoru' to catch on. With 'Ue wo muite arukō' becoming a hit, we know that Japanese teenagers and American teenagers are the same. Japanese pop songs are no longer an underdeveloped country. With my generation, at last Japan has become an international power" ("Kyū-chan America wo seifuku su"). In the same article, he is quoted again, this time on the plane ride home, to the effect that the best part of the trip was when an executive for Capitol Records told him that if he could produce two more hits, he would get his own star on the sidewalk in front of Graumann's Chinese Theatre. Given the

Orientalist nature of the follow-up single, the location was perfect. But "China Nights" peaked in the low fifties on the hit charts, and Sakamoto never got his star on Hollywood Boulevard.

Japanese music journalists in 1963 were well aware of the exoticization involved in retitling Sakamoto's song as "Sukiyaki."[8] The song's lyricist, Ei Rokusuke, also found this translation a jarring experience. He happened to be traveling in the United States just as the song was starting to break. In a travel diary published at the time, he describes the envy he felt for the song's composer, Nakamura Hachidai. Nakamura's music can be appreciated by anyone, no matter what language they speak.

> When he sits down at a piano, he doesn't need any words. But my work uses the Japanese language.
>
> When I write poetry, when I write prose, only people who can read Japanese — no, really, only a part of those who can read that language — understand my work.
>
> In New York, I heard "Ue wo muite arukō." The melody was exactly the same, but the title written on the record label was "Sukiyaki." In the lyrics were words like "geisha baby" and "Fujiyama." (Ei, "Rokusuke America noshiaruki")

Ei goes on to analyze the situation: "Even if someone were to translate my Japanese, it still wouldn't be my words, because it would be a translation." His article concludes emphatically, " 'Ue wo muite arukō' is *not* 'Sukiyaki'!" It's unclear which version of "Sukiyaki" Ei heard in New York, but it is quite clear that he, like many others caught up in neocolonial power relationships, had inadvertently discovered that translation was "a significant technology of colonial domination" and that the colonial subaltern "exists only 'in translation,' always already cathected by colonial domination" (Niranjana 21, 43).

Ironically, the dish sukiyaki, chosen here for its exotic resonance, was a modern creation, a product of the Meiji period (1868–1912) and the reintroduction of beef eating into Japan after a thousand-year-long prohibition due to the influence of Buddhism. In Meiji, the dish signified the ingestion of Western modernity, not the preservation of Japanese tradition. Obviously, these overtones had been lost in both Japan and the West by 1963 and it was for the signification of Japaneseness that the word was chosen and the song lyrics left untranslated. It should also be noted that one reason the word "sukiyaki" had entered the vocabulary of many

Americans was the large number of returned American soldiers who had encountered the dish during their tours of duty in Japan and Okinawa.

Why were the lyrics left untranslated? Perhaps we can speculate that while Sakamoto singing in English could only produce a sense of alienation, Sakamoto singing in Japanese could be consumed and enjoyed — just like the markings of Japaneseness found on JAL airplanes. Gilroy notes that the "discourse of authenticity has been a notable presence in the mass marketing of successive black folk-cultural forms to white audiences" (99); with "Sukiyaki" Sakamoto discovered that Japan also could function as a commodity. What was to be communicated was not the semantic content of the song's lyrics, but the semiotic content of the music and the ethnicity of the performer and his language.[9]

To borrow Sakai's words, Sakamoto singing in Japanese to an English-speaking audience provided a reassuring *"experience of understanding the experience of not comprehending"* (Sakai, *Translation & Subjectivity* 6; emphasis original). English-speaking listeners could represent their incomprehension tidily through the schema of cofiguration: they did not understand Sakamoto because he was singing in a foreign language. Sakamoto could even be the object of great praise: "Even in its praise of 'extraordinary cultural achievements by other civilizations,' the narcissism of the West seeks only to find in other cultures and civilizations what distinguishes the West from the rest of the world, and continually expects the others to respond to its narcissistic demand for acknowledgement of its distinction" (Sakai, *Translation & Subjectivity* 70–71). Rather than a troubling experience of discommunication, Sakamoto's Western listeners were permitted to enjoy what was quite literally a harmonious misunderstanding. It was a different sort of misunderstanding from, for example, the panic set off by the cryptic English-language lyrics of the Kingsmen's 1960 hit single, "Louie Louie," or by any number of Little Richard singles from the 1950s, when parents feared that the slurred lyrics might contain obscene passages.

Moreover, given the Cold War context of 1963, I would argue that only by singing in Japanese could Sakamoto demonstrate that he — and the nation of Japan, which had so recently exploded in violent protest against the United States — was in fact singing in our language all along. "Sukiyaki" signified a Japan that was ready to take its place within the U.S.-dominated security order for East Asia. It was an exotic, peripheral member of this community, speaking a kind of marginal dialect — and yet nonetheless a member. In the schema of configuration that became hegemonic during the Cold War, Japan was "one of us." Unlike Red China or North Korea, it belonged to the community on this side of the Iron Curtain. Performing this role was, it seems, the precondition for Sakamoto to enjoy the status of a globally famous pop singer. It is also true, however, that by singing in Japanese Sakamoto — unlike, for example, the Beatles — condemned himself in the West to the status of a one-hit wonder, more specifically an ethnic novelty act, akin to Chinese acrobats, even as his global success helped pave the way for the Beatles.

Given the racializing and gendered tendencies of Orientalism in its Cold War guise, whatever potential Sakamoto Kyū had for creating a minority discourse lay not so much in a translation like "Sukiyaki" as it did with one like "GI Blues." "A minor literature doesn't come from a minor language; it is rather that which a minority constructs within a major language" (Deleuze and Guattari 16). Sakamoto's "GI Blues" was a major hit in Japan (albeit in the relatively marginal cultural world of popular music), where it only reinforced hegemonic notions about America and Japan. But had it been released in America, the same song might well have unleashed the sort of troubling force that Deleuze and Guattari associate with Kafka and his ilk. It could have become what Niranjana calls a "disruptive translation," a form of colonial mimicry that undermined notions of the authenticity of Elvis's (and America's) rockabilly. Sakamoto's ability to adopt the posture of an honorary white man had one effect in Japan, but it also had the potential to produce a different effect on American listeners. But the song remained unheard beyond Japan, its potential unrealized.

There is, then, something tragic about the story of Sakamoto, who in America is remembered as a one-hit wonder, because his numerous hit records in Japan don't count. With "Sukiyaki," Sakamoto finally chose to represent Japan rather than rockabilly music.[10] In subsequent years, he would be trotted out again and again whenever Japan needed an "official youth spokesman" for international expos and the like. And, like Elvis in the early 1960s, Sakamoto drifted away from the marginal genre of rockabilly and into mainstream pop ballads. Eventually, he became better known as a television personality than as a singer — although Sakamoto tried more than once to revive his music career. In 1975, timed to coincide with the first visit to America by Emperor Hirohito, Capitol Records invited Sakamoto to return to Los Angeles to record new material, mainly English-language versions of songs that had been hits for other artists in Japan. A single, "Elimo," with the B side "Why," was released in the

United States in October 1975. Although it received some media coverage in Japan, it sank without denting the American charts. Then again, just days before his death, Sakamoto approached Ei and Nakamura, the songwriting team that had produced "Ue wo muite arukō," to ask their help in restarting his singing career. But unlike Elvis, Sakamoto was never going to have his great comeback — at least not during his lifetime.

Still, along with tragedy, there is also something astonishing about Sakamoto's story, that of a pimply-faced Japanese teenager who went from singing "Hound Dog" to U.S. soldiers in Japan to worldwide fame in just five years. No one told him that he couldn't become a rockabilly star, that he didn't have the right passport, and so, for a brief moment, he did. In the hands of the subaltern, as Lydia Liu reminds us, translation can become a weapon for the production of agency and for disrupting the hierarchies that divide "original" from "copy."

Thousands of mourners gathered for Sakamoto's funeral on 9 September 1985. Like the plane crash, it was a major media event. In the weeks before and after, Japanese musicians of all generations and genres paid tribute to him. One musician was quoted as saying he was surprised to find himself more deeply affected by Sakamoto's death than he was by John Lennon's (Ei, *Sakamoto Kyū monogatari* 10).

When Sakamoto died, the Japanese economy was near its bubble peak, as the nation enjoyed unprecedented prosperity. Japan was the world's wealthiest, healthiest, and best-educated nation; its products and services set global standards for excellence. Flights into and out of Japan were booked to capacity, as Japanese traveled abroad in astonishing numbers to enjoy their new prosperity. The contrast with the United States, stuck in its post-Vietnam economic doldrums, was lost on no one. While JAL flourished, American airlines like Braniff (1982), Pan American (1991), and TWA (1992) were going bankrupt. Japanese didn't screw things up, the way Americans did. The drug-related death of Elvis Presley in 1977 and the murder of John Lennon in New York City in 1980 helped contribute to the image of an America whose undisciplined culture threatened its position as hegemon in East Asia. Japan seemed poised to take its place as the next superpower.

In retrospect, it now seems that the 1985 JAL crash signaled the beginning of the end for that version of Japan. Although Japan's economy would continue to boom for another five years, anyone who was there at the time of the crash will remember the obsessive news coverage of the incident (television networks suspended regular programming for days to devote airtime to the disaster) and the way it left an indelible scar on Japanese public self-confidence. Enormous efforts were made to determine which side of the border blame rested on — was JAL or the (American) Boeing Corporation at fault? The eventual finding, that sloppy maintenance work at Boeing caused the crash, provided little comfort (Davies 476–484). In the late 1980s, the Japanese government slid into another series of ugly bribery scandals, and then in the early 1990s the economic bubble burst and hard times began. Privatized in 1987, JAL struggled to survive in a new environment of cutthroat competition.

Given the timing and significance of his death, it is perhaps unsurprising that even today, Sakamoto continues to hold a unique place in Japanese popular memory. Despite repeated efforts, no Japanese artist has broken through in Western pop charts the way he did. On 31 December 2000, during *Kōhakuō uta gassen*, the annual musical extravaganza broadcast on the NHK network, the producers marked the end of the twentieth century by having all of the performers gather on stage together to sing "Ue wo muite arukō," with Sakamoto's widow and daughters present in the audience. And with Japan still sunk in seemingly endless recession, 2001 would see a Sakamoto Kyū nostalgia boom, centered on a rediscovery of his 1963 single "Ashita ga aru sa" ("There's Always Tomorrow"), a lively big-band number. If Sakamoto is remembered as a one-hit wonder in the West, in Japan he more and more becomes the unshakable ghost haunting a once high-flying empire.

What can we learn from all the translations Sakamoto performed — and that were performed on him? For starters, that whereas a "minor literature" might need to be written in a major language, Sakamoto's example forces us to realize that "language" here does not necessarily mean "national language." "Sukiyaki" was a major international hit despite — because of — its being in the exotic language of Japanese. Translation takes place in many guises, and the boundaries it draws can be ideological rather than linguistic. Second, Sakamoto shows us that what makes a text minor or major depends as much on its historical situation as it does on any internal quality belonging to the work itself. During the back-and-forth movements of translation, minor and major can swap places fluidly.

And what can we learn from Sakamoto's ill-fated career as an airline passenger? That overly simple models of the postmodern situation as transnational miss the ways that capitalism redraws boundaries of nation (and race, gender, class, etc.) even as it promises to erase them. When Sakamoto's personal effects were recovered from the JAL crash site, it was learned that he had carried on board with him a portable tape player. The song on the tape was USA for Africa's "We Are the World," a fact simultaneously pathetic, ridiculous — and telling. According to his widow, Sakamoto loved the song and sang it frequently in the months before his death (Kashiwagi 161). On the one hand, we see here the bad taste and sentimentality that led Sakamoto to follow not the early Elvis but rather the bland pop of Pat Boone and Paul Anka (or, for that matter, the Hollywood Elvis). On the other hand, perhaps we see yet another sign of the tragedy of Sakamoto's life. Having been pigeonholed as an Oriental novelty act, he was unable to secure his star in front of Graumann's Chinese Theatre. Had things turned out differently, had "China Nights" or "Elimo" become hits, Sakamoto might well have been one of the superstars who jetted into Los Angeles for the "We Are the World" session. As it was, the song simply repeated a familiar pattern. It was performed almost exclusively by North American and English musicians who nonetheless confidently proclaimed (in English, of course) that they, indeed, were the world. No translation needed. No Asian performers appeared on the recording.

Sakamoto the air traveler crossed national, ethnic, and racial boundaries, but some lines he could not cross. A few years before his death, Sakamoto would look back on his whirlwind airplane trip to Los Angeles in 1963. "On the way back from Los Angeles, we stopped in Hawaii. There was this really pretty beach there. But when I tried to go there with my friends, they told us no coloreds allowed. I went, 'Huh? Oh, I get it — I'm colored.' I was just stunned. I felt like I had yet again brushed against the hugeness, the complexity of America" (qtd in Aikura 180–181).

This is Hawaii, Elvis's home away from home, a regular stopover for JAL flights since 1959, and the only American state whose population in 1960 included a *majority* of persons of Asian ancestry, and where Japanese constituted the single largest ethnic group. In translating rockabilly, Sakamoto crossed the color line, only to find that the color line stood intact — even in Hawaii. To become an international star, he was required to perform as an "authentic" Japanese, and that meant staying to one side of the color line. His claims to translate rockabilly, likewise, have to be denied implicitly by those who would tie the genre's authenticity to American culture.

But if we listen carefully to Sakamoto's translations, and if we pay close attention to the trajectories of his flight paths, we can perhaps trace not the clash of civilizations, not the clash between civilizations, but the clash within, the noise disrupting the myth of a homogeneous national culture. Perhaps we can hear a sonic boom that cannot be explained away either as a foreign language or as a marginal dialect of some national tongue. Perhaps we can obtain hints about how to translate outside the schema of cofiguration, about how to fly airplanes that don't simply return us to the same identities they promised to transgress.

Notes

This paper began in an exchange of e-mails with Joseph Murphy, who first pointed out to me the complexity of "sukiyaki" as a translation. I am also grateful to Tess Orth for research assistance. She unearthed, among other things, the main title of this article, a 1960s JAL advertising slogan. Finally, I am thankful to the participants in the Multicampus Research Group, whose comments on an earlier version of this paper helped me to rethink the project in many useful ways. Translations from Japanese language sources are mine, except where noted. Japanese personal names appear in the original order (family name first, given name second), except in references to English-language sources, where the order has been reversed.

1   The transnational career of rockabilly is clearly a symptom of Paul Virilio's dromological power, whereby speed itself becomes the central form of domination in contemporary society. But, as I hope to demonstrate here, this is not (à la Paul Virilio) solely a matter of the erasure of territory; it is also simultaneously and necessarily an issue of reterritorialization.

2   Peter Guralnick describes the reaction of Sam Phillips, head of Sun Records, to the first successful studio session with Elvis, when his debut single "That's All Right (Mama)" was recorded: "[Phillips] knew that something was in the wind. He knew from his experience recording blues, and from his fascination with black culture, that there was something intrinsic to the music that could translate, that *did* translate. 'It got so you could sell a half million copies of a rhythm and blues record,' Sam told a Memphis reporter in 1959, reminiscing about his overnight success. 'These records appealed to white youngsters just as Uncle Silas [Payne's] songs and stories used to appeal to me. . . . But there was something in many of those youngsters that resisted buying this music. The Southern ones especially felt a resistance that even they probably didn't quite understand. They liked the music, but they weren't sure whether they ought to like it our not. So I got to thinking how many records you could sell if you could find white performers who could play and sing in this same exciting, alive way" (Guralnick, *Last Train* 96).

3   There are other instances in the early history of rock 'n' roll of "literal reading" as a means of effecting a distinction between mainstream and peripheral culture — comedians, for example, who would parse the lyrics to rock 'n' roll songs as if they were difficult grammar exercises. This strategy for enforcing hierarchies within the speech community apparently has a long history. In E. M. Forster's *A Room*

with a View (1908), for example, we encounter Mrs. Honeychurch, "who hoped to cure her children of slang by taking it literally" (95).

4 Although most of Sakamoto's early singles in Japan were covers of American pop hits, only two were included among the twelve songs on his U.S. album, *Sukiyaki and Other Hits* (Capitol Records, 1963): "Good Timing" and "Goodbye Joe." The lyrics for both were translated into Japanese, and neither was released as a U.S. single.

5 Wanda Jackson, who appeared as an opening act on a number of Elvis's early concerts, was a rare exception, though she considered herself more a country-and-western singer than a rockabilly queen. Her 1959 visit to Japan (she too arrived on a Pan American jet), after her version of "Fujiyama Mama" unexpectedly became a hit there, created a sensation among Japanese rockabilly fans (Kurosawa, *Roots* 68–71).

6 "Kangei ni kimo tsubusu: America de no Kyūchan." Sakamoto also hoped to meet Audrey Hepburn, but was told that she likewise was too busy. His third request, to visit Disneyland, was fulfilled. Sakamoto's 1963 visit to Los Angeles was ignored by the *Los Angeles Times*, but received heavy coverage in the local Japanese American newspaper, the *Rafu Shimpo*, in both its English- and Japanese-language sections.

7 Sakamoto's version of "Shina no yoru" was released in the United States on 3 August 1963. The song, from a film of the same name, had been a wartime hit for the film's star, Li Ko Ran (Yamaguchi Yoshiko, known in Hollywood in the 1950s as Shirley Yamaguchi), a Japanese actress who masqueraded as a Japanophilic Chinese in a series of wartime films (Silverberg).

8 "Probably to give the image of 'Japan,' it has been given its new title, which bears no relation whatsoever to the song's original title in Japanese" (Ishioka). Following its success abroad, in late 1963 the song was rereleased by Toshiba in Japan under the title "Sukiyaki," whereupon it reentered the Japanese hit charts.

9 On Orientalist exoticism in Japan-related popular music, see Hosokawa.

10 Other singers from the late-1950s rockabilly boom, including Mickey Curtis and Kamayatsu Hiroshi, would retain "rock" credibility through the turbulent 1960s and 1970s and beyond. They, on the other hand, never enjoyed anything like the international success accorded Sakamoto, although their 1960s bands, the Spiders (Kamayatsu) and the Samurais (Curtis) would tour in the West.

Works Cited

Aikura Hisato. "Sukiyaki song de zenbei wo sekken shita Sakamoto Kyū." *Bungei Shunjū* (October 1981): 179–181.

Davies, R. E. G. *Airlines of Asia Since 1920*. London: Putnam, 1997.

Deleuze, Gilles, and Félix Guattari. *Kafka: Toward a Minor Literature*. Trans. Dana Polan. Minneapolis: University Minnesota Press, 1986.

Ei Rokusuke. "Rokusuke America noshiaruki." *Fujin kōron*. (May 1963): 244–250.

———. *Sakamoto Kyū monogatari: Roku-Hachi-Kyō no Kyō*. Tokyo: Chūo Kōron, 1990.

Forster, E. M. *A Room with a View*. 1908. New York: Vintage Books, n.d.

Gilroy, Paul. *The Black Atlantic: Modernity and Double Consciousness*. Cambridge: Harvard University Press, 1993.

Guralnick, Peter. *Careless Love: The Unmaking of Elvis* Presley. Boston: Little, 1999.

——. *Last Train to Memphis: The Rise of Elvis Presley*. Boston: Little, 1994.

Hogan, Ed. "Kyu Sakamoto." *All Music Guide*. 22 Aug. 2003. http://www.allmusic.com/cg/amg.dll.

Hosokawa, Shuhei. "Martin Denny and the Development of Musical Exotica." *Widening the Horizon: Exoticism in Post-War Popular Music*. Ed. Philip Hayward. Sydney: John Libbey, 1999. 72–93.

——. "Soy Sauce Music: Haruomi Hosono and Japanese Self-Orientalism." *Widening the Horizon: Exoticism in Post-War Popular Music*. Ed. Philip Hayward. Sydney: John Libbey, 1999. 114–144.

Ishioka Ritsuko. "Kongetsu no spot: Kyu Sakamoto," *Music Life* (Sept. 1963). Kurosawa 246–247.

"Kangei ni kimo tsubusu: America de no Kyūchan." *Asahi shinbun*, evening edition. 20 Aug. 1963: 5.

Kashiwagi Yukiko. *Ue wo muite arukō*. Tokyo: Fuji Terebi shuppan, 1986.

Kitanaka Masakazu. *Nihon no uta: sengo kayōkyoku shi*. Tokyo: Shinchōsha,1995.

Kurosawa Susumu, ed. *Roots of Japanese Pops 1955–1970*. Tokyo: Shinkō Music, 1995.

"Kyū-chan hoshi wo mitsuketa." *Mainichi graph* 14 July 1963: 22–27.

"Kyū-chan America wo seifuku su." *Shūkan josei* 4 Sept. 1963: 120–122.

Lee, Yeounsuk. *Kokugo to iu shisō: Kindai Nihon no gengo ninshiki*. Tokyo: Iwanami shoten, 1996.

Liu, Lydia H. *Translingual Practice: Literature, National Culture, and Translated Modernity: China, 1900–1937*. Stanford: Stanford University Press, 1995.

Lovegrove, Keith. *Airline: Identity, Design and Culture*. New York: teNeues, 2000.

Marcus, Greil. *Mystery Train: Images of America in Rock 'n' Roll Music*. 1975. 4th rev. ed. New York: Plume, 1997.

Niranjana, Tejaswini. *Siting Translation: History, Post-Structuralism and the Colonial Context*. Berkeley: University of California Press, 1992.

"Rising Son." *Newsweek*. 1 July 1963: 64.

Sakai, Naoki. *Translation & Subjectivity: On "Japan" and Cultural Nationalism*. Minneapolis: University Minnesota Press, 1997.

——. *Voices of the Past: The Status of Language in Eighteenth-Century Japanese*. Ithaca: Cornell University Press, 1991.

Schilling, Mark. *The Encyclopedia of Japanese Pop Culture*. New York: Weatherhill, 1997.

Schnapp, Jeffrey T. "Propeller Talk." *Modernism/Modernity* 1.3 (1994): 153–178.

Silverberg, Miriam. "Remembering Pearl Harbor, Forgetting Charlie Chaplin, and the Case of the Disappearing Western Woman: A Picture Story." *positions* 1.1 (1993): 24–76.

Take Hideki. *Yomu J-POP: 1945–1999 shiteki zenshi*. Tokyo: Tokuma, 1999.

Torpey, John. *The Invention of the Passport: Surveillance, Citizenship and the State*. Cambridge: Cambridge University Press, 2000.

Virilio, Paul. *Speed & Politics*. Trans. Mark Polizzotti. New York: Semiotext(e), 1977.

PART IV
SPATIALIZING

Cartographies of Globalization,

Technologies of Gendered Subjectivities

The Dub Poetry of Jean "Binta" Breeze

It is generally recognized that an academic use of "African diaspora" grew out of the civil rights movement, anticolonial struggles, and the building of pan-African movements (Hall 222–237; Gilroy, *Black Atlantic* 111– 145; Patterson and Kelly 14; Edwards 46–48). What is less acknowledged, perhaps, is how the current usage of "diaspora" as a category of analysis is implicated in today's global cultures. "Globalization," in its simplest terms, refers to the transnational mobility of capital, labor, technology, consumer goods, art forms, and media images. As a cultural phenomenon, the term refers to the labor diasporas that straddle national borders, existing in a state of "cultural flux" (Appadurai 44). It also denotes a decentering that allows for new hybrid cultures to emerge through an "indigenization" of metropolitan culture (32). As a sociological phenomenon, it means that remote events can have an effect on local ways of life despite the distances separating geographically removed locations (Giddens 64). Marshall McLuhan coined the term "global village" to describe a world in which new media, advanced telecommunications, and rapid transportation shrunk distances between continents and nations. Yet, as Arjun Appadurai observes, McLuhan's metaphor is conceptually inadequate to a world that has become more "rhizomic" in the sense that identities are no longer rooted in a single geographical place (29).

The paradigm shift of "African diaspora" from signifying cultural survivals, commonalities, and continuities to denoting cultural hybridities, difference, and discontinuities reflects the new conditions of globalization. One of the studies that has been instrumental in this conceptual shift is Paul Gilroy's *The Black Atlantic: Modernity and Double Consciousness* (1993).

Guided by a discourse of travel rather than an ideology of return, the book seeks to demonstrate the "rhizomorphic, fractal structure of the transcultural, international formation" that is the black Atlantic (4). Gilroy suggests multiple centers and points of migration that can account for the mutations and hybridities of black culture on both sides of the Atlantic. It is primarily through black popular music that he makes his case. Ronald Judy is correct to identify the third chapter, " 'Jewels Brought from Bondage': Black Music and the Politics of Authenticity," as central to the book's argument (22–29). The value Gilroy ascribes to music as an expressive form has to do with its marginalization in Western systems of knowledge, a history in which a slave's access to literacy was denied or restricted, and its antiphonal (call and response) form that decenters "Africa" as a fixed point of reference for the disapora (72–110). As he explains, "the circulation and mutation of music across the black Atlantic explodes the dualistic structure which puts Africa, authenticity, purity, and origin in crude opposition to the Americas, hybridity, creolisation, and rootlessness" (199). The transatlantic circulation of black popular music, however, is inseparable from a corporate industry responsible for its marketing as a cultural commodity. And although a globalization of the recording industry means that Anglo-American corporate control has been replaced with transnational corporations that are not headquartered in any one nation, all of these corporations operate out of "wealthy, developed nations" (Colista and Leshner 183). It is not accidental, then, that most of the recording artists Gilroy discusses are located in First World cities.[1] Indeed, the old metropolitan centers of New York, London, and Paris — now expanded to include Los Angeles, Tokyo, and Hong Kong — occupy a privileged place in academic discussions of transnational cultures. A consideration of minor transnationalism would necessitate examining the transatlantic traffic between locations that are remote to the global city centers.

The Black Atlantic has received criticism for its narrow definition of the black Atlantic, one that excludes Africa, the Caribbean, and Latin America (Gikandi, Byfield). An absence of the Caribbean as a space of intellectual and cultural production is particularly conspicuous due to the centrality of Afro-Caribbean culture to Gilroy's rethinking of modernity. Although he admits to having "said virtually nothing about the lives, theories, and political activities of Frantz Fanon and C. L. R. James, the two best-known black Atlantic thinkers," he is less aware of how his examples of transatlantic cultural practices are rooted in global city centers (xi). The Soul II Soul song "Keep on Moving," which serves as an icon for the restlessness of the black Atlantic world he wants to chart, is an indication of how the Caribbean that is everywhere in the book is also nowhere to be found. The song appeals to Gilroy as an instance of "transnational black Atlantic creativity" because it was recorded by the British-born descendents of Caribbean settlers in north London and remixed in a dub format in New York by an African American DJ who sampled from American and Jamaican records (16). Although there is a distinctive Jamaican sound or style to the song, Jamaica exists not as a geographical location but only in its British diasporic form, or as "raw materials" for American DJs to sample. "Keep on Moving" was produced in London and remixed in New York because these are centers of the music industry. In this regard, the global village — as a metaphor derived from an agrarian way of life — is no village at all but a series of interconnected urban centers.

To consider London and New York as global city centers is to recognize the degree to which Gilroy's mapping of the black Atlantic follows a cartography of corporate globalization. As a dialogic engagement with African American intellectuals, the book is a transatlantic exchange between Britain and the United States that passes through the Caribbean. In this regard, the absence of Africa, the Caribbean, and Latin America in the black Atlantic is better understood as an effect of the center and periphery structures that are maintained by corporate globalization, despite new transnational cultures that make such structures appear obsolete. On the one hand, globalization breaks down center-periphery relations through a two-way traffic that cannot be explained simply as cultural imperialism and which allows independent artists and cultural producers access to an international market. On the other hand, neocolonial relations are maintained through the uneven distribution of resources in the global marketplace, the unlevel playing field established by the World Trade Organisation (WTO), International Monetary Fund (IMF), and World Bank, and a global assembly line that draws primarily on cheaper Third World female labor (Anderson). In addition, the tendency to regard globalization as a transurban phenomenon elides its effect on rural economies. The growth of agribusiness and biotechnology, accompanied by the need for expanding agricultural markets, has destroyed small farms and their related industries throughout the Third World (Shiva 91–125). Any theory of diaspora that follows a cartography of corporate globalization risks reproducing its structures of power and knowledge.

Not only does the transatlantic travel of black popular music in Gilroy's study take place between First World city centers; the unacknowledged subject of black modernity is also Western, urban, and male. Alluding to Toni Morrison's observation that "modern life begins with slavery," Gilroy argues for black modernity as a thoroughly diasporic, transcultural, and creolized experience (cited in *Atlantic* 221), establishing his definition of modernity through black popular music.[2] His interest in black music as a modern diasporic cultural form lies in its constitutive role in the formation of a black British subjectivity. At the end of the third chapter, he describes his own experience of growing up in a London where "the Caribbean, Africa, Latin America, and above all black America contributed to our lived sense of a racial self" (109). To be fair to Gilroy, he states at the outset that his primary interest in a black Atlantic world lies in defining the cultural politics of Britain's black citizens. However, since his model of a transatlantic black culture is becoming institutionalized as a general theory of the African diaspora, it is necessary to recognize its limitations.

Feminist scholars have shown how the chronotope of mobility in Gilroy's transatlantic model is gendered male (DeLoughrey 205–223; Gunning 32–69). A similar argument could be made about his discussion of black music as a transatlantic phenomenon. Gilroy considers the consumption of music to be an activity that plays a central role in the formation of a black identity, describing this identity as gendered because so many songs are about "the conflict between men and women" (201–202). Yet nowhere does he explain what the music means for black women, or how their listening pleasures might differ from men's. Nor does he explain how female performers have contributed to the diasporic music he describes. Rather, his discussion centers on distinguishing male musicians who give a "respectful and egalitarian representation of women" from their more misogynistic brothers (85). He relies on "dubbing, scratching, and mixing" as technological innovations that "joined production and consumption together" for decentering the musician as artist (103–108). The "cutting and mixing techniques through digital sampling" so characteristic of contemporary black music hold a particular appeal for Gilroy as creative acts that are both modern (because technologically driven) and synchretic (because they sample from global cultures) (103).[3] By "sampling" a few notes or lines from a recording and remixing them with the beats of synthesized drum machines, the musician plays the role of technician rather than creator. Although digital sampling undermines traditional notions of originality and authorship, the artistic creativity of the musician is reconstituted around technological innovations associated with masculinity (Bradby 155–176).[4] It is not just that the musical innovations emerged from the "electronic wizardry" of male DJs who built and repaired sound systems. Music critics and producers also promote the creativity of these musicians as a form of "mastery." The celebration of a "cut-and-mix style" for its blurring of the boundaries between production and consumption nonetheless recenters black popular music around the disc-jockey as producer.

To theorize the black Atlantic in terms of the decentering that Gilroy so admirably proposes, one would have to consider it as the site of multiple heterogeneously produced subjectivities. A theory of modern black subjectivities that are Third World, rural, domestic, and female is available in the work of a diasporic Jamaican female performer, Jean "Binta" Breeze, who employs reggae music and radio technology for staging Jamaican women's cultural identities. Reggae, and its offspring dub and dancehall, has spread throughout the African disapora — there are even Nigerian and South African reggae bands. In its Jamaican birthplace, however, reggae is not simply one among several black musical styles; it is the one that predominates. Its rhythm, from early roots to its most recent incarnation as dancehall music, can be heard booming from large store-front sound systems, ghetto blasters, and the radios that people listen to in their homes, cars, at work, and on the streets. If, as Gilroy claims, music is central to a black sense of self, then one can make an even stronger case for the constitutive power of music in Jamaica. More records per capita are produced there than in any other part of the globe (Oumano, "Reggae" 24). By invoking the mediation of the music through the radio and rhythm box, Breeze decenters the DJ as artist through Jamaican women's consumption of music rather than a cut-and-mix style that consigns them to a more passive role.

Jean "Binta" Breeze grew up in Patty Hill, a small village in the rural hills of Hanover on the northwestern side of the island before moving to Kingston in 1978 to study at the Jamaica School of Drama, where she met the dub poets Oku Onuora, Mikey Smith, and Mutabaruka (Breeze, "Dub Poet" 47). "Dub" is a term used for the B side or instrumental version of records over which DJs "toast" their rhymes (Hebdige 83).[5] Dub poetry, however, fuses reggae beats with the spoken word so that the voice itself is an instrument. Incorporating a Rastafarian style of testimony and prophecy, dub poets merge their voices with those of the people through their use of oral speech patterns or patois and popular sayings to protest imperialism, racism, bourgeois norms, and political corruption. Breeze first performed onstage in 1981 with Mutabaruka in Montego Bay and went on to record a number of songs that received airplay on Jamaica's popular reggae stations. She soon became recognized as the first woman dub poet in a male-dominated field ("Dub Poet").[6] Linton Kwesi Johnson, Britain's leading dub poet, heard her perform and brought her to London, where she has lived since 1985, although she spends a few months each year in Sandy Bay, a coastal town in Hanover, to be with her children. She is part of the transnational economic migration responsible for the popular saying that "anywhere in the world you go, you find Jamaicans."

Breeze's early poems, written while she still lived in Jamaica, were strident political messages that condemned the severe austerity measures imposed after Prime Minister Michael Manley signed with the IMF in 1978. "Aid Travels with a Bomb" shows the "structural adjustments" made to encourage foreign investments to be yet another form of colonization. The designation of factories as export free zones meant that the government received no compensation for providing cheap labor and could not prevent them from relocating to more cost-effective locations:

> They love your country
> They want to invest
> But your country don't get
> When it come to the test
> Dem gone home wid all de profit
> Your government left
> Upholding a racket. (Breeze, *Answers* 14)

In "To Plant," Breeze is critical of the IMF recommendation that agriculture be shifted from produce for local consumption to cash crops for export. She sings about how these recommendations have contributed to world hunger:

> For de hungry getting rampant
> An de food is growing scarce
> De prices getting steeper
> De lan space jus kean waste (8)

These early poems are spoken out of a national pride that positions itself against the complicity of the national bourgeoisie and nation-state with the forces of neocolonialism. But the national voice is also gendered female. In "To Plant," Breeze assumes the traditional role of the woman as food provider in order to criticize the government for following the IMF recommendations that it shift agricultural production to cash crops and import food for local consumption. She is also critical of the dumping of surplus food and destruction of the land used to store nuclear waste in "Aid Travels with a Bomb." The neocolonial relations Breeze exposes in her early poems have not disappeared but have only deepened with globalization.

The effect that an integrated economy has had on a small Caribbean nation like Jamaica is further marginalization, through Jamaica's inability to compete in a world marketplace even though, by virtue of its enormous debt, it must. Manley aptly describes the problem as going "up the down escalator." Although Jamaica has increased its production of cash crops, it has been unable to compete in a market overseen by the WTO, which favors global giants. In 1997, the Jamaican government found itself facing a lawsuit led by the Clinton administration on behalf of Chiquita and Dole that challenged the special preferences European nations gave to Caribbean bananas, which was a holdover from their colonial interests in the region (Blustein).[7] The U.S. insistence on a free-market policy meant that, in the absence of such preferences, Jamaican bananas were too expensive to produce, despite agricultural workers receiving the same wages as those in Haiti, the lowest paid workers in the Western hemisphere (A. Bolles 111). Jamaica now faces the problem of having to import produce for local consumption while being unable to export its cash crops. Jamaican women have traditionally been employed sewing inexpensive underwear and T-shirts at garment factories in export free zones in Kingston and Montego Bay. Although they have constituted a larger percentage of the workforce than women in other undeveloped countries, due to the international stock exchange, civil unrest, and the ease with which manufacturers can move to more cost-effective regions, there has been a 40 percent decline in employment since 1988 (Dunn). Not only does the globalization of labor hurt women as wage earners, the scarcity of goods and soaring consumer prices that are a direct result of IMF policies also undermine their ability to manage households (L. Bolles 138–160).

Breeze's *Riddym Ravings* — which was published in 1988 and several poems of which were included on her 1989 LKJ Records release *Tracks* — stages the financial, emotional, and psychological difficulties that working-class Jamaican women experience. Her own diasporic existence between London and Sandy Bay is perhaps what gives this collection its keen sense of how global cultures are woven into the fabric of everyday life in Jamaica. In sharp contrast to her earlier work, in which a female-gendered voice was embedded into the public voice of the nation, the poems in this collection include dramatic monologues expressing Jamaican women's thoughts and experiences that are distinct from a larger discourse of nation. *Riddym Ravings* denotes Breeze's break with dub poetry, in terms of both its reggae rhythm and its testimonial delivery style. As she explains, "I lost the need to teach or preach, especially to audiences already converted, and found the courage to tell" ("Dub Poet" 49). But the poems do not only stage the economic and social marginalization of Jamaican women; they also produce a black female subjectivity out of reggae's dancehall culture.

Dancehall, which is the new synthesized and electronic music that emerged from reggae in the 1980s, is often characterized as a black Atlantic sound linking Kingston, New York, and London (Gilroy, *Ain't No Black* 187–192; Chude-Sokei 219). But at the local level the term refers to the mobile sound systems traveling throughout Jamaica, bringing an urban sound to remote rural areas.[8] Anyone who crosses the border zone between city and country will quickly notice that the culture of preliterate (i.e., orally based) societies is also technologically driven, even if it is not the cybertechnology of postliterate societies like our own. Crews load up enormous speakers, multiple turntables, and high-decibel amplifiers into open-air trucks and travel on dirt roads to the far reaches of the island to set up their sound systems on street corners and in school yards for Saturday night parties. The observation of one music critic is an indication of the important linkage to the city that dancehall offers rural districts: "The border crossing where St. Andrew parish gives way to St. Mary — where city cedes to country — is marked not by guards or even a sign but by jerry-built sound boxes blasting reggae at eardrum-splitting volume" (Oumano, "Reggae" 25). The traveling sound systems were popular in rural parishes, where people could not afford the steep prices of live performances, as far back as the early 1950s. A dancehall session consisted of a "selector" or DJ spinning discs, while the "toaster" or MC spoke from ghetto experience about unemployment, inflation, and the "dirty tricks" of politicians. Today, with the growth of the recording industry's promotion of stars, the DJ is no longer a technician but a singer, songwriter, and performer (Cooper, *Noises* 138–139; Barrow, Dalton, and Buckley 234; Levin 226–230; Stolzoff 97–99).

Despite dancehall music's antiauthority stand and rootedness in ghetto culture, its politics are generally considered the antithesis of those espoused by dub poets. Since the music has increasingly been taken over by gun talk and "slackness" — the propensity of DJs to make sexual puns and wordplay, particularly ones that are demeaning to women — it is associated with the consumerism and free market liberalism promoted by Edward Seaga, who became Jamaica's prime minister after the violent 1980 general election (Hebdige 122–127). Gilroy contrasts dancehall, as the music of the pro-Reaganomics Seaga regime, to dub poetry and roots reggae, which expressed the utopian vision of Michael Manley's socialist government (*Ain't No Black* 188). The authors of *Reggae: The Rough Guide* characterize dancehall as a "conservative and inward-looking" reaction to the deepening of the class gap that resulted from the free market policies of the new government (Barrow, Dalton, and Buckley 231). These critical views from Britain are confirmed by Jamaica's leading dub poet, Mutabaruka, who has his own show on the popular IRIE-FM reggae station:

> Some people have said that dancehall music is anti-establishment; this is not true. The dancehall music is the most pro-establishment culture ever come inna Jamaica. It is dealing with exactly what the society is dealing with. The lewdness, the downgrading of women, the slackness, materialism, gun violence. The establishment is not against any of these things that dancehall personifies. I personally don't give any credence to dancehall culture. I think it is the worst thing that ever happen to Jamaica culture. (Ama 8)

Breeze does not share Mutabaruka's sentiments, and this difference is also the sign of a gender difference in the subjects of her poems. Although she castigates DJ slackness in the poem "Get Back," saying "We tired of degradation," she also credits dancehall music with breaking down the middle-class mores that reinforced double standards for men and women. "The DJs were saying jump and spread out, jump and chuck out," she explains, "and women broke out in the dancehall" (*Bad Language*). Although most dancehall sessions take place in the Kingston metropolitan area, the mobile sound systems also bring its synthesized rhythm and ghetto culture to rural Jamaica.

The (mostly working-class) women don electric-colored synthetic wigs or extensions, large false eyelashes, glittery sequined, fringed, or plastic outfits consisting of not much more than G-strings and push-up bras to step out at night in the dancehall. "It does not matter if the women are fat," explain Paulette McDonald and Carolyn Cooper. "Fat is hot" ("Dancehall Revisited" 30). Cooper characterizes dancehall women as "disdainful, inaccessible sexual beings" who revel in the "DJ's 'bigging up' of her person as desired and desiring subject — not mere sex object" (Cooper, *Noises* 166; Cooper, "Lady Saw" 79; Ross 65–67). Despite the reduction of women to their body parts in songs like Shabba Ranks's "Love Punaany Bad," women are greater fans of these songs than are men (Barrow, Dalton, and Buckley 295). The appeal slack lyrics have for women has to do with their being sung by DJs (like Shabba Ranks) who have a lover-man reputation. But slackness also expresses ambivalence about female sexuality that allows women to assume sexual agency within dancehall culture. Since the singer expresses his sexual prowess through his ability to satisfy women, he indirectly acknowledges women's need for satisfaction.[9]

In two poems depicting the pleasure women derive from dancehall culture, Breeze turns slackness inside out by making it into a source of female self-empowerment. "Dubwise" presents the erotic gyrations of a dancehall diva as a ritualized dance between the sexes for control of the floor. The words of the poem snake across the page in imitation of the female dancer's "wining," which consists of pelvic rotations to the beat of the music. The idea of the dance as a simulated sex act is made evident through the poem's sexually explicit language:

'cool an
deadly'
snake
lady
writhing
'roun
de worlie'
wraps
her sinews
roun his
pulse
and grinds
his pleasure
and disgust
into a
one dance
stand (*Riddym Ravings* 28)

The ambivalence the male dancer feels toward his partner's grinding of his pelvic region has to do with her sexual aggressiveness that turns *him* into an object of desire:

to equalise
he grins
cockwise
at his bredrin
and rides
a 'horseman scabie'
or bubbles a
'water
bumpie'
into action. (28)

The male dancer's hypermasculine dance style is represented here as a defense mechanism, his effort to recuperate the control he has lost to his female partner, or which he perhaps did not have from the start. The dance — which is a ritualized enactment of the battle between the sexes in which pleasure is derived from the "fight" — ends when the DJ "smilingly / orders / 'Cease'" (28). The DJ occupies a godlike position, controlling the dance floor through the music. As Gilroy explains, "The DJ and the MC or toaster who introduces each disc or sequence of discs, emerge as the principal agents in dialogic rituals of active and celebratory consumption" (*Ain't No Black* 164).

As much as women play a central — and flamboyantly visible — role in the dancehall, they are removed from the male-dominated technical fields of dubbing, mixing, and versioning and from the verbal mastery of the MC. There appears to be a gendered division of labor with women being associated with "sexuality, the body, emotion, and nature," while men are associated with "culture, technology, and language" (Bradby 157). This gender division, however, is blurred through the skill with which the women manipulate and rotate their bodies on the dance floor — an activity that mirrors the selector's technical expertise and MC's verbal dexterity. One cannot help but marvel at the dancer's rhythmic interpretation of the music and skillful contortions of her body in such styles as "head-top dancing," where she places both head and feet on the floor to emphasize her buttocks. Countering the male technical skills through dance and the hypersexualized female body, the women dancers assert an agency that parallels the technological innovations of the music.

Since Breeze's collection of poems first appeared, a number of women have emerged as DJ/singers, although the selectors who operate the sound systems are still men (Stolzoff 117–118). The most popular of the female

DJs is Lady Saw, whose satirical wit, compelling stage presence, and mike skills have earned her the title of First Lady of Dancehall. Behind the story of her achieving international fame in dancehalls from London to New York is the story of how Jamaica's mobile sound systems enabled her to make the journey from the rural parish of St. Mary to Kingston. Born Marion Hall, she grew up in Galina, a coastal town east of Ocho Rios, and got her start by taking a turn at the mike of touring sound systems. As Lady Saw explains: "I was begging the selector, 'Gimme a talk on the mic, gimme a talk!' But he didn't pay me any attention, I think because I was dressed like a real country girl, in some ugly shoes, and some stockings and shorts. And they were thinking, 'What's she got?'" (qtd. in Dreisinger).

The "country girl" soon earned the reputation of having "mashed up" three veteran DJs. She made her way to Kingston, where in 1994 she recorded her first international hit, "Find a Good Man," which, as a prayer for the miracle of finding a good man, became the "ladies' anthem."

Lady Saw soon discovered that the only way she could break into the male-dominated field of deejaying was through slack lyrics. "In those early days, when I was busting out, I did X-rated songs [on records], but now I only do them onstage," she reports; "I've shown people that I can succeed on my talent alone" (Oumano, "V.P." 8). She soon earned notoriety for outdoing the male performers in slackness. By using the same raw language to undermine the sexual boasting of men who claimed to be "strong black stallions," she demanded that they work harder at pleasing the ladies: "You can't grind good and you can't fuck straight. Stab out the meat! Stab out the meat!" Songs like "Stab Out the Meat" and "Good Wuk" exploit the humor and wordplay of slackness in order to reverse its signification. Lady Saw's appearance onstage in a push-up bra and G-string, grabbing her crotch (as she reminds her detractors Michael Jackson did), similarly displays female sexuality in the act of parodying the hypermasculinity of male DJs. When the guardians of middle-class morality criticized her slack lyrics and scandalous performances, she responded with "What Is Slackness," which lambasted them for their double standards for men and women and pointed to the government's own slackness in providing basic social services for Jamaican people. As Cooper explains, "Lady Saw's brilliant lyrics, reinforced by her compelling body language, articulate a potent message about sexuality, gender politics and the power struggle for the right to public space in Jamaica" ("Lady Saw" 83). The dancehall divas and female DJs constitute a more visible form of women claiming male-dominated territory through a technologically driven female sexuality. But there are also less dramatic ways in which Jamaican women assert themselves in public space.

While the female DJ explicitly weds the eroticized female body to the mike, in "eena mi corner," a companion poem to "Dubwise," Breeze metaphorically transforms the female body into a technological device. The speaker appears to be a passive observer of the dancehall scene, standing on the sidelines and moving in steady rhythm to the music, except that she has turned her body into a radio so she can tune in to the sexual energy being generated. The bass sound and synthesized reggae rhythm that reverberate through the woman's body as a site of sexual energy are reproduced in the onomatopoeia of the Jamaican speech patterns in the poem:

> im jus a
> im jus a
> a eh i oh oooh
> im way troo
> de mos complex part
> a mi lunar system. (*Riddym Ravings* 26)

Hans Enzensberger, building on Frantz Fanon's writings on the radio as an instrument for advancing the Algerian revolution, saw the revolutionary potential of the radio to turn actors into authors. He explains, however, that as an instrument for change, the radio would have to be able to transmit as well as receive signals (97–98). In her use of the radio as a metaphor for female sexual energy, Breeze imagines a woman who can turn her receiver into a transmitter through the mere flick of a switch:

> an jus
> flip a switch
> tun mi receiva
> to transmitta
> checking anadda one
> wanderin troo
> de sonic boom of a bassline. (*Riddym Ravings* 27)

In contrast to the dancehall diva's explicit display of her sexuality, the woman standing quietly in the corner equalizes gender relations by sending her sexual desire through the sound waves of the music. Breeze uses the cyborgian image of a woman whose body is inhabited by a radio for representing a black female subjectivity that is rooted in the vernacular of Jamaica's dancehall culture. This subjectivity is not to be equated with a consciousness, because the rhythm box is in the woman's body rather than her mind. The question is not whether dancehall produces a revolutionary consciousness but how Jamaican women insert themselves into a popular cultural form in order to assert themselves in a world over which they have little control.[10]

Breeze also fuses the female body with radio technology in "riddym ravings (the mad woman's poem)," where the ravings of a pregnant country woman issue from a radio embedded in her head. The poem is delivered in the voice of one of those crazy women seen wandering the city streets, singing and talking to themselves. Breeze has remarked that it "represents the whole dislocation of a rural agricultural community into an urban setting of mass unemployment" ("Interview" 57). Dislocation is one aspect of modernity belonging to globalization, and in "riddym ravings" we see the effect that the IMF's "structural adjustments" have had on the rural poor. The country woman in "riddym ravings" has been evicted for failing to pay her rent and ends up on the streets with nothing but her "Channel One riddym box." That same night a DJ flies into her head and plays this song:

> *Eh, Eh,*
> *no feel no way*
> *town is a place dat ah really kean stay*
> *dem kudda — ribbit mi han*
> *eh — ribbit mi toe*
> *mi waan go a country go look mango.* (*Riddym Ravings* 58)

"Ribbit" (rivet) is a DJ term for describing the state of being caught in a heavy dub beat. In the song the woman hears in her head, the term refers to her being caught in the city but nonetheless able mentally to escape to the country through music. For her, the city is not a place of meeting and mobilization for "the migrants, the minorities, the diasporic," which is how Homi Bhabha describes a global city like London (169). In a Third World city like Kingston, an unemployed country woman has no claim to a home, or even to the public space of the streets. After her landlord evicts her, she is picked up and sent to Bellevue, which is both a poorhouse and a mental hospital.

The homeless woman's madness is the overt manifestation of her effort to avert her dehumanization in the city through the memory of country life back home. In identifying slavery as the first modern experience, Morrison characterizes madness as a strategy for survival: "Certain kinds of madness, deliberately going mad . . . 'in order not to lose your mind' " (qtd. in Gilroy, *Black Atlantic* 221). The idea of "deliberately going mad" makes madness into the exercise of control over the mind in the face of an absence of control over one's own body:

> an a ongle one ting tap mi fram go stark raving mad
> a wen mi siddung eena Parade
> a tear up newspaper fi talk to
> sometime dem roll up
> an tun eena one a Uncle But sweet saaf
> yellow heart breadfruit
> wid piece a roas saalfish side a I. (*Riddym Ravings* 59)

Although the woman appears to be controlling the song she hears, it is not clear whether it originates in her mind or in the outside world, as she hears the same song playing on the bus she attempts to take back home:

> an sometime mi a try board de bus
> an de canductor bwoy a halla out seh
> 'dutty gal, kum affa de bus'
> an troo im no hear de riddym eena mi head
> same as de tape weh de bus driva a play, seh. (*Riddym Ravings* 59)

The constant clamor of music blasting from huge storefront speakers, boom boxes, and tiny transistor radios makes it difficult to locate the country song in any one place. By virtue of its mediation through a technology of reproduction, it has no single origins.

When talking about the mobility of today's global cultures, it is important to distinguish between the movement of cultural forms and people. In "riddym ravings," the homeless woman lacks the ease of mobility belonging to the music that travels from country to town and perhaps back again. As a social being rather than a cultural form, she suffers the consequences of dislocation. It is not simply the case that she is unemployed; she is also stranded in a large impersonal city like Kingston. Cut off from her extended family that allows her to "make do" (which is the Jamaican term for women's ability to survive on little or no money), she is ignored, laughed at, or run off for being dirty and ragged. She wants to go home, but she does not have the money for bus fare. When, faint from hunger, she attempts to pick up a piece of banana dropped by a girl, she is sent back to Bellevue, where the doctor and landlord pull the radio plug out of her head. But as soon as she is back on the street, she pushes it back in so she can continue to hear the song.

The mad woman then decides to walk home, the same way her grandmother used to walk to town to sell food. Here, Breeze invokes the memory of country higglers or market women, who dominated the informal economy of selling locally grown produce in the cities and providing people who lived in rural areas with news, gossip, and goods from town (Durant-González 2–12; LeFranc 15–17). However, the domestic network in which the madwoman's grandmother participated is no longer available to her. In a modern world of rapid transportation, the journey from town to country on foot signifies the inability to "make it" in the city. Taking pride in her appearance, the mad woman strips naked to bathe herself in water running from an open pipe so that she can be clean when she arrives home. However, she is arrested for indecent exposure and returned to the mental hospital. This time the doctor and landlord remove the entire radio from her head, but when they are not looking, she grabs it and pushes it up in her belly for her baby to hear:

> fah even if mi nuh mek i
> me waan my baby know dis yah riddym yah
> fram before she bawn. (*Riddym Ravings* 60)

By moving the radio from her head to her belly, the woman, like her sister standing in the corner of the dancehall, turns her receiver into a transmitter so that her baby can hear the sounds of the country. Her action of relaying the song to her unborn child transmutes one of the most normative and naturalized significations of the female body — maternity — into a technologically mediated relation.

The poem ends with the mad woman hearing the DJ scream — "*Murther / Pull up Missa Operator!*" — the same moment the doctor and landlord send an electric shock through her body (61). These words, also from dancehall culture, allude to a particularly good or "murderous" track that an audience wants to hear again. In response to the crowd's enthusiasm, the DJ pulls up the needle and places it at the beginning of the song again. Breeze performs a word play on "mother" and "murder" and the DJ and doctor as "operators" through which the attempt to kill the music on the operating table is transformed, through dancehall language, into an act in which the song ends abruptly only so that it might be repeated once again. No matter how many times the forces of law and order attempt to "cure" the woman by killing the song in her head, they cannot destroy the memory of her home or prevent her from passing on that memory to the next generation.

Breeze draws on the language of deejaying for articulating the consciousness of an unemployed rural woman who is otherwise classified as "mad." Yet she does not simply extend the DJ's voice to the woman. Rather, she reworks it in a manner that inauthenticates both the presupposed masculinity of his voice and the rural origins of the song. As Joan Dayan remarks about the poem, the voice the mad woman hears does not express the male bravado of toasting, which is the name for the slick rhymes the MC or DJ speaks over the music. The wistful expression of a desire to be in the country suggests that the woman "inhabits the DJ voice" rather than the other way around (60). The image of country life as one of looking for mangoes perhaps displays a romantic nostalgia for a pastoral way of life that no longer exists. But that would be far too literal a reading of the song. For, even as the woman inhabits the DJ voice, the song is inhabited by DJ language ("rabbit"), thus undermining its authenticity as an instance of folk culture. This "inauthentic" — in the sense of James Clifford's explanation of being "caught between cultures" — and mechanized — because mediated through the radio — song is the sound of the country caught in the web of globalization (Clifford 11). The woman has made her way to the city in search of work because an integrated market has destroyed Jamaica's rural economies. At the same time, a global reggae culture connects her with the rural origins from which she is removed.

The radio not only provides a woman seeking employment in the city with a connection to her home, it also brings the rest of world into the domestic space of women who stay home. In "ordinary morning," Breeze weaves the national and international news relayed through the radio into the daily struggle of one unemployed, unmarried mother to survive. The poem linguistically connects the life of an ordinary Jamaican woman to the news she hears on the radio about "Israel still a bruk up / Palestine / an Botha still have de whole world han / twist back a dem" (*Riddym Ravings* 48). The woman knows that, as in the case of the problem of nation in Israel and South Africa, there is no way out of her daily struggle:

> so it did hard fi understand
> why de ordinary sight of
> mi own frock

heng up pon line
wid some clothespin
should a stop mi from do nutten
but jus
bawl. (49)

    If the woman cries at the sight of her frock hanging on the clothesline, it is not because she lacks an understanding of her life. Rather, she knows all too well that the ordinariness of the morning means that the future looks much the same as the past. The woman reveals, in the course of her musings, the effect that Jamaica's debt crisis has had on working-class women, whether they are part of the workforce or not. The currency devaluation and austerity programs imposed by the IMF are responsible for "de price rise pon bus fare / an milk an sugar" (49) that has contributed to the burden of everyday life for an unmarried mother like herself. While "Dubwise," "eena mi corner," and "riddym ravings" show women claiming public space, this poem weaves the outside world into domestic space. It reworks the personal/political opposition to illustrate how so private a world as a woman's domestic musings is shot through with the shards of global culture.

    The women who appear in *Riddym Ravings* challenge the perception that rural populations somehow exist outside the transnational cultures of globalization, that their entry into modernity has been stalled. Modernity is not just a transurban, diasporic experience; it is also the experience of forced migration from rural to urban areas and the fact that few parts of the world remain untouched by today's global cultures. Breeze's poems disrupt the taken-for-grantedness of modernity being equated with cosmopolitanism and global city centers. They use radio technology for shifting the signification of black popular music from production to consumption, while making consumption into a two-way process through the idea of the radio as both a receiver and transmitter. They also extend the power of the DJ's voice to the female body in order to assert black women's ability to act upon a world in which the agents of control increasingly exist elsewhere. In short, they provide a theory of gendered subjectivities that is derived from the cultures and everyday experiences of ordinary Jamaican women.

    An academic discourse on diaspora and transnational cultures escapes the critique of being parochial precisely because its scope extends beyond the national level. But unless we locate our theoretical models within the geopolitical dimensions of their production, we risk turning the category of "transnationalism" into a new universalism. By examining the cultures that are unique to particular societies rather than globalizing our own, we can consider how heterogenously produced subjectivities might be part of the new world system known as globalization. Then we might begin to see that the shrinking world being mapped is just a little bit less global.

Notes

1 Gilroy makes brief mention of Nigerian Fela Ransome Kuti's integration of African American funk into Afro-beat, but it is only from the perspective of James Brown's characterization of Fela as "the African James Brown" (*The Black Atlantic* 199).

2 "Music," explains Judy, "is the principal mode in which and through which a distinctly 'black' modern subjectivity is constituted" (25).

3 "Unlike synthesizers, which generate tones artificially," explains Robert Burnett, "samplers record real sounds. Anything audible is eligible: prerecorded music, drumbeats, human voices. Samplers transform these sounds into digital codes, which in turn can be manipulated to produce melodies, rhythm tracks and other sound patterns" (93).

4 My discussion of the gendering of technological innovations in popular music is indebted to Bradby's provocative essay.

5 A Jamaican record producer describes the dub version of a title track as "just the bare bones . . . just a naked dance rhythm" (cited in Hebdige 83).

6 For a discussion of women dub poets in Jamaica and the diaspora, see Habekost 201–208.

7 Stephanie Black's documentary film *Life and Debt* shows how the problem of globalization is not simply that of Jamaican farmers being able to compete both internationally and locally. Many agricultural sectors — dairy, bananas, produce for local consumption — have been destroyed through the marketing of less expensive American imports perceived as superior.

8 For a historical and ethnographic account of Jamaican dancehall, see Stolzoff.

9 For a more detailed reading of the ambivalence male DJs have toward female sexuality, see Cooper, *Noises* 136–173. In "Masculinity and Dancehall," Jarret Brown reads slackness less optimistically than does Cooper, arguing that the imaginary violence enacted against women in these songs maintains them in a submissive position.

10 Although I am primarily interested in Jamaican women as consumers of dancehall music, there is an entire transnational trade in dancehall clothing connecting Kingston to Miami and New York, through which higglers, or informal commercial importers (their government-designated name), have managed to carve out a space of economic independence for themselves. For a gendered model of globalization derived from the transnational practices of Barbadian pink-collar higglers, see Freeman.

Works Cited

Ama, Imani Tafari. "Muta and Yasus Defend the Culture." *Sistren* 16 (1994): 8.

Anderson, Sarah, ed. *Views from the South: The Effects of Globalization and the WTO on Third World Countries*. Oakland: Food First, 2000.

Appadurai, Arjun. *Modernity at Large: Cultural Dimensions of Globalization*. Minneapolis: University of Minnesota Press, 1996.

Barrow, Steve, Peter Dalton, and Jonathan Buckley, ed. *Reggae: The Rough Guide*, 1st ed. London: Rough Guides, 1997.

Bhabha, Homi K. *The Location of Culture*. London: Routledge, 1994.

Black, Stephanie, dir. *Life and Debt*. Tuff Gong Picture Production, 2001.

Blustein, Paul. "Caribbean Could Wonder Where the Yellow Went." *Washington Post* 19 March 1997: C9, C12.

Bolles, Augusta Lynn. *Sister Jamaica: A Study of Women, Work, and Households in Kingston*. Lanham: University Press of America, 1996.

Bolles, Lynn. "Kitchens Hit by Priorities: Employed Working-Class Jamaican Women Confront the IMF." *Women, Men, and the International Division of Labor*. Ed. June Nash and María Fernández-Kelly. Albany: SUNY Press, 1983. 138–160.

Bradby, Barbara. "Sampling Sexuality: Gender, Technology, and the Body in Dance Music." *Popular Music* 12 (1993): 155–176.

Breeze, Jean "Binta." *Answers*. Kingston: Masani, 1983.

———. *Bad Language: The Delights of Improper Language*. London: ICA Video, 1993.

———. "Can a Dub Poet Be a Woman?" *Women: A Cultural Review* 1 (1990): 47–49.

———. "An Interview with Jean Breeze." *Commonwealth* 8 (1986): 51–58.

———. *Riddym Ravings and Other Poems*. Ed. Mervyn Morris. London: Race Today Publications, 1988.

Brown, Jarret. "Masculinity and Dancehall." *Caribbean Quarterly* 45 (1999): 1–16.

Burnett, Robert. *The Global Jukebox: The International Music Industry*. New York: Routledge, 1996.

Byfield, Judith, ed. *Rethinking the African Diaspora*. Spec. issue of *African Studies Review* 43 (2000).

Chude-Sokei, Louise. "Postnationalist Geographies: Rasta, Ragga, and Reinventing Africa." *Reggae, Rasta, Revolution: Jamaican Music from Ska to Dub*. Ed. Chris Potash. New York: Schirmer, 1997. 215–227.

Clifford, James. *The Predicament of Culture: Twentieth-Century Ethnography, Literature, and Art*. Cambridge: Harvard University Press, 1988.

Colista, Celia, and Glenn Leshner. "Traveling Music: Following the Path of Music Through the Global Market." *Critical Studies in Mass Communication* 15 (1998): 181–194.

Cooper, Carolyn. "Lady Saw Cuts Loose: Female Fertility Rituals in Jamaica Dancehall Culture." *Dancing in the Millennium: An International Conference Proceedings*. Ed. Juliette Willis and Janice D. LaPointe-Crump. Washington, D.C.: Congress on Research on Dance, 2000. 79–83.

———. *Noises in the Blood: Orality, Gender, and the "Vulgar" Body of Jamaican Popular Culture*. Durham: Duke University Press, 1995.

Dayan, Joan. "Caribbean Cannibals and Whores." *Raritan* 9 (1989): 45–60.

DeLoughrey, Elizabeth. "Gendering the Oceanic Voyage: Trespassing the (Black) Atlantic and Caribbean." *Thamyris* 5 (1998): 205–230.

Dreisinger, Baz. "Dancehall Star's Key to Success." *Miami Herald* 27 October 2002.

Dunn, Leith L. *Women Organising for Change in Caribbean Free Zones: Strategies and Methods.* The Hague, Netherlands: Institute of Social Studies, 1991.

Durant-González, Victoria. "The Occupation of Higglering." *Jamaica Journal* 16 (1983): 2–12.

Edwards, Brent Hayes. "The Uses of *Diaspora.*" *Social Text* 109 55, 19:1 (spring 2001): 45–73.

Enzensberger, Hans Magus. *The Consciousness Industry: On Literature, Politics and the Media.* Trans. Stuart Hood. New York: Seabury, 1974.

Freeman, Carla. "Is Local : Global as Feminine : Masculine? Rethinking the Gender of Globalization." *Signs* 26 (2001): 1007–1037.

Giddens, Anthony. *The Consequences of Modernity.* Stanford: Stanford University Press, 1990.

Gikandi, Simon, ed. *The Black Atlantic.* Spec. issue of *Research in African Literatures* 27 (1996).

Gilroy, Paul. *Black Atlantic: Modernity and Double Consciousness.* Cambridge: Harvard University Press, 1993.

———. *'There Ain't No Black in the Union Jack': The Cultural Politics of Race and Nation.* London: Hutchinson, 1987.

Gunning, Sandra. "Nancy Prince and the Politics of Mobility, Home and Diasporic (Mis)Identification." *American Quarterly* 53 (2001): 32–69.

Habekost, Christian. *Verbal Riddim: The Politics and Aesthetics of African-Caribbean Dub Poetry.* Amsterdam: Rodopi, 1993.

Hall, Stuart. "Cultural Identity and Diaspora." *Identity: Community, Culture, Difference.* Ed. J. Rutherford. London: Lawrence & Wishart, 1990. 222–237.

Hebdige, Dick. *Cut 'n' Mix: Culture, Identity, and Caribbean Music.* London: Methuen, 1987.

Judy, Ronald A. T. "Paul Gilroy's Black Atlantic and the Place(s) of English in the Global." *Critical Quarterly* 39 (1997): 22–29.

LeFranc, Elsie. "Higglering in Kingston: Entrepreneurs or Traditional Small-Scale Operators." *Caribbean Review* 16 (1988): 15–17.

Levin, Jordan. "Dancehall DJs in the House." *Reggae, Rasta, Revolution.* Ed. Chris Potash. Farming Hills, Mich.: Gale, 1998. 228–230.

Manley, Michael. *Up the Down Escalator: Development and the International Economy: A Jamaican Case Study.* Washington, D.C: Howard University Press, 1987.

McDonald, Paulette, and Carolyn Cooper. "Dancehall Revisited/Kingston," *Review: Latin American Literature and Arts* 50 (1995): 29–30.

Oumano, Elena. "Reggae Says No to 'Politricks.' " *Nation* 25 August 1997: 24–26.

———. "V.P. to Make Known Lady Saw's 'Passion.' " *Billboard* 109 28 June 1997: 8–9.

Patterson, Tiffany Ruby, and Robin D. G. Kelly. "Unfinished Migrations: Reflections on the African Diaspora and the Making of the Modern World." *African Studies Review* 43 (2000): 11–35.

Ross, Andrew. *Real Love: In Pursuit of Cultural Justice*. New York: New York University Press, 1998.

Shiva, Vandana. "War against Nature and the People of the South." Anderson 91–125.

Stolzoff, Norman C. *Wake the Town and Tell the People: Dancehall Culture in Jamaica* Durham: Duke University Press, 2000.

The Double Logic of Minor Spaces

In his semiotic analysis of culture, Yuri Lotman has argued that the establishment of any culture as semiotic space (or "semiosphere") is premised upon the fundamental demarcation of space between inside and outside. The opposition between internal and external space, according to Lotman, is typically imbued with specific values, dividing what is structured and bounded from what is unbounded and heterogeneous; it also organizes various conceptual oppositions, such as the difference between civilization and barbarism.[1] Within such an organization of space, Lotman writes, the boundary (or boundaries, for they are always multiple, as are languages within a semiosphere) serves a double function; the boundary exists both inside and outside and forms a "membrane," a mechanism for translation and filtration. Lotman writes: "The notion of boundary is an ambivalent one: it both separates and unites. It is always the boundary of something and so belongs to both frontier cultures, to both contiguous semiospheres. The boundary is bilingual and polylingual" (136–137).

What has been theorized as "minor literature" can be seen to exist precisely within the context of such ambivalent and heterogeneous borderlines, fulfilling a double function of both deterritorializing a major literature or language and also providing its necessary boundary or limit. This essay examines this double function of the minor in relation to discourses of national culture in Japan, focusing on conceptualizations of territoriality in the production of the minor — as well as the attempt to deconstruct such concepts through the representation of spaces situated in between communities. In particular, it looks at the ways in which the formation of discourses of national culture in Japan (particularly in relation to dominant civilizations of Asia or the West) has tended to produce a double space for marginal cultures and communities — "borderline spaces" marked both by exclusion or abjection from, as well as appropriation into, the national essence. The primary trope for this double space is the image of the storehouse (or repository) which, in some sense, also functions as a crypt. This double function (which is perhaps also the double function of literature itself) was formed during the period of empire, yet, as a work by writer Nakagami Kenji (1946–1992) illustrates, still generates effects in contemporary discourse.

As a number of scholars have pointed out, the processes of nation building and empire building in Japan were in many ways coextensive. For example, in his study of imperial language policy, *Teikoku Nihon no gengo hensei* (*The Organization of Language in Imperial Japan*, 1997), Yasuda Toshiaki argues that the very concept of a "national language" (*kokugo*) was worked out in the context of the state's expansion into neighboring territories. Yasuda points out that it was only in the period following the Sino-Japanese War of 1894–1895, which led to the annexation of Taiwan and a rise of nationalist sentiment, that the ideological and institutional foundations for a national language took shape. The early scholars who helped to construct the concept of a national language were on the one hand conscious of following the example of European nations in establishing a unified language as a necessary step in the process of modernization, but their writings are also permeated by the perceived need for a codified and standardized language in order to spread it throughout Asia and in order to use it as a tool of colonial administration (Yasuda 5–9).[2] Various scholars have also argued that the "colonization" of the northern island of Hokkaido — its incorporation into the boundaries of the nation-state and the formation of state policies toward indigenous Ainu inhabitants — served as a template for colonial policies later carried out in Taiwan and Korea.[3]

The relationship between the concepts of nation (*kokka*) and empire (*teikoku*) in prewar Japanese intellectual discourse was often quite complex and conflicted, as might be expected. At times there were significant contradictions between these ideas (expressed, for example, in competing theories of "homogenous" and "mixed" Japanese ethnicity), while at other times one flowed into the other.[4] The precise boundaries of the "national body" (*kokutai*) were thus in many cases quite fluid, and the borderlines between what were called the "inner territories" (*naichi*) and the "outer territories" (*gaichi*) were never entirely stable. For example, in *Nihonjin no kyōkai* (*The Borderlines of the Japanese*, 1998), a review of various discourses on ethnicity in modern Japan, Oguma Eiji has shown how the undecidability of these boundaries generated a great profusion of theories concerning the limits of the nation and of Japanese identity. Oguma focuses on particular "borderline" spaces — namely Taiwan, Korea, Hokkaido, and Okinawa — which were imbued with a charged significance as topographies staging essential conflicts in the constitution of Japanese modernity.

Within this state of flux, the attempt to map out both the material and conceptual borderlines of the nation became a significant theme of cultural discourse; in particular, this cartographic impulse can be identified in certain key works of modern literature. One of the foundational texts of modern fiction, for example, is Kunikida Doppo's "Musashino" ("The Musashi Plain," 1898), an attempt to map out a well-known literary terrain, shifting it from the context of premodern Japanese texts into the context of Western writings.[5] Within the processes of territorial mapping, in literature and in other discourses, the topos of the borderline accrues a particular significance and plays an important role in producing a consciousness of minority cultures — those situated precisely within such in-between topographies (both literally and figuratively). In the 1920s and 1930s in particular, in intellectual discourse and in literature, such spaces served as sites of ideological contestation and as vessels into which were projected anxieties concerning the boundaries of national and racial subjectivity. For example, the fictional works of perhaps the most prominent modernist writer in 1920s Japan, Yokomitsu Riichi (1898–1947), revolve around the representation of colonial and semicolonial spaces; these topographies are used to highlight the ambivalent cultural and racial identifications between Japanese and other Asian characters and Westerners.[6] These borderline topographies were imbued with a double significance — on the one hand, they existed as sites of abjection, markers of what is necessarily excluded or foreclosed in establishing the boundaries of national community.[7] On the other hand, these peripheral spaces are valorized and included within the concept of national essence as markers of the often-cited Japanese capacity for assimilation — what the writer Akutagawa Ryūnosuke (1892–1927) formulated as the "power to remake," in contrast to what he termed the West's "power to destroy" (183–185).

In addition, the cultures of the periphery were at times incorporated into certain conceptions of Japanese culture that represented the nation itself as a minor culture in relation to external dominant civilizations (primarily the West).[8] In this context, the peripheral spaces of the nation become charged with a special value as markers of a national essence coded precisely as peripheral or marginal, and thereby recuperated into a conception of Japanese cultural and national identity. This double logic has, in various ways, shaped the production of minority discourse (discourse both *on* minorities and *by* minorities) in Japan. As Oguma's study shows, there were diverse theories of minority cultures, as well as responses by Taiwanese, Korean, Ainu, and Okinawan writers and intellectuals; each maintained its own specificity and they cannot all be discussed in the same way. Indeed, there is a need to maintain this heterogeneity and to point out the various fractures and conflicts among different groups. At the same time, however, as Murai Osamu and others have noted, there is a certain critical value in linking the question of minority discourse to the general framework of colonialism — especially in light of the postwar tendency to make a sharp break between the representation of Okinawa and Hokkaido on the one hand, as existing within national borders, and Taiwan and Korea on the other, as existing outside of them (An 16). What should be questioned is precisely how such borders were established in the first place.

In the same way, although the double logic of abjection and assimilation was forged in the process of imperial expansion and maintains a historical specificity, it is possible to discern its effects in contemporary literary and cultural discourse. The diverse writings situated within the category of "minor literature" in Japan today — which includes in particular writings by ethnic Koreans, Okinawans, and *burakumin* (or "outcaste") and which has become a significant force in the Japanese literary world — are in many ways shaped by this legacy. In this context, this essay will also look at the ways in which one of Japan's most celebrated contemporary writers, Nakagami Kenji, has engaged this question of the positioning of minority culture in his literature. At stake is an attempt to represent a space situated on the borderlines of national community which escapes this process of appropriation — that is, a space that evades the double structure of abjection and incorporation, both of which merely reinforce the phantasmal boundaries of the nation.

The prototypical example of the positioning of Japan as a peripheral culture in the early twentieth century can be found in a well-known text by Okakura Kakuzō (1862–1913), *Ideals of the East*, which was published in English in 1903. In this work Okakura argued that the uniqueness of Japanese civilization derived from its position at the margins of the two dominant civilizations of Asia, India and China. Japan, Okakura wrote, functioned as a "museum" of Asian civilization, a type of storehouse or repository preserving what had now been lost in those countries themselves (7). The notion of the peripheral status of Japanese culture is accompanied by its characterization as a type of mixture—a space of exchange located at the intersection of diverse civilizations. Okakura's argument presents a counterpart in the realm of aesthetics to the racial theories analyzed by Oguma—the positing of an originary mixture or heterogeneity as the foundation of Japanese identity. Okakura's repository is based on an idea of assimilation and ingestion that would provide a framework for subsequent articulations of Japanese uniqueness. Of course the idea of "preserving" Chinese and Indian civilizations inevitably suggests that these civilizations are either in decline or already in ruins. And it should also be pointed out that while Oguma correctly underscores the very real conflicts that existed between writers who proclaimed the "purity" of Japanese blood and those who proclaimed its essentially hybrid character, there is a sense in which Japanese ideology functioned not in spite of such contradictions, but rather precisely because of them. For example, Okakura presents a picture of a mixed national culture, a container for traces of other cultures, that is nonetheless able to maintain its "purity" (16).

In certain influential accounts of native culture, there is a transposition of this image of storehouse or repository onto the marginal spaces of the nation. Perhaps the best-known example is represented by Yanagita Kunio's (1875–1962) ethnology (*minzokugaku*), which emerged in the 1910s as a study of borderline communities. Yanagita's writings on the origins of Japanese culture, and his attempt to record and preserve the traces of what he saw as an original folk culture, have had tremendous influence on both scholarship and on popular consciousness of Japanese culture. Hashimoto Mitsuru has argued that Yanagita's theories were based in large measure on a positioning of Japan as the periphery of the West; he furthermore notes that this was also reflected in the attempt to recuperate a native essence preserved in Japan's outlying regions. According to Hashimoto, Yanagita believed that "however much Japan modernized its center and however well it dressed itself in modern clothes, it still maintained indigenous characteristics deep in its core. In this view, Japan itself was the periphery (*chihō*) of the global modern world" (143).[9]

There was, in other words, a transposition of the storehouse image that Okakura had used to describe Japan onto Japan's minorities—the peripheral spaces where an originary culture was supposedly preserved intact. Yanagita's initial attention focused on the "mountain people," whom he claimed were the descendents of Japan's indigenous inhabitants who had been defeated by a race of newcomers; after this defeat, according to his theory, the indigenous population had mostly assimilated into the conquering peoples, while some had fled into the mountains (Yanagita, "Yama no jinsei" 226). For the early Yanagita, the mountain people of contemporary Japan — those who were vanquished but who refused to assimilate — thus preserved traces of an originary Japanese culture.[10] As Hashimoto notes, a temporal relationship (modern-ancient) was translated into a spatial relationship (center-periphery) (137).

The critic Murai Osamu has pointed out that Yanagita's study of the mountain people was generated at precisely the same time as his direct involvement in the annexation of Korea, through his role as a government bureaucrat dealing with agricultural administration. Murai argues that Yanagita's conception of the mountain people was essentially based on his knowledge of the indigenous inhabitants of Taiwan and Korea; in addition, the mountain people served for Yanagita as a phantasmatic conglomeration of diverse minority populations in Japan, including the Ainu and *burakumin*.[11] In this context, then, the study of the defeat and assimilation of the indigenous inhabitants by the "invading" peoples served as the production of a historical precedent for Japan's contemporary policy of colonization and assimilation. At the same time, Murai and others point out that Yanagita's emphasis on the mountain people can also be seen to mark a general concern for outsiders to Japanese society, those who inhabit its marginal spaces. This concern would largely dissipate in his later work.

As has been frequently noted, Yanagita eventually dropped his emphasis on the mountain people and turned instead to the topos of the "southern islands" (a designation that includes the islands of Okinawa and Amami) and to a conception of the *jōmin*, or common folk; in the southern islands, he would rediscover the storehouse of originary Japanese culture for which he had been searching — one that was located outside the boundaries of written culture.[12] The southern islands become appropriated as the essential space of Japanese culture, preserving its original form. For example, in *Kainan shōki* (*On the Southern Sea*, 1925), Yanagita wrote that "seen from our perspective, Okinawa is a storehouse of language. Since the most ancient times, all of the goods placed in there remain, bearing the marks of intervening ages" (Yanagita, *Zenshū* 1: 370–371).[13]

This conception of the southern islands as repository of cultural history can be situated within a broader discursive strategy to legitimate the annexation of Okinawa; similarities can also be found with the theories of "common origins" between Korea and Japan, which, as Oguma points out, were used to justify the annexation of Korea — an action that was in fact referred to as a "union" or "merger" (*heigō*). The annexation could thus even be presented as a return to an originary identity, rather than an erasure of difference (Oguma, *Tan'itsu minzoku* 87–116). Murai, stressing Yanagita's involvement in the development of colonial policy in Korea, argues that his discourse on Okinawa is based not only on an erasure of the history of Okinawa's colonization, but also on a sublimation of the annexation of Korea.

Of course, the gesture of assimilation presents its own forms of violence. In the first instance, the appropriation of the margins for a national identity is typically accompanied by strategies of exclusion and abjection. Even more, the very notion of assimilation, or *dōka* — literally, "making same," the elimination of difference — indicates an obliteration of an existing identity. Murai quotes the Naturalist writer Iwano Hōmei (1873–1920), who in 1909 noted the need to preserve the culture of the Ainu, which he referred to as a dying race. This discourse of disappearance is also, as Murai points out, the barely concealed violence of the rhetoric of "preservation," whereby the storehouse becomes, in effect, a crypt. Hōmei asserts that what he wants to preserve from the Ainu is not their "rotting bear-skins or their utensils" but rather their "language and literary art" (Murai 143). There is here a rejection of a materiality perceived as filthy, unclean, and corporeal — this process of abjection is symbolic of the erasure of a history of discrimination and violence, which is subsumed into the disembodied categories of "culture" or "literature." At the same time, the notion of a dying race (in effect, as Murai says, a race being killed off) makes explicit the violence underlying policies of assimilation. It is also worth noting that the concept of literature as linguistic art was precisely being installed in Japan around this time; Hōmei's statement in this sense suggests a certain violence inherent in this institution of literature itself.[14]

As mentioned earlier, this double gesture can be placed within the broader context of colonial discourse in Japan, whose strategies of exclusion and differentiation were often submerged within a rhetoric of assimilation and incorporation.[15] In particular, they can be situated within the rhetorical attempt to distinguish between Western colonialism — based on discrimination and conceptions of racial difference — and the Japanese variety — based, ostensibly, on racial affinity and the eradication of difference. For this reason, there are important differences in the discourses on minority culture between prewar and postwar Japan. These differences have recently been examined by Oguma in his book *Tan'itsu minzoku shinwa no kigen* (*The Origins of the Myth of the Homogenous Nation*, 1995). In particular, there is a fundamental transformation in the status of both ethnic Koreans, who changed from imperial subjects to foreign nationals, and Okinawans, who found themselves under American occupation after the war. Oguma's central argument, in fact, is that many of the dominant accounts of Japanese identity during the period of empire were explicitly cast in terms of multiple ethnicities, while in the postwar period the discourse of Japaneseness was more typically based upon the notion of a homogeneous race. Despite this important historical shift, we can also see the survival of the discourse of appropriation in certain contexts in postwar and contemporary Japanese literature. One of the reasons for this, as Murai points out in his book, is that beginning in the late 1960s there was a powerful resurgence of Yanagita's ethnology, especially among those disillusioned with the failures of left-wing political movements (11).

Ethnology provides an important context for Japanese literature in this period, and its effects can also be seen in those writings that might be categorized as minor, which emerged, especially in the late 1960s and 1970s, as a powerful force in the literary establishment. As commentators have remarked, this is a period that, with the collapse of the New Left, the return of Okinawa to Japanese sovereignty, and the nation's emergence as an economic power (as Japan once more established itself as the dominant economic presence in Asia), is seen to mark the end of the postwar period. The rise of minor literature in the literary marketplace was marked by the awarding of the Akutagawa Prize — the most prestigious literary prize given to new writers — to Ōshiro Tatsuhiro for "Kakuteru pāti" ("Cocktail Party," 1967); Ri Kaisei for "Kinuta o utsu onna" ("The Woman at the Fulling Block," 1971); Higashi Mineo for "Okinawa no shōnen" ("Child of Okinawa," 1971); and Nakagami Kenji for "Misaki" ("The Cape," 1975).

To give a few examples of the use of ethnology in the literature of this period, Kuroko Kazuo situates Ōe Kenzaburō's novel *Man'en gannen no futtobōru* (*The Silent Cry*, 1967), with its exploration of the topos of the remote valley and forest of Shikoku, within the resurgence of ethnology in the 1960s and the attempt to discover a critique of modernity in the space of the native (*dochaku*) or the folk (*minzoku*) (Kuroko 27–35). In addition, Ōba Minako's figure of the "mountain witch," the cannibalistic, threatening female figure who lives in the mountains and outside of the boundaries of the village, can be placed within the general context of Yanagita's mountain people.[16] In fact, the mountain witch is one of the figures discussed by Yanagita in his work "Life in the Mountains." Another example is Tsushima Yūko's story "Danmari ichi" ("The Silent Market," 1982), which represents her relationship to Japanese society through the opposition of the mountain people versus the villagers; these are two communities that exist separately, yet which periodically intersect in certain borderline spaces to trade and communicate. Tsushima, in effect, situates herself within this in-between space of commerce.[17]

The discourse of ethnology also provides the general context for Nakagami's celebrated novel *Sennen no yuraku* (*A Thousand Years of Pleasure*). Nakagami has been the focus of a great deal of critical attention in both Japan and abroad—as others have noted, among literary scholars he has clearly emerged as a central figure of contemporary literature (Monnet 13–14; Dodd 11). In Japan, he has been discussed and praised by critics writing from a wide range of ideological viewpoints. Nakagami's novel, which was published as a book in 1982, is one of a series of his works set in the burakumin community of Shingū, where he was raised, and which is heavily marked by discrimination suffered at the hands of mainstream society.[18] *A Thousand Years of Pleasure* is organized as a series of six stories filtered through the consciousness of a woman named Oryū no Oba, an elderly midwife who stores in her memory the history and individual narratives of the community (which is referred to as the *roji*, which literally means "alley" but could also be translated as "ghetto"). She is something of a mythic figure, who is described at one point as an embodiment of the community itself (149); the narratives that she stores in her memory stretch back a thousand years and also extend into the future (144).

As Asada Akira has written, Nakagami's writing, beginning with his first collection of stories, "Jūkyūsai no chizu" or "The Map of a Nineteen-Year-Old," is based on a certain cartographic impulse, a literal mapping out of specific cultural and social topographies (Asada 8). In particular, a number of his most prominent works revolve around the space of the roji, Nakagami's term for the outcaste village; on the one hand the roji embodies the history of discrimination suffered at the hands of majority society, materialized as the spatial positioning of the village at the margins of the castle town. At the same time, the roji also serves as a source of creative imagination and vitality.

The appropriation of Nakagami's writings for a narrative of national essence is exemplified by Etō Jun's well-known essay on *A Thousand Years of Pleasure*. Etō, one of the most prominent literary critics of the postwar period, praised the work as a "fundamental rejection of modernity" and in particular as a rejection of postwar Japan, which he describes as a "landscape of desolation" (283 and 291). He notes that Nakagami's roji circumscribes a space on the margins of the castle-town, which represents mainstream society and its structures of power. The roji is a space characterized by oral narrative, a world that transcends morality, situated against the space of the city, heavily encoded and regulated by writing and modernity. Etō sees the roji as an opening onto "another world" (*takai*). He writes that such entryways into the other world are often found in everyday spaces, such as the garden, the hedge, or the *tokonoma* alcove inside the Japanese house. In fact, this space of otherness in Nakagami's work will be subsumed into a narrative of a lost cultural essence that existed prior to the encroachment of foreign civilization.

Because of the overarching figure of Oryū no Oba, the midwife who literally facilitates the birth of the male protagonists of the novel and metaphorically gives birth to countless narratives, the roji has sometimes been described by critics as a maternal space. Indeed, Nakagami describes Oryū no Oba as the "roji itself" which in turn is "like a woman's womb" (149).[19] It would not be difficult to establish an opposition between such an apparently maternal space and the symbolic world of the law — and in effect, this is what Etō does (although not by recourse to psychoanalysis). For example, Etō points out that Oryū no Oba, who is illiterate, is described as someone existing outside the world of moral prohibition. In contrast, the castle town on whose margins the roji is positioned is "a world of everyday order governed by morality. Spatially, this world is regulated by the written law, and temporally, it is situated within the normative perspective of history" (Etō 257).

Etō's analysis then shifts to a discussion of the eighteenth-century nativist scholar Motoori Norinaga; Etō cites Norinaga's condemnation of Chinese writing (and morality) and his privileging of the world of oral transmission. Etō recuperates Nakagami's roji into this space of a native, oral culture, one that is premodern, and even prehistorical. The space that is heavily inscribed by discrimination and destitution in Nakagami's work is thus transformed into a purified space of native culture. He writes that "this linguistic space is one that is completely free from any trace of 'foreign learning' which attempts to 'change' or 'confuse' its 'native-born spirit'" (282). In Etō's reading, the association of the burakumin with animals and death becomes transformed into the basis for an originary national culture that excludes the foreign. He thus writes of the roji: "This space in which nature and human beings, people and insects and beasts and birds, the living and the dead, coexist harmoniously—we used to call this space Japan" (285). Etō subsumes Nakagami's roji according to the same double logic analyzed by Murai—positing a space of difference and marginality that is then assimilated into a larger homogenizing narrative of national culture. Thus for Etō, the protagonists of the story—the men of the Nakamoto family, who are each physically marked with signs of difference—are "without exception the most Japanese of Japanese" (288). This erasure of the materiality of the body, and the transformation of the abject into something approaching the sacred, can be read as an elision of the history of discrimination based precisely on such tropes of corporeality.[20]

Which is not to say that Etō's reading is entirely without basis. In some ways, the possibility for this type of appropriation already exists within the novel. As Eve Zimmerman has noted, there are certain mythic narratives deployed in Nakagami's work; in particular, the protagonists of the novel are said to be descended from a noble family that was defeated in an ancient war; this is said to be the origin of their "sacred yet polluted blood" as well as of the cycle of violence in which they are trapped. This notion of a simultaneously sacred and defiled identity seems to mirror Okakura's notion of a culture that is a storehouse of foreign cultures and yet is nevertheless "pure." Zimmerman writes that in using these myths,

> Nakagami implicitly equates [the outcastes] with the emperor of Japan, whose origins are similarly shrouded in the mists of time. During [a] 1989 interview, Nakagami equated the *burakumin* and the emperor, stating that neither of them could be said to have an *ie* or family line that can be traced back through history. Instead their origins lie in myth. For this reason Nakagami considered them to be two sides of the same coin . . . and, at the same time, sacred outcastes. (137)[21]

Nakagami also wrote that he considered the emperor and the burakumin to be the two ends of the structure of Japanese society, both, in a sense, existing outside of it—and at any moment, he notes, the profane has the potential of becoming the sacred (Nakagami, Noma, and Yasuoka 10).

Yet Nakagami's novel ultimately resists assimilation into any narrative of national community. As Etō writes, Nakagami did conceive of the roji as a space in opposition to mainstream society and its institutions of power, an opposition that is materialized as a conflict between writing and oral narrative. Yet for Nakagami, this alienation from the world of majority culture does not open a path of return to an originary national community; rather, it is precisely such a community that is the origin of discrimination. For example, in one chapter of *A Thousand Years of Pleasure*, set immediately after the war, Oryū no Oba recalls a transitional moment in the history of the roji: the passage of the Meiji-era law abolishing outcaste status. She recalls how at that time, all across the country, farmers attacked the homes of burakumin, burning them down; and in one area, ten men who had escaped into the mountains were hunted down and killed like animals (131). Oryū no Oba refers to the farmers who killed the men of the roji as *jōmin*, Yanagita's term for the common folk (138). It is precisely within the discourse of equality that this murderous violence takes place — just as, Oryū no Oba thinks, the violence against Koreans after the 1923 earthquake took place within the discourse of assimilation.

The roji is ultimately an ambivalent space for Nakagami; it provides the imaginative wellspring for his writings, and at the same time it is a place from which he is constantly trying to escape. Thus the roji can be represented only through contradictory images, embodied, as Watanabe Naomi has pointed out, by characters who are depicted as either extremely beautiful or disfigured (139). Yet, there is also no easy line of flight from the roji that does not result in reterritorialization into the space of the nation. For example, one attempted escape from the roji is represented by the character known as Yasu of the Orient, who had been conscripted into the military and had served in China during the war. When he returns to the roji, Yasu dreams of establishing a utopian community outside of Japan; yet his dream is ultimately nothing more than a repetition of the Japanese imperialist project, the construction of a new Manchukuo in South America. The movement beyond Japanese borders is thus simultaneously the assumption of a national identity.

Nakagami once related a story about a number of people from the *buraku* traveling to Brazil with other Japanese. On the ship, he said, everyone was friendly, but once they reached the other shore, the familiar discrimination started up anew (Nakagami, Noma, and Yasuoka 17). In this sense, it is only in the process of movement between fixed locales, what Shu-mei Shih referred to as "spaces of transit," that Nakagami's

characters are able to escape the double structure of abjection and assimilation (or the profane and sacred). Ultimately, Nakagami tries to position
the roji as precisely such an in-between space, something on the order of
what Karatani Kōjin refers to as "communicative space," which decon-
structs the opposition between inside and outside ("Kōtsū kūkan" 31–35).

It is perhaps for this reason that the novel ends with another kind of
movement, an invisible, secret displacement from one minority community to another. Tatsuo, the protagonist of the last story, goes to work in
the coal mines in Hokkaido, where he meets an Ainu youth and visits an
Ainu village, which is described as an uncanny replica of his own village
(there is even an old woman who is a counterpart to Oryū no Oba). Here,
at the end of the work, the roji, which structures the world of the narrative, replicates itself and multiplies. At the very end of the chapter, the
Ainu youth takes the place of Tatsuo, who has been killed in an uprising of
coal miners; he comes to the roji and assumes Tatsuo's name and identity.
Ultimately, it is only through this displacement — a cryptic, hidden movement along the borders of the nation-state — that the legacy of the "noble
yet polluted blood" of the Nakamoto family is finally broken. The substitution of the Ainu youth for Tatsuo, and the movement from one roji to
another, can perhaps be considered a type of "mimicry" that takes place
along the margin — between minority groups, rather than between colonizer and colonized.[22] It is this identification that offers a line of flight
from the type of reterritorialization essayed by Etō.

In effect, this is the direction Nakagami was working toward near the
end of his life. Asada Akira has noted that Nakagami's works move along
two trajectories — what he refers to as "intensive" and "extensive" movements. On the one hand, there is a burrowing toward the center, into a
mythic past in which ultimately the distinction between emperor and
outcaste is dissolved. On the other hand, Asada writes that Nakagami sets
the margins in motion, linking up, in a nomadic movement, with other
borderline spaces (13–15).[23]

In one of his last speeches, delivered in 1991 and published the following year, Nakagami wrote that while he had conceived of the roji as rooted
in Japanese culture, he was also conscious of links between the roji and
other spaces in other cultures. In this piece, he writes of walking the
streets of Paris and feeling an identification with Walter Benjamin, who,
for Nakagami, represented a certain experience of fear in the face of the
power of the nation-state, race, and language (Nakagami, "Shōsetsuka no
sōzōryoku 2" 356). He writes of sensing an affinity between the roji (liter-

ally, "alleyway") and Benjamin's "arcades" (*passages*) and expresses a desire to write a novel about Benjamin's last days, tracing his steps from Paris to his death at the border with Spain. The roji, he writes, is a strange space that is both inside and outside — it is, precisely, a border (*kyōkai*). "When one is walking in the roji, without knowing it one is suddenly outside of it. You don't know how you got out. When you are walking outside, all of a sudden you find yourself inside of it, without knowing how you got in" (349). Nakagami writes of the disorienting experience of walking in the roji and unexpectedly finding himself in some completely other space; as he does so he finds himself questioning his place within the national community. "In other words, I pass through nation and language and ethnicity. I question all of these things and transcend them. Once you transcend them, there is nothing but fear, but that is where I end up. This is the strange power of the roji that I have continually thought about" (358).

Notes

1 As Karatani Kōjin has noted, Lotman's topographical structure can also be applied to various other conceptual oppositions as well — for example, to the oppositions between consciousness and the unconscious, culture and nature, information and noise ("Kōtsū kūkan" 24).

2 On the origins of the concept of national language in Japan, see also Lee.

3 This point is made by Karatani in *Origins* 40–41. On Hokkaido as "domestic colony," see Tamura.

4 For an extended analysis of such contradictions, see Oguma, *Tan'itsu minzoku shinwa no kigen*.

5 The story begins with the author studying a map of Musashino, a famous topography featured in a number of historical and literary works. He sets out to discover the present-day Musashino, to see it directly with his own eyes. Ironically, he comes to appreciate the beauty of the natural scenery only after reading a translation of a particular work by Turgenev, which is cited at length in the text (101–102).

6 The most prominent of these works is his novel *Shanghai* (1928–1932), in which the semicolonial city marks a double identification between Japan and the Western imperial powers, on the one hand, and with the Chinese, on the other.

7 In this context, see Michael Bourdaghs' discussion of the complex relationship between the character Ushimatsu and the community in Shimazaki Tōson's novel *Broken Commandment* ("Disease of Nationalism, Empire of Hygiene" 657).

8 The notion of Japanese culture as minor in relation to the West is examined by Michael Bourdaghs in his contribution to this volume ("The Calm Beauty of Japan at Almost the Speed of Sound: Sakamoto Kyū and the Translations of

Rockabilly"); in this analysis of postwar Japanese and American popular music, Bourdaghs shows how discourses of the minor can be used to both consolidate and disturb the borderlines between dominant and peripheral cultures.

9 See also Harootunian's analysis of Yanagita's ethnology and its attempt "to compensate for the loss experienced in modern life by recalling the memory of a prior form of existence whose traces, presumably, remained available in the countryside" (146).

10 Hashimoto writes: "The *sanka* represented a forgotten world that could still be discovered in unwritten legends, which had been kept alive in the minds of the ordinary people from generation to generation. Therefore, Yanagita began his folklore studies by collecting those stories. From them, he attempted to reconstruct an archaic Japanese life that only survived deep in the 'worm-eaten and rotten' fragmentary memories of ordinary people" (136).

11 See Yanagita, "Iwayuru tokushu buraku no shurui." Also, Yanagita draws connections between the *sanka*, one of his subcategories of mountain people, and the so-called special villages (" 'Itaka' oyobi 'Sanka' " 464).

12 Irokawa Daikichi writes that "after Yanagita abandoned the inquiry into the mountain people, he once more discovered the most static matrix of ethnic oral transmission among the rice-cultivating peoples who had assimilated the indigenous peoples of the same race as the mountain people" (37). For Murai, this shift from the "mountain people" to the "common folk" is precipitated by the March First Movement in Korea in 1919 and the massacre of Koreans in Tokyo following the 1923 earthquake, which demonstrated the failure of colonial policy in Korea (16–51). In *Tan'itsu minzoku shinwa no kigen*, Oguma argues that the shift is explained by Yanagita's experience abroad as part of a League of Nations delegation in Switzerland. There, Oguma writes, Yanagita became aware of Japan itself as a "minority" within the world system (213–220).

13 Harootunian writes of Yanagita's treatment of Okinawa: "He was persuaded to believe that Okinawa offered a treasure trove of unchanging religious beliefs and practices, which were fundamental to the figure of an enduring Japanese daily life. Yanagita viewed Okinawa as a surviving reminder of what Japanese life must have looked like in archaic times. In an act of misrecognition noted by Orikuchi, Okinawa appeared to Yanagita as a vast, living replica or even a laboratory of seventh-century Japan in the present" (155).

14 On the question of the complicity between literature and discrimination, see Watanabe 195–96 and Fowler 34–37.

15 This point has been analyzed by Tessa Morris-Suzuki, who writes that "because they attempted to juggle two essentially contradictory principles — the principle of the nation-state on the one hand and the principle of colonialism on the other — official definitions of nationality and national identity in the Taishō period were almost inevitably fraught with insoluble paradoxes" (159). It goes without saying that the doubleness or ambivalence of colonial discourse is hardly unique to Japan, yet it should also be noted that in the Japanese case this discourse also arises from a particular imperative — to simultaneously identify with and dissociate from Western colonialism. For this reason, the emphasis on "as-

similation" or incorporation was in many cases used in an attempt to distinguish between Japanese and Western imperialism. See, for example, Choi 82–85.

16 On the figure of the mountain witch in Japanese literature, see Viswanathan.

17 Tsushima's novel *Yama o hashiru onna* (*Woman Running in the Mountains*, 1980) has also been linked to the discourse of the mountain witch (Viswanathan 241).

18 For an excellent overview of writings by and about burakumin in Japanese literature, see Fowler.

19 On Nakagami's use of folklore in relation to the representation of gender, see Cornyetz; also, see Monnet for a critical reading of the role of violence in Nakagami's representations of gender and sexuality.

20 For a discussion of Nakagami's treatment of the link between discrimination and "animal nature," see Dodd 4–8.

21 In this sense, it is possible to point to similarities between Nakagami's view of the burakumin and a certain conception of jōmin, or common folk, which Yanagita claimed, in a famous remark of 1957, to include the imperial household. Zimmerman points out the simultaneously subversive and reactionary qualities of Nakagami's gesture of equating the outcastes and the emperor (137).

22 Komori Yōichi notes the gradual infiltration of this substitution of the Ainu youth for Tatsuo into the language of the text, beginning with its acceptance in the discourse of Oryū no Oba to its acceptance within the third-person narration, and argues that at this point the coherency of identity in the narrative is undermined (164).

23 Asada notes that the "extensive" movement is developed further in the novel *Izoku*, left unfinished at Nakagami's death (13). On this point, see also Nakagami and Karatani 25.

Works Cited

Akutagawa Ryūnosuke. "Kamigami no bishō." *Akutagawa Ryūnosuke zenshū*. Vol. 5. Tokyo: Iwanami shoten, 1977. 173–192.

An Ushiku, et al. "Sabetsu to bungaku." *Hihyō kūkan* 2:2 (July 1994): 6–33.

Asada Akira. "Nakagami Kenji o saidōnyū suru." *Hihyō kūkan* 1:12 (Jan. 1994): 6–17.

Bourdaghs, Michael. "Disease of Nationalism, Empire of Hygiene." *positions* 6.3 (1998): 637–673.

Choi, Chungmoo. "The Discourse of Decolonization and Popular Memory: South Korea." *positions* 1.1 (1993): 82–85.

Cornyetz, Nina. "Nakagami Kenji's Mystic Writing Pad; or, Tracing Origins, Tales of the Snake, and the Land as Matrix." *positions* 3.1 (spring 1995): 224–254.

Dodd, Stephen. "Japan's Private Parts: Place as a Metaphor in Nakagami Kenji's Works." *Japan Forum* 8.1 (1996): 3–11.

Etō Jun. "'Roji' to takai: Koe to moji to buntai." Nakagami, *Sennen no yuraku*. 252–291.

Fowler, Edward. "The *Buraku* in Modern Japanese Literature: Texts and Contexts." *Journal of Japanese Studies* 26.1 (2000): 1–39.

Harootunian, Harry. "Figuring the Folk: History, Poetics, and Representation." Vlastos 144-159.

Hashimoto Mitsuru. "*Chihō*: Yanagita Kunio's 'Japan.'" Vlastos 133-143.

Irokawa Daikichi. *Yanagita Kunio: Jōmin bunkaron.* Tokyo: Kōdansha, 1978.

Karatani Kōjin. "Kōtsū kūkan ni tsuite no nōto." *Yūmoa to shite no yuibutsuron.* Tokyo: Chikuma shobō, 1993. 22-35.

———. *Origins of Modern Japanese Literature.* Translation edited by Brett de Bary. Durham: Duke University Press, 1993.

Komori Yōichi. "*Sennen no yuraku* ron: Sa'i no gensetsu kūkan e." *Nakagami Kenji. Kokubungaku: Kaishaku to kanshō* special issue. Ed. Sekii Mitsuo. Tokyo: Shibundō, 1993. 159-165.

Kunikida Doppo. "Musashino." *River Mist and Other Stories.* Trans. David Chibbett. Tokyo: Kōdansha International, 1982. 97-112.

Kuroko Kazuo. *Ōe Kenzaburō ron: Mori no shisō to ikikata no genri.* Tokyo: Sairyūsha, 1989.

Lee Yeounsuk. *Kokugo to iu shisō: Kindai Nihon no gengo ninshiki.* Tokyo: Iwanami shoten, 1996.

Lotman, Yuri M. *Universe of the Mind: A Semiotic Theory of Culture.* Trans. Ann Shukman. London: I. B. Tauris & Co., 1990.

Monnet, Livia. "Ghostly Women, Displaced Femininities and Male Family Romances: Violence, Gender and Sexuality in Two Texts by Nakagami Kenji." 2 Parts. *Japan Forum* 8:1 (1996): 13-34 and *Japan Forum* 8:2 (1996): 221-239.

Morris-Suzuki, Tessa. "Becoming Japanese: Imperial Expansion and Identity Crises in the Early Twentieth Century." *Japan's Competing Modernities.* Ed. Sharon A. Minichiello. Honolulu: University of Hawai'i Press, 1998. 157-180.

Murai Osamu. *Nantō ideorogii no hassei: Yanagita Kunio to shokuminchi shugi.* Tokyo: Ōta shuppan, 1995.

Nakagami Kenji. *Nakagami Kenji hatsugen shūsei.* Vol. 6. Ed. Karatani Kōjin and Suga Hidemi. Tokyo: Daisan bunmeisha, 1999.

———. *Sennen no yuraku.* Tokyo: Kawade shobō, 1992.

———. "Shōsetsuka no sōzōryoku 2." Nakagami, *Nakagami Kenji hatsugen shūsei* 6: 347-358.

———, and Karatani Kōjin. "Roji no sōshitsu to ryūbō." *Kokubungaku: Kaishaku to kyōzai no kenkyū* 36.14 (1991): 12-33.

———, Noma Hiroshi, and Yasuoka Shōtarō. "Shimin ni hisomu sabetsu shinri." Nakagami, *Nakagami Kenji Hatsugen shūsei* 6: 9-61.

Oguma Eiji. *"Nihonjin" no kyōkai: Okinawa, Ainu, Taiwan, Chōsen shokuminchi shihai kara fukki undō made.* Tokyo: Shinyōsha, 1998.

———. *Tan'itsu minzoku shinwa no kigen: Nihonjin no jigazō no keifu.* Tokyo: Shinyōsha, 1995.

Okakura, Kakuzō. *Ideals of the East.* Tokyo: Tuttle, 1970.

Tamura Sadao. "Naikoku shokuminchi toshite no Hokkaidō." *Shokuminchi teikoku Nihon.* Iwanami kōza: Kindai Nihon to shokuminchi 1. Tokyo: Iwanami shoten, 1992. 87-99.

Viswanathan, Meera. "In Pursuit of the Yamamba: The Question of Female Resistance." *The Woman's Hand: Gender and Theory in Japanese Women's Writing*. Ed. Paul Gordon Schalow and Janet A. Walker. Stanford: Stanford University Press, 1996. 239–261.

Vlastos, Stephen, ed. *Mirror of Modernity: Invented Traditions of Modern Japan*. Berkeley: University of California Press, 1998.

Watanabe Naomi. *Nihon kindai bungaku to 'sabetsu.'* Tokyo: Ōta shuppan, 1994.

Yanagita Kunio. " 'Itaka' oyobi 'sanka.' " Yanagita, *Yanagita Kunio zenshū* 4: 454–482.

——. "Iwayuru tokushu buraku no shurui." Yanagita, *Yanagita Kunio zenshū* 4: 483–506.

——. *Kainan shōki*. Yanagita, *Yanagita Kunio zenshū* 1: 297–523.

——. "Yama no jinsei." Yanagita, *Yanagita Kunio zenshū* 4: 77–254.

——. *Yanagita Kunio zenshū*. Vols. 1 and 4. Tokyo: Chikuma shobō, 1989.

Yasuda Toshiaki. *Teikoku Nihon no gengo hensei*. Tokyo: Seori shobō, 1997.

Zimmerman, Eve. "In the Trap of Words: Nakagami Kenji and the Making of Degenerate Fictions." *Ōe and Beyond: Fiction in Contemporary Japan*. Ed. Stephen Snyder and Philip Gabriel. Honolulu: University of Hawai'i Press, 1999. 130–152.

National Space as Minor Space

Afro-Brazilian Culture and the Pelourinho

I begin with a reference to a recent essay by Pierre Bourdieu and Loïc Wacquant that raises some of the issues that frame my study. In "On the Cunning of Imperialist Reason," Bourdieu and Wacquant argue that topics stemming from particular scholarly debates in the United States are imposed, in dehistoricized form, upon the whole planet, and thus produce an apparent universalism that submerges the effects of U.S. imperialism (42). They claim that social relations and cultural practices are being refashioned "after the U.S. pattern" in a process now "accepted with resignation as the inevitable outcome of the evolution of nations" (43). Choosing comparative studies of racial relations in the United States and Brazil as an example of this imposition, they ask, "How are we to account for the fact that the 'theories' of 'race relations' which are but thinly *conceptualized transfigurations*, endlessly refurbished and updated to suit current concerns, of the most commonly used racial stereotypes that are themselves only primary justifications of the domination of whites over blacks in one society, could be tacitly . . . raised to the status of universal standard whereby every situation of ethnic domination must be analysed and measured?" (45). Their answer is the globalizing power of the U.S. academy:

> The fact that this racial (or racist) sociodicy was able to "globalize" itself over the recent period, thereby losing its outer characteristics of legitimating discourse for domestic or local usage, is undoubtedly one of the most striking proofs of the symbolic dominion and influence exercised by the USA over every kind of scholarly and, especially, semi-scholarly production, notably through the power of

consecration they possess and through the material and symbolic profits that researchers in the dominated countries reap from a more or less assumed or ashamed adherence to the model derived from the USA. (46)

While it is certainly true that globalization can submerge the effects of imperialism, in their essay, Bourdieu and Wacquant insist that U.S. scholars are transposing their North American conceptualizations of race onto a Brazilian society that is without racism. In so doing, they employ a schematized view of transnational intellectual circulation and mischaracterize the current dialogue on the African diaspora in the Americas by presenting the last several decades of research on race in Brazil as a unilateral U.S. imposition on a society without racial prejudice (French 110).

Ironically, then, Bourdieu and Wacquant reproduce precisely what they argue against and perpetrate what they themselves decry as "ethnocentric intrusions" (44). They offer a simplistic view that both erases a longstanding process of transculturation involving Brazilian appropriation of so-called foreign ideas and completely ignores the fact that researchers and activists against racism and racial inequality do not consistently adhere to U.S. racial theories based on "a rigid dichotomy between blacks and whites" (44). Their incorrect assertions must be countered for several reasons, the most simple and powerful being that their work reaches a wide international audience, something that the writings of Brazilian scholars on race and ethnicity rarely do. Furthermore, as John French notes, in "adopting a shared posture of victimhood with Brazil at the hands of U.S. imperialism," these French scholars "appear to display the same 'vainglorious nationalism' as Brazilians do when they preempt critical self-examination by judging their country only and positively, against the USA in terms of race" (122).

Bourdieu's and Wacquant's misinterpretation points to the need to examine the specifics of racial ideas in Brazil and their relationship to dominant interpretations of the African diaspora. Brazil is not a static victim of foreign racial theories, nor do Brazilians embrace specifically North American ideas about race. To suggest that ideas about race in Brazil are somehow locally pure and may be contaminated by contact with "foreign ideas" is to overlook the history of the formation of Brazil's myth of racial democracy, an ideology that has its roots in late-nineteenth-century responses to European social theories. Given the country's high rates of racial mixture, Brazil's intellectuals could not fully accept scientific racism — especially the Spencerian notion that miscegenation would lead to a doomed race of mongrels — without condemning their nation to perpetual inferiority. The solution they fashioned allowed them to maintain the assertion of white superiority while simultaneously allowing for the possibility of eliminating the black "stigma" through further miscegenation. Subsequent developments in racial thinking, particularly Gilberto Freyre's thesis of Luso-tropicalism (based on his notion of the "super-capacity" of Portuguese colonizers to mix and mingle), tended toward a valorization of the mulatto and led to a common belief in Brazil's racial exceptionalism: the idea that Brazil, unlike other multiracial societies, was not a country of racial inequalities. Despite ample evidence to the contrary, including empirical confirmation that browns and blacks have unequal access to education, health care, employment, housing, and other quality-of-life indices, this remains the prevalent view of race relations in Brazil today.

The apparent static nature of Brazilian ideas about race, the ideology of racial democracy blindly reinforced by Bourdieu and Wacquant, belies the fact that they are always in flux. Race is continually being transformed and recast as cultural, political, and global developments shape our sense of who we are. New conflicts have generated new ideas and perceptions about racial identity and politics, including the meaning of race in everyday life. The interrelationship of race, cultural production, and political power can be linked to broader ruminations on the politics and production of space in political and social theory, and the role of subaltern groups in dominant social spaces (Lefebvre). As in other multiracial societies, racial prejudice and discrimination have spatial and territorial dimensions in Brazil. Multiple spaces bear the mark of marginalized Afro-Brazilians who have made a formerly exclusive or uninhabited space their own. One site of debate over the meaning of black racial identity in Brazil is the city of Salvador, Bahia.

Nowhere are the clashes between old and new forms of thinking about race and its cultural significance more evident than in the historic center of Salvador known as the Pelourinho. Salvador has held national symbolic importance for more than four centuries as Bahia has moved from being a donatary captaincy, to the seat of the Portuguese colonial government, to a province, and finally to statehood. As the port of entry for most of the millions of Africans forced to migrate there and the state with the largest black population, Salvador has long been understood as the spiritual and cultural center of black Brazil, sometimes imagined as a "Black Rome."

More than a historic place, the Pelourinho is a space shaped by the activities and relationships that occur within it. Examination of that space lends itself to an interdisciplinary approach that allows for discussion of several issues that face Afro-Brazilians today. Among these are closely related questions about the advantages and disadvantages of the cultural affirmation of blackness, the marketing of Brazilian blackness or *negritude* for the purposes of tourism, and the need and desire for a true racial democracy. The space of the Pelourinho is an example of the complex dynamic whereby people of African descent populate the margins of Brazilian society but are at the heart of its national culture.

The history of Salvador is central to the history of Bahia and to the national identity of Brazil. The overwhelmingly nonwhite population of the city today reflects Bahia's heritage as a slave plantation colony. The Largo do Pelourinho is the site of the Igreja Rosário dos Pretos, home to Salvador's black Catholic brotherhood, founded in 1685. The Sociedade Protetora dos Desválidos, a black mutual aid society, was also founded there in 1832. These continue to serve as important points of reference for both the Pelourinho and the Afro-Bahian community. Yet for most of its history, the Pelourinho was not a black neighborhood. The colonial two- and three-story mansions for which it is best known were, for over two hundred years, the homes of planters, public servants, and military men — the cultural elite of the Bahian capital (Mattos 20).

Paradoxically, the Pelourinho, symbolic center of black Brazil, was built by and for a Bahian elite who identified themselves culturally with Europe. In fact, the neighborhood comprises the largest urban grouping of colonial architecture in Brazil and within its limits are some of the country's most important examples of civic and religious architecture dating to the seventeenth and eighteenth centuries. The area is of particular interest to those who study art and architecture and appears in numerous travel writings, novels, and song lyrics about Salvador. Stemming from popular usage, the denomination "Largo do Pelourinho" maintains the memory of the last site of the city's pillory (*pelourinho*), where criminals were publicly tortured and the condemned were executed. The stone pillar or whipping post to which those being punished were shackled at the neck and wrists was moved there in 1807. In the eighteenth century it had been located at the nearby Terreiro de Jesus, but the Jesuits had it removed from that site because the screams of those being punished interrupted the religious ceremonies of their church (Mattos 117).

The name Largo do Pelourinho has endured for nearly two centuries despite the fact that the actual pillory was eliminated in 1835 and the plaza was officially named in 1932 after Brazil's nineteenth-century novelist José de Alencar. This act of popular resistance — or perhaps popular persistence — characterizes the contrasts to be found in the Pelourinho. The site draws the attention of those interested in its magnificent art and architecture and simultaneously retains the name of the instrument of torture that once stood there. The persistent memory of the whipping post also foregrounds the question of the shifting symbolic meaning of the Pelourinho, originally designed for those who, wishing to distinguish themselves from Africans, sought to emulate Europeans.

By the end of the nineteenth century, most of those upper-class families had moved south to other neighborhoods along the coast, and the Pelourinho mansions were occupied by fabric stores, notions shops, jewelry stores, and other small businesses. They housed the workshops of goldsmiths, funnel makers, engravers, sculptors, tinsmiths, and other artisans (Mattos 27). Much of the property remained in the hands of wealthy families and religious orders that rented space to the new occupants. As the city expanded, the Pelourinho became isolated and the area was increasingly cut off from the routes of public transportation.

The Pelourinho neighborhood had become both socially and economically marginalized by the mid–twentieth century and was populated by those who could not afford to live elsewhere. Prostitution was relocated there from other areas of Salvador by the police in 1932 (Mattos 33). Migrant workers from rural regions arrived in large numbers in the 1940s and crowded into the decaying subdivided buildings. This is the poor population of prostitutes, immigrant shopkeepers, vagabonds, and spiritualists fictionalized in *The Two Deaths of Quincas Wateryell* (1961), *Tent of Miracles* (1969), *Tereza Batista Home from the Wars* (1972), and other works by Bahia's world-renowned novelist Jorge Amado (1912–2001).

In the 1960s, Salavdor saw a wave of industrialization that included the development of a large-scale industrial center (the Centro Industrial de Aratu) and later the Camaçari Petrochemical Complex. A city center developed around a new state government administration complex and a new central bus terminal was constructed. All were built far from the old city, which declined further with this new commercial and residential expansion.[1] In sum, the Pelourinho suffered the consequences of administrative decentralization and commercial marginalization as capital markets were redirected to the periphery.

The late 1960s simultaneously mark the first move toward conservation of the neighborhood. In 1967, a restoration program was mounted as part of a regional cultural conservation plan. The government sought advice from UNESCO, and Michel Parent was sent from France to tour Brazilian historical sites in 1966 and 1967. UNESCO subsequently declared the historic center of Salvador a World Heritage Site and what later became known as IPAC (the Institute of Artistic and Cultural Patrimony) was founded to coordinate the restoration of the old city. To this end, in November of 1969, a socioeconomic survey of the Pelourinho was completed. One of its most impressive findings was that in that year, approximately 58 percent of all females of reproductive age in the Pelourinho worked as prostitutes (Bacelar, *Família* 54). In his foreword to a bilingual (Portuguese/English) book acclaiming the recent restoration of the area, titled *Pelourinho: Historic District of Salvador-Bahia: The Restored Grandeur*, Bahia's governor, Antônio Carlos Magalhães, recalls the purpose of the survey was to "evaluate the possibility of developing one of the largest tourist centers in South America" (4). Magalhães's role in the renovation process dates back to the 1960s, when he was mayor of Salvador. His post facto framing of the project in 1994 forcefully reminds us that government conservation policy since the 1960s has been principally motivated by the desire to increase tourism.

The first efforts to restore the Pelourinho coincided with the rise of a black consciousness movement. In Salvador, this involved the revival of *afoxés*, and the creation of *blocos afros*, Afrocentric carnival societies that became cultural standard-bearers of the new movement. The blocos came to dominate cultural political activities in the Northeast in the 1980s. In conjunction with the MNU (Unified Black Movement against Racial Discrimination), they reinforced pride in African heritage and called for redemocratization during the military regime. The most powerful of these groups, Olodum, was established in the Pelourinho. In the words of its current president, João Jorge Rodrigues, "Olodum was founded in 1979 by prostitutes, homosexuals, people associated with the *jogo do bicho* [an illegal lottery], dope smokers, bohemian lawyers, and intellectuals," precisely those marginalized people that many believed gave the neighborhood its bad reputation ("Olodum and the Black Struggle" 47). The group established its headquarters in the Pelourinho. In fact, the Casa do Olodum, reconstructed by architect Lina Bo Bardo from an abandoned mansion, served as a pilot for the larger neighborhood restoration project (Rodrigues, *Olodum* 41).

Olodum successfully drew public attention to the Pelourinho with its weekly music performances. These, combined with a 1990 collaboration with Paul Simon on his *Rhythm of the Saints* album and video, underscored the commercial viability of the blocos as tourist attractions and businesses. According to Rodrigues, Olodum shared the government's interest in revitalizing the Pelourinho, but with the goal of bettering the lives of its (then) residents ("O Olodum" 83). The group sought to recycle black dollars and reinvest in the Afro-Bahian community by providing jobs and financing educational programs. Yet, Olodum and other community activists were unable to prevent the evictions of hundreds of poor people from the Pelourinho when large-scale renovation began in 1991.

This latest conservation project differed from earlier attempts at restoration in that it was characterized by radical disregard for the local population. Residents were forced to relocate and some were paid compensation averaging between $400 and $800 dollars ("Indenizações" 5). The state police removed resisters under threat of force. Once removed, undesirable or "marginal" people were and continue to be kept out of the area by the military police, who have a new station in the Pelourinho near the Casa do Olodum.

While nearly everyone praises the recuperation of the built environment of the historic district, some critics question both the means of the recent renovation (especially the forced removal of longtime residents) and its ends. In an essay titled "Could the New Pelourinho be a Trick?" journalist Roberto Marinho de Azevedo states an opinion echoed by many others: "The Pelourinho was transformed into a stage set. That neighborhood where you used to feel old Salvador, today looks like a theater where Salvador is represented for tourists" (131).[2] The representation or performance of Salvador, and particularly black Salvador, to which Marinho de Azevedo refers, is a product of the wholesale reorientation of the area to draw tourism. Community housing was not central to the project when the Pelourinho was redesigned as a tourist hub rather than a dynamic residential or business district.

As the work of Brazilian sociologist Jocélio Teles dos Santos shows, state agencies have been actively involved in commodifying Afro-Bahian culture to promote tourism since the 1970s (119). Their determination to publicly demonstrate Brazil's harmonious multiracialism renders static, folkloric representations of African-based culture. The relegation of Afro-Brazilian cultural production to the realm of the folkloric robs it of its

Figure 1. The Pelourinho before renovation.

Figure 2. The Pelourinho after renovation.

dynamism and potential agency, ignoring the centrality of cultural exchange to its formation. Africanisms are thus separated from other influences on Brazilian culture and circumscribed as quaint, unthreatening vestiges of the past in a move that actually contradicts the longstanding Brazilian ideology of race mixture (119).

The commodification of "blackness" or "Africanness" for tourism is an obvious component of the Pelourinho renovation. One example of this process is the naming of the new plazas formed in the interior of city blocks and intended for public music and dance performances. These plazas were named after characters in Jorge Amado's novels: Largo de Quincas Berro D'Água, Largo de Tereza Batista, Largo de Pedro Arcanjo. Renaming sections of the Pelourinho after Amado's fictional creations entails an unthreatening reification of the portraits of poverty and ethnicity in his novels. Why, one might ask, were they not instead named after important Afro-Brazilian citizens?

To encourage tourism, the state emphasizes equality and promotes an idealized image of Bahian society as a model of Brazil's harmonious racial coexistence. Despite the fact that it is now a predominantly commercial area and has few actual residents, the Pelourinho is central to this promotion. In reality, Salvador is a highly segregated city and the majority of Afro-Bahians live in all-black neighborhoods (Telles 94).

Caetano Veloso and Gilberto Gil evoke the complicated crossings of race and class in the setting of the Pelourinho in the song "Haiti" recorded on their album *Tropcália II*, released in 1993:

> When you are invited up on the terrace
> Of the Casa de Jorge Amado Foundation[3]
> To watch from above the row of soldiers; almost all black
> Beating on the necks of the black good for nothings
> Of mulatto thieves and other almost white ones
> Treated like the black ones
> Just to show the other almost black ones
> (And they are almost all black)
> How it is that blacks, poor men and mulattoes
> And almost white ones, so poor they're almost black are treated
> And it doesn't matter if the eyes of the whole world
> Might be for a moment turned to the square
> Where the slaves were punished
> And today a pounding of drums pounding of drums

With the purity of boys in secondary school uniforms
On parade day
And the epic grandeur of a people in formation
Attracts us, astonishes us and stimulates us
Not one thing matters: not the trace of the mansion's architecture
Not the camera lens from Fantástico, nor Paul Simon's record
No one, no one is a citizen
If you go to the party there at Pelô,[4] and if you don't go
Think about Haiti, pray for Haiti.
Haiti is here, Haiti is not here.

The entire *Tropicália II* album addresses questions of identity and is referred to by critics Ivo Lucchesi and Gilda Korff Dieguez as "an epic of the identity of the Brazilian being" (222). Within that epic, Veloso's lyrics for "Haiti" call up cinematic images of the Pelourinho that detail the violence of poverty in its complicated relation to Brazilian racial practices and ideologies. Violence here — less explicitly political than the violence of the period immediately following the release of the first *Tropicália* album in 1968, when both Veloso and Gil were exiled by the ruling military regime — is both racialized and inclusive, part of the structure of Brazilian social life. *Mestiçagem* (miscegenation) is not portrayed as any guarantee of social harmony. The beatings described in the first verse of Caetano's lyrics are linked to the whippings at the pillory of the slavery period: "And it doesn't matter if the eyes of the whole world / Might be for a moment turned to the square / Where the slaves were punished." In the juxtaposed instances of the colonial and postcolonial beatings at the Pelourinho, the violent action is implicitly condoned by the larger society. Drawing the comparison between them, the lyrical voice prods listeners to contemplate the multiple meanings of that space. Don't be awed into complacency by the contemporary performance of the Pelourinho, the pounding of Afro-Brazilian drums that represent "the epic grandeur of a people in formation," Caetano sings, "Not one thing matters: not the trace of the mansion's architecture / Not the camera lens from Fantástico / Nor Paul Simon's record." Rather than simply party in the Pelourinho, as so many do, we are encouraged to think of that space as what Saidiya Hartman calls a "scene of subjection," a site of spectacle where blackness is performed and black suffering and violence are minimized through an emphasis on "good times" (25).

The song's refrain, "Think about Haiti, pray for Haiti / Haiti is here, Haiti is not here," both alludes to the violence and poverty that have wracked Haiti in the twentieth century and echoes an oft-cited late-nineteenth-century quotation from Brazilian intellectual Sílvio Romero. Fearful of the free black majority in Haiti and the threat it represents to Euro-Brazilian society, Romero argues in his 1881 (preabolition) essay, "The Emancipation of the Slaves," that "Brazil is not, and should not be, Haiti" (qtd. in Brookshaw 43). Following the refrain, the lyrics move from the Pelourinho to the streets of Rio de Janeiro to the site of an infamous prison massacre in São Paulo, and finally beyond Brazil, to Cuba and the Caribbean: "And when you go on holiday in the Caribbean / and when you have sex without a condom / and participate intelligently in the blockade of Cuba / think about Haiti." The violence depicted in the first verse travels outward in the second, its manifestations local, yet broadly recognizable within their Latin American context.

The renovation of the Pelourinho and the marketing of blackness for tourism serve as an example of how Afro-Brazilians populate the margins but are at the heart of Brazil's national culture.[5] Though the architecture was recuperated, the "marginal" inhabitants of the buildings were evicted. While the state wished to maintain a sense of a black cultural presence in order to attract tourists, it was the poor — a population in which Bahia's people of African descent are vastly overrepresented — who were removed from the Pelourinho. They were replaced by Quincas Berro D'Água, Tereza Batista, and Pedro Arcanjo. I return to Amado's characters because of the questions they raise and their relevance to the way this reclamation of space is understood. Do they represent romanticized images of poverty and ethnicity? Do they show a creative response to domination, an alternative, perhaps antiracist, mode of social experience? There is not one answer to what they signify. Like the space of the Pelourinho, they are invested with multiple meanings.

The debate about the place of cultural expression within social struggle is a longstanding one in Brazil's black movement. Historian Kim Butler contends that Afro-Bahians' struggles for self-determination have taken shape around the areas of culture, rather than race, because Afro-Bahians developed a cultural rather than a racial ethnicity. An ethnicity based on African culture was made possible by the large and diverse black population of Bahia (58). The controversy surrounding the renovation of the Pelourinho offers an example of the complexities of race and class in Brazil and, as Butler argues in her comparison of São Paulo and Salvador, shows that the dynamics of Afro-Brazilian ethnicity are not identical throughout the country.

On one side of the discussion about black cultural production are groups like Olodum that see their efforts as a means of social and economic empowerment. João Jorge Rodrigues insists that Olodum has remained true to its goals and asserts: "Through it all we have constructed and are still constructing a patrimony that has not been given to us by any politician" ("Olodum and the Black Struggle" 48). Others, like Brazilian sociologist Jeferson Bacelar, argue that jobs in the culture industry are supervalued by Afro-Bahians, creating the false impression that blacks are fully participating in the labor market ("Blacks" 100). For him, "mythical, romanticized valorization of black culture qua product has achieved various things, among them racial segregation and a total lack of changes in the position of blacks in the class structure" ("Blacks" 99).[6] Despite the problems of co-optation — the move to transform the cultural production of blacks into "portraits of Bahianness" as seen in the new Pelourinho — Bacelar does not deny the benefits of the cultural affirmation of blackness: "Culture is life and danger, strength and temptation. Those who were familiar with Salvador in the 1950s and 1960s, when 'blacks knew their place,' however, know the advances that culture has provided and the significance of being able to say that one is black. It has been, and continues to be, the path of blacks in the construction of their racial identity in Salvador" ("Blacks" 100).

The Pelourinho is strongly associated with the affirmation of black Brazilian culture. Study of this site and the debates taking place within and around it must be part of a larger discussion that addresses recent Afro-Brazilian cultural production with reference to the African diaspora. Attention to the dynamics of the production of Afro-Brazilian culture may help reshape current understandings of the black Atlantic, an idea customarily defined with little or no reference to Brazil, the country with the largest population of African descent outside Africa. Despite the warnings of Bourdieu and Wacquant, we must attend to the racial and cultural politics of Brazil. Not only is Brazil not an "exception" in its ideas about race, but lately scholars of comparative race studies — Howard Winant is one example — argue convincingly that the United States is becoming ever more like Brazil. In recent years, a new resistance to acknowledge racism and racial difference and an accompanying insistence that we live in a "color-blind" society has emerged in the United States. We are told by some that it is racist to study the ways in which race shapes our daily reality. Meantime, in Brazil, a new racial consciousness is emerging and is most evident in the work of the modern Afro-Brazilian movement, which is linked to the consolidation of the expansion of democracy. As this consolidation takes shape, we must view Afro-Brazilians not only as cultural subjects, victims of racial inequality, or of imperialist theorizing, but as active, though unequally situated, participants in one of the world's largest multiracial societies.

Notes

1   This is a continuing process. Ford is currently building the world's largest car manufacturing plant in the periphery of Salvador.
2   All translations from the Portuguese are mine unless otherwise noted.
3   Reminders of Amado and his work can be found throughout the Pelourinho and include not only this foundation building, but plaques placed on buildings referring to the activities of some of his characters as if they had occupied that space.
4   "Pelô" is a nickname for "Pelourinho."
5   Vianna's *The Mystery of Samba* is a recent study of this process.
6   For a similar view, see my interview with journalist and activist Fernando Conceição.

Works Cited

Amado, Jorge. *Tent of Miracles*. Trans. Barbara Shelby. New York: Knopf, 1971.
———. *Tereza Batista: Home from the Wars*. Trans. Barbara Shelby. New York: Knopf, 1975.
———. *The Two Deaths of Quincas Wateryell*. Trans. Barbara Shelby. New York: Knopf, 1965.
Azevedo, Roberto Marinho de. "Será o novo Pelourinho um engano?" *Revista do Patrimônio Histórico e Artístico Nacional* 23 (1994): 131–137.
Bacelar, Jeferson. "Blacks in Salvador: Racial Paths." *Black Brazil: Culture, Identity, and Social Mobilization*. Ed. Larry Crook and Randal Johnson. Los Angeles: UCLA Latin American Center, 1999. 85–101.
———. *A família da prostituta*. São Paulo: Ática, 1982.
Bourdieu, Pierre, and Loïc Wacquant. "On the Cunning of Imperialist Reason." *Theory, Culture and Society* 16.1 (1999): 44–58.
Brookshaw, David. *Raça e cor na literatura brasileira*. Trans. Marta Kirst. Porto Alegre: Mercado Aberto, 1983.
Butler, Kim. *Freedoms Given, Freedoms Won: Afro-Brazilians in Post-Abolition São Paulo and Salvador*. New Brunswick: Rutgers University Press, 1998.
French, John D. "The Missteps of Anti-Imperialist Reason: Bourdieu, Wacquant, and Hanchard's *Orpheus and Power*." *Theory, Culture and Society* 17.1 (2000): 107–128.

Hartman, Saidiya V. *Scenes of Subjection: Terror, Slavery, and Self-Making in Nineteenth-Century America*. New York: Oxford University Press, 1997.

"Indenizações baixas podem prejudicar obras no centro." *A Tarde* 14 April 1992: 5.

Lefebvre, Henri. *The Production of Space*. Trans. Donald Nicholson-Smith. Cambridge, Mass.: Blackwell, 1991.

Lucchesi, Ivo, and Gilda Korff Dieguez. *Caetano. Por que não? Uma viagem entre a aurora e a sombra*. Rio de Janeiro: Leviatã, 1993.

Magalhães, Antônio Carlos. "Foreword." *Pelourinho: Centro histórico de Salvador-Bahia: A grandeza restaurada/Pelourinho: Historic District of Salvador-Bahia: The Restored Grandeur*. Salvador: Fundação Cultural do Estado da Bahia, 1994.

Marchant, Elizabeth. "Interview with Fernando Conceição." *Callaloo* 25.2 (2002): 613–619.

Mattos, Waldemar. *Evolução histórica e cultural do Pelourinho*. Rio de Janeiro: SENAC, 1978.

Rodrigues, João Jorge. "Olodum and the Black Struggle in Brazil." *Black Brazil: Culture, Identity, and Social Mobilization*. Ed. Larry Crook and Randal Johnson. Los Angeles: UCLA Latin American Center, 1999. 43–51.

——. "O Olodum e o Pelourinho." *Pelo Pelô: História, cultura e cidade*. Ed. Marco Aurélio A. de Filgueiras Gomes. Salvador: Editora da Universidade Federal da Bahia, 1995. 81–91.

——. *Olodum: Estrada da paixão*. Salvador: Fundação Casa de Jorge Amado, Grupo Cultural Olodum, 1996.

Santos, Jocélio Teles dos. "A Mixed-Race Nation: Afro-Brazilians and Cultural Policy in Bahia, 1970–1990." *Afro-Brazilian Culture and Politics: Bahia, 1790s to 1990s*. Ed. Hendrik Kraay. Armonk, N.Y.: M. E. Sharpe, 1998. 117–133.

Telles, Edward E. "Ethnic Boundaries and Political Mobilization Among African Brazilians: Comparisons with the U.S. Case." *Racial Politics in Contemporary Brazil*. Ed. Michael Hanchard. Durham: Duke University Press, 1999. 82–97.

Veloso, Caetano. "Haiti." Trans. Arto Lindsay. Music by Gilberto Gil and Caetano Veloso. *Tropicália II: Caetano e Gil*. Elektra Nonesuch 9793392, 1994.

Vianna, Hermano. *The Mystery of Samba: Popular Music and National Identity in Brazil*. Chapel Hill: University of North Carolina Press, 1999.

Winant, Howard. "Racial Democracy and Racial Identity: Comparing the United States and Brazil." *Racial Politics in Contemporary Brazil*. Ed. Michael Hanchard. Durham: Duke University Press, 1999. 98–115.

Alternate Geographies and the Melancholy of Mestizaje

Esperanza, the adolescent narrator of Sandra Cisneros's 1984 book *The House on Mango Street*, walks through her Chicago neighborhood with her friends when she turns suddenly: "Look at that house . . . it looks like Mexico." Before her friends have the chance to laugh at her, Esperanza's sister Nenny speaks up: "Yes, that's Mexico all right. That's what I was thinking exactly" (18). Each sister translates her urban space into a familiar referent, locating herself within a hostile and threatening environment. The source of these threats lies in the economic disempowerment and ethnic antagonisms experienced by the members of their Chicago barrio. More centrally for the narrator, hostility derives from Esperanza's gendered position within a world of male privilege and sexual violation.

The fact that both sisters interpret their geographies through similar conceptual grids places them within a shared spatial, cultural, and familial relation. The connection between self, family, and national/ethnic origin is concretized through their shared interpretive tactics. The characters serve as examples of how Chicano/a culture conceptualizes geography differently (and differentially) as it articulates images of identity and place that often strive toward an oppositional stance.

One durable example of this opposition has been the deployment of Aztlán as a cultural icon. Another has been the more recent (and some would say already clichéd) configuration of the borderlands as a site of hybridity or — in a phrase favored by poststructural theorists from Homi Bhabha to Edward Soja — a Thirdspace.

This essay examines the manner in which land as both home and border, as site of place and displacement, finds its representation in Chicano/a public art. This art helps situate the role that land plays in the perpetually moving border of Mexican/American experience, one that blurs national boundaries. In this sense, Chicano art participates in the formation of a cultural and personal consciousness that engages with the transnational: Chicano/a art, culture, identity, and politics become transnational practices breaking down fixed notions of a bounded nation and opening a vista that situates Chicana/o subjectivity within a broader context.

Chicano/a artists have maintained a peculiar relationship to local geography within a U.S. context. Unlike the Asian or African American minorities, whose histories are those of displacement (diasporic movements through immigration or enslavement), Chicano and Chicana subjectivities occupy an ambiguous space. Their transnationalism is not one borne of the movement from a national context to another. Rather, it is one that is produced by the historical realities of shifting borders in the southwestern United States. The borders here are linguistic, social, and economic borders negotiated and crossed by Chicano subjectivities working through multilingual cultural identities and dissident practices.

If the borderlands names the space of Chicano subjectivity, it does so as a transnational space connecting this subjectivity to economies, social orders, identities, cultures, and histories not fixed by U.S. national borders. Chicano public art maps the possibilities of this new terrain, drawing on varied visual representations of land in order to name new significance. One way land has been given new significance within a Chicana/o context is the use of the term "Aztlán" to name a home amid a profound sense of homelessness.

Aztlán, ostensibly situated in the present Southwest of the United States, names the mythic homeland of the Aztecs before their migration to the high valley of central Mexico. It was introduced to Chicano discourse with "El Plan Espiritual de Aztlán," drafted in March 1969 for the Chicano Youth Conference held in Denver, Colorado: "Brotherhood unites us and love for our brothers makes us a people whose time has come and who struggle against the foreigner "Gabacho," who exploits our riches and destroys our culture. . . . Before the world, before all of North America, before all our brothers in the Bronze Continent, We are a Nation, We are a Union of free pueblos, We are Aztlán" (403).

Aztlán—as a mythic homeland—provides a discursive and cultural claim to primacy, an image of legitimacy, a means by which to understand the United States neither as a sovereign nation state nor as an end point of migration, but as a part of a more extensive political, economic, and cultural landscape. Ironically, the United States, acting as a sovereign nation, has served to foster this alternate geography, first with the Bracero Program (1942–1964), on the heels of which followed the Border Industrialization Program in 1965, and since 1994 the North American Free Trade Agreement. All these initiatives have served in one form or another to foster social and familial bonds that encourage rather than discourage continued movement from Mexico to the United States and back.

The significance of Aztlán as an oppositional geography in Chicano cultural discourse cannot be overstated. In part, Aztlán serves to distinguish Chicanos from other immigrant groups. As the popular saying goes, "We didn't cross the border. The border crossed us." This rejection of the immigrant experience causes problems between Chicano articulations of subjectivity and constituencies whose sense of self is bound to notions of diaspora and immigration. In part, the centrality of Aztlán comes from the very fact of its performativity. Aztlán is more myth than locale, more prescriptive than descriptive. While in its most assertive register "Aztlán" can name a kind of nationalist or nativist claim to place and land, in fact it serves a rather complex "transcultural" and performative identity evoking but moving beyond historically situated discourses of national identity. By asserting an Aztec past to legitimate one's claim to place, the use of Aztlán replicates the strategic reliance on Aztec civilization found in the postrevolutionary discourse of Mexican nationalism. The evocation of Aztlán is always a performative gesture, one meant to call up and move beyond key historical moments in the conceptualization of Chicano cultural, ethnic, and racial identity.

Aztlán in particular, and the idea of borderlands more generally, relies on the dynamic of hybridity implicit in Chicano conceptualizations of *mestizaje* — racial (and cultural) mixture. Though it seeks to evoke connection to a pre-European moment and call up the possibility of a contemporary Chicano self free from the delimiting influences of colonization, Aztlán yet exists only in relation to that moment and those influences. Quite literally, the imagining of an originary Chicano space rests upon the racial mixture that has been a key feature of the colonial experience in the Americas. This is significant because mestizaje has, in many ways, become a dominant trope within the criticism and creation of Chicana/o culture.

This trope has not been without controversy. Josefina Saldaña, for example, argues that historically the idea of racial mixture has served as the biological metaphor for the corporativist government policies of the Mexican ruling party, the Partido Revolucionario Institucional (PRI). A progressive teleology in Mexico has thus been produced, one that posits the Indian as a point of origin in an evolutionary history (407). This history buries Indian identity in a still past, one that means any reference to the Indian on the cultural level only serves to cite a noble yet tragic descent into oblivion.

Within Mexican national discourse, the counterpoint to mestizaje is the ideology of *indigenismo*. The central notion of indigenism, as Peter Wade explains, is that "Indians needed special recognition and that special values attached to them. Very often it was a question of exotic and romantic symbolism, based more on the glorification of the pre-Columbian Indian ancestry of the nation than on respect for contemporary Indian populations" (32). The embrace of mestizo bodies within a Mexican nationalist discourse excludes Indian concerns from present national agendas.

But what of mestizaje in a Chicano context? Do the same patterns of erasure and oblivion hold true? Saldaña argues: "In our Chicano reappropriation of the biologized terms of mestizaje and indigensimo, we are also always recuperating the Indian as an ancestral past rather than recognizing contemporary Indians as coinhabitants not only of this continent abstractly conceived, but of the neighborhoods and streets of hundreds of U.S. cities and towns" (413). The erasure enacted in Mexico by the trope of mestizaje, she suggests, functions similarly in the Chicano deployment of mixed-racial identification. I would modify this view only by elaborating further the difference between a Mexican nationalism and the subnational context of Chicano cultural production.

While there certainly has been a steady romanticizing of the *indio* in Chicano discourses (particularly those nationalist discourses developed in the 1960s and reshaped by feminist writers like Gloria Anzaldúa in the 1980s), the conditions under which this romantic recasting has taken place are not innocent. That is, certain quarters have deployed a strategic use of indigenismo to achieve concrete political gains. While mestizaje has been used to inform Mexican national identity, in the United States mestizaje has been used for quite the obverse reason: to challenge accepted notions of American identity, notions often premised on the exclusion of the racial in the service of the national.

Mestizaje as a trope in Chicano discourse is involved in a process that values interstitiality, a transnational sense of being betwixt and between common to many minority discourses. Implicit in this position is a dynamic of both reclamation and absence, of redemption and loss. The tensions inherent in developing a minoritarian position — tensions that shift from anticolonial triumph to melancholy — are clearly visible in the visual and literary history of Chicano cultural production.

It is worth recalling Hayden White's observation that "troping is both a movement *from* one notion of the way things are related *to* another notion, and a connection between things so that they can be expressed in a language that takes account of the possibility of their being expressed otherwise" (2). This movement from one notion to another — compounded with an awareness that they can otherwise be expressed — parallels the slippery signification of mestizaje within Chicana cultural production and criticism. Be it the border criticism of Renato Rosaldo, the new mestiza consciousness proposed by Gloria Anzaldúa, the borderlands criticism that has, as José Saldívar observes, "contributed to the 'worlding' of American studies" (xiii), the notion of mixture is a common concern in Chicana studies. In some ways, mestizaje remains the touchstone, an instance of how in a Mexican and Chicana context mixture has served as a defining act of reproduction, self-identification, and representation.

Mestizaje bears the trace of a historical material process, the result of a violent racial/colonial encounter. In articulating the idea of mestiza consciousness, Gloria Anzaldúa tropes José Vasconcelos's notion of *la raza cosmica*: "From [a] racial, ideological, cultural and biological crosspollinization an 'alien' consciousness is presently in the making — a new *mestiza* consciousness, *una conciencia de mujer*. It is a consciousness of the Borderlands" (77). I do not mean to cite Anzaldúa as the authoritative word on mestizaje and borderlands. Nor do I take her characterization — as I believe some critics do — to be an articulation of the borderlands as a site of absolute, free-floating alterity. In evaluating notions of the borderlands, we should keep in mind Yvonne Yarbro-Bejarano's suggestion that we need to contextualize the idea of the borderlands historically and critically in order to "avoid the temptation to pedestalize or fetishize" it (9). Thus the borderlands is where body, history, culture, and consciousness cross with self-identity. Mestizaje derives from a complex history involving both a sense of dispossession and empowerment, a dynamic process that variously devalues and esteems indigenous ancestry.

Quite simply, Chicano culture moves dynamically through and between numerous geographic, cultural, and social spaces. The betweenness of Chicano culture, its interstitial quality, allows it to draw from a large variety of discursive practices that come to form its repertoire. From the histories and traditions it constructs to the motifs and speech acts it evokes, the poetic expression of Chicano culture employs a type of recuperative strategy akin to the pastiche associated with the condition of postmodernity. Within the postmodern debates, the contemporary deployment of different historical styles has been critiqued as a type of historical eclecticism that expresses a simplistic neoconservative nostalgia. Although it does employ a type of historical pastiche, the counterdiscursive quality of Chicano culture precludes the easy conclusion that cultural eclecticism necessarily signals a reactionary ideology.

As critics such as Andreas Huyssen have argued, the postmodern invocation of historical styles can "express some genuine and legitimate dissatisfaction with modernity and the unquestioned belief in the perpetual modernization of art" (12). The demand to "make it new" cannot be an imperative when what is "old" — traditional forms of discredited knowledge passed on through families and communities — has from a "majoritarian" position been denied. The historical connectivity made evident in Chicano cultural production refuses to become either a meaningless play of empty historical signifiers or a neoconservative reinscription of a regime of tradition. It marks a profound reexamination and critique of history. It questions the narratives that comprise that history, proposing alternate and critical narratives that seek to counterpoise disempowering subject positions and limiting discourses.

Chicano cultural production provides, in other words, a counterdiscourse that draws on history and simultaneously interrogates it. Or, as Ramón Saldívar has articulated this process, Chicano literary production is marked by a double move, the "paradoxical impulse toward revolutionary deconstruction and toward the production of meaning" (88).

This double movement, at once interstitial (between hermeneutics and deconstruction) and resistant (advocative and interrogative) manifests itself in numerous ways. The celebration of the racial and cultural mestizaje that, during the 1920s and beyond, found valorization in the construction of Mexican national identity resonates, during the 1960s and beyond, throughout the development of Chicano cultural identity. The sense of joining and conjoining implied by mestizaje expands exponentially within a Chicano cultural space comprised of seemingly infinite conjunctions between a variety of historically marked cultural matrices. Chicano culture, in short, forms a type of radical mestizaje.

Mestizaje informs the metaphor of cultural borderlands, a site where Chicano identity is borne out of national and racial displacement. This leads to a complex valuation of interstitiality — both as a site of utopian imagining and a naked manifestation of power. Chicano culture locates

Figure 1. "Retablo of M. Esther Tapia Picón," from *Miracles on the Border: Retablos of Mexican Immigrants to the United States,* by Jorge Durand and Douglas S. Massey. © 1995 The Arizona Board of Regents. Reprinted with permission of the University of Arizona Press.

itself within a complex third space neither Mexican nor American but in a transnational space of both potential and constraint.

The borderland stands as that region between home and not home. Living between worlds involves negotiating through a ruptured terrain: "To survive the Borderlands / you must live *sin fronteras* / be a crossroads." To live without borders means that the multiple subjectivities Gloria Anzaldúa's poetry evokes stand at the intersection of various discursive and historical trajectories.

The geography of the borderlands incessantly places the subject in relation to matrices of meaning, identity, and power. Cultural practices translate this new space into signifying systems that highlight multivalent tactics of survival and opposition at work within the postmodern geography of the borderlands.

Figure 1 offers a visual representation of the U.S.-Mexican border by an anonymous Mexican painter commissioned as an offering (or *ofrenda*), giving thanks for surviving a treacherous journey across the border and back. (The lettering reads, "We give thanks to the Virgin of San Juan for saving us from the migration authorities on our way to Los Angeles. León, Guanajuato. María Esther Tapia Picón.") This *retablo*, found in the church sanctuary of San Juan de los Lagos in Jalisco, Mexico, brings together both the technological developments of advanced capitalism and the religious piety of premodern times. The earliest example of a retablo in Mexico dates to 1781, and its form can be traced back to the Middle Ages (Durand and Massey, 5).

This ofrenda represents the border as an alien and menacing site; simultaneously it reclaims and transforms that geographic space. The ex-voto accommodates the alienating and dangerous experience of border crossing through aesthetic and religious practice into a contained and reordered spatial formation. Indeed, the triangulation of the retablo is significant both in terms of the religious iconography the formation evokes and the semiotics of the representation. The border crossers — hidden — spy upon the INS agents; the Virgin of San Juan gazes benignly upon the border crossers; and the INS, significantly, sees nothing. The border undergoes a cultural reclamation, a rescripting, in an effort to affirm a comprehensive — and comforting — geography carved from an overwhelmingly menacing landscape.

The religious symbolic system in which the painting functions suggests a sense of closure and completion in relation to the border. María Esther Tapia Picón has obviously returned home and completed a sense of religious obligation by commissioning the ofrenda. The representation of land in the painting as a site of conflict is offset by the context of the painting in the sanctuary of San Juan de los Lagos. The sanctified land on which the sanctuary sits represents a return to home, a resolution of the relation between self and place.

When visual art is free to circulate in other symbolic systems of exchange, the sense of security and reclamation the ofrenda suggests is altered. Figure 2 shows a poster used for political organizing by the United Farm Workers Union (UFW). The pose of the dispirited mestizo family speaks quite clearly to the indigenous roots of the farm laborers — an identification underscored by the stylized Aztec eagle that serves as the symbol for the UFW. The iconography of the Indian — the bare chested man, the swaddled baby, the braided mother — suggests the view that Europeans and Euro-Americans have unjustly occupied native land. The poster posits a Chicano/a identity that predates national borders, but it also highlights the creation of other borders. The figure of the family indicates how the Chicano movement naturalized the ideology of heterosexuality and a patriarchal family order. The family structure is already

Figure 2. *The Land Is Ours*, artist unknown,
United Farm Workers Union poster.

scripted within the new national formation of a Chicano "Aztlán," an ideological order that later Chicana work seeks to undo.

In the background the silhouettes of children, workers, and picketers march in an act of political solidarity. The juxtaposition of the somber and isolated mestizo family against the political activism on the horizon suggests a kind of transforming reality. The invocation of a racial/historical mestizaje is marked by the corporeality of the family in the foreground, indicating the rightful claim Chicanos have to the land on which they stand. The poster recognizes an indigenous past in order both to challenge relations of power in the present and to envision a future that may potentially be more empowered and more collective. The defeat suggested by the expressions in the foreground is offset by the act of defiance in the background. The horizon thus forms a kind of imagined border of possibility, one which seeks to undo alienation, which suggests a movement from a problematic past through a reforming present toward a more fully realized and just future.

The sense of political engagement and resistant positioning evident in *This Land Is Ours* manifests itself in numerous ways throughout the

Figure 3. *Argentina . . . One Year of Military Dictatorship*, by Malaquias Montoya, 1976–1977. Reprinted with permission of Malaquias Montoya.

history of Chicano poster art. Figure 3 shows a poster used to organize political protest in Berkeley, California, on behalf of *los desaparecidos* half a world away. The image of the barbed wire conveys a sense of the horrific Argentinean prisons where students, journalists, writers, and artists considered dangerous to the state were taken during Argentina's "dirty war" from 1976–1983. Argentina's military dictatorship arose, as is well known, as a result of a military coup fully supported by the U.S. government. The message of the poster is meant to be direct and forceful and thus draws on obvious symbolism to convey its point: the bleeding flower reflects the brutality endured under the military junta, the barbed wire obviously symbolizes state repression and violent power.

In these last two posters, land gets conceived as a site infused with political significance. The Montoya poster suggests that the Americas form a hemispheric geopolitical unit where the struggle for justice within the national borders of the United States should be understood as part

Figure 4. *Seven Views of City Hall*, by Alfredo de Batuc, 1987. Reprinted with permission of Alfredo de Batuc.

of an international dynamic. As with figure 2, the question of national boundaries and its relation to personal and political agency comes into question.

In a more humorous vein, figure 4 also invokes images of political power, here crossed with religious imagery. The City Hall of Los Angeles assumes the spatial position of the Virgen de Guadalupe. On the one hand, this conflation claims the city and its iconic landmarks as part of an ethnic identity. After all, no icon has proved more durable for Mexican national and Chicano/a cultural identity than has the Virgin. On the other hand, it parodies the power structure — indexed by the multiple figures of City Hall — that has historically failed to represent Chicano/a political concerns adequately. The imagery evokes a sense of placement and displacement within new and problematic spatial relations.

By echoing the luminous halo that surrounds the Virgen de Guadalupe, De Batuc displays City Hall as either a glowing abstract Madonna or

Figure 5. *Break It!* by Otoño Luján, 1993. Reprinted with permission of Otoño Luján.

as a floating phallus. The object of reverence and worship can suggest both political power and homosexual desire. This sense of ambiguity is echoed by the title of the lithograph. Are these indeed seven views of City Hall, or simply one repeated mechanistically over and over? The landmark, in any case, becomes part of an altered and reconfigured geography: the seat of city government becomes the basis for De Batuc's aesthetic play. Is this parody or reverence? If parodic, what is the ironic object: secular state power or traditional religious iconography? If reverential, what is the idea revered: the phallus or — pardon the pun — the seat of city government? De Batuc's work plays with significations evoking a sense of alienation and geographic dislocation. The mestizaje of his work tropes on the idea of home, land, power, and religious/ethnic identification.

Representations of land within Chicano/a graphic arts reveal ways in which identities of the self and of the nation conjoin and conflict with quite naked forms of power. Land forms a metonymic connection to an extensive political and economic geography, one whose smoldering revolutionary fervor is reflected in figure 5. The "it" of the lithograph's title refers, of course, to the militarized border signified by the barbed wire in the background. The fiery reds, browns, and oranges of the poster stand in stark contrast to the white jagged outline highlighting the breached border. The clenched fists of the two rifle-toting figures, the sharp knives clutched in their hands, and the crossed bandoliers across their chests match the militancy of the imperative title. (The bandoliers should, as well, invoke images of the Mexican Revolution, whose figures of male and female resistance — the *soldado* and his *adelita* — are recast here as urban guerrillas.)

What subtlety the poster may lack on the semiotic level is offset by the implication of its political message connecting the struggle to reform, resist, and repeal U.S. immigration policies with revolutionary action. A fervor fuels the desire to tear down barriers to immigration. The smoldering emotions evoked by the lithograph suggest how strongly immigration and border policies are felt. At the same time, the representation of urban guerrillas as icons of political change in a work of art from 1993 marks how changed the political landscape has become from the revolutionary fervor of the 1960s and early 1970s. The male and female images are meant to convey political passion, yet within the political context of the early 1990s they serve not so much as a political tool for mobilization as a personal expression of anger at U.S. border policy.

The passions evoked by the U.S.-Mexico border were in part responsible for the articulation of Aztlán within Chicano political and cultural discourse. While the notion of Aztlán has been invoked within a kind of nationalist (and often separatist) minoritarian politics, the usefulness and resiliency of Aztlán lie not in its ability to name a Chicano homeland or nation — a way of looking to the past in order to identify a sense of identity and place — but rather in the plasticity and elasticity of its significance. Aztlán is more myth than place, an idea rendered well in figure 6. The poster plays with verbal and visual puns, contrasting phrases like "La Frontera" with "The Border," "Aztlán" with "Acquired," "Rodillas" with "Rodino." This last pairing is a metonymic connection, the knees suggesting submission and Rodino the name of the legislator who passed immigration reform in the 1980s. The poster makes visual references to the dollar bill, the U.S. Constitution, and the two-faced border with its indigenous profile and its Spanish conquistador. These all serve to convey the conflicted sense of history that land makes present. These playful, painful, and ironic turns are characteristic of Chicano aesthetics. As explained by such critics as Tomás Ybarra-Frausto and Alicia Gaspar de Alba, these aesthetics are sometimes characterized as *rasquache*: a type of reverential kitsch, a complex irony at once satiric and compassionate.

Aztlán is at times employed within this framework as a way to provide an ironic remapping of the United States, one that both recognizes and

Figure 6. *Border Mezz-teez-o*, by Victor Ochoa, 1993. Reprinted with permission of Victor Ochoa.

inverts the notion of periphery and center. In this respect, Aztlán challenges secured boundaries, confirmed norms, and social facts such as nation, citizenry, and home by questioning notions of loyalty, citizenship, nationhood, and belonging. Such a remapping of self and place is necessary in order to undo dominant notions of identity and, simultaneously, to resist rigidly defined codes that sometimes arise in the redefinition of what it means to be Chicano.

In figure 6, Victor Ochoa's poster turns the mythic and the utopian notions of Aztlán into an icon that signals how the self is always in the process of becoming and transforming. This process and its numerous contradictions are reflected and interrogated by many works of contemporary Chicano art. They deploy the metaphor of land — implicitly or explicitly evoking the idea of Aztlán — in order to map alternate geographies, ones that reveal the complexities involved in the representation and identification of a Chicano/a self.

These posters highlight the visual representations of land where forms of national power in both a domestic and international setting are made present. The imagery helps one understand in more global terms how the misuse of military power is a repressive act, whether that power be wielded in the name of immigration control or the establishment of military order. In both cases, the use of violence defends national and social interests at the cost of human life, freedom, and dignity. These artistic efforts reveal an understanding of geographic space that encompasses all of the Americas, connecting a people's suffering from Tijuana to Tierra del Fuego. Land turns into an extended metaphor for the suffering endured by the poor, the helpless, the powerless who struggle to better their plight by either fighting or fleeing. These representations highlight the significance of land not simply within a national context. They map quite a different geography.

This new geography traces the interconnection between land and self, a necessary circuit in the circulation of various forms of power. Thematically we have seen how self-identification and place are inflected — in some ways determined — by economic power, national interest, and racial construction. So too does the body serve as a site where numerous other borders cross. Cherríe Moraga, for one, has conceived of the complicated relationship between space and subject in a Chicana context. Her essay "Queer Aztlán" relocates Chicano nationalist concerns associated with Aztlán by simultaneously expanding and contracting its metaphorical qualities, reconnecting the idea of Aztlán to numerous forms of social struggle. Thus Aztlán as a metaphor for land stands as an overdetermined signifier: "For immigrant and native alike, land is . . . the factories where we work, the water our children drink, and the housing projects where we live. For women, lesbians, and gay men, land is that physical mass called our bodies" (173). The site of conflict becomes enmeshed in a broader context. Her work highlights the interconnection between localities of work and environment, community and family, land and body across national boundaries.

La Ofrenda by Ester Hernandes (1984) exemplifies some of the controversy that such an interconnection can evoke. Her work has inflamed passions because of its elision of religious iconography and Chicana lesbian desire. This furor has not allowed for there to be a discussion of the many levels of sanctity, holiness, and offering that are evoked in this work. The tattooed back of the butch lover forms a human altar before which a fleshy rose is placed. The evocation of vaginal images underscores a sense of both erotic and religious delight. The idea of ofrenda (offering) points to both the traditional religious offering of flowers made to the Virgin during a Mexican wedding mass and the offering of love and passion symbolized by the voluptuous pink flower. While the figure of the Virgin is placed within a scenario of quite explicit homosexual desire, there is no overt irreverence. Indeed, it could be said that the lithograph serves to venerate the feminine power of the Virgin. Hernandes thus draws together an icon of Mexican identity, a reference to the Nahuatl earth goddess Coatlapeuh to which the figure of the Virgin refers, the mixture of Indian and Spanish religious culture, and a celebration of same-sex love.

Hernandes's poster works to undo the assumption of heterosexuality and patriarchal roles as norms within a Chicano/a context. The images of the poster question the socially constituted notions of masculinity and femininity and the gender roles ascribed to sexual bodies. The work helps concretize the ways in which the idea of borderlands has been deployed by Chicano/a aesthetics to form a realm of commentary on issues of hybridity and transformation, but ones in which the body and social discourse coalesce.

Mestizo/a conceptualizations of the self and the borderlands serve to highlight the way power circulates in relation to politics, to religion, to race, to national identity. The crossroads of the borderlands is a site where one looks not to the past for a sense of wholeness or completion but to the present as a constantly negotiated and troubling terrain.

One tension in the discourse developed around mestizaje is the simultaneous sense of gain and loss implied in its use. Many Chicano artists have sought to reclaim the resistant and discarded implicit in Chicano racial and cultural mestizaje. Yet the dynamic of loss — an actively sought loss of indigenous ties, a movement away from that stigmatized as dark and barbaric — is implicit in Latin American notions of mestizaje and whitening. From a slightly different perspective, the hybridity of Chicano culture, as it incorporates Mexican and American influences, is faced with a threatened loss of uniqueness and identity. That is, the loss of the Mexican into the American and the loss of agency in the face of industrial and postindustrial capitalism curbs the celebratory embrace of mestizaje as a dominant trope in Chicano discourse.

Consequently, loss is a strong charge carried by the trope of mestizaje. Many aesthetic and critical texts that explicitly or implicitly address notions of mestizaje cannot but raise issues of absence, search, and fulfillment. This may signal a sense of loss that Julia Kristeva calls the "impossible mourning for the maternal object" (9), the experience of "*object loss* and of a *modification of signifying bonds*" (10). Within a minority framework, the loss of the maternal object can be read as a loss of a personal or cultural identity, a loss of nation or language, a series (potentially unending) of losses leading inevitably to a general sense of humanity's anxiety in being.

In discussing the nature of Chicano identity, cultural critics often foreground the trope of search or location in the conceptualization of their critical projects. Luis Leal, for example, has written on "The Problem of Identifying Chicano Literature" and has discussed being "In Search of Aztlán." Marcienne Rocard is concerned with "The Chicano: A Minority in Search of a Proper Literary Medium for Self-Affirmation." Juan Rodríguez has titled his article "La busqueda de identidad y sus motivos en la literatura Chicana" ("The Search for Identity and Its Motives in Chicano Literature"). Francisco Jiménez has edited a collection called *The Identification and Analysis of Chicano Literature*. The titles of these works convey the sense of loss that permeates these discussions, concerned as they are with search and identification. They help to strike a dominant (and decidedly dark) key in the realm of Chicano culture.

One reason loss in Chicano culture emerges as such a strong subtext can be traced to the discursive configurations of identity and solitude Octavio Paz has posited as central in understanding Mexican national and cultural identity. Loss has, in a Chicano context, already been thematized as a central force in the national constellation of Mexican identity.

There is, Paz argues in his 1950 collection of essays, *The Labyrinth of Solitude*, a sense of violation inherent in Mexican self-identity that haunts the national character. Even in the curses Mexicans use, this sense of violation is present. Paz notes: "The *Chingada* is the Mother forcibly opened, violated or deceived. The *hijo de la Chingada* is the offspring of violation, of abduction or deceit. If we compare this expression with the Spanish *hijo de puta* (son of a whore), the difference is immediately obvious. To the Spaniard, dishonor consists in being the son of a woman who voluntarily surrenders herself: a prostitute. To the Mexican it consists in being the fruit of violation" (79–80). The Mexican character carries with it a sense of primordial violation — one significantly associated with the figure of the mother — that cuts to the heart of one's standing in and comprehension of the world. To Paz, the power of melancholy in the Mexican spirit is determined by a history that has produced a people born into absence. The loss of a centered being, loss of an empowered self, loss of the Indian connection, and loss of a Cartesian whole manifests itself over and over.

Earlier in *Labyrinth*, Paz argues that the figure of the zoot-suited *pa-*

chuco — the Mexican American dandy — represents the apex of both Chicano self-representation and abjection. Standing outside both U.S. and Mexican society, the pachuco "actually flaunts his differences. The purpose of his grotesque dandyism and anarchic behavior is not so much to point out the injustice and incapacity of a society that has failed to assimilate him as it is to demonstrate his personal will to remain different" (14–15). Torn from the anchoring influence of nation, the pachuco flaunts his difference not as a form of social or political critique, but as a form of willful spite. Paz implies that the pachuco imposes a self-willed alienation and isolation and thus stands in contrast to the Mexican whose isolation derives from an elemental abandonment. Loss, according to Paz, becomes for the Chicano not a condition for the uncertainty of existence, but a force driving the Chicano toward a sense of perverse difference.

The influence of Paz on and rejection of him by Chicano critical thought is undeniable. Yet it is not possible to view loss and melancholy as that which connects Mexican national identity with the minoritarian condition of Chicano identity. In *The Cage of Melancholy*, Roger Bartra demonstrates that there is no ontological basis for perceiving Mexican culture as one inevitably imbued with a sense of loss. On the contrary, he argues, the reliance on melancholy as a defining trait of Mexican national consciousness is a means by which a Mexican nationalist discourse reinscribes and reasserts relations of power. Bartra closes his book with the observation that there are agents at work affirming the sense of loss and helplessness in order to define Mexican and national culture:

> In Mexico, the suffering through melancholy and metamorphosis that I have described is precisely the strange medium through which the intelligentsia have revived and given form to popular sentiments. This process activates a structure of mediation that serves as an imaginary bridge between the elite and the people. But it is clear that the result of this bridge building is not an exact reflection of popular sentiments: it is a unification and identification that, in its turn, must be accepted by the widest sectors of the population as the national essence distilled by Mexico's intellectuals upon "reviving" and "appropriating" popular sentiments. (166)

The formation of a melancholic state enables the stability of a national state, one in which members of an elite class build imaginary bridges between themselves as rulers and the people as the led. The complex interaction between the intelligentsia and the people creates a condition in which popular sentiment is produced and distributed in order to forge a nationalist consciousness and preserve an unequal distribution of power.

This same condition does not apply (even by analogy) to a Chicano context. Here there is no nationalist discourse of melancholy employed to delimit the social role of Chicanos. Yet the power of the melancholic remains, even in the often celebratory tones employed in embracing cultural and racial mestizaje, as a critical component of Chicano identity. How can one account for this persistence? The temptation is to locate the melancholic as a characteristic traceable to national origin. Yet the idea of a Chicano mestizaje, and the sense of gain and loss it implies, is a concept developed beyond any given national context. Roger Bartra's critique of Paz reveals the impossibility of transposing the social dynamics of one place onto another and so illustrates the difficulties in translating minority identities in a transnational context.

How much can one generalize, then, about melancholy, loss, identity, and hybridity when discussing minority discourses? Within a Chicano context, the idea of mestizaje has served as a trope that seeks to express the sense of gain and loss seemingly inherent in Chicano culture. The various forms of cultural mestizaje signify how race and identity and citizenship are related to and dislocated from nation, place, and community. This process of signification takes into account the possibility that these relations can at any point always be expressed otherwise.

This ambivalence casts the trope of mestizaje in a melancholic light. Despite its assertion of new historical subjectivities identified by the terms "Chicana" and "Chicano," Chicano mestizaje implies a fluidity of identity, one that gains and loses simultaneously. As the visual texts discussed above illustrate, Chicano culture manifests this fluidity as a central component of Chicano mestizaje. The critical use of mestizaje represents a highly valued — though not unproblematic — conceptual tool in contemporary Chicana/o critical discourse. Mestizaje embodies the idea of multiple subjectivities, opening up discussions of identity to greater complexity and nuance. Radical mestizaje locates how people live their lives in and through their bodies as well as in and through ideology. I do not mean to imply a kind of universal position of resistance, nor an all-encompassing always-already-present position of resistance in using the term "radical." Rather, I argue that a disjuncture or rupture in ideology occurs through the dislocation experienced by mestizo/a bodies. Ideological constructs of subjectivity cannot always successfully hail Chicano/a subjects because they undergo a dislocation of identity. The use of mestizaje within Chicano/a culture has been a means by which artists, writers, and critics have articulated the critical nature of ideological dislocation. As such, a radical mestizaje implies irony and ambiguity, empowerment and melancholic loss, all at the same time.

Certainly in the United States, where the one-drop rule still informs dominant constructions of a binary racial identity, people who identify themselves as mixed-race experience a certain dislocation. This dislocation represents a rupture in racial ideology. Mestizaje not only marks this rupture but signifies the embodiedness of power, the incarnation of colonial histories, the ways the body is disciplined, formed, and deformed by ideology. The mestizaje of Chicano bodies represents the physical trace of a historical process, an often-violent encounter in which identities of race (as well as gender and sexuality, class and ethnicity) become inextricable from the material conditions of colonial and neocolonial histories.

Chicana mestizaje represents the double nature of Chicano identity. It allows for the forging of new multivalent identities *and* it imbeds identity in already constraining social relations. For this reason, land has served as one of the icons used to imagine Chicano subjectivity. Land seems to represent the stable and stolid ground upon which we all, despite our subjective positions, stand. Yet, as several critics have noted, land is mediated through culture. Chicano visual arts help make clear the nature of this mediation and what is at stake in how land is constructed and, alternately, how this construction shapes subjectivity. As Mary Pat Brady has noted, the social production of space has "an enormous effect on subject formation—on the choices people can make and how they conceptualize themselves, each other, and the world" (8). Whether understood as a developing border zone, a hemispheric geopolitical unit, or an absent homeland, the image of land shapes alternate geographies expressed by Chicano culture, geographies that make plain the ways land is shaped by and helps shape human subjectivity.

An interest in the specificity of minor transnationalisms should serve to keep one attuned to the ways in which notions of identity, agency, place, and the past interpenetrate and mark each other. Chicano culture expresses how that interpenetration reveals a loss: of nation, of innocence, of language, of power. Simultaneously, it expresses that which remains: a belief in political transformation, a powerful outrage, a hope for a more just future, faith in the fulfillment of desire. The rendering of land in Chicano expressive culture forms a site where the intertwining of gain and loss, self and other, home and placelessness become embodied. This embodiment both celebrates an evolving hybrid culture and mourns what remains an unnamable and ever-present loss.

Works Cited

Anzaldúa, Gloria. *Borderlands/La Frontera: The New Mestiza*. San Francisco: Spinsters/Aunt Lute, 1987.

Bartra, Roger. *The Cage of Melancholy: Identity and Metamorphosis in the Mexican Character*. Trans. Christopher J. Hall. New Brunswick: Rutgers University Press, 1992.

Brady, Mary Pat. *Extinct Lands, Temporal Geographies: Chicana Literature and the Urgency of Space*. Durham: Duke University Press, 2002.

Cisneros, Sandra. *The House on Mango Street*. New York: Vintage, 1991.

Durand, Jorge, and Douglas S. Massey. *Miracles on the Border: Retablos of Mexican Migrants to the United States*. Tucson: University of Arizona Press, 1995.

Gaspar de Alba, Alicia. *Chicano Art: Inside/Outside the Master's House*. Austin: University of Texas Press, 1998.

Huyssen, Andreas. "Mapping the Postmodern." *New German Critique* 33 (Fall 1984): 5–52.

Jiménez, Francisco, ed. *The Identification and Analysis of Chicano Literature*. New York: Bilingual Press/Editorial Binlingüe, 1979.

Kristeva, Julia. *Black Sun: Depression and Melancholia*. Trans. Leon S. Roudiez. New York: Columbia University Press, 1989.

Leal, Luís. "The Problem of Identifying Chicano Literature." *The Identification and Analysis of Chicano Literature*. Ed. Francisco Jiménez. New York: Bilingual Press/Editorial Bilingüe, 1979. 2–6.

———. "In Search of Aztlán." Trans. Gladys Leal. *Denver Quarterly* 16 (Fall 1981): 16–22.

Paz, Octavio. *Labyrinth of Solitude*. Trans. Lysander Kemp, Yara Milos, and Rachel Phillips Belash. New York: Grove, 1985.

"El Plan Espiritual de Aztlán." *Aztlan: An Anthology of Mexican American Literature*. Ed. Luís Valdez and Stan Steiner. New York: Knopf, 1973 [1969]. 402–406.

Rocard, Marcienne. "The Chicano: A Minority in Search of a Proper Literary Medium for Self-Affirmation." *Missions in Conflict: Essays on U.S.-Mexican Relations and Chicano Culture*. Ed. Renate von Bardeleben. Tübingen: Gunter Narr Verlag, 1986. 31–40.

Rodríguez, Juan. "La busqueda de identidad y sus motivos en la literatura Chicana." *The Identification and Analysis of Chicano Literature*. Ed. Francisco Jiménez. New York: Bilingual Press/Editorial Bilingüe, 1979. 170–178.

Rosaldo, Renato. *Culture and Truth: The Remaking of Social Analysis*. Boston: Beacon, 1989.

Saldaña-Portillo, Josefina. "Who's the Indian in Aztlán? Re-Writing Mestizaje, Indianism, and Chicanismo from the Lacadón." *The Latin American Subaltern Studies Reader*. Ed. Ileana Rodríguez. Durham: Duke University Press, 2001. 402–423.

Saldívar, José David. *Border Matters: Remapping American Cultural Studies*. Berkeley: University of California Press, 1997.

Saldívar, Ramón. "A Dialectic of Difference: Towards a Theory of the Chicano Novel." *MELUS* 6 (fall 1979): 73–92.

Wade, Peter. *Race and Ethnicity in Latin America*. Critical Studies on Latin America. Ed. Jenny Pearce. London: Pluto, 1997.

White, Hayden. *Tropics of Discourse: Essays in Cultural Criticism*. Baltimore: Johns Hopkins University Press, 1978.

Yarbro-Bejarano, Yvonne. "Gloria Anzladúa's *Borderlands/La Frontera*: Cultural Studies, 'Difference,' and the Non-Unitary Subject." *Cultural Critique* 28 (fall 1994): 5–28.

Ybarra-Frausto, Tomás. "Rasquachismo: A Chicano Sensibility." *Chicano Art: Resistance and Affirmation, 1965–1985*. Ed. Richard Griswold del Castillo, Teresa McKenna, Yvonne Yarbro-Bejarano. Los Angeles: Wright Art Gallery, University of California, Los Angeles: 1991. 155–162.

CONTRIBUTORS

Moradewun Adejunmobi is an associate professor in the African American and African studies program of the University of California, Davis. She is the author of *JJ Rabearivelo, Literature and Lingua Franca in Colonial Madagascar* (1996) and has just completed work on a book to be titled *Vernacular Palaver: Imaginations of the Local and Non-Native Languages in West Africa*.

Ali Behdad is an associate professor of English and comparative literature at the University of California, Los Angeles. He is the author of *Belated Travelers: Orientalism in the Age of Colonial Dissolution* (Duke University Press, 1994) and *A Forgetful Nation: On Immigration and Cultural Identity in the United States* (Duke University Press, forthcoming). He has also published numerous articles on postcolonial theory and cultural politics of representation.

Michael K. Bourdaghs is an associate professor of modern Japanese literature in East Asian languages and cultures at the University of California, Los Angeles. He is the author of *The Dawn That Never Comes: Shimazaki Toson and Japanese Nationalism* (2003) and the translation editor of Kamei Hideo, *Transformations of Sensibility: The Phenomenology of Meiji Literature* (2002).

Suzanne Gearhart is a professor of French and critical theory at the University of California, Irvine. She is the author of *The Interrupted Dialectic: Philosophy, Psychoanalysis and Their Tragic Other* (1992) and articles on philosophy, psychoanalysis, and culture.

Susan Koshy is an associate professor of English in the Asian American studies department at the University of California, Santa Barbara. She has published numerous articles on globalization, comparative racial formations, feminism, human rights, and whiteness in the *Yale Journal of Criticism, boundary 2, Social Text, Diaspora, differences,* and *Transition*. Her book *Sexual Naturalization: Asian Americans and Miscegenation* is forthcoming.

Françoise Lionnet is chair of the department of French and Francophone studies at the University of California, Los Angeles, and is codirector of the University of California Multicampus Research Group on Transnational and Transcolonial Studies. She is the author of *Autobiographical Voices: Race, Gender, Self-Portraiture* (1989), *Postcolonial Representations: Women, Literature, Identity* (1995), and numerous essays on francophone literature and culture. She is the coeditor of several special issues of journals such as *Yale French Studies, Comparative Literature Studies, MLN*, and *Signs*.

Seiji M. Lippit is an associate professor of modern Japanese literature at the University of California, Los Angeles. He is the author of *Topographies of Japanese Modernism* (2002) and the editor of *The Essential Akutagawa* (1999).

Elizabeth Marchant is an associate professor of Spanish and Portuguese at the University of California, Los Angeles. She is the author of *Critical Acts: Latin American Women and Cultural Criticism* (1999) and is presently at work on *Brazil and the Black Atlantic: Afro-Brazilian Cultural Expression and the Politics of Identity*.

Kathleen McHugh is an associate professor and teaches in English and the School of Film and Television at the University of California, Los Angeles. Her publications focus on feminism, film melodrama, and cinematic autobiography. She is completing a book-length study of Jane Campion's films and an edited volume on South Korean melodrama.

David Palumbo-Liu is a professor of comparative literature and director of the Program in Modern Thought and Literature at Stanford University. He is also coeditor of *Streams of Cultural Capital* (1997) and author of *Asian/American: Historical Crossings of a Racial Frontier* (1999). His recent articles have appeared in the *New Centennial Review* and *boundary 2*.

Rafael Pérez-Torres is an associate professor in the Department of English at the University of California, Los Angeles. He is the author of *Movements in Chicano Poetry: Against Myths, against Margins* (1995) and the coauthor (with Ernest B. López) of *Memories of an East L.A. Outlaw: To Alcatraz, Death Row, and Back* (forthcoming). He has published articles on Chicano/a literature and culture, postmodernism, multiculturalism, and contemporary American literature in such journals as *Cultural Critique, American Literary History, Genre, Aztlán: A Journal of Chicano Studies*, and *American Literature*.

Jenny Sharpe is a professor of English and comparative literature at the University of California, Los Angeles. Her publications include a recent book, *Ghosts of Slavery: A Literary Archeology of Black Women's Lives* (2003). Her current research engages questions of nation, gender, and technology in diasporic cultures.

Shu-mei Shih is an associate professor of East Asian languages and cultures, comparative literature, and Asian American studies at the University of California, Los Angeles, where she directed the Center for Comparative and Interdisciplinary Research on Asia (2000–2004) and codirects the University of California Multicampus

Research Group on Transnational and Transcolonial Studies. She is the author of *The Lure of the Modern* (2001), "Global Literature and Technologies of Recognition" (2004), and other works.

Tyler Stovall is a professor of history at the University of California, Berkeley. He specializes in modern French history, especially that of labor, colonialism, and race. He is the author of *The Rise of the Paris Red Belt* (1990) and *Paris Noir: African Americans in the City of Light* (1996) and the coeditor (with Sue Peabody) of *The Color of Liberty: Histories of Race in France* (Duke University Press, 2003).

INDEX

disciplines, 1; and Elvis Presley, 245; function of, 283; and minor literature, 283; and translation, 243–244, 254. *See also* Border

Bourdagh, Michael, 18

Bourdieu, Pierre, 301–302, 313

Brady, Mary Pat, 336

Brathwaite, Edward Kamau, 204

Brazil: and the African diaspora, 302–303; black racial identity in, 303; national culture of, 19–20; national identity of, 304; racial consciousness in, 314; tourism in, 307–308, 312; and violence, 311–312. *See also* Pelourinho, the

Break It! (poster), 328–329

Breeze, Jean "Binta," 19, 261–279; "Aid Travels With a Bomb," 266–267; background of, 265–266; and dance-hall women, 270; "Dubwise," 273, 278; "Eena mi corner," 278; "Get Back," 269; and Jamaican women's cultural identities, 265; and languages of deejaying, 276–277; "Ordinary morning," 277–278; *Riddym Ravings*, 267–268, 273–274, 278; "To Plant," 266–267

Bricktop's (night club), 137, 139, 143–145

Buhler, Reverend, 183

Burakumin ("outcaste"), 286, 291, 293–294

Burke, Kenneth, 67–68

Butler, Kim, 312

The Cage of Melancholy (Bartra), 334–335

Caillaux, Henriette, 141

Caillaux, Joseph, 141

Calavita, Kitty, 226

"Candle in the Wind" (*Labouzi dan labriz*) (Virahsawmy), 215

"The Cape" ("Misaki") (Nakagami Kenji), 290

Caribbean, 262–263. *See also* Jamaica

CEDAW (Convention on the Elimination of All Forms of Discrimination Against Women), 122–123

Césaire, Aimé, 204, 214–216

Chakrabarty, Dipesh, 12, 208

Chamoiseu, Patrick, 210

Chancé, Dominique, 208, 210

Chatterjee, Partha, 112

Chicano/a art: religious symbolism in, 327–328, 331–332; representation of land in, 317–318, 328–331, 336–337; sexuality in, 332; and U.S.-Mexican border, 318

Chicano/a context, *mestizaje* in, 320–321

Chicano/a culture: "betweeness" of, 321–322; and the borderlands, 317; and geography, 317–337; and the homeland, 20–21; and loss, 336; production of, 322; and the United States, 318–319

Chicano/a identity, 322–325, 333–336

Children, sale of. *See* Human trafficking

China, ethnic minorities in, 14

"China Nights" (Shina no yoru), 249–250

"Chinese," and affect, 75–76

"Chinese," identity as, 79–80

Chinese and Japanese languages, separation of, 242

"Chineseness," limits of, 95–98, 97

Chinese New Left, 88–89

Chinese people, residing outside of China, 14

Chinese women: diasporic, 89–92; identity of, 94–95; liberation of, 83–85, 87–88; as scholars, 89–92; under Maoism, 104 n.11; and the West, 81–83, 86, 91

Chiu, Monica, 53

Choice, rational. *See* Rational choice

Chow, Rey, 96

Chraïbi, Driss, 18, 223, 228, 232, 234

Cisneros, Sandra, 317

Citizenship: defined, 12–13; and human rights, 128; and immigrants, 34; norms of, 8

Cixous, Hélène, 3

Clifford, James, 227

Clinton, Bill, 43

"Cocktail Party" (Kakuteru pāti") (Ōshiro Tatsihiro), 290

Cold War, and Japan, 251–252

Coleman, J. S., 46

Colonialism: and assimilation, 187–188; and European nations, 11; and Japan, 284, 289–290, 297 n.15; and minor literature, 224; and translation, 250; and vernacular literacy, 181–182, 182–183; and the West, 289–290

Communities: and discourses of the vernacular, 191–192; of immigrants, 224–228; transnational, 37, 110–111

Confiant, Raphaël, 216

Contact, face-to-face versus virtual, 13

Convention on the Elimination of All Forms of Discrimination Against Women (CEDAW), 122–123

Cooper, Carolyn, 269, 272

Crawford, James, 189

Creole, Mauritian, 203–207, 218 n.2; as written language, 202–205. See also Mauritius

Creolization, of cultures, 8–9

Crimes of passion, French tradition of, 136–137, 140–143

Crispin, Philip, 214

Cross-cultural studies, boundaries of, 74–75

Crucero / Crossroads (Puerta, Verdecchia), 16, 159, 166–173; as autobiographical film, 167; the border in, 166–169, 173; characters in, 167–169, 171; history in, 169–172; narrative of, 166–167

Crutcher, Leon: background of, 137–139; murder of, 139–143; portrayal of, 143

Crutcher, Marie: acquittal of, 140, 148; background of, 137–139; character of, 142–143, 145; murder of husband, 142–143, 147; trial of, 139–140

Crutcher murder case, 135–149; as crime of passion, 140–143; examination of, 15–16; and French colonial life, 146–148; media coverage of, 143

Cultural ambivalence, 32

Cultural difference, 77–78

Cultural forms, diasporic, 264

Cultural production, 103 n.8, 262–263, 313

Cultural transversalism, 8

Cultural workers, minority, 9

Culture: and civility, 40; and creolization, 8–9; minority (see Minority culture); and repression, 31–32; as semiotic space, 283; as term of action, 12; transnational, 37

Curtis, Mickey, 246

Dancehall culture and music, 269–274

Danny Iida and the Paradise kings, 246

Dayan, Joan, 214, 277

De Certeau, Michel, 6

Declaration on the Elimination of Violence Against Women, 123

Deconstructing the Nation (Silverman), 228, 233

Deconstruction, in theoretical discourse, 3, 78–79

Deejaying, language of, 276–277

Deleuze, Gilles, 2, 224, 244, 252

Derrida, Jacques, 2, 3

Dialects, and otherness, 243. See also Language

Diaspora: African 261–262, 302–303; for Chinese women scholars, 89–92, 93–95; and cultural forms, 264; for intellectuals, 227–228; for minorities, 227–228; and postmodern subjects, 118

Dieguez, Gilda Korff, 311

Dirlik, Arif, 91

Discipline, as term of action, 12

Discourse: of the "beyond," 111; deconstruction in, 3; of minorities, 10–11, 15, 232, 252; of national culture, 283–284; of Orientalism, 14; of rational choice, 67; of universalism, 78–79; of the vernacular, 179–194

Dislocation, and racial identities, 336

Displacement, geographical, 225–227

DJs: as artists, 264–265; in dancehall music, 271; female, 272–273; language of, 276–277; male, 279 n.9; and slackness, 269–270

Documentary, autobiographical. *See* Autobiographical film

Doezema, Jo, 122, 123–124

Dub poetry, 19, 265–266, 268–279. *See also* Breeze, Jean "Binta"

"Dubwise" (Breeze), 270, 273, 278

Dunye, Cheryl, 155, 157–158

Durand, Jorge, 323

Dystopic visions, of globalization, 6

Economics: and human trafficking, 121; and transnational communities, 110–111

Education, and Africans, 185–187, 192–193, 195 n.6

"Eena mi corner" (Breeze), 278

Ei Rokusuke, 248–250, 253

Elster, Jon, 47–49

Emotion, and storytelling, 47–48

Empire (Negri, Hardt), 110–113, 115

English, Africans writing in, 187, 194 n.2

English Only movement, 189–190

Enlightenment, new, 86–88

Enzenberger, Hans, 273

Epistemology, in *Toufann*, 217–218

Equality, state-induced gender, 80–81, 83–84, 87–88, 103 n.10

Ethical manipulation, 58; in *My Year of Meats*, 54

Ethics: and affect, 48, 98–102; and literary narrative, 49–50; and recognition, 98–102; in transational context, 13; and transnational encounters, 73–102

Ethnicity: and feminism, 85–95; and language, 179

Ethnic minorities. *See* Minorities: ethnic

Ethnic studies: "arrival" in, 4; and diaspora studies, 73; and globalization theory, 109–130; inspiration of, 3–4; and the nation, 4–5, 11–12; the subject in, 117–118

Ethnology, and Japanese literature, 290–291

Etō Jun, 292–293

Euro-American dominance, 112–113. *See also* Colonialism; Universalism

European advocates, of vernacular literacy, 183–184, 186, 188

European languages: and Africans, 181, 195 n.6; and indigenous languages, 193–194

Exclusion, politics of, 9–10

Exile intellectuals, 224–228, 231–232

An Exploration of Women's Aesthetic Consciousness (Li Xiaojiang), 87

Fabian, Johannes, 85–86, 193

Face-to-face contact, and ethics, 13

Facundo (Sarmiento), 167

"Facundo," in *Crucero / Crossroads*, 167, 168, 171

Fagunwa, Daniel, 194 n.2

Fanon, Frantz, 3, 146, 224, 228, 229, 262, 273

Feeling, structures of, 69–70

Female bodies and sexuality. *See* Women

International Institute of African Language and Cultures (IALC), 184, 186–187
International Monetary Fund (IMF), 115–116, 266–267
Iwano Hōmei, 289
Iyer, Pico, 231

Jamaica, 19; economy of, 267, 279 n.7; women from, 265, 267–268. *See also* Breeze, Jean "Binta"
James, C. L. R., 262
JanMohamed, Abdul, 156, 168, 179–180, 224, 233
Japan: and air travel, 239–241; and the Cold War, 251–252; and colonialism, 289–290, 297 n.15; discourse in, 283–285; minor literature in, 286; mountain people in, 288; nation building in, 284; Sakamoto as representing, 252–253, 255; as superpower, 253–254
Japan Airlines (JAL), 239, 240–241, 253–254
Japanese Americans, internment of, 159–161, 163, 172
Japanese: autobiography, 160–161; cultural identity, 285–286; language, 242–243, 250–252; literature, 290
Jiménez, Francisco, 333
Johnson, Linton Kwesi, 266
Journal of the African Society (*African Affairs*), 184
Judy, Ronald, 262
Justice, and fiction, 48, 50

Kainan shōki (Yanagita Kunio), 288
Kamayatsu, Hiroshi, 246
Kaplan, Caren, 225, 226
Karatani, Kojin, 14
"Keep on Moving" (Soul II Soul), 262–263
Kelsen, Hans, 114

Kiefer, Anselm, 50
King Lear (Shakespeare), and *toufann*, 205
Korea, and colonization, 285–286, 288–289
Koshy, Susan, 15
Kourouma, Ahmadou, 214
Kristeva, Julia, 81, 84, 332
Kunikida Doppo, 285
Kuroko Kazuo, 290

The Labyrinth of Solitude (Paz), 333–334
Lady Saw, 271–272
Lamming, George, 204, 232
Land, representations of, in Chicano art, 317–318, 328–331, 336–337
Language: and African nations, 192–193; and identity, 17, 180–181, 214–216; national, 242–243, 284; postcolonial approach to, 18; and psychoanalysis, 28–29; as symbol of ethnicity, 179; and transcolonial networks, 213–218. *See also* Vernacular
Largo do Pelouinho, 304. *See also* Pelourinho, the
Lauretis, Teresa de, 87
Leal, Luis, 333
Lederer, Laura J., 121
Ledikasyon pu Travayer (Education for the Workers), 215
Legal recourse, for immigrants, 127–128
Lennon, John, 253
Lentricchia, Frank, 67
Les Boucs ("The Butts") (Chraïbi), 18, 223, 224, 232; characters in, 228; as "counterhistory," 229–230; plot of, 228; reading of, 228, 232–234
Les Misérables, 205
The Letter (film), 135, 149 n.2
Levinas, Emmanuel, 2, 14, 100
Levine, Les, 50

Lévi-Strauss, Claude, 36
Le Zoute, Belgium, conference at, 184–185
Li ("The Prisoner of Conscience") (Virahsawmy), 204
Lin, Maya, 50
Lionnet, Françoise, 17–18
Lippit, Seiji, 19, 243
Literacy, transnational, 115–116
Literacy, vernacular. *See* Vernacular literacy
Literary aesthetic, modern, 44
Literary narrative, and affect, 49–50, 58
Literature: and borderlines of nations, 285; and ethnology, 290–291; and information, 45–46, 64; and knowledge, 201–202; postcolonial approach to, 18; and rational choice, 44–52; role and function of, 13–14; sentimentality in, 66–67
Literature, minor. *See* Minor literature
Liu, Lydia, 253
Li Xiaojiang, 14, 85; and "Chineseness," 96–98; rejection of Western feminism, 73–74, 81–82, 86–92; as representative of Chinese women, 95; on "transvaluations," 101–102; and women's studies in China, 83
Lloyd, David, 156, 168, 179–180, 224, 233
Logic: and rational choices, 46–47; of translation, 202
Lotman, Yuri, 19, 283
"Love Punaany Bad" (Shabba Rank), 270
Lucchesi, Ivo, 311
Lugard, Frederick, 185, 188
Lukács, Georg, 50
Lutzenberger, Jose, 42, 43, 46

Madness, as strategy for survival, 274–275
Magalhães, Antônio Carlos, 306

Maghrebi immigrants, 228
Mainstream narrative and minority filmmakers, 16
Major discourse, of the vernacular, 179–194
Majority, as term, 28
Majority culture, minority cultures becoming, 28, 36
Malkki, Liisa H., 129
Malloy, Sylvia, 167, 169
Manipulation, of sentiment, 58, 65; ethical, 54, 58; and propaganda, 67–69
Manley, Michael, 267, 269
Maoism, women under, 81–82, 84–85, 104 n.11
"The Map of a Nineteen-Year-Old" ("Jukysai no chizu") (Nakagami Kenji), 291
Maravall, José Antonio, 208
Marchant, Elizabeth, 19 -20
Marcus, Greil, 237, 238
Marginalized populations, and discourses of the vernacular, 190–191
Marinetti, F. T., 239
Marks, Stephen, 114
Masako (singer), 248
Massey, Douglas S., 323
Mauritian audiences, and *Toufann*, 208–209
Mauritian Creole, 202–207, 218 n.2
Mauritius, 201–218
McAlmon, Robert, 139, 145
McClintock, Anne, 231
McDonald, Paulette, 269
McHugh, Kathleen, 16
McLuhan, Marshall, 261
Media: information in, 45–46; in *My Year of Meats*, 57–58
Melancholy, and Chicago identity, 334–335
Memmi, Albert, 224

Men: black, and white women, 143–
145; and black music, 264–265; as
DJs, 279 n.9; under Maoism, 104 n.11.
See also Gender; Women

Mestizaje (racial mixture), 20–21; and
the borderlands, 319; in Chicano/a
context, 320–321, 335; and Chi-
cano/a identity, 322–323, 336; melancholy of, 317–337; and sense of
gain and loss, 332–333

Mexican national discourse, *indigenismo*
in, 320

Mexican national identity, and loss, 334

Mexican-U.S. border, visual representations of, 323–331

Mexico, identity in, 320, 324–325. *See
also* Chicano/a culture

Mignolo, Walter, 201–202

Migration: versus traveling, 98; between
West and non-West, 13. *See also*
Immigration

Min, Anchee, 73–74, 93–98

Minami, Kazumi, 245–246

Minor: condition of being, 223–224;
forms available to the, 43; what constitutes the, 10

Minor culture, and rockabilly music,
238–239

Minor discourses, of the vernacular,
179–194

Minorities: ethnic 14; experience of,
227–228; and solidarity, 232

Minority: meaning of term, 28; as object
of interior exclusion, 12–13; what
constitutes the, 10

Minority bodies, 16–17

Minority culture: becoming majority
culture, 28; exhibiting transnational
perspectives, 27, 35–36; and immigration, 33–34; and majority cultures,
36; and power, 27–28; and psychoanalysis, 28–29; as site of abjection
and incorporation, 19; as term, 27

Minority discourse, 10–11, 232. *See also*
Discourse

Minority filmmakers, 16, 155–156, 158

Minority groups: arrival of, 4; and
autobiographical filmmakers, 155–
156; cultural practices of, 6–7;
newly created versus immigration-
created, 38

Minority literature, reading, 223–225,
228–234

Minority politics, 179–180

Minority populations, recognition of,
100–102

Minority subjects, and the mainstream, 2

Minor literature, 2; as boundary, 283; in
Japan, 286; and postcolonial theory,
223–234; reading, 18, 232–234

Minor spaces, 283–296, 301–314

Minor transnationalism, 5–12; conception of, 6–7; as consequence of
globalization, 5; versus global capitalism, 116, 238–239

Minor transnationality, 8

Missionaries, and vernacular literacy,
183–184, 186, 190

Modernism, and progressive politics,
49–50

Modernities, baroque, 207–212

Modernity, and autobiographical film,
156–157

Modernization, and indiginous languages, 196 n.12

Modern literary aesthetic, 44

Mohanty, Chandra, 85

Molière, 205

Montmartre, in 1920s, 137, 144. *See also*
France

Montoya, Malaquias, 326

Moraga, Cherríe, 331

Morrison, Toni, 264, 274–275

Motoori Norianga, 292

Mountain people, in Japan, 288,
297 n.12

Psychoanalysis, and social analysis, 27–40

Puerta, Ramiro, 16, 158–159, 166–167, 172. See also *Crucero / Crossroads* (Puerta, Verdecchia)

Queerness, 210–212

Rabossi, Edouardo, 51

Race: and crimes of passion, 136–137; in Jazz Age Paris, 135–149; in the Pelourinho, 310–312; and postcolonial relations, 147–148

Radio: and black female subjectivity, 19; revolutionary potential of, 273; and women, 273–274, 276–278

Ramaiah, D., 120

Rational choice, 41–70; discourse of, 67; and irrational choices, 41–70; and storytelling, 47; theory, 13–14, 44–45, 49

Rationality, and propaganda, 68

Recognition: and ethics, 98–102; of female subaltern subject, 121; and minority populations, 102

Red Azalea (Min), 73, 93–94

Reggae: The Rough Guide, 269

Reich, Wilhelm, 29, 35

Religious symbolism, and the U.S.-Mexican border, 324, 327–328, 331–332

Repression, and culture, 31–32

Republicanism, French version of, 2

"Retablo of M. Esther Tapia Pìcon," 323

Retrieval, politics of, 9–10

Rhizome, in globalization, 2

Rhythm of the Saints (Simon), 307

Riddym Ravings (Breeze), 267–268, 274–276, 278. See also Breeze, Jean "Binta"

Ri Kaisei, 290

Rocard, Marcienne, 333

Rockabilly music, 18; global circulation of, 242; and language, 242; translations of, 237–256; as transnational minor culture, 238–239; in the United States, 247

Rock 'n' roll, and airplanes, 239

Rodrigues, João Jorge, 306–307, 313

Rodríguez, Juan, 333

Roji ("outcaste village"), 291–292, 294; and "arcades," 295–296; as border, 296; as in-between space, 294–295; notion of, 19

Romero, Sílvio, 312

Rorty, Richard, 50–52, 54, 65, 67

Rosaldo, Renato, 321

Ross, Kristin, 148

Rushdie, Salman, 50

Sadness, forms of, 66

"Sad stories," 51, 60

Said, Edward, 224, 231

Sakai, Naoki, 242–243

Sakamoto Kyū: as air traveler, 254–255; death of, 239, 253; debut of, 240; and "GI Blues," 244–246; and "Hound Dog," 240; in Japanese popular memory, 254; as representing Japan, 252–253, 255; and rockabilly, 237–256; and "Ue wo muite arukō," 247–248; vocal mannerisms of, 246

Saldaña, Josefina, 319–320

Saldívar, José, 321

Saldívar, Ramón, 322

Salvador, Bahia (Brazil), 304, 306. See also Pelourinho, the

Sampling, in music, 264–265

Santos, Jocélio Teles dos, 307

Sarmiento, 167

Sartre, Jean-Paul, 216

Sasaki, Isao, 246

Sassen, Saskia, 126, 128–129

Schiwy, Freya, 201–202

Schmidt, W., 186

Scott, James, 6

Women: Chinese (*see* Chinese women); and dancehall music, 269–273; domestic space of, 277; Jamaican (*see* Jamaican women); white (*see* White women)

Women, A Distant and Beautiful Lengend (Li Xiaojiang), 87

Women's bodies: and dancehall culture, 269–273; and radio technologies, 273–274, 276, 278

Women's studies, in China, 83

Women's time, 99

Workers skilled versus unskilled, 126–127

World Bank memo, 41–42, 44

World Charter for Prostitutes' Rights, 123

World Trade Organization (WTO), 113, 115–116

Yamamoto, Traise, 160
Yanagita Kunio, 287–288, 291
Yarbro-Bejarano, Yvonne, 321
Yasuda Toshiaki, 284
Ybarra-Frausto, Tomás, 329
Yeats, William Butler, 213–214
Yokomitsu Riichi, 285

Zabus, Chantal, 210, 212
Zachernuk, Philip, 181, 193
Zhang Jie, 76–77, 83
Zimmerman, Eve, 293
Zitzewitz, Eric, 66

Library of Congress Cataloging-in-Publication Data

Minor transnationalism / Françoise Lionnet and

Shu-mei Shih, editors.

p. cm.   Includes bibliographical references and index.

ISBN 0-8223-3478-x (cloth : alk. paper)

ISBN 0-8223-3490-9 (pbk. : alk. paper)

1. Pluralism (Social sciences) 2. Transnationalism.

3. Arts and globalization. 4. Arts, Modern — 21st century.

I. Lionnet, Françoise. II. Shih, Shu-mei.

HM1271.M4555 2005

305 — dc22   2004018754